ACCOUNTING
ACE 911 ™

VOLUME 1

Gregory R. Mostyn, C.P.A., M.B.A.

ACCOUNTING ACE 911 ™

VOLUME 1

Gregory R. Mostyn, C.P.A., M.B.A.

MISSION COLLEGE

ACCOUNTING PRINCIPLES

BEFORE YOU BUY OR USE THIS BOOK, YOU SHOULD UNDERSTAND ...

Copyediting, interior design and composition by Joanne Shwed, Backspace Ink

Cover design by Mike Chrumka, In-House Studio

Publisher's Cataloging-in-Publication

Mostyn, Gregory R.
   Accounting ace 911. Volume 1 / Gregory R. Mostyn. --
1st ed.
   p. cm.
   Includes index.
   LCCN: 00-191805
   ISBN: 0-9703719-3-4

   1. Accounting.   I. Title.

HF5635.M67 2000   657
QBI00-823

Acknowledgements

Many people have contributed to the improvement of this book. In addition to my students, I wish to especially acknowledge the following individuals, practitioners, and educators for their excellent suggestions, useful criticism, and creative ideas:

William E. Bjork, J.D., C.P.A., M.B.A.
George Dorrance, C.P.A., M.B.A.
Richard Hobbs, M.A.
Ernestine Porter, C.P.A., M.B.A.
Joanne Shwed, Backspace Ink
Mike Chrumka, In-House Studio

And a special thanks to

Carl Goldman and Michole Nicholson of **Rising Star Press** for their generous help and dependable guidance, for which I am truly grateful.

To my parents, Bob and Melita, who by word and deed

have taught me the value of lifelong learning

and

Daisy, who has always been exactly right

about the importance of long walks in the park

Contents

Learning Goals Index

How to Use This Book

This is a **"Read What You Need"** book. Once you decide what you need to study, just look in the Subject Index (beginning on page 657). The Subject Index has all subjects arranged alphabetically and will show you the page number of your desired topic.

IF you need ...

explanations of specific topics ...

... then look in the index for the name of the topic. *Example:* you need to review what "revenue" is, and how it is recorded. The Subject Index shows four references for "**revenue**":

> Revenue
> confirming added value, 17
> defined, 119
> element of owner's capital, 394
> recording rules, 400, 410–411

Using the page number references, you can now go directly to whichever topics you want.

---

problems to practice specific topics ...

... then look in the index for the name of the topic. Use the page number reference to find the topic. All practice questions and problems with their answers appear **at the end of each learning goal**. So the questions and problems you want will be at the end of the learning goal that contains your topic.

You can also find a Learning Goals Index on page viii.

---

cumulative tests ...

... then look in the index for **Cumulative tests** to locate which practice test you want.

---

math review ...

... then look in the index for the name of the particular math topic you want. ("Essential Math for Accounting" begins on page 517.)

---

vocabulary review and practice ...

... then look in the index for the specific word you need, or
... **Vocabulary tests** to find the vocabulary test you want.

Note: See the Glossary on page 654.

---

a self-study course ...

This book is written so that it can be used as a comprehensive self-study of accounting fundamentals, by reading all sections in sequence.

How to Study Accounting

Acquire a balanced understanding

Accounting is a system of activities which processes, communicates, and interprets financial information about a business or other entity. If you wish to acquire a clear understanding of this system, you will need to spend some time studying three important areas of accounting knowledge:

- how a business operates
- processing accounting information
- preparing and interpreting financial reports

Each of these areas is very important in its own right and should not be underestimated. For example, an understanding of:

- "how a business operates" is needed by accountants, managers, management consultants, operations specialists, investors, and lenders

- "processing accounting information" is needed in bookkeeping, auditing, and information system use (or design), especially in new "intranet" systems which integrate all kinds of accounting and other information

- "preparing and interpreting financial reports" is important for accountants and managers. Interpreting financial reports is also very important for investors, bankers, voters, union members, and everyone and anyone with a financial or social interest in business and the economy

At some point in your future career, you might become a specialist or be involved in work that is related to any one of the three areas just mentioned. However, because all of these areas interact with and affect each other, and because you cannot be entirely sure where your career will take you, it would be wise to make sure that you acquire some working knowledge in each area. This book and other good introductory accounting textbooks introduce you to each of these areas in a balanced and careful way.

STUDY TECHNIQUES

Overview

The following suggestions are study tips that really work. Each additional one that you are able to consistently use is "money in the bank" toward success in your accounting study.

Consistent study in small amounts

This is probably the *most important and powerful technique* of all. For a great many people, it is also the most difficult to apply. Many people will often put off a task until a large block of time becomes available. This is very inefficient, because:

- Large blocks of time do not frequently become available.
- You can learn only a limited amount before you become tired.
- You will not have frequent repetition, which is essential.

> *Rule:* Use any small amount of time and **give yourself permission to stop after doing only one or two small things.** You can do more, but always make it acceptable to stop before you complete an assignment, **because you will use another small period of time soon.** You will be surprised at how this method of using many small time periods eases anxiety and increases your cumulative output.

Join or form a study group

Controlled research studies have demonstrated that students who belong to a study group perform significantly better in class than those students who are not in study groups. Whether the group is small or large, meet regularly. It will make you feel much better.

Know what you don't know

Always be very aware of what you don't understand. As you are reading (or listening), be aware of *exactly where* the confusion or uncertainty begins. Make a note, so you can develop a list of "confusion points." Then you can focus on these particular items that you know will give you trouble.

Do not miss any classes

Even if you have the most boring, record-setting, dullest teacher in the history of education, keep going to class. You will pick up important class content by just being aware of the subjects that the teacher likes to emphasize: this alone will give you clues for exams. More likely though, you will also pick up important explanations that will save you a great deal of study time.

Ask, ask, ASK!

You have probably heard this a million times: "Never be afraid to ask questions." We are always anxious about looking foolish or ignorant, but remember this: you are putting in your valuable time, effort, and money on this subject! Your teacher *owes you* the best and most patient explanation possible, or he/she is not doing a professional job.

If someone acts impatient or rushed, maybe that person is just having a bad day. Politely suggest another time, but be persistent. (Persistence is always a good habit to develop anyway.)

Examination strategy

- Do *not* begin to work on the first question immediately.
- *Do* scan the test. If the test has individual problems, find a problem that:
  — you know how to solve, AND
  — is worth a lot of points.

Work these kinds of problems **first**! By doing this, you know that you are getting the most points as fast as possible. This will *relax* you and give you *confidence*. This way you will perform and think better when you do the other problems.

Mistakes are not a disaster!

Sad but true, we often learn the most by making mistakes. (In a class, the best idea is to make most of your mistakes on homework, where they will hurt you the least.) However, even the occasional bad exam score can serve as good motivation. Mistakes and failure can almost always serve as guides to success, but you must be smart enough to see that this is how things work in the world.

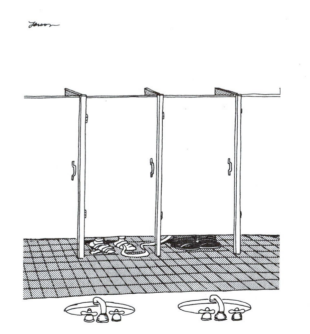

"*It was an innocent mistake, but nevertheless, a moment later Maurice found himself receiving the full brunt of the mummy's wrath.*"

An Accounting Teacher's Dirty Little Secret

After having taught hundreds of beginning accounting students over the years, I want you to know that I have seen plenty of suffering in my time. Sometimes, it has seemed rather like watching one of those nature programs where some of the weaker antelope on the African savannah begin to fall behind the herd, and then *whammo!* … a predator appears out of nowhere and the stragglers are gone. Years of watching these scenes re-enacted every fall and spring have revealed something about the nature of beginning accounting classes, a little secret that I am sure I share with all other experienced accounting teachers, which is this: ***a student who does not learn the early material probably will never catch up***—a lame antelope that becomes easy prey for the cruel jaws of the midterm exams.

This happens because not all the chapters in textbooks used for accounting principles classes are created equal. The early chapters are by far the most important; they contain material that is the foundation, and everything else builds on the information in these early chapters. The early material deserves extra class time and resources, but for various reasons, this is frequently not possible.

This book, with Volume 2, provides extensive explanations and practice that concentrate on the **critical foundation topics** of accounting principles. These are the essential topics that must be mastered in order to successfully continue on in accounting, either in the classroom or on the job. Additionally, if you do not feel completely secure in your math skills, a comprehensive basic math review is also available for you here, called "Essential Math for Accounting."

You do not have to read everything in these pages. When you use the book, you can look in the index for the topics you want to review, and study only what you feel you need. However, keep an open mind, because the more you learn the better off you will be. Learn all the basics, and you'll do far more than survive … you'll succeed!

SECTION I

What Is a Business?

Overview: what this section does	This section introduces you to the fundamental features of a business: ● purpose ● how a business operates ● basic financial structure ● economic entities ● ownership types
Use this section if ...	... you are unfamiliar with *any* of the above features. Learning Goal 3, Learning Goal 4, and Learning Goal 5 are especially important.
Do NOT use this section if ...	... you already understand all the elements listed above. You can begin with Section II starting on page 80, analyzing the transactions that change a business.

"Welcome to the territory of business!"

• •

LEARNING GOAL 1
Explain What a Business Is and What It Does

WELCOME

Speak the language of business ...

Welcome! Thank you for selecting me as your guide in this part of your journey through the territory of business and commerce. To prosper in this territory and to enjoy your journey, you will need to learn the languages of the region. The most important language to learn is called "accounting."

When educated people in this region want to describe a business or explain what has happened to it, they often use the language of accounting. When you use this book, you will be carefully and thoroughly trained in the fundamentals of this language.

... but first learn what a business is.

A common dilemma for beginning accounting students is the double burden of struggling to learn accounting while at the same time being expected to understand what a "business" is—the thing that the accounting is trying to describe. The student is expected to learn what a business is by having to learn the language that describes it. This would be like me telling you, in a new language, all the details about some beautiful tree while you are not exactly sure what a tree is.

I suggest that we try something more interesting and fun. Instead of beginning right away with the details of accounting, let's first take a little time to understand what a business is and how it operates. After that, accounting discussions will make more sense to you.

If you decide to extend your study of accounting, you will later learn that, with small modifications, accounting can also be used to describe nonbusiness activities, such as governments and charities. However, business is where accounting is used the most.

In Learning Goal 1, you will find:

▼ Identify a Business

BUSINESS CHARACTERISTICS

Definition:
a business

A "business" is an organization with the primary goal of accumulating wealth by creating valuable new resources and selling them to customers.

Note: Valuable resources have a dollar value, so they are also called ***economic resources.***

Examples of businesses ...	Desired resource created ...
an automobile manufacturer	automobiles
an automobile dealer	a selection of automobiles to buy
a veterinarian	medical services for animals
an accounting firm	accounting and tax services
a movie theater	entertainment
a bakery	delicious bread and desserts

Learning Goal 1: Explain What a Business Is and What It Does

BUSINESS CHARACTERISTICS (continued)

Not a business	• a public university (its primary purpose is not accumulating wealth) • a charitable organization (its primary purpose is not accumulating wealth) • your city government (its primary goal is public service, not accumulating wealth)
Important difference	Government or nonprofit organizations (such as charities) do carry on business-like activities such as detailed record-keeping, paying bills, incurring expenses, commercial transactions, and so on. However, because the primary goal of these organizations is not the accumulation of wealth, none of them would be called a "business."

THE TWO KINDS OF RESOURCES

Overview	Only two kinds of resources can be created: property and services.
Property and services	A business creates and sells valuable resources that people want. There are only two possible kinds of resources that can be created and sold: • ***Property:*** any resource that can be *owned*. Property generally (but not always) has a dollar value. Examples are a computer, a book, a car, or a loaf of bread. • ***Services:*** the *use of* labor or the *use of* someone else's property. Services generally (but not always) have a dollar value. Examples are repairing a truck, delivering a pizza, giving financial advice, teaching a class, renting out a copy machine, or renting out an apartment.
Synonym	Property and services are often referred to as "goods and services."

"I'm bored. Let's go into business!"

●　　●

CLASSIFYING A BUSINESS

Classify by type of resource created

● A *service business* creates services. Examples of services are repairs, communication, legal advice, entertainment, and medicine.

● A *merchandising business* offers the service of providing a convenient selection of merchandise to customers. Merchandising businesses do not make products. Examples of merchandising businesses are a grocery store, a bookstore, a clothing store, and an automobile dealer.

● A *manufacturing business* creates new property. Examples are an automobile manufacturer, a food manufacturer, and a computer manufacturer.

Combined types

It is not unusual for one business to combine activities. Examples are an automobile dealer (a merchandiser) that may also do repairs (services), or a bakery (a manufacturer) that may also sell to the public (a merchandiser).

Learning Goal 1: Explain What a Business Is and What It Does

▼ *Business Operations*

WHAT IS WEALTH?

Overview

Because the primary goal of a business is to accumulate wealth, it is important that we agree on exactly what "wealth" means.

Wealth defined

Wealth is property that has a dollar value.

The idea of wealth

"Wealth" refers to the *dollar value* characteristic of property. If the property is in the form of money, its value is easy to know, and it can be used to buy things and pay debts. Other property that has value, but that is not money, can be sold or exchanged for money (example: selling equipment).

Although most property is also physically useful (like equipment), the idea of wealth ignores this utility and focuses only on the dollar value.

Wealth is important, because its value can be used to acquire any other resource.

Wealth examples

- money
- equipment that you could sell for $500
- *account receivable* (the legal right to collect money from a customer)
- shares of stock that you could sell
- clothing for sale in a store
- land that is worth $100,000
- a car that you can sell for $5,000
- a calculator that you can sell for $5
- office supplies worth $900

  Note: All of these examples both have dollar value and can be owned.

WHAT IS WEALTH? (continued)

Not wealth

This item ...	is not wealth because ...
Old broken equipment that no one wants	it has no value.
Shares of stock in a bankrupt business	it has no value.
Food that is spoiled and dangerous	it has no value.
The services of an employee	a service cannot be owned (because it is immediately consumed).
The telephone service you receive	a service cannot be owned (because it is immediately consumed).
The financial advice that you receive from an accountant	a service cannot be owned (because it is immediately consumed).
The rental of a computer	a service cannot be owned (because it is immediately consumed).

Property and services compared

The table below helps you compare property and services, and indicates whether or not they can be called wealth.

Resource	Useful?	Can it have dollar value?	Can it be wealth?
Services	Yes	Yes	No, because it cannot be owned.
Property	Yes	Yes	Yes, because it can be owned.

Coming up next ...

Exactly *how* does a business operate so that it can accumulate wealth?

CHECK YOUR UNDERSTANDING

Fill in each blank space with the correct word. The answers are below.

A business is an organization which creates and sells new resources, and which has the primary goal of accumulating _____. This is property which has a dollar _____.

There are only two kinds of resources that can be created and sold. They are _____ and _____. Only _____ can be wealth, because it can be owned.

ANSWERS

A business is an organization which creates and sells new resources, and which has the primary goal of accumulating wealth. This is property which has a dollar value.

There are only two kinds of resources that can be created and sold. They are property and services. Only property can be wealth, because it can be owned.

HOW A BUSINESS ACCUMULATES WEALTH

Overview	A business accumulates wealth by creating and selling things (resources) that people (customers) need. Because these resources have value, the business is paid other valuable property by the customers.
Examples	The table on page 10 shows you some examples of how a business creates resources and accumulates wealth.

HOW A BUSINESS ACCUMULATES WEALTH (continued)

A business does this:	so it created the valuable resource of ...	and the business accumulates wealth because ...
performs computer repairs for $300	computer repairs (service)	the customer pays $300 cash for the value of the repairs received
shows a movie	entertainment (service)	the customers pay for the value of the tickets and to be entertained
makes and sells 1,000 loaves of fresh bread to a store	loaves of bread (property)	it receives money for the value of the bread
makes and sells 100 new computers for $200,000	computers (property)	the customers pay $200,000 cash for the value of the computers
operates a grocery store that sells 1,000 loaves of bread and other foods	providing a selection of bread and other foods (service)	the customers pay the store for the value of the food and the service provided

HOW A BUSINESS CREATES A NEW RESOURCE

Overview

By now you know that a business creates and sells new resources, but that does not yet explain *how* a business creates the new resources. The discussion below tells you how that is done.

HOW A BUSINESS CREATES A NEW RESOURCE (continued)

**Resources
are used up**

A business creates valuable new resources by using up other valuable resources. In other words, a business creates new property and services by using up other property and services.

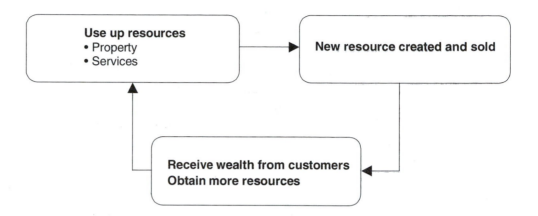

In the table below, notice that the only two kinds of resources used up are property and services, in order to create new and different property or services.

Business action	The resource created is ...	and examples of resources used up by the business are ...
Richland Bakery makes and sells 1,000 loaves of fresh bread.	1,000 loaves of bread, a resource which did not exist until it was produced,	the flour, water, and other ingredients of the bread dough; employee and manager labor; the equipment wear and tear.
Brookhaven grocery store sells the bread to shoppers.	the service of providing access to a selection of different breads,	employee and manager labor; electricity for light, heat, and power; the bread that the store had to purchase in order to sell.
El Paso Company manufactures 100 new computers.	a computer, which did not exist until it was manufactured,	employee and manager labor; metal and plastic components in the computer; the air and water of the city where the business is located.
Your local theater group presents Shakespeare's "Hamlet."	the service of entertainment,	the rental of the theater; the use of actors' labor; the wear and tear on the costumes.

HOW A BUSINESS CREATES A NEW RESOURCE (continued)

Business term: expenses	People in business have a name for the dollar amount of a resource consumed in the operations that create a new resource. The *dollar cost* of any resource used up in the process of creating a new resource is called an ***expense.***

> *Note:* "Used up" or "consumed" means not replaced by any other resource.

It does not make any difference what kind of resource is consumed. Services, supplies, equipment, merchandise, or any other kind of resource can be used up in order to create a new resource. Whatever the cost of the resource consumed, that is the amount of the expense.

Examples of expenses	• $100 of office supplies used up is called "Office Supplies Expense."

• $2,000 of cash paid to employees is called "Wages Expense."
• The bread sold to customers by a grocery store cost the store $500. When the bread is sold, the store has $500 "Cost of Sales Expense."
• A furniture maker uses wood, nails, and fabric to make chairs. When the chairs are sold, the cost of these materials are "Cost of Sales Expense."

Not expenses	• A business uses up $10,000 to pay off a bank loan. This is not an expense because paying a debt is not part of the process of creating a new resource for customers.

• A business gives up $100 cash in order to buy $100 of supplies. This is not an expense because one resource is simply replacing another (supplies for cash). Total value of resources remains the same.

HOW MUCH VALUE IS CREATED?

Overview	The entire purpose of using up resources is to create a new resource *that is valuable*. A business is not interested in creating something that has little or no value because no one will buy it. A business tries hard to create as much value as it can for every dollar of resources used up.

HOW MUCH VALUE IS CREATED? (continued)

| *Added value* | The total dollar value of a new resource that a business creates is called ***added value***. The process of incurring expenses to create a new, valuable resource is sometimes called *adding value*. |

The table below shows you some examples of added value and the expenses that create it.

The resource created:	so the added value is …	and value was added by incurring expenses such as …
Blinn Bakery makes *muffins* that can be sold for $1 each,	$1 each,	Wages Expense, Supplies Expense, and Cost of Sales Expense.
Blinn Bakery makes *walnut muffins* which can be sold for $1.25 each,	$1.25 each,	walnuts, which increased expense, but also increased the added value by $.25 per muffin.
Laredo Plumbing Service does *plumbing repairs* and charges the customer $375 for the job,	$375 for the job,	Labor Expense and Parts Expense.
Computers are manufactured by San Antonio Company. A computer can be sold for $1,000,	$1,000 each,	Labor Expense, Utility Expense, Rent Expense, Supplies Expense, and Cost of Sales Expense.
Kilgore Nursery offers *a selection* of young pine trees for $20 each,	$20 each,	Utilities Expense, Fertilizer Expense, and Labor Expense.

Warning to businesses!

Expenses do not always add value.

As you have seen in the examples, a business consumes resources because it is trying to add value. Unfortunately, while producing a new resource, businesses often consume resources that actually add very little or even no value. These expenses are wasted, because little or no value is added. The customer will not pay for the amount of these expenses as part of the price of the resource created. A successful business eliminates as much of this nonvalue-added resource consumption as possible.

HOW MUCH VALUE IS CREATED? (continued)

Examples of NO value added

The resource created:	The business has this expense:	and the expense does not add value because …
Jones Company manufactures and sells a computer.	$10,000 for *storing the computers* before they are sold,	customers will not want to pay more just because the company made too many computers and had to pay for storage.
Jones Company manufactures and sells a computer.	the company president *uses the company airplane* to fly his dog back and forth between New York and Los Angeles,	the cost of these flights, and wear and tear on the airplane, do not make the computers more useful or valuable to customers. Use of the company airplane in this way will not help to add value, even though it makes the dog happy.
Jones Company manufactures and sells a computer.	$25,000 *labor time* required to repair manufacturing mistakes,	customers do not want to pay for the cost of fixing new merchandise. Customers want a product that works properly the first time.

*"Really? And just how much value
do you add with that stupid flag?"*

• • •

HOW MUCH VALUE IS CREATED? (continued)

**Added value
is difficult to predict**

In reality, the amount of added value that a business creates is only an educated guess until the resource created is actually sold. A business can never be completely sure of the total added value until it sells what it has created. It is the customer who finally determines the actual added value by purchasing the resource and paying for it.

Regardless of how carefully a business designs or sells the resource it is creating, "value" is still just a feeling in the mind of the customer. This can change at any time. Moreover, customers are different, and some will perceive value differently than others.

Here are some interesting examples of how added value can be unpredictable:

If a company …	then we would guess that the added value will be …	because …
uses higher quality parts in the toasters it makes,	probably greater than before	many people want improved reliability and quality, and will pay more for it.
offers Christmas tree ornaments for sale on December 1 for $25 each,	$25 each	customers are willing to pay this amount because they are excited about Christmas and want new ornaments.
offers the same Christmas ornaments on February 1 for $25 each,	probably a lot less than $25 each	people are not so excited about Christmas anymore. Changing the time of the year reduced the total amount of added value.
angers potential customers because it damages the environment,	anywhere from a little less to a lot less than before	people become so angry that they refuse to purchase the company products. (*Note:* this actually happens. Example: customers boycotted tuna products until tuna sellers agreed to stop killing dolphins in tuna nets.)
pays for a big advertising promotion for a product, although not changing the product in any way,	probably greater	even though the product itself has not changed, it may have improved in the *minds* of the customers! Resources used for repeated advertising can add significant value, even if a product is actually unchanged.

HOW MUCH VALUE IS CREATED? (continued)

The value chain

Every business has a value chain. The *value chain* is the sequence of all the activities that consume resources for the purpose of adding value. Together, all the expenses in the value chain result in the total cost of all resources consumed.

> *Note:* The name "value chain" might be a little misleading, because as we know now, not all resources consumed will always add value.

Example of value chain

Bad Apple Cider Company has to pay for fertilizer, water, and labor to maintain the apple trees. Then it pays for processing the apples into cider. After that, it pays for the cost of distributing and selling the cider. All during operations, the business also pays for the cost of management.

> *Question for the owner:* Do all parts of this value chain add significant value?

CHECK YOUR UNDERSTANDING

Fill in each blank space with the correct word. The answers are below.

A business accumulates wealth by creating and selling new resources. New resources can only be created when a business uses up other_____. The business term for the dollar cost of resources used up for this purpose is _____.

The dollar value of the new resources that a business creates is called _____ _____. This is usually (easy/difficult) _____ to precisely predict. As a general rule, (all/not all) _____ expenses will add significant value.

ANSWERS

A business accumulates wealth by creating and selling new resources. New resources can only be created when a business uses up other resources. The business term for the dollar cost of resources used up for this purpose is expense.

The dollar value of the new resources that a business creates is called added value. This is usually difficult to precisely predict. As a general rule, not all expenses will add significant value.

CONFIRMING THE VALUE CREATED

Overview	You know that added value is difficult to predict. The point at which a business finally knows exactly how much total value has been created is when a sale is made to a customer.
Business term: revenue	When a business actually makes a sale to a customer, the true total of added value is confirmed. Businesspeople have a special name for this final amount: revenue. ***Revenue*** is the dollar value of a sale. It is the amount the customer pays for the resource created.
Example #1 of revenue	Blinn Bakery incurs expenses in order to make 100 muffins which can be sold for $1 each. So far, the company has sold 70 muffins for a total of $70.

- The total amount of added value that the company believes has been created is $100, because 100 muffins will normally sell for that amount.
- The total revenue is $70, because this is the actual dollar value of sales up to now. The company has received $70 from customers. This means that $70 of added value has been confirmed so far.

Example #2 of revenue	Vancouver Company makes glazed clay pots for gardens. The company incurs expenses in order make 20 blue pots and offers the pots for sale at $10 each, based on past experience. So the added value of the 20 pots appears to be $200.

- The company sells 10 of the clay pots, so it has $100 of revenue. This confirms the added value of 10 clay pots as $100.
- However, the company is unable to sell the remaining 10 blue pots and must reduce the price to $8 per pot. At this price, all the remaining pots are sold. The company has $80 of revenue for the remaining 10 pots, thus confirming their added value.

The total revenue of $180 for all 20 pots confirms that their real added value was actually $180. (The company has received $180 in wealth from customers.)

Example #3 of revenue	Artie the golf pro owns the golf shop next to the municipal golf course. Artie offers golf lessons for $100 per hour. Artie sold 20 hours of paid golf instruction this month. Artie says, "The business earned $2,000 of instruction revenue." This means that the business wealth increased by $2,000 because the business created and sold $2,000 of added value in the form of golf instruction.

CONFIRMING THE VALUE CREATED (continued)

Not revenue

- Burnaby Company collected $10,000 from a bank loan. This is not revenue because it does not come from making a sale. It must be repaid.
- The owner of Surrey Company invests $10,000 in his business. This is not revenue because it does not come from making a sale.

Do not confuse revenue with wealth

"Revenue" refers to the dollar amount of a sale. Making a sale is one particular source of wealth.

"Wealth" is the dollar value of the *property* that is received. This property could be anything—cash, accounts receivable, gold, supplies, land—although, in reality, it is almost always cash or accounts receivable.

SUCCESS OR FAILURE?

The owner's difficult dilemma

To be successful, the owners and managers of businesses must determine which combination of resources adds the most value. This is not easy to do because, as we have seen, the amount of value added is only an estimate until whatever is created is actually sold.

In spite of all this difficulty, the method by which a company utilizes its resources *does affect* the actual added value—the revenue—by *some* significant amount.

Example of combining resources

Bad Apple Cider Company makes and sells apple cider. The company makes 200 gallons of apple cider which the managers estimate can be sold for $10 per gallon, an added value of $2,000. When the cider is actually sold, the company has $2,000 of revenue, confirming the amount of value created.

The owners of Bad Apple Cider Company say, "We have earned $2,000 of cider revenue." The owners must figure out precisely what combination of resources created the total added value. Is it some combination of the types of apples used to make the cider? How about the method of processing? The quality of the apples? The convenience of the store? The selection of ciders in the store? The time of year? ... Business is tricky.

Learning Goal 1: Explain What a Business Is and What It Does

SUCCESS OR FAILURE? (continued)

Success	If a business creates and sells more value than the cost of the resources consumed in the value chain, then a business is successful. This means that revenues are greater than expenses. When *revenues are greater than expenses,* the business has a *profit.* People in business call this by the name ***net income.*** Net income makes the wealth of the business increase and the business grows.

Failure

If *revenues are less than expenses,* the business has a loss. This is called a ***net loss***. This is bad, because the business is using up a greater value of resources than it is receiving from customers. Wealth is decreasing. There are two possible reasons for this:

- The expenses (resources used up) cannot add enough total value.
- The business is not charging enough for the actual value that it is creating.

This is why businesses lose money and go out of business.

Example #1: net income

The price charged by Swell Computer Manufacturing Company is $2,500 per computer, and the company makes and sells 100 computers. The cost of the resources consumed (expenses) is $1,500 per computer. So, the business has total revenue of $250,000 and total expenses of $150,000. This is a net income of $100,000. Even though some of the $150,000 expenses might not add value, other expenses created enough value so there was a net income.

Example #2: net loss

At the end of the year, Jiffy Tax Services has $300,000 of revenue for all the tax returns that it prepared. Expenses were $400,000. Jiffy has a net loss of $100,000. There are two possibilities:

- The expenses do not add enough total value. The business must change the way it uses resources or go out of business. This means:
  — Use the resources more efficiently so total expenses are less.
  — Use the resources in a different way so greater value is created.

- The business is not charging enough for the actual value that it is creating. In this case, the business should increase what it charges customers.

☞*QUICK REVIEW*☜

● A business is an organization which has the primary goal of accumulating wealth by creating and selling new and valuable (economic) resources.

● There are only two economic resources: property and services.

● "Wealth" is property that has value.

● A business creates a new economic resource by consuming other resources in order to add value. The cost of a resource consumed to add value is called an "expense."

● Unfortunately, not all expenses will add value, and final added value is difficult to predict.

● What the new resource actually sells for is called "revenue." Revenue confirms the actual added value.

● In a successful business, revenues exceed expenses. In an unsuccessful business, revenues are less than expenses.

☞*VOCABULARY*☜

Account receivable: an amount owed by a customer to a business (page 7)

Added value: the value created when a new resource is created (page 13)

Economic resource: a resource that can be valued or measured in dollars (page 4)

Expense: the cost of a resource used up in the process of creating a new resource (page 12)

Net income: when revenues are greater than expenses (page 19)

Net loss: when expenses are greater than revenues (page 19)

Property: any resource that can be owned (page 5)

Revenue: the dollar value of a sale—what a customer pays for a new resource (page 17)

Services: the use of labor or the use of someone's property (page 5)

Value chain: the sequence of activities that consumes resources for the purpose of adding value (page 16)

PRACTICE FOR LEARNING GOAL 1

SOLUTIONS FOR LEARNING GOAL 1 BEGIN ON PAGE 24.

Learning Goal 1 is about defining and identifying a business. Use these questions and problems to practice what you have learned about a business.

MULTIPLE CHOICE
On the line provided, enter the letter of the best answer for each question.

1) A business is ____
   A) an easy way to get rich.
   B) an organization which has the purpose of accumulating wealth.
   C) an organization that always adds value.
   D) an activity that provides little or no benefit to society.
2) The way a business operates is by ____
   A) borrowing and obtaining investments.
   B) using up resources.
   C) avoiding all risk.
   D) using up resources in order to create and sell new resources.
3) When a business is creating a new resource that customers will want, the business is said to be ____
   A) adding value.
   B) making sales.
   C) doing market research.
   D) advertising.
4) "Bad Apple Cider Company had $200 of revenue." This statement refers to ____
   A) cash, in the amount of $200.
   B) an increase in business wealth in the amount of $200, caused by making a sale.
   C) a profit of $200.
   D) all of the above.
5) In order to add value, a business always has to ____
   A) make a profit.
   B) consume resources.
   C) make a sale.
   D) both B and C.
6) Expenses ____
   A) will always add significant value.
   B) may add little or no value.
   C) require a nonvalue-added activity.
   D) none of the above.
7) Added value results from any expense which ____
   A) is not excessive.
   B) is cost-effective.
   C) makes the final product more valuable or useful to customers.
   D) uses up resources.
8) The actual amount of revenue (total added value) is always determined ____
   A) by business management.
   B) by the productivity of the employees.
   C) by how much the customers decide to pay for the resource created.
   D) by a predetermined mathematical calculation for each product.

PRACTICE FOR LEARNING GOAL 1

SOLUTIONS FOR LEARNING GOAL 1 BEGIN ON PAGE 24.

9) A business knows that it has net income when _____
    A) revenues are greater than expenses.
    B) expenses are greater than revenues.
    C) it is still able to repay its loans.
    D) it is certain that it is adding value.

10) Which of the following expenses probably do not add any value? _____
    A) The $500 cost of the utilities to air-condition an accounting office.
    B) The $15,000 cost of the employee wages in the computer assembly operation.
    C) The $2,000 cost of the cookie dough that was spoiled in the bakery refrigerator.
    D) The $750 cost of the janitorial service.

___

REINFORCEMENT PROBLEMS

1) **How is value being added?** For each of the following situations, write a short and clear explanation of how the business is adding value.

    A) A restaurant prepares a meal.

    B) A bank advertises its new services and low loan rates.

    C) An automobile manufacturer crash-tests the new models.

    D) A doctor studies new surgical techniques.

___

2) **Determine the amount of added value.** In each situation below, give your advice about what you think the final value will be.

    A) Thinking that they have created the greatest new product since sliced bread, executives at Great Products Company produce liver-flavored toothpaste. Each tube costs $1.50 to produce, and this cannot be changed. The management wants to sell the product for $2 per tube. The managers have heard about added value, and they want you—a consultant—to tell them if their proposed selling price is a good estimate of the added value of their product.

    B) Management at Green Bay Company is thinking about spending $100,000 to install on-site exercise and child-care facilities for its employees. However, to pay for this, the company will have to cancel the purchase of four new delivery trucks. Management wants to maximize added value, and is not sure how their decision will affect the added value of the products. Write a brief response to the managers.

___

Learning Goal 1: Explain What a Business Is and What It Does

SOLUTIONS FOR LEARNING GOAL 1 BEGIN ON PAGE 24.

3) **Learning Goal 1 Cumulative Review.** Jerry Berg recently graduated from veterinary school and received his license to practice veterinary medicine. A few months ago, he opened a veterinary clinic. The clinic provides medical care for animals and also sells pet-care merchandise that customers frequently need. Last month, the clinic billed customers a total of $38,500 for medical care services. At the beginning of the month, the merchandise was marked up to a total selling price of $2,500. However, for various reasons, the merchandise sold for only $2,200. $10,000 of the cash received from customers was used to purchase new equipment.

In order to operate the clinic, Dr. Berg employs a medical staff of five people. Employee wages last month totaled $21,200. The clinic also pays $2,000 per month for rent, and utilities of $450. The cost of the merchandise was $2,000. Repair services to repair equipment that was damaged by a poorly trained employee was $1,100. Supplies were an additional $800. The clinic advertises its services in local magazines and papers, and this costs $400 per month. Finally, accounting and management services are $750 per month.

Answer the questions below about the clinic.

A) Would you classify this business as service, merchandising, or manufacturing?

B) How does this business add value? What kind of new resource is being created?

C) What was the actual added value as determined by the revenue? Was this different in any way from what was expected?

D) What kinds of resources does this clinic use up in order to add value?

E) Describe the value chain for this business. What was the total expense in the value chain?

F) Did all expenses in the value chain add significant value?

G) As a business, was the clinic successful or unsuccessful for the month? How much did the wealth of the business change?

SOLUTIONS FOR LEARNING GOAL 1

PRACTICE QUESTIONS FOR LEARNING GOAL 1 BEGIN ON PAGE 21.

MULTIPLE CHOICE

1) B.
2) D.
3) A.
4) B. "Revenue" is a word that confuses many people. Usually they think revenue is the same thing as wealth (like cash, or some other valuable thing). Revenue is not a *thing*. Revenue is expressed as a dollar value; however, revenue is really an explanation of *why* wealth increased.
5) D. A business does not know how much value was added by consuming resources until a sale is made.
6) B.
7) C.
8) C.
9) A. Notice that "D" is incorrect, because a business can be adding value and still have a loss. This is because it is not adding *enough* value!
10) C. Customers do not want cookie prices increased because of resources consumed by waste and loss.

REINFORCEMENT PROBLEMS

1) A) A meal is created using various resources such as labor, food, and equipment. The meal provides valuable pleasure and energy to the customer, who pays for it.
   B) Information is made available that will inform people of the availability of new services and low-cost loans. People will want this information and want to borrow money, which the bank will charge for.
   C) The automobiles are made safer, which customers will perceive as adding to the total value of the automobile, making it more desirable. At a minimum, the cost of testing resources will be added to the price of the new car. The customer will probably pay it—and probably much more—very willingly.
   D) People are willing to pay more for better, safer surgery.
2) A) Unless you think that people will like liver-flavored toothpaste (personally, I find it revolting), I would say that the total added value of the toothpaste is zero (unless it might be sold as a joke novelty) because I think no one will buy it at any price. So, the cost of the resources used to produce it will be lost, because thousands of tubes of the toothpaste will have to be disposed of, probably in a toxic-waste site.
   B) This is a difficult question, but typical of the uncertainty managers have to deal with. My own feeling is that the exercise and child-care facilities will probably add more value than the value received from using four new trucks, depending upon how many other trucks are available and the need for the new ones. This is because healthy employees and employees with peace of mind will be far more careful and creative. They will produce and create quality things that ultimately increase the total added value (revenue). Secondly, cost of production will probably decline, employee turnover and training costs will be reduced, and company loyalty might be created, so total expenses will also probably be reduced. This reduces the amount of resources used, even if total added value is not changed at all.
3) A) This is a combination business. It is both a service (veterinary service) and a merchandising (pet-care products) business. However, it is primarily a service business.
   B) The clinic adds value primarily by providing veterinary medical care, which people need and are willing to pay for. Secondarily, the clinic adds value by offering a selection of pet-care merchandise, which people also need and will pay for. Two new resources are being created: 1) veterinary medical services, and 2) pet-care merchandise selection.
   C) Total added value confirmed by the revenue was $40,700 ($38,500 + $2,200). Based on the initial prices, the clinic apparently thought the merchandise had an added value of $2,500, instead of $2,200 it actually sold for.
   D) 1) Service resources consumed: $25,900 ($21,200 + $2,000 + $450 + $1,100 + $400 + $750)
      2) Property resources consumed: $2,800 ($2,000 + $800)

Learning Goal 1: Explain What a Business Is and What It Does

PRACTICE QUESTIONS FOR LEARNING GOAL 1 BEGIN ON PAGE 21.

3) *continued*

E) The value chain includes consuming both services and property. Wages, rent, utilities, repairs, supplies, advertising, accounting and management, and cost of merchandise sold are the items that we know about. Total expenses in the value chain were $28,700.

F) No. The repairs to the damaged equipment caused by poor training did not add value. Also, I have some doubts about the wages of the poorly trained employee adding much value in the future.

G) The wealth of the business increased by $12,000 during the month ($40,700 – $28,700). Because the business had this $12,000 net income, I would say that last month was successful. *Note:* using the $10,000 cash to purchase equipment does not diminish wealth; it simply changes form from cash into equipment.

Your Questions?

It is *very* important to be aware of what you need to understand better. What do you need to understand better about this learning goal? Use this space to write the questions that you want to discuss with your classmates, instructor, or supervisor. Try to be very specific about what is bothering you, such as explanations that you do not fully understand.

DO YOU LIKE A GOOD STORY?

It might help you to remember better

Sometimes people remember information better when it is part of an interesting story. The story that begins on page 27 tells about how mankind first discovered what a business really is. The story has adventure, mystery, and romance—all for your enjoyment! So, if you think a story might help you remember better, of if you just want to have some fun, go ahead ... the adventures of Darius await you.

Technical content

This part of the story contains the following technical content:

- the basic financial structure of any business
- the definition of "asset"
- asset valuation basics
- claims on assets
- using the accounting equation

You can skip the story

If you prefer to study the above technical content more quickly, you can skip the story and go directly to page 36, where the normal presentation and practice continue.

AN HISTORICAL FABLE

The Wealth of Darius

PART I

How Darius Came to Be a Merchant

 ong, long ago, when civilization was just beginning, when the world was fresh, and when the Greek people believed that gods lived far above the clouds on the heights of great Mount Olympus, there lived a youth named Darius. What happened to Darius changed the world forever.

Darius was the child of a poor family, with many brothers and sisters, but he was lucky. The gods had given Darius the gifts of the artist. Everyone in the village admired the child for his fine drawing and painting. His skill surprised everyone, for none of his brothers or sisters nor his mother or father had ever shown the slightest of such talents.

Darius grew into a dark-haired and athletic young man, and became an apprentice to a painter who painted walls and frescoes, and sometimes pottery for wealthy collectors. Darius had such exceptional talent that it was not long until he became more skilled than his master, a friendly man named Ammon.

One day Ammon came to Darius and said, "Young man, it is time for you to be on your own. There is nothing more that I can teach you now. Your beautiful designs, bright colors, and expert painting show the world that you are already better than the master. I am getting old, and it is time for me to enjoy the rest of my life without the worries of business."

Ammon continued. "You have such great talents, Darius. I would be honored if you would buy my shop from me and carry on the name of this honorable business. I will sell it to you for 7,000 gold coins, even though I might be able to get more."

When he heard Ammon say these things, Darius' heart rose and then fell. He had almost no money. He had no chance to buy the business.

But Ammon continued. "I know that you are still a poor apprentice. I will wait seven years, and then you can pay me for the business. By that time, I think you will be a rich and famous painter. In the meantime, I only ask that you allow me to work for you as your employee for two gold coins per week so that I may have some income. I also ask two additional gold coins per week for allowing you to have the seven years to pay me."

Darius' eyes filled with tears of gratitude. He and Ammon signed an agreement according to Ammon's terms. Poor but talented young Darius became the owner of his own business. He earned the admiration of all who saw and purchased his beautiful and original work.

Darius' Troubles

Darius worked very, very hard to prove to Ammon that he could succeed. However, Darius was worried, and every day he prayed to the gods on Mount Olympus to help him.

Darius had the talents of an artist, not a businessperson. So, when Darius began to be responsible for the business, he soon felt confused and frightened. He did not dare ask Ammon for too much advice, because he did not want to worry and trouble the old man. Besides, Darius was sure that neither Ammon nor any other merchant would have the answer to the most frightening worry of all.

What worried Darius most of all was that he did not know a way to determine what kind of condition the business was in. How does one know if a business is successful or unsuccessful? Even if there were many customers, would there be enough money to pay back the debt to Ammon? A few times, Darius asked other merchants how they would know if a business was successful, but he always received different answers from different people.

One merchant answered, "Well, that is easy! The more gold you have, the more successful you are." Another merchant said, "Success is when the business does not have debts." Still another said, "Many customers means success." Darius just became more confused than before.

At first, Darius would sometimes wonder about whether he was any more prosperous because he owned a business. But after a while, he stopped thinking about his own prosperity because all he thought about was paying Ammon. Even worse, Darius then remembered that there were other people to whom the business also owed money: Aulis, the merchant who sold paint and glaze; and Hela, the merchant who supplied the paper, ink, and drawing tools Darius used for designs.

Darius tried to think: "Let me see … the business has some gold now. The business owes money to Aulis and Hela, and will have to pay Ammon four gold coins per week. But there is still some paint that I bought last month, and the prince Cronos has not yet paid for the large wall painting that was finished last week, and there are brushes and drawing tools, and … aaahh! How does all that tell me if the business is any better or worse than when I bought it? How do I know if I will ever be able to pay Ammon? I will be shamed in front of the world. I am sorry Ammon, sorry, *sorry!*"

When Darius returned to his house that evening and lay down to sleep, the worry demons whispered and giggled in his ears the entire night, and he never closed his eyes.

The Gods Intervene

The gods, who can observe all that mortal man does, had been watching Darius. The immortal gods reposed in the garden of eternal life on Mount Olympus, and debated what they should do with Darius. The god Hermes (pronounced *her-meez*) was especially interested. Hermes wore winged sandals, and was the god of commerce and the marketplace. Of all the gods, Hermes was the cleverest and most cunning, and he was forever causing discord and arguments among the other gods.

"I think it is time for mankind to learn a secret of commerce from us," Hermes said. "These foolish mortals pretend to do business, they buy and they sell, they count their worthless little coins, and still they have almost no idea of what a business is or what they are doing. Let us give them new knowledge."

"Yes," said Apollo, the god of music, truth, and light. "It is time to give humanity a secret. After all, we make the dull little beasts suffer enough with our games."

"What! Give them a secret of the gods? Never!" said Artemis, the goddess of hunting and of all wild things. "What a waste it would be. They would never know what to do with a secret of ours, and this fool Darius only knows how to paint pictures."

"Well," rumbled Hades (pronounced *hey-deez*), the god of the dead and the world below, who had heard the discussion and appeared from his lands under the earth, "it will do them no good when they come to spend their time with me," at which Hades and Artemis laughed heartily, while Apollo frowned.

Hermes had started another argument and felt pleased with himself. Now he was ready for his next trick. "So," he said, "if none of the gods themselves can decide, let us wager that Darius can decide for us! I will test this mortal, and if he passes my test I will reward him with a secret of the gods that will end his worries. If he fails my test, then Artemis may turn him into a wild pig to be hunted anytime she wishes."

"Yes, excellent!" they roared, Artemis shouting the loudest.

Hermes was happy with himself again. He had tricked the gods into gambling one of their secrets on the test of a human which, as we all know, no one can ever be sure about.

A Strange Event

Darius felt exhausted, confused, and full of worry when he left his house the next morning. He walked down the road to a small favorite lake, where he planned to bathe and regain his energy after a night with no sleep. He had been walking for perhaps ten minutes when he observed a dark form next to the road. As he approached the object, Darius began to notice a foul odor coming from the shape. To his surprise, the form was a filthy old beggar woman, disgustingly soiled and infested with lice.

The woman screeched, "I am hungry! I have no place to stay. Give me food and a place to stay! I am too tired to walk. Carry me to a place to rest!" Darius was already burdened with his own worries and concerns. He did not want another problem, so he walked away from the repellent woman. After a few steps, however, he thought, "Her problems are just as important to her as mine are to me. Who knows? If I fail in my business, as seems likely now, someday I may be nearly the outcast she is today."

With that thought he turned, picked up the disgusting woman, and carried her back to his house. He gave her bread, what meat he had left, heated some water for her bath, and told her to rest as long as she wished. As Darius prepared to leave his house the second time, a brilliant light filled the room, momentarily blinding him. As he regained his vision, he saw the old woman disappear. A large, powerful-looking man wearing winged sandals replaced her at the center of the light.

"You have passed," proclaimed the figure. Darius also heard the sounds of laughter and angry voices, but he could not see anyone else in the room. In that moment, he knew that he was in the presence of a god. Darius threw himself to the floor, trembling.

"Yes," said Hermes, who had disguised himself as the foul old woman, "you may be full of your own concerns, but you did not abandon someone even more hopeless than yourself, poor mortal." With that, the imposing god threw back his head, his thundering laughter filling the room, and pronounced, "You have defeated the gods!"

The huge, brilliant figure spoke again. "And now, Darius, as the god of commerce, I reward you with a secret of the gods that will end your present confusion. I thereby bring you peace of mind, for now. Rise up and listen, so that I may give you the secret of knowing the condition of your business at any time you wish."

As Darius slowly rose, the god continued. "Listen carefully to what I tell you now, mortal. The true picture of a business is simply this: wealth and claims on the wealth. That is all.

"At any time you choose, you may determine the condition of your business. First, determine the wealth of the business. Business wealth means any valuable things that belong only to the business. These things are called 'assets.' Assets are the business wealth. They are also used by the business to operate.

"Next, determine the claims on the assets. There are no more than two kinds of claims. The owner, of course, has a claim on the assets. But if there are business debts, which are the claims of creditors, then the creditors have first claim. Whatever value of all assets exceeds the claims of the creditors, then this excess may be claimed by you, the owner."

Finishing, the god said, "Here is how to remember what I have told you today: First, determine the value of all the assets. Next, determine the claims on the assets—the creditors and the owner. The total claims always equal the total assets . . . but the creditors have first claim.

"Remember this well, mortal, for it is the essence of every business. I expect you to understand this. I will visit you again in one year, when I will decide if you have learned to properly use the gift of knowledge that I have given to you."

With that, the god and the bright light disappeared in a shower of arching golden sparkles, leaving Darius dazzled and speechless. There was a roll of parchment paper on the wooden table in the center of the room. Written on the paper in gold print were the words:

ASSETS = CREDITORS' CLAIMS + OWNER'S CLAIM

Darius Tries Out The Secret

When he recovered his senses, Darius looked at the words on the paper and felt happier than he had felt since he had bought the business. He thought, "No longer will I operate my business in darkness! I will learn to use this at once!" Excitedly, Darius grabbed the paper and raced toward town, passing the place where he had met the old woman, and ran the entire distance to his shop.

Ignoring everyone else in the shop, Darius flew straight to his table in the back, where he did his planning and drawing. Slowly he took a deep breath, found a piece of paper to write on, and began to think.

"Let me see," he thought, "first I determine the wealth of the business. The name for this is assets. Hermes himself told me that an asset is anything with value that belongs to the business. So, what assets does my business have?"

Slowly and carefully, Darius began to list the assets belonging to the business, along with their values:

Gold *$2,500*
Receivable from Prince Cronos *500*
Painting equipment ....

As he was about to write down a number for the painting equipment, Darius began to hesitate. "What is the value of this equipment? I think I could sell it for $3,000 because Thrice, that bandit, offered me only $1,500 for it last week. Everyone knows that he never offers more than half." Still hesitating, Darius thought, "Yet, I cannot be certain until I actually sell it."

Then Darius had an excellent idea. "I know! I will use the cost that I paid for the equipment when I bought it. At least this is a number of which I can be completely certain. Only when I actually sell the equipment will I find out if it has some other value. This is acceptable."

And so, using this rule, he continued writing:

> Painting equipment......................2,700   (my cost)
>
> Painting supplies............................ 1,900   (my cost)
>
> Other supplies..................................... 300   (my cost)
>
> Other assets.. 800   (my cost)

These were all the assets that he could see. He tried to think if there were any other assets that might belong to the business. "The building!" he thought. But then he remembered that the building was actually owned by Amar, the landlord, and Darius paid Amar $25 in gold each month to use the building. So, the building really belonged to Amar.

Then Darius thought about Ammon. "Is Ammon an asset?" he wondered. Ammon was still a very valuable employee, but did he actually belong to the business like the equipment and supplies?

What do you think?
If you could help Darius answer this question before he decides what to do, how would you advise him? Should Ammon be considered a business asset? Write your answer:
After giving the problem much thought, Darius remembered that Hermes said that an asset must not only have value, but that it must also belong only to the business. So Darius decided that he could not include Ammon, since Ammon did not belong to the business like a table or a chair.

Darius then added up the assets and wrote the total on a piece of paper:

> Total assets: $8,700

This was beginning to make sense! Under his breath, he thanked the gods one more time. Anxiously, Darius now began to write down the total business debts:

Owing to Ammon........................$7,000

Owing to Aulis...............................400

Owing to Hela................................600

He could not think of any more debts, except he wondered if Ammon's future wages were a business debt. Also, Darius owed his neighbor one gold coin for some meat he had bought when he prepared dinner for his family last week. He stopped writing and thought hard about these two items.

What do you think?

If you could help Darius answer this question before he decides what to do, how would you advise him? Are Ammon's future wages a business debt right now? How about the money that Darius owes to his neighbor? Write your answer.

Darius thought for a long time. He slowly began to realize that Ammon's wages could not be a debt if Ammon had not yet done the work. The business did not owe money for things that it had not yet received, and so it did not owe Ammon for work that was not yet done.

As to the one gold coin owing for the meat—well, that was a debt, all right, but it was not a business debt. It was Darius' personal debt because he was the one who had received the meat. Again, the business itself had not received anything, and so it did not owe anything.

Darius then added up the total business debts: $8,000.

Darius looked again at the words on the paper Hermes had left for him. He remembered that Hermes said that the owner's claim on the business wealth was whatever value of assets exceeded what was owed to the creditors.

The Owner's Claim

Darius realized that now all he had to do was simply make the totals on each side be equal. To do this, he needed to determine if the assets' value exceeded the creditors' claims. This excess would be the amount of owner's claim, if there was any. Darius started writing down the total assets and total creditors' claims. He already knew the total assets and creditors' claims, so he only had to fill in …

$$\textit{Assets} = \textit{Creditors' Claims} + \textit{Owner's Claim}$$
$$\$8,700 \qquad \$8,000$$

Before Darius could write anymore, he realized what was happening and his heart leaped into his throat. He held his breath. Electricity flashed down his spine. He stood up and sat down. He stood up and sat down again. And again. Then he jumped into the air and shouted out, "Oh yes, by the gods, I am worthy!" People in the shop stopped and looked at him.

What made Darius so deliriously happy was that the calculation showed that the condition of his business was such that the business had enough wealth ($8,700) to pay *all* the $8,000 of debts (including Ammon!), and still leave $700 which Darius could claim for himself as owner. He had not failed as an owner!

Finally, when his heart was beating more slowly, Darius sat down again and finished writing the calculation:

Assets = *Creditors' Claims* + *Owner's Claim*

$8,700 $8,000 $700

Darius was an artist, so he drew a picture of the condition of his business, because he knew this would help him to remember it better. His picture looked like this:

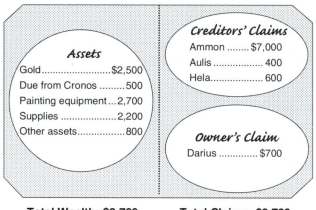

Assets

Gold $2,500
Due from Cronos 500
Painting equipment ... 2,700
Supplies 2,200
Other assets 800

Creditors' Claims

Ammon $7,000
Aulis 400
Hela 600

Owner's Claim

Darius $700

Total Wealth: $8,700   **Total Claims: $8,700**

It was all clear as day to him. Darius realized that now he had the power at any time to clearly see the picture of his business. This made him remember what Hermes had said: "The picture of a business is simply wealth and claims on that wealth."

How Darius Used His Knowledge

At first, Darius was so excited about his newfound power that he wanted to calculate the condition of his business almost every day. However, because the condition changed so little from one day to the next, he began the habit of calculating the condition at the end of each month. When he did this, Darius could clearly see the change in the condition of the business every month.

He discovered that the total wealth—that is, the total of the assets—would change. Sometimes the total of the assets would increase a little and sometimes a lot, and sometimes it would even decrease. Not only did the total amount of the assets change, but Darius discovered that the individual assets also changed. For example, sometimes the business would have more gold or less gold than before, or more supplies or less supplies than before, and so on.

Also, the total amount owing to the creditors would change. Sometimes the business would owe more to creditors than before and sometimes less. Darius watched the debts carefully.

Darius felt so good that he found a piece of paper and made a list of all the wonderful things that the calculation had made possible:

What I can see now but I could not see before:
- *I now see that the condition of my business is made up of assets and an equal amount of claims on those assets:*
  - *— Assets are wealth (and are also used by the business).*
  - *— The two types of claims on the assets are the creditors' and the owner's.*
- *I can know the condition of my business any time I want to by calculating these values.*
- *I can observe how the condition of my business is changing by doing the calculation every month.*
- *By watching the changes, I can make better decisions.*

Because of the success of the business, Darius was able to withdraw a little more money from the business for himself. His greatest enjoyment was to prepare dinners and parties for his mother and father and brothers and sisters, who had always been poor.

As the seasons passed, Darius continued on in this way. He worked hard, calculated the condition of his business, and was good to his family and friends.

But Darius had forgotten something important: Hermes' promise. It was now exactly a year since Hermes had promised to return.

To be continued …

LEARNING GOAL 2
Define and Identify Assets

OVERVIEW

Introduction

In business, the word for property is "assets." Assets (especially the right kind) are what make a business wealthy, successful, and powerful.

However, before we begin discussing business assets, we will do a quick review of all resources—property and services—just to make sure that these basic ideas are clear.

In Learning Goal 2, you will find:

▼ *A Review of Resources*

RESOURCES IN A BUSINESS

Resources consumed to add value	A business consumes resources for the purpose of creating and selling more valuable resources. This is often called "adding value."
Only two kinds of resources	On the planet earth, there are only two kinds of resources that can be bought and sold: property and services. These are also called "goods and services."

- *Property* is any resource that can be owned.
- *Services* are the use of labor or the use of someone else's property.

   Note: Because they can be bought and sold at some money amount, goods and services are sometimes called "economic" resources.

A business creates both kinds	A business can add value by producing either property or services, or both.
Example	Your business makes and sells fresh bread. The business has created bread, a valuable resource which can be owned. Your business also delivers the bread to restaurants and charges for this service. The delivery service is another valuable resource that customers want; however, the delivery service—although valuable—is not something that can be owned (services are immediately used up).
Which resource is most important?	Both property and services are essential to any business, because both are needed in order to make a business operate. For example, a bread company needs ovens (property) and oven repairs (services) to operate.

Besides being a useful resource, however, property has another feature that makes it more important than services: Besides being useful, property is also wealth.

▼ *The Dual Nature of Property*

PROPERTY AS RESOURCE AND WEALTH

Property provides two benefits	Most property has a dual nature that allows it to be used in two ways. First, property can be consumed as a *useful resource* in the adding-value process. Secondly, property is also *wealth*.
Property as a useful resource	A business obtains benefits by *consuming* property. In the examples below, each property item provides benefits as the item is used up or worn out in the adding-value process of operations.

Property	Benefits
computer equipment	calculations, projections, document preparation
book	knowledge
insurance policy	protection from losses
truck	delivery and transportation
coffee supplies	nourishment

Property as wealth	Wealth is property that has a dollar value. Because wealth is property, wealth can be owned and kept for future use. This makes it extremely useful for obtaining other resources.

Wealth (property)	which has value because ...
computer equipment	it could be sold for cash (used to obtain other resources).
book	it could be sold for cash (used to obtain another resource).
... and so on, for all the other property listed above.	

Exceptions	Some property has only monetary value. This kind of property is not a resource that is physically consumed in the adding-value process. Money is the best example of this kind of property. Another example is accounts receivable. These items are strictly wealth.

▼ *The Three Essential Characteristics of Assets*

OVERVIEW

Introduction

People spend a lot of time thinking about assets. It probably has been that way from the time that two cavemen argued about who was entitled to sleep on the bearskin. Assets seem to appease deep psychological needs for security, power, and pleasure.

Human beings are amazing in the ways that they can think of creating different assets and exchanging them back and forth. Common examples of business assets can be simple things like cash, office supplies, automobiles, or land. Sometimes assets can be strange and unusual things, like a "capitalized lease" or a "financial market derivative" (who ever thought up those things?). You will learn more about assets as you progress in your study of accounting and business.

ASSETS: THE EVERYDAY MEANING AND THE BUSINESS MEANING

Everyday assets

It is important to distinguish the everyday meaning of the word "asset" from the business meaning. In everyday language, we usually use the word "asset" to mean anything useful or beneficial, such as:

- cash (because you can buy things with it)
- a car (because it provides transportation)
- a computer (because you can use it to do calculations)
- an education (because it will help you get a good job)
- beauty (because it helps you meet people and get invited to parties)
- a sense of humor (because it helps you make friends)

ASSETS: THE EVERYDAY MEANING AND THE BUSINESS MEANING (continued)

"Assets, sir. Everywhere you look!"

● ●

Business assets

In business, the general idea of **asset** is similar to the everyday meaning—something useful or beneficial. However, for business purposes, *general beneficial qualities are not enough*. First, an asset must be property. Then, the property must have the following three specific qualities to qualify as an asset:

- The property must provide future benefits to a business.
- The property must have a dollar value determined by a past event.
- The property must belong to a business.

ASSETS: THE EVERYDAY MEANING AND THE BUSINESS MEANING (continued)

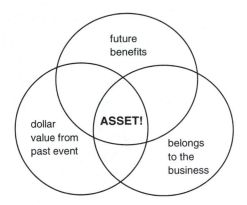

You can visualize the necessary qualities of an asset as three different circles. An asset is described only in the space where all three circles intersect.

THE "FUTURE BENEFIT" CHARACTERISTIC

Future benefit (property is useful)

A future benefit of an asset is whatever benefit or advantage an asset will bring to a business at any time in the future.

The asset must benefit the business in some way in the future, whether the benefit is five minutes in the future, five years in the future, or any other future time. Past benefits are gone. Only future benefits can help a business.

Note: Sometimes these future benefits are called ***service potential.***

EXAMPLES OF FUTURE BENEFITS (SERVICE POTENTIAL)

	For a business to …	**Using the asset releases benefits**
Cash	… get a different asset, it might exchange its cash for a computer. … operate and grow, it might exchange its cash for employee services. … pay debt, it might use its cash to pay a bank loan.	By exchanging its cash for assets or services, or using its cash to pay debt, a business can … 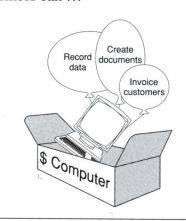
Noncash: computer	… operate and grow, it might consume its computer by using it to: • record revenues and expenses • create marketing documents • e-mail bills to customers *Analogy:* driving a car wears it out and therefore uses it up. Similarly, using office equipment wears it out.	As it uses up or wears out its computer, a business can …
Noncash: supplies	… operate and grow, it might use up or consume its office supplies to: • write letters to customers and vendors • make copies of documents • prepare bills for customers	By using up or consuming its supplies, a business can … 

THE "DOLLAR VALUE FROM A PAST EVENT" CHARACTERISTIC

Dollar value and past event	The asset must have *a measurable dollar value* as a *result of a past event*. • *Dollar value:* The correct amount of dollar value to use and how to measure it has been a long, ongoing controversy, but the basic rule is this: use whatever has been paid for the asset. This basic rule is called the **historical cost principle**. • *Past event:* A past event is a completed transaction (the transaction has taken place). It provides proof of who acquired an asset and for how much. This proof is known as **objective evidence**.
Objective evidence	"Objective evidence" generally means documents that prove the amount of cost, and when and where an asset was acquired. Examples of objective evidence are invoices, receipts, canceled checks, and other documents.
Examples	• A business purchased a truck for $15,000. The truck normally costs $21,000. The historical cost principle requires that the truck be recorded for $15,000. • A business owns land that cost $50,000, but is now worth $1,000,000. The historical cost principle requires that the higher value be ignored. The business does not change its records.

THE "BELONG TO THE BUSINESS" CHARACTERISTIC

"Belongs" means ...	If property belongs to a business, it means that a particular business has complete control over any use of the property, as long as the use is legal. Property qualifies as an asset only when a business has the freedom to use the property in any way it wishes, including selling or disposing of it. *Note:* Property that is rented from someone else does not belong to the business that is operating it. The property is owned by and belongs to whomever is allowing someone else to use it. Renting property is often called **leasing**.

EXAMPLES OF ASSETS AND THEIR CHARACTERISTICS

Cash

Cash is the most useful of all assets; its dollar value is clear, and it provides the most kinds of future benefits. This is because cash can easily be used to obtain any other kind of resource—whether property or services—or to pay debts.

Examples:

● It is easy to use cash to purchase a new truck. (It is not easy if you have to exchange some other asset to acquire the truck.)

● If you are in the bread-baking business, it is easy to use cash to pay your employees for their services. (It is not easy to pay them with bread.)

● Most creditors will only accept cash as payment for a debt.

"Cash is the most useful of all assets."

●   ●

Noncash assets

Noncash assets are any assets other than cash.

Examples:

● office supplies (small items that are quickly used up in the office such as pens, pencils, paper, diskettes, and coffee for employees)

● office equipment (long-lasting equipment that is used in the office such as desks, file cabinets, computers, and copy machines)

● accounts receivable (the legal right to collect money that is owed from your customers because your business allowed them to defer payment, usually for 30 to 60 days)

● automobiles

● land

EXAMPLES OF ASSETS AND ALL THEIR CHARACTERISTICS (continued)

Not assets

- **Employees:** Although employees are a valuable resource, people are not property, and *they do not belong to the business.*
- **Rented truck:** Although the truck is useful to the business that uses it, the truck *does not belong to that business.* It is an asset of the business that actually owns it, and that rents it to other businesses. Renting is a service.
- **Broken calculator:** If the calculator is broken and cannot be repaired, it will never function and will not provide future benefits (no service potential). It will not work and cannot be sold, so it will give *no future benefits.*
- **Repair service:** *Services cannot be owned* because they are immediately consumed. Services are never assets.
- **Good credit:** The good credit does belong to the business, is very important, and surely will provide future benefits. However, there is *no dollar value from an identifiable past event.* Good credit is not something that can be acquired in a transaction, even though it belongs to the business.

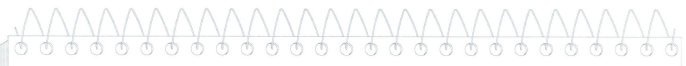

⌐QUICK REVIEW⌐

- There are only two kinds of economic resources available to a business:
    - — services, which are useful in the operations, and
    - — property, which is both useful *and* is wealth.
- A business property is called an "asset."
- To qualify as an asset, the property resource must meet three requirements:
    - — It must provide future benefits.
    - — It must have a dollar value determined by a past event.
    - — It must belong to the business.
- A business has both cash and noncash assets.

⌐VOCABULARY⌐

Asset: business property (page 40)

Historical cost principle: the requirement that transactions be recorded at actual cost (page 43)

Leasing: renting property (page 43)

Objective evidence: proof provided by a past transaction (page 43)

Service potential: the future benefits that any asset provides (page 41)

PRACTICE FOR LEARNING GOAL 2

SOLUTIONS FOR LEARNING GOAL 2 BEGIN ON PAGE 49.

Learning Goal 2 is about defining and identifying assets in a business. Use these questions and problems to practice what you have learned about assets.

REINFORCEMENT PROBLEMS

1) **Characteristics of an asset.** This exercise will help you remember and understand the correct definition of the word "asset." Fill in each blank space in the sentences below with the correct word.

    An asset is _____ that _____ to a business. Every asset must be able to provide a future _____ to the business to which it belongs. The asset must have _____ value as demonstrated by a _____ event.

    _____

    Write a short, clear answer to each of the following questions:

2) What is the everyday, nontechnical meaning of the word "asset"?

    _____

3) Name the three essential qualities of an asset for business purposes.

    _____

SOLUTIONS FOR LEARNING GOAL 2 BEGIN ON PAGE 49.

4) **Identify assets and nonassets.** In the table below, see if you can identify what items are assets and what items are not. If an item is *not* an asset, identify the *missing* quality. The first two items have been done as examples.

| | It is … | | *Missing* Quality | | |
Business Item	An Asset	Not an Asset	Future Benefits	Belongs to the Business	Dollar Value from a Past Event
A) The supervisors you employ		●		●	●
B) Office supplies	●				
C) Cash in the checking account					
D) The legal right to collect $500 that customers still owe the business					
E) The new airport to be built next year, 5 miles from your business					
F) A 12-year-old computer that is no longer functional					
G) An expensive French impressionist painting purchased to hang in the lobby of your office					
H) A building that your company rents from Multnomah Company					
I) A prepaid $700 fire insurance policy					
J) The business owner's Master's degree					
K) The computer that your business rents and uses to produce marketing brochures					
L) A promise by a good customer to buy $10,000 of merchandise from your business					
M) The $5,000 increase in value of the French painting that your business bought six years ago and still owns					
N) A mission statement explaining company goals that managers prepared					
O) Money that your business owes to vendors					

P
R
A
C
T
I
C
E

■

P
R
A
C
T
I
C
E

■

P
R
A
C
T
I
C
E

■

P
R
A
C
T
I
C
E

■

P
R
A
C
T
I
C
E

■

P
R
A
C
T
I
C
E

PRACTICE FOR LEARNING GOAL 2

SOLUTIONS FOR LEARNING GOAL 2 BEGIN ON PAGE 49.

5) **Identify the type of resource.** In the table below, identify each resource item as property or service by placing a mark in the correct box. The first item has been done for you as an example.

Item	Property	Service
A) The aircraft of a commercial airline company	●	
B) A medical examination by your doctor		
C) The medical equipment in the doctor's office		
D) The gasoline in your car		
E) The cash in a savings account		
F) The classroom lecture from your accounting instructor		
G) The rental of a computer to a business that does not own one		
H) A six-month fire insurance policy paid in advance		

6) **Make up an example of an asset.** Using a bicycle as your subject, create your own example that compares the bicycle used as an everyday asset (meaning a nonbusiness asset) to the bicycle used as a business asset. (*Tip:* when writing the example, think of the essential qualities of a business asset. An everyday asset will be missing some or all of those essential qualities. A business asset will have all of them.)

SOLUTIONS FOR LEARNING GOAL 2

PRACTICE QUESTIONS FOR LEARNING GOAL 2 BEGIN ON PAGE 46.

REINFORCEMENT PROBLEMS

1) An asset is <u>property</u> that <u>belongs</u> to a business. Every asset must be able to provide a future <u>benefit</u> to the business to which it belongs. The asset must have <u>dollar</u> value as demonstrated by a <u>past</u> event.
2) The everyday, nontechnical meaning of the word "asset" is anything that has a beneficial quality or trait.
3) The three essential qualities of a business asset are: A) It must provide future benefits to a business. B) It must have measurable value from a past event. C) It must belong to a particular business.
4)

Business Item	It is ...		Missing Quality		
	An Asset	Not an Asset	Future Benefits	Belongs to the Business	Dollar Value from a Past Event
A) The supervisors you employ		•		•	•
B) Office supplies	•				
C) Cash in the checking account	•				
D) The legal right to collect $500 that customers still owe the business	•	*Note: The legal right to collect money owed by customers is called an account receivable.*			
E) The new airport to be built next year, 5 miles from your business		•		•	•
F) A 12-year-old computer that is no longer functional		•	•		
G) An expensive French impressionist painting purchased to hang in the lobby of your office	•				
Note: The art provides a kind of advertising benefit. Art makes the business appear successful and it makes customers feel good.					
H) A building that your company rents from Multnomah Company		•		•	
Note: The building provides benefits, there is a dollar value transaction, but your business doesn't own the building.					
I) A prepaid $700 fire insurance policy	•	*Note: Prepaid insurance provides the future benefit of protecting the business from the risk of fire loss.*			
J) The business owner's Master's degree		•		•	
K) The computer that your business rents and uses to produce marketing brochures		•		•	
L) A promise by a good customer to buy $10,000 of merchandise from your business		•	•	•	•
Note: Not a past transaction; certain legal details aside, your company has nothing but a promise.					
M) The $5,000 increase in value of the French painting that your business bought six years ago and still owns		•			•
Note: Any "increase" in value is only an estimate and not really measurable until a sale actually takes place.					
N) A mission statement explaining company goals that managers prepared		•	• ?		•
O) Money that your business owes to vendors		•			
Note: This is a DEBT, which is the claim of someone else on your assets! Were you fooled? Don't worry, we talk more about debts and assets in the next learning goal.					

SOLUTIONS FOR LEARNING GOAL 2

PRACTICE QUESTIONS FOR LEARNING GOAL 2 BEGIN ON PAGE 46.

5)

Item	Property	Service
A) The aircraft of a commercial airline company	●	
B) A medical examination by your doctor		●
C) The medical equipment in the doctor's office	●	
D) The gasoline in your car	●	
E) The cash in a savings account	●	
F) The classroom lecture from your accounting instructor		●
G) The rental of a computer to a business that does not own one		●
H) A six-month fire insurance policy paid in advance	●	
Note: Anything prepaid is property, even prepayment of a service as in this case. A prepayment is owned by whomever made the prepayment, and the benefit is the right to receive future fire insurance coverage. We will talk more about prepaid items in later sections of this volume and in Volume 2.		

6) Your answer will be different than this answer. Nevertheless, notice how the everyday example of an asset excludes some of the necessary qualities of a business asset, and the business example includes all three of the necessary qualities. You should look for this in your own examples.

Everyday Asset: "I love my bicycle! I found it sometime last summer in a park, so I did not pay anything for it, and I'm not even sure what it would cost. It looks old, is rusting, is slow, and has only one speed, but people like to look at it and ask questions because it's an antique! That's how they become my friends. And the bike gives me pleasure because while I *slooowwwly* pedal it, I notice more flowers and trees. And by doing all this pedaling, I have lost eight pounds."

In this story, the bicycle provides the benefits of pleasure and a way to make new friends, but these are not business benefits. Also, we cannot be certain of who really owns the bicycle. There was never any kind of dollar value transaction that took place to acquire it, nor do we know what date it was acquired.

Business Asset: "We use a bicycle in our business to provide fast, inner-city delivery of documents. Our business bought the bicycle on August 10 for $800. The employee assigned to use the bicycle can make deliveries in half the time of a professional courier service."

In this story, all three qualities of a business asset are set forth: the business benefits it provides (speedy delivery); it is owned by the business; and it has a dollar value from a past transaction with objective evidence.

Your Questions?

It is *very* important to be aware of what you need to understand better. What do you need to understand better about this learning goal? Use this space to write the questions that you want to discuss with your classmates, instructor, or supervisor. Try to be very specific about what is bothering you, such as explanations that you do not fully understand.

LEARNING GOAL 3

Define and Identify the Two Claims on Assets

OVERVIEW

Introduction

In the previous learning goal, you learned how to identify business assets. In this learning goal, you will learn who gets to claim these assets and why … and it is not always just the owner!

Rules for claims on assets

- There is always at *least* one kind of claim on business assets—the owner's.
- There are never more than two possible claims—the owner's and the creditors'.

"Equity" means a claim

Equity, as used in business, means the legal right to claim the value of assets. Another way of expressing the same idea is to say that equity means a legal claim on the business wealth.

In Learning Goal 3, you will find:

▼ *The Owner's Claim and the Creditors' Claims*

▼ *The Owner's Claim and the Creditors' Claims*

OWNER'S EQUITY AND CREDITORS' EQUITY DEFINED

Two possible kinds of equity	The two kinds of legal claims on assets that can exist are: • the owner's equity • the creditors' equity
Definition of owner's equity	*Owner's equity* is the owner's legal claim on the value of business assets. This is the most basic claim on the assets. There is always an owner's equity for every business. Other terms used for owner's equity (synonyms) are ***net worth*** and ***net assets***.
Example of owner's equity	Ramos Enterprises has a $10,000 value of various kinds of assets, consisting of cash, accounts receivable, supplies, equipment, and so on. Andy Ramos (the owner) has the legal right to claim the entire $10,000 value of the business assets for himself if there are no business debts to pay.
Definition of creditors' equity	Creditors' equity is a legal claim on the value of business assets by a creditor. This kind of claim is usually called a ***liability***. Liability simply means a debt of the business.
Examples of creditors' equity	• an unpaid bank loan (the bank is the creditor) • amount owing to vendors (for supplies purchased on credit) • wages owing to employees (who are creditors until they are paid) • an unpaid telephone bill (the telephone company is the creditor)
What is the amount of a liability?	The amount of a liability is the value of the resources provided. When a business pays the liabilities, the creditors' equity disappears.
Not liabilities	• A contract is signed for $5,000 of accounting services to be performed next month. No resources (services) have yet been provided, so no liability exists. • Totally defective supplies are received from a vendor. No acceptable resources (supplies) have yet been provided, so no liability exists.

WHY THE TWO CLAIMS EXIST

Overview of the two claims

Directly or indirectly, the owner and the creditors provide all the resources to a company, both assets and services.

- *The owner* invests his/her own assets into a business. The owner also invests services—time and energy—and by doing this creates a business operation that adds value and obtains wealth from customers.
- *Creditors* directly supply both assets and services to a business.

Why owner's equity exists

The owner's equity claim exists because the business belongs to the owner.

Why creditors' equity exists

The creditors' equity (liabilities) exists because the creditors provided additional resources to the business which the business has not yet paid for.

When ...	and ...	then ...
resources are provided by someone other than the owner	the resources are not immediately paid for,	a liability is created (creditor's equity).

Claims are usually on the total assets

The liability claims and owner's equity claim are normally against the entire dollar value of all assets, and not against the value of any specific asset.

Exception: Sometimes a creditor's claim may be "secured" by a particular asset. This means that a creditor has the right to seize and sell a particular asset to pay a debt, if the debt is not paid on time. The particular asset is said to be **security** for the debt.

A supplier of goods or services is sometimes called a **vendor**. "Vendor" means the same as "seller."

COMPARE THE CLAIMS

The most important difference

Owner's equity claim and the liability claim are different in several ways, which are listed for you in the comparison table on page 55. However, the *most important difference* is that they do not have the same priority for payment.

Liabilities have first priority

Liabilities have first priority over owner's equity. This means that if a business does not have enough assets to pay both the creditors and the owner, then the creditors must be paid first.

If all liabilities were to be fully paid, then any asset value still remaining can be claimed by the owner.

Examples of liability priority

● Tishomingo Enterprises has a $10,000 bank loan coming due this week. The owner must make sure there is sufficient asset value to pay the loan before considering how much asset value might be available for himself.
● Wilmington Company has $90,000 of assets and $50,000 of liabilities. The company decides to cease operations and go out of business. Therefore, all company debts are now due and payable. The owner must wait and make sure that all the debts are fully paid before he can claim any of the asset value for himself.

Owner's equity is residual

Whenever there are liabilities, the owner's equity is the amount of asset value that would be left over if all the liabilities were fully paid. Therefore, the owner's equity is always a residual amount. The formula is:

$$\textbf{Assets – Liabilities = Owner's Equity}$$

Example of owner's equity residual

Georgetown Company has $52,000 of total assets and $35,000 of various kinds of liabilities. To calculate the amount of the owner's equity, calculate the value of assets that would be left over if the business were to pay off all its liabilities: $52,000 – $35,000 = $17,000 owner's equity.

"It says: 'There are no more than two kinds of claims on assets.'"

•   •

COMPARE THE CLAIMS (continued)

Liabilities compared to owner's equity

This table compares the three important characteristics of liabilities and owner's equity.

Compare …	Liabilities …	Owner's Equity …
priority of payment	always have first priority	is second priority
when it must be paid	• the day a debt becomes due, according to its terms, or • when the business terminates	has no requirement to be paid at a particular time
intended risk	none, because the creditor expects to be fully paid	resources that are invested can be lost

---

CHECK YOUR UNDERSTANDING

Fill in each blank space with the correct word. The answers are below.

There are two kinds of claims on the assets of a business. The owner's claim is called
_____ _____ and the creditor claims are called _____. Directly or indirectly,
the owner and the creditors together provide all the _____ to a company, both assets
and services.

The (owner's equity/liabilities) _____ always has (have) legal priority for payment.
Liability claims are usually against (total assets/a particular asset) _____.

ANSWERS

There are two kinds of claims on the assets of a business. The owner's claim is called
owner's equity and the creditor claims are called liabilities. Directly or indirectly, the
owner and the creditors together provide all the resources to a company, both assets and
services.

The liabilities always have legal priority for payment. Liability claims are usually against
total assets.

MANAGEMENT OF A BUSINESS CHANGES THE OWNER'S EQUITY

Good management

Regardless of whether an owner manages a business or employs other people
to do the management, management can be good or bad. Good management
will cause the business assets to grow because the managers will operate the
business so it will create and sell more value than the value of resources it
uses up. When assets increase this way, owner's equity also increases.

Bad management

Bad management will cause the business to use up more resource value than
the value that is created and sold. This will cause assets to decrease as more
resources flow out than come in. When assets decrease this way, owner's
equity decreases.

☞QUICK REVIEW☜

- There are only two possible types of claims on business assets:
  — creditors' claims, which are called liabilities.
  — owner's claim, which is called owner's equity.
- The owner's equity exists because the owner owns the business and provided assets and services to the business. The creditors' claim exists because the creditors provided assets and services which have not been paid for.
- The claims do not have equal rights; the creditor always has priority. This means:
  — Debts must be paid when they are due.
  — Debts have first claim if a business is liquidated.
- Liabilities are normally against the entire total dollar value of the assets.
- The most important cause of change in the owner's equity is the manner in which a business is managed.

☞VOCABULARY☜

Equity: a claim on asset value (page 51)

Liability: a debt; a creditor's claim on assets (page 52)

Net assets: a synonym for owner's equity (page 52)

Net worth: a synonym for owner's equity (page 52)

Owner's equity: an owner's claim on assets (page 52)

Security: the particular asset or assets a creditor can claim for nonpayment of a debt (page 53)

Vendor: any seller of goods or services (page 53)

P
R
A
C
T
I
C
E
.
P
R
A
C
T
I
C
E
.
P
R
A
C
T
I
C
E
.
P
R
A
C
T
I
C
E
.
P
R
A
C
T
I
C
E
.
P
R
A
C
T
I
C
E

PRACTICE FOR LEARNING GOAL 3

SOLUTIONS FOR LEARNING GOAL 3 BEGIN ON PAGE 60.

Learning Goal 3 is about identifying the claims on assets. Use these questions and problems to practice what you have learned about a business.

REINFORCEMENT PROBLEMS

1) **What creates and changes claims on assets?** Claims on the wealth of a business (the assets) result from only two providers of resources.

   A) Who are these two providers of resources? What do they provide?

   B) Why do they have claims on the wealth of a business?

   C) Why isn't the owner's claim equal to the value of whatever assets the owner invested minus the value of whatever the owner has withdrawn?

   D) Do the owner's services have a fixed dollar value, like wages of an employee?

2) **Explain changes in equities.**

   A) A supplier sells merchandise to a business for $800 on credit. Does the supplier have a claim on the assets? How much?

   B) A computer repair service charges a business $500 on credit for repairs made. Does the repair service have a claim on the assets? How much? If the business later pays $100 of the liability, does the claim change?

   C) An owner invests $5,000 in his small video store. Does this affect the owner's claim on the assets? By how much?

   D) The owner of a video store invests 500 hours of his time managing the store. He thinks his time is worth $30 per hour. Does this affect the owner's claim on assets? By how much?

3) Write a short, clear definition of "owner's equity."

4) Write a short, clear definition of "liabilities" and give three examples.

Learning Goal 3: Define and Identify the Two Claims on Assets

PRACTICE FOR LEARNING GOAL 3

SOLUTIONS FOR LEARNING GOAL 3 BEGIN ON PAGE 60.

5) **YOU be the teacher!** While I was writing this book, a student made the following suggestion about how to describe the meaning of equities. He said:

> "Why not just say that equities are a claim against assets because the equities were the source of those assets? So, you could look at equities as *simply direct sources of assets and also as claims on assets.* That's all there is to it!"

I appreciated his good suggestion, but why is he not quite complete in his description of equity claims? How do I answer him? (*Hint:* Is there more than one kind of resource that a business has to pay for?)

6) **Explain the priority of liabilities.** "The creditors' liability claims always have priority over the owner's claim." Does this mean that an owner cannot withdraw money from his business until he pays off all the debts first?

7) **Identify the kind of claim.** For each separate item described, indicate in the space provided if it is a creditors' equity claim or an owner's equity claim.

Description of Equity Characteristic	Creditors' Equity	Owner's Equity
A) It always has the first claim on assets.		
B) It is increased by the owner's hard work and risk-taking.		
C) It is usually called "liabilities."		
D) It is known as a "residual" claim on assets.		
E) They are the debts of the business.		
F) It is increased when the owner invests in his/her business.		
G) It is created when someone other than the owner provides assets or services to the business that are not immediately paid for.		
H) Together they always add up to the total amount of assets.		

SOLUTIONS FOR LEARNING GOAL 3

PRACTICE QUESTIONS FOR LEARNING GOAL 3 BEGINS ON PAGE 58.

REINFORCEMENT PROBLEMS

1) A) Creditors and the owner(s). They provide property and services.
   B) The creditors have provided resources to the business for which the business has not paid them. The owner also provided resources and has the legal right to claim the value of the assets, *except* for the amount needed to pay the creditors.
   C) Because the owner's management efforts will cause the total business assets (wealth) to increase or decrease, and this changes the owner's claim.
   D) Owner services do *not* have a fixed dollar value like wages. Owner services are an investment of time and effort whose value shows up as the increase or decrease in the wealth of the business, which changes the owner's claim. (However, this is different in a corporation, where an owner can also be an employee; see Learning Goal 5.)

2) A) Yes. $800.
   B) Yes. Initially $500, and then the claim is reduced to $400 after the payment is made.
   C) Yes. The owner's claim increases by $5,000.
   D) The effect of the owner's services can only be measured by the change in the wealth of the business as a result of business operations. Owner's services are not wages—the owner is not an employee of himself—so the $30 per hour is irrelevant.

3) "Owner's equity" is the owner's claim on the assets. It is secondary to the creditors' claim.

4) "Liabilities" are debts of the business. They have the first claim on assets. Some examples are wages owed to employees, debts to vendors, and unpaid bank loans.

5) While it is true that the creditors and the owner directly provide assets to a business, they also provide services. So the equity claims on the assets arise not only for the assets provided, but also for services provided.

6) No. "Priority" means: A) all business debts must be paid when they are due, regardless of what the owner might want, and B) when a business is terminated and liquidated, all existing debts have priority over the owner's claim on assets. The owner can withdraw assets at any time. However, debts still have to be paid in the manner stated above, and if the owner withdraws too much, he is legally obligated to reinvest enough to make sure the debts are paid.

7)

Description of Equity Characteristic	Creditors' Equity	Owner's Equity
A) It always has the first claim on assets.	●	
B) It is increased by owner's hard work and risk-taking.		●
C) It is usually called "liabilities."	●	
D) It is known as a "residual" claim on assets.		●
E) They are the debts of the business.	●	
F) It is increased when the owner invests in his/her business.		●
G) It is created when someone other than the owner provides assets or services to the business that are not immediately paid for.	●	
H) Together they always add up to the total amount of assets.	●	●

Your Questions?

It is *very* important to be aware of what you need to understand better. What do you need to understand better about this learning goal? Use this space to write the questions that you want to discuss with your classmates, instructor, or supervisor. Try to be very specific about what is bothering you, such as explanations that you do not fully understand.

LEARNING GOAL 4
Use the Accounting Equation to Show the Condition

OVERVIEW

The most basic question

The most fundamental and basic question about any business is: "What is the condition *right now*?" This is the question that every business owner and every investor will ask hundreds of times during the life of a business.

What "condition" means

The "condition" of a business as used in this book means the total value of the assets and the total claims on the assets, at any specified point in time. This simply means the wealth and the claims on the wealth.

Synonym

Another word used to refer to the condition of a business is *position*.

Purpose of this learning goal

In this learning goal, we will study how the condition of a business can always be expressed by the accounting equation. Then we will practice using the equation to show condition.

You will also learn a way to visually picture the condition of a business.

In Learning Goal 4, you will find:

▼ *The Financial Condition of a Business*

▼ *The Financial Condition of a Business*

THE ACCOUNTING EQUATION

The final result of business activities

The daily operations of a business can be quite complex, involving marketing, finance, production, research and development, and a complex flow of resources into and out of the business. **But the final result of all these activities always shows up like this simple picture:**

$ $ $ **Assets** $ $ $	**which value can be claimed by …** ⟶	**whoever has a legal claim on the assets**

This is the fundamental condition of any business.

Assets and the claims on assets are the essential elements of the condition of any business entity. That is why we have taken such a long time to talk about them. No matter how complex the business operations might be, the result of all the activities can still be expressed like this simple picture.

The accounting equation

Instead of drawing a picture, we can use the accounting equation as a clear and powerful way of describing the condition of a business:

$$\text{Assets} = \text{Liabilities} + \text{Owner's Equity}$$

or

$$A = L + OE$$

This means that the total dollar value of the assets is claimed by no more than two providers of resources: the creditors and owner. This is a very powerful idea and it applies to any business. In fact, it even applies to charities, governments, or you and me! We all have assets and equity claims on the assets.

Rearranging the equation

The equation can also be rearranged to show:

- Liabilities: $A - OE = L$
- Owner's equity: $A - L = OE$

CHECK YOUR UNDERSTANDING

Last month, your aunt Minnie opened up an appliance repair business. She is thinking about applying for a loan, and wants to know how to show the bank the financial condition of her business at the end of the first month. At the end of the month, she provides you with the following information from her business records:

- cash in the bank: $7,500
- debts to suppliers: $2,000
- office supplies on hand: $300
- car belonging to the business: $10,000
- tools belonging to the business: $4,000
- owing to employee: $500

On a separate piece of paper, show the condition of aunt Minnie's business at the end of the month by using the accounting equation. To do this, identify each of the individual asset and equity items and then show their totals.

What do you think about the financial condition of aunt Minnie's business?
Do you think the business looks strong or weak now? Using the accounting equation, if you had to explain to aunt Minnie what would make her business be stronger or weaker, what would you say?

ANSWERS

Assets	=	Liabilities	+	Owner's Equity
$21,800		**$2,500**		**$19,300**
($7,500 cash + $300 supplies + $10,000 car + $4,000 tools)		($2,000 debts to suppliers + $500 owing to employee)		(assets of $21,800 less the liabilities of $2,500)

The business looks strong now. Creditors have only a $2,500 claim on $21,800 of assets. (This is only 11.5% of assets needed to pay debts.) Stronger or weaker? If the liabilities were lower or the assets were greater, the business would be stronger because more wealth would be available for operations. The reverse situation would make the business weaker. Owners and managers spend a lot of time worrying about this!

VISUALIZING THE CONDITION

**Most people are
visual learners**

Most people do a lot of their learning by remembering mental pictures. Using a picture in your head is called "visualizing." If I were to say the word "car" to you, the first thing you probably would think of is a picture of some kind of car. This is a very good way to remember and understand.

**Visualize the
condition of
a business**

For many people, it is helpful to visualize the condition of a business in addition to using the accounting equation of A = L + OE.

Suppose for a moment that I gave you a "magic" camera. You can point this magic camera at any business and the camera will give you an accurate picture of the condition of the business in its most basic form. The picture would always come out like this:

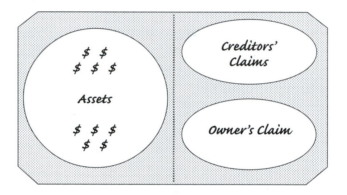

**Continue to
visualize ...**

Soon, we will spend a lot of time watching how business events can cause changes in the three parts of the picture, but remember that the financial condition of every business can always be visualized like this picture.

Any change or business event you might encounter in an accounting book (or in "real life") can always be understood by visualizing how it affects the three basic parts of the business. If you can, try to keep this picture in mind as you study the rest of the book.

Learning Goal 4: Use the Accounting Equation to Show the Condition

PRACTICE FOR LEARNING GOAL 4

SOLUTIONS FOR LEARNING GOAL 4 BEGIN ON PAGE 66.

Learning Goal 4 is about using the accounting equation. Use these questions and problems to practice what you have learned.

REINFORCEMENT PROBLEMS

1) **Make the equation balance.** In the table below, fill in the missing amounts in the accounting equation.

	Total Assets =	Total Liabilities +	Owner's Equity
A) Mohawk Company (June 30, 2000)	$251,000	$200,000	?
B) Nez Perce Company (December 31, 2001)	?	$18,500	$22,200
C) Lakota Company (October 31, 2001)	$50,000	?	$35,000
D) Modoc Company (March 31, 2001)	?	$45,000	$180,000
E) Cherokee Company (April 30, 2000)	$200,000	$251,000	?

What is the meaning of situation E in the table above? Is situation E actually possible?

2) **Identify specific items in the accounting equation.** In the space to the right of each item, indicate if the item is an asset (A), a liability (L), owner's equity (OE), or none of the above (none).

Item	A, L, or OE
A) Money owed to a supplier	
B) Cash	
C) Office supplies	
D) Money owed to the bank for a loan	
E) The amount of assets that would go to the owner after the all creditors are paid	
F) A signed contract requiring us to provide services next month	
G) A computer	
H) Computer software	
I) A bill from the telephone company for this month's service	
J) Land	
K) An employee	
L) An office building our company is renting	
M) Money owed to us by our customers	

3) **What does the accounting equation explain?** Someone in another business class who has never studied accounting wants to know if it is true that the accounting equation somehow "explains any business." Write a brief, but complete, answer to this person here:

4) **A practical application.** The Schuykill River Rowing and Sailing School has a bank loan. The bank requires that total liabilities including the loan (which is $80,000) can never be more than 40% of the company's assets. What is the minimum amount of assets that the company must maintain if there are no other debts? What is the minimum amount of owner's equity?

SOLUTIONS FOR LEARNING GOAL 4

PRACTICE QUESTIONS FOR LEARNING GOAL 4 BEGIN ON PAGE 65.

REINFORCEMENT PROBLEMS

1) A) $A - L = OE$ (OE = $51,000).
   B) $A = L + OE$ (A = $40,700).
   C) $A - OE = L$ (L = $15,000).
   D) $A = L + OE$ (A = $225,000).
   E) $A - L = OE$ (OE = – $51,000).
   Meaning of situation E: Yes, this is not unusual. It means that a business has consumed so many assets that there are not enough assets left to pay the creditors. This negative owner's equity means that the owner will have to invest $51,000 more so the business can pay all the liabilities, if the business were to be terminated today.

2) A) L.
   B) A.
   C) A.
   D) L.
   E) OE.
   F) None (perhaps some undetermined legal liability, but no measurable amount).
   G) A.
   H) A.
   I) L.
   J) A.
   K) None (it doesn't meet the definition of asset).
   L) None (somebody else owns the building).
   M) A.

3) Any business consists of three fundamental financial elements: Assets, Liabilities, and Owner's Equity. They are always related to each other in this way: $A = L + OE$, so this relationship will always explain the essential financial condition of any business.

4) This is a feature sometimes written into business loans. If $80,000 is the only debt, then $80,000 is 40% of what amount? $80,000 / .4 = $200,000 amount of assets. So if the assets were $200,000 and the liabilities were $80,000, then owner's equity would be $120,000.

Your Questions?

It is *very* important to be aware of what you need to understand better. What do you need to understand better about this learning goal? Use this space to write the questions that you want to discuss with your classmates, instructor, or supervisor. Try to be very specific about what is bothering you, such as explanations that you do not fully understand.

LEARNING GOAL 5
Define "Entity" and Identify Different Types

OVERVIEW

Introduction

In the prior learning goal, you learned how to calculate the basic financial condition of a business. In this learning goal, you will see that in order to calculate a condition, something else must be done first: an "entity" must be identified. Unless this is done, it is impossible to calculate the condition of a business.

In Learning Goal 5, you will find:

▼ *Economic Entities*

THE ECONOMIC ENTITY EXPLAINED

Definition of an entity	An *economic entity* is any activity for which the financial condition or financial information is to be reported separately. An economic entity is also called an *entity*.

Examples of economic entities	• A candy store business is an economic entity. A hardware store business is a different economic entity. Another candy store is a different entity.
	• The owner of a business and the business that she owns are two separate economic entities.
	• A charity is an economic entity.

The more specific the entity, the more detailed the financial information can be.

• A large company is an economic entity. However, the management of the company wants more detailed information about the operations of the company. The company is therefore divided into different divisions, and financial records of business activity will be kept for each division. Each division is an entity. If each division is divided into departments and financial records are kept for each department, then each department is an entity.

• A government is an economic entity. Each department within the government is also an entity, if the department must report its operations separately.

Not economic entities	• Your Wednesday night chess group is not an economic entity because the group is a social entity and not an economic one. There is no intention of preparing financial reports concerning the group.
	• You own three businesses and you do not keep separate records for any of the individual business activities. The individual operations are not economic entities because there is no way to identify their separate activities. It is impossible to report their financial information individually. Only the combination of the three activities is an economic entity. This is not very useful information.

THE ECONOMIC ENTITY ASSUMPTION

Assumption	The *economic entity assumption* states that it must be possible to correctly identify an economic entity for which accounting is to be done.
A priority requirement	The economic entity assumption is the most fundamental requirement in accounting.
Why is it important?	If there is no identifiable entity, then accounting will be impossible.
	Before you can calculate financial condition or report financial activities, you must identify the entity for which you are doing the calculating and reporting. If no entity can be identified, no reporting can be done. If the operations of different entities are all mixed up like scrambled eggs, then financial reporting will be all mixed up like scrambled eggs.
Example	You own a video rental store, an ice cream store, and a real estate sales office. You do not identify them as separate entities and you make no effort to keep separate records of the business activities.
	Result: You will not be able to determine the condition of any of the businesses or analyze the operations of each business.

HOW TO IDENTIFY AN ECONOMIC ENTITY

Follow these steps

Step	Action	
1	Identify an activity.	
2	**IF** someone needs to make financial decisions concerning this activity …	**THEN** go to Step 3. Otherwise, this is not a economic entity.
3	Maintain separate financial records concerning only this activity.	

Learning Goal 5: Define "Entity" and Identify Different Types

HOW TO IDENTIFY AN ECONOMIC ENTITY (continued)

*Examples of separate
recording-keeping*

Once an economic entity is identified, accounting principles require that each entity keep separate records of its financial activities, apart from any other entity. This is the only way to accurately identify the true financial condition of an entity.

- Dave's dry cleaning business has $275,000 in various assets such as cash, supplies, and equipment, as well as business debts. Dave personally owns another $190,000 in various assets that are not part of the business. Dave wants to make financial decisions about both the operations of the business and his own personal affairs, so he must keep completely separate records for the business and for himself. These records will show assets, claims on assets, income, expenses, and so on.
- Eduardo owns a yogurt shop and a motorcycle repair shop. Therefore, he must keep separate records for three entities: the yogurt business, the motorcycle repair business, and himself.
- Diana owns a beauty salon business and uses only one credit card for purchases of beauty supplies and cash advances. She uses some of the purchases and cash in her beauty salon business; the rest of the beauty supplies and cash she uses personally. Without a tremendous amount of reconstruction, Diana will *not* know:

  — How much of the credit card debt is personal and how much is for the business.
  — How much of the cash and beauty supplies were actually used in the business operations, and how much she used personally.

CHECK YOUR UNDERSTANDING

Fill in each blank space with the correct word. The answers are below.

The _____ assumption means that each economic _____ can be _____. Once this is done, then separate_____ must be maintained. An airline company (is/is not) _____ an economic entity, and each individual ticket agent for the airline (is/is not) _____ an economic entity of the airline.

You are tutoring accounting. A student asks you this: "Why keep a separate checking account for my business? If I own the business, then I own the cash in the business. So why not just keep that cash with my personal cash all in one account?"

ANSWERS

✔

The **entity** assumption means that each economic entity can be **identified**. Once this is done, then separate **records** must be maintained. An airline company **is** an economic entity, and each individual ticket agent for the airline **is not** an economic entity of the airline.

The issue is not just that all the cash belongs to her. The issue is knowing how to account for it. Otherwise, she will manage her business poorly.

Can the student identify exactly where all the cash came from—how much from business activities and how much from personal activities? The student probably will not know how much is business cash and how much comes from personal activities, such as investments, loans, gifts, or another job. If she says, "I keep a record of all the deposits and checks," then she has the potential to reconstruct separate records for each entity, but it will be a very slow and difficult process.

▼ *How Businesses Are Owned*

CLASSIFICATION BY OWNERSHIP

Three classifications

It is common practice for people to classify a business entity by the way in which the business is owned. There are three common forms of business ownership:

- proprietorship
- partnership
- corporation

Each of these forms of ownership has certain advantages and disadvantages, and there is no one "best" type for everyone.

THE PROPRIETORSHIP

Definition

A **proprietorship** (also called a *sole proprietorship*) is a business that is owned by one person. The business cannot be a corporation.

Attributes of a proprietorship

The following table describes the important attributes of a proprietorship.

Proprietorship Attribute	Description
Number of owners	One
Who manages it?	The owner
How difficult to start?	A proprietorship is easy to start. Only a limited amount of money is needed, and very little documentation is required for legal approval (business license, resale application, etc.).
How common is it?	It is the most common form of business. There are more proprietorships than any other kind of business.
Type of business	Any kind of business can be a proprietorship, but usually small service businesses and small retail merchant operations are proprietorships.

THE PROPRIETORSHIP (continued)

"Economic entity" compared to "legal entity"	As you know, every business must be identified as a separate *economic* entity. "Economic" refers to identifying financial activity for record-keeping purposes. This is done so the operations are correctly identified and the financial condition is properly reported.

However, legal rights and responsibilities are also a part of being in business. These legal rights and responsibilities must always connect to some particular person. A **legal entity** is a person with legal rights and responsibilities.

For a business, a legal entity can be different than an economic entity. A perfect example of how these two entities can be different for a single business is the proprietorship. A proprietorship is a separate *economic* entity from its owner and other businesses. The owner keeps separate records for the business and himself or herself.

But *legally*, there is no distinction between the owner and the business! It is the owner who has the ultimate obligation to pay the business debts and who legally owns the business assets. There is **one** *legal* entity—the person who is the owner. However, for financial record-keeping, there are **two** *economic* entities: the business operations and the owner's personal financial activities.

Example #1

Al owns a flower shop proprietorship which has $75,000 of assets, including a $35,000 delivery van. Even if the van is used only by the business, Al's name is on the state motor vehicle department records that show he owns the van. If Al permanently withdraws the van asset from the business operations and uses the van personally, the van still belongs to the same legal entity: Al.

However, for the purpose of identifying financial assets and claims on assets, the van has moved from one economic entity (the business) to a different economic entity (Al).

Example #2

The flower shop has $50,000 of liabilities. Suppose the business cannot sell its assets for enough money to pay these business debts. Al, the owner of the business, is *personally* responsible to pay the business debts with his own personal assets. The personal obligation to pay business debts is called **personal liability**. Even though the business is a separate economic entity for record-keeping purposes, the *legal* entity that has the ultimate obligation to pay the debts is Al.

THE PROPRIETORSHIP (continued)

Example #3

If Al works in the business and pays himself cash from the business, this is not an expense of the business even though Al calls it a "salary." Like all the other proprietorship assets, the cash is already owned by Al. Even though Al might be taking the money out of the business bank account, he is simply paying himself what he already owns. It is just a withdrawal of an asset by the owner.

THE PARTNERSHIP

Definition

A *partnership* is a business that is owned by two or more people, acting together as partners.

Attributes of a partnership

The following table describes the important attributes of a partnership.

Partnership Attribute	Description
Number of owners	Two or more, acting together as partners
Who manages it?	The partners
How difficult to start?	Technically, as easy as a proprietorship. Only a verbal agreement is legally required, but this is very unwise. For practical purposes, partnerships can be extremely tricky to properly form. A written partnership agreement should be used, along with the help of a lawyer and an accountant experienced in partnerships.
How common is it?	Less common than proprietorships and corporations.
Type of business	Any kind of business can be a partnership. Usually partnerships are businesses that require more investment than a proprietorship.

THE PARTNERSHIP (continued)

General vs. limited partnership	The kind of partnership we are discussing is called a ***general partnership***.
	Like a proprietorship, the partners in a general partnership have personal liability for partnership debts.
	A different kind of partnership is a ***limited partnership***. These are special partnerships in which certain partners do not have personal liability; however, these partners cannot manage the business.

THE CORPORATION

Definition	A ***corporation*** is a business that is *one* combined legal *and* economic entity given "life" by the laws of the state in which the corporation was formed.
General features of a corporation	• The document that creates a corporation is called a ***charter***.
	• The charter creates the corporation as a legal "person." The corporation is *both* a combined legal and economic entity, and the owners of a corporation do *not* have personal liability or ownership of the business assets.
	• The ownership of a corporation is divided into many small shares, called ***common stock***. Anyone can buy shares of the stock, so it is possible that the stock may be owned by just one or many thousands of people. These people are called ***stockholders*** or ***shareholders***. Large corporations obtain millions of dollars of investment money because there can be many stockholders. Corporations are the largest business.
	• A corporation has an unlimited life.
	• A corporation is the most complex of all businesses to form and operate.

THE SAME BASIC PRINCIPLES FOR ALL BUSINESS TYPES

Use the same principles	Regardless of the kind of business, use the same principles to determine the financial condition of the business. The business classification will have no effect.

Learning Goal 5: Define "Entity" and Identify Different Types

THE SAME BASIC PRINCIPLES FOR ALL BUSINESS TYPES (continued)

Example

If Bill Smith owns a proprietorship, but then changes it to a partnership by signing a partnership agreement with Louise and Dave, the basic principles of business condition are exactly the same. The only difference is that the ownership claim is divided among three people, which is more time-consuming to analyze.

Later on, if the partners agree to make the business a corporation, the basic accounting principles are still exactly the same, even though there might be many stockholders. Now the ownership claim is called "stockholders' equity." There may be certain special stockholder equity transactions; however, that is only a refinement of the basic principles, which still apply.

Visual picture of condition for the three types

Below are pictures of the condition of the business as proprietorship, partnership, and corporation. Notice that the idea of assets and claims on assets is exactly the same. In all cases, the accounting equation is still A = L + OE. The only difference is how the owner's equity is described.

A Proprietorship

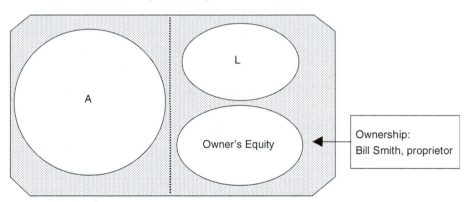

A Partnership

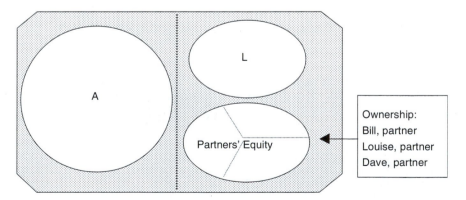

THE SAME BASIC PRINCIPLES FOR ALL BUSINESS TYPES (continued)

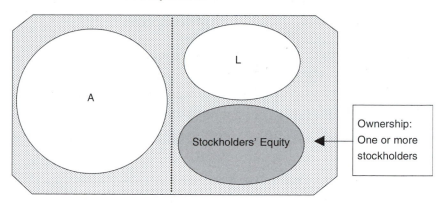

A Corporation

OVERVIEW OF ORGANIZATION FEATURES			
Feature	**Proprietorship**	**Partnership**	**Corporation**
Ownership	1 owner	2 or more partners	1 or more stockholders
Owner personal liability?	Yes	Yes (unless a limited partnership)	No
Life	Limited (to termination or life of owner)	Limited (fixed period or same partner group)	Unlimited
Separate records kept?	Yes	Yes	Yes
Same accounting rules?	Yes	Yes	Yes
Main advantages	• Easy to start • One person controls the business • Simple records	• Greater resources than a proprietorship • Greater flexibility in allocating profits and losses to owners than a corporation	• No personal liability (with limited exceptions) • Potentially greater resources • Often easier ownership transfer
Main disadvantages	• Personal liability • Limited resources	• More complex and expensive to start, operate, and manage • Personal liability • Potential for partner conflict is high	• Also complex and expensive to start, operate, and manage • Corporate income is taxed twice: on the profits and on the dividends

Learning Goal 5: Define "Entity" and Identify Different Types

⌒ QUICK REVIEW ⌒

- An economic entity is any activity or operation for which financial condition or financial information is to be reported.
- The economic entity assumption means that it must be possible to correctly identify an economic entity for which accounting is to be done.
- Once an entity is identified, separate financial records must be maintained for that entity.
- It is necessary to distinguish between economic entities and legal entities.
- Business entities are commonly identified by the nature of their ownership:
    — proprietorship (one owner)
    — partnership (two or more owners acting as partners)
    — corporation (one or more stockholders)

⌒ VOCABULARY ⌒

Charter: the legal document that creates a corporation (page 75)

Common stock: ownership shares of a corporation (page 75)

Corporation: a business that is a combined legal and economic entity, and is owned by one or more individuals as stockholders (page 75)

Economic entity: any activity or operation for which the financial condition or financial information is to be reported (page 68)

Economic entity assumption: assumption that it is possible to identify an individual economic entity for which financial reporting is to be done (page 69)

Entity: another term for economic entity (page 68)

General partnership: a partnership where all partners have personal liability and full management authority (page 75)

Legal entity: the entity that has legal ownership of assets and legal responsibility for debts (page 73)

Limited partnership: a partnership in which certain partners do not have personal liability (page 75)

Partnership: a business with two or more owners acting as partners (page 74)

Personal liability: being personally responsible to make good all business debts (page 73)

Proprietorship: a noncorporate business that is owned by one person (page 72)

Shareholder: another word for stockholder (page 75)

Stockholder: an owner of stock of a corporation (page 75)

PRACTICE FOR LEARNING GOAL 5

Learning Goal 5 is about defining the meaning of "entity" and identifying different types of entities. Use these questions and problems to practice what you have learned about entities.

MULTIPLE CHOICE

On the line provided, enter the letter of the best answer for each question.

1) A general partnership _____
   A) is not an economic entity.
   B) is not a legal entity.
   C) cannot be created by only a verbal agreement.
   D) all of the above.
2) A proprietorship _____
   A) is not a separate economic entity from the owner.
   B) is difficult and time-consuming to start.
   C) cannot be easily managed by the owner.
   D) is the most common form of business organization in the United States.
3) The economic entity assumption means that _____
   A) separate recording-keeping is important.
   B) it must be possible to correctly identify a particular financial activity.
   C) if an entity cannot be identified, accounting cannot be done.
   D) all of the above.
4) Which of the following is *not* an economic entity? _____
   A) a bowling club
   B) a stockholder
   C) the marketing department of a corporation
   D) a group of accountants that meet every Wednesday night just to go bowling
5) Which of the following is both a combined economic entity and legal entity? _____
   A) the De Anza Partnership Company
   B) the West Valley Corporation
   C) the Mission Proprietorship
   D) none of the above.
6) The owners of a corporation are usually called _____
   A) stockholders.
   B) partners.
   C) proprietors.
   D) investors.

SOLUTIONS FOR LEARNING GOAL 5

MULTIPLE CHOICE

1) B. The partners are personally liable for all partnership debts and together have legal ownership of the assets.
2) D.
3) D.
4) D. No financial activity takes place that needs to be reported for the Wednesday night group.
5) B.
6) A.

Transactions—
Analyzing and Visualizing

Overview: what this section does	This section shows you how to analyze and see the effects of transactions, so you can understand how they change the condition of a business.
Use this section if ...	... you do not fully understand how transactions affect a business, or ... you want more practice analyzing transactions before studying debits and credits.
Do NOT use this section if ...	... you already know how to analyze the effects of transactions. If you want to learn about debits and credits, go to Section V on page 364. To get an easy introduction to debits and credits, go to Section III on page 219.

DO YOU LIKE A GOOD STORY?

It might help you to remember better

Sometimes people remember information better when the information is part of an interesting story. The story that continues on the next page is the second part of a three-part adventure, mystery, and romance story. If you have not read the first part of the story, you can return to the beginning on page 27 to find out how it all began or you can start here. So, if you think a story might help you remember better, of if you just want to have some fun, go ahead! The adventures of Darius continue.

Technical content

This part of the story contains the following technical content:

- identifying transactions
- how to analyze the effects of transactions
- revenues and expenses explained
- identifying all changes in owner's equity

You can skip the story

If you prefer to study the above technical content more quickly, you can skip the story and go directly to page 97, where the normal presentation and practice continue.

THE WEALTH OF DARIUS

PART II

t happened when Darius least expected it. Early in the morning, just after sunrise, Darius was walking in the marketplace toward the vegetable seller's stall when he felt a hand on his arm.

Darius heard a shrill, cackling voice say to him, "Come here, young man!"

He turned instantly and saw that an old woman, dressed in black, was grasping his sleeve. It was the same woman who he had helped a year ago. She pulled his sleeve and her voice rattled. "You come with me."

Remembering her and what she had become, Darius felt his strength drain from him. He fought to keep his legs from folding. In a moment, the old woman pulled Darius out of the market and around a corner. Darius was at once blinded by a flash of intense white light. For an instant, he felt himself being lifted off his feet by a strong wind, and then he remembered nothing.

When Darius awoke, he was standing in his shop. The large, dazzling Hermes loomed before him. They were alone. "Well?" Hermes boomed. "I promised you that I would return in exactly one year, and here I am!"

Darius threw himself down and whispered to the floor, "I have used what you have given me and I have given it much thought. I am grateful beyond words! I thank you daily!"

"Up, mortal!" the god ordered. A force snapped Darius back into a standing position. "Yes, I know," Hermes continued, "and I am pleased that you say you have given this valuable gift much thought. Tell me what you have thought about it."

Darius tried hard to think clearly. Then with relief he remembered that he had made a list of all the things that the formula, which he had received from the god, had made possible. He found the paper and timidly handed it to Hermes. In a shaky voice, Darius said, "I have given much thought to the correct value to use for the assets when I calculated the condition of my business."

"You did well to use the price that you paid for the assets," Hermes responded.

"I gave much thought to what assets and debts to use in the calculation. I have never included assets or debts that did not belong to the business."

"You did well again," the voice rumbled.

"Each time I prepared the calculation, I have carefully watched the changes in the total assets and the changes in the total debts. Sometimes this helped me make better decisions about when to buy more assets and how much debt I will allow the business to have."

Hermes looked down at Darius and spoke. "You have done correct things, but I expected no less from you. After all, you have received a great gift, have you not?"

"Yes, a very great gift," Darius said.

"Very well, then. You spoke of changes in the condition of your business. How do you explain those changes?"

Darius began to tremble, because he had nothing else to say. His mind raced. What had he overlooked?

"You have nothing else to tell me or to ask me after an entire year?" The force of Hermes' voice was now vibrating the tools lying on the table. "You have no other questions concerning what you have seen happening?"

As if he were a forest animal caught in a bright light, poor Darius was so paralyzed that he could only stare, transfixed by the sparkling brilliance around Hermes. Darius could no longer think.

Hermes softened his voice. "Darius, you have calculated the condition of your business. You learned to use the formula A = L + OE. That is good. But isn't there something else that you need to know each time you use the formula?"

Silence.

"Mortal, you try my patience!" The tools bounced off the table. "Very well, the gods will teach you!"

In a white blaze, Hermes was gone. Darius remained frozen, staring into the space Hermes had just occupied. In the distance, like a faraway echo, Darius heard, "… gods will teach you … gods will teach you …"

What Darius Forgot

Another perfect day warmed the fields of blooming clover on the distant heights of Mount Olympus. Gentle zephyrs puffed and nudged the sweet blossoms, and borrowed their fragrance to bring to the gods, who relaxed among a grove of oak trees in a grand garden.

"So, Hermes," said Artemis, goddess of hunting and all wild things, "tell us about your visit to that mortal Darius."

"He demonstrates that mortals remain flawlessly impaired."

"Yes," replied Artemis, "in their own way, they are as perfect as we are."

Aphrodite (pronounced *afro-dye-tee*), the goddess of love and beauty, asked, "He is such a handsome young man. What did you find deficient in him, Hermes?" She lifted a silver cup of ambrosia to her lips.

"What I find deficient," replied Hermes, "is that Darius faithfully calculates the condition of his business, yet he does not bother to ask himself *why the condition changes*! He watches the changes but does nothing to discover the reasons. He does not appreciate my gift! After all I did for him!"

"Really. They are such simple beings," said Athena, the goddess of wisdom and courage.

"And worst of all, worst of all," Hermes continued, "is that he has done nothing to explain the reasons why his owner's claim on the wealth has changed. What could be more important to a merchant or a businessperson than explaining why the owner's claim on the business wealth has increased or decreased?"

Apollo, god of truth and music, had been listening the whole time and added, "I would think that explaining all the changes in his claim on the business wealth would be the first thing an owner would always do. It would be the first thing the owner would want to understand. After all, if an owner can explain the reasons why his claim on the wealth has changed, then he can begin to control the causes of the change! He is thereby sure to improve his claim."

"Exactly," replied Hermes. "You describe it perfectly, Apollo."

"Perhaps he has become too satisfied," Apollo said. "After all, his owner's claim has only been increasing. Why should he trouble himself to find out?"

"Yes," Hermes said. "So far, he has not had a good reason to learn what causes the changes in his business—especially the changes in the owner's claim. I believe it is time for me to give him a reason to learn. I will ask Aphrodite to help me."

"What are you going to do?" all the others asked at once, as they turned to look at Aphrodite.

"Oh, nothing really," smiled Hermes. "I will simply give him reasons to want to know."

Hermes' First Trick On Darius

After the second visit from Hermes, Darius tried to go about his business as if nothing had happened, and for a while nothing at all was different.

He watched his business grow. He was grateful and thanked the gods. Darius now prayed to the gods even more frequently, but in his heart he was not sure if he wanted his prayers answered or not.

He worked hard. He carefully observed the calculation each week, and observed the changes in the amounts of assets and claims on assets. What more could the gods want?

One day, Darius had been working in the back of his shop and did not notice the increasing buzz of conversation and gossip in the front. Then

Ammon's daughter, Dana, who now sometimes worked in the shop, said, "Darius! Can you believe it? What are you going to do?"

"Do about what?" Darius asked.

Dana smiled gently at him. Darius was always too intent on his work to notice that Ammon's attractive daughter never smiled in the same way for anyone else. "Look across the street, Darius."

As Darius looked out the front of his shop, he saw that the shop directly across from him did not look the same. It had been a sandal maker's shop, but the sandal maker was gone. To Darius' great amazement, paintings of every size were displayed in front of the shop.

Another painter had moved into the shop directly across from Darius' painting business! The new painter's name was Somnus. He had traveled many miles from his old town to settle in Darius' village and open a new shop. Somnus later told people that he moved because of a powerful dream that he had. In that dream, he heard the god Hermes telling him to move. Then, in the dream, he had seen Darius' village.

Darius soon discovered that Somnus was an artist of great experience and talent. He was about the same age as Darius but, unlike Darius, Somnus was a businessman. Somnus always spent extra time with customers or gave them small gifts. He would tell each customer what great artistic understanding the customer had.

Because there was another painter, Darius noticed that customers did not buy paintings from his shop quite so quickly as before. Even regular customers did not always choose to have Darius design a fresco or wall painting anymore. Now they would always speak to Somnus before deciding.

Darius began to notice something else happening when he did his monthly calculation. The assets of the business no longer seemed to be increasing so quickly, and the owner's claim hardly changed at all.

After two months, something happened that Darius had never seen before: slowly at first, then faster, his owner's claim began to decrease. As the business lost its wealth, the owner's claim began to diminish. Darius did not understand the reasons for this, and so he could only watch helplessly as the business began to dissolve like a small piece of candy.

Unexpected Help From a Friend

Month after month, Darius watched as his owner's claim decreased. Finally, at the end of a year, to Darius' dismay, the calculation showed:

Assets	=	Creditors' Claims	+	Owner's Claim
$14,700		$7,700		$7,000

The creditors' claims were now again greater than the owner's claim—something Darius had promised himself to never let happen again.

While Somnus continued to create new wall designs and find new customers, Darius watched as his own business sank further. At the end of the next month, his calculation showed:

$$\text{Assets} = \text{Creditors' Claims} + \text{Owner's Claim}$$
$$\$10,400 \qquad \$7,700 \qquad \$2,700$$

The causes of the changes seemed unknowable and beyond Darius' control. Darius had no idea what to do!

Darius tried to find some comfort with friends. He still gave his dinners for neighbors, especially the poorest ones. On the evening of the same day that he had done his last calculation, Darius had prepared a large birthday dinner for Ammon and his family.

Darius was unable to enjoy the party. He smiled and wished Ammon a happy birthday, but each time he spoke with Ammon the old worries returned. At a quiet moment, after the toasts were finished, Ammon's daughter, Dana, approached Darius and looked into his eyes.

"Darius, I know you. I watch you every day in the shop. Something is troubling you. What is wrong?"

Darius began to say that everything was fine and deny that he was worried, but instead he found himself saying, "Dana, you are a clever girl. I have seen how well you bargain with the other merchants. If you can keep a secret, I will show you something tomorrow at the shop. If you have any of your clever ideas, now is the time that I can use them."

The next day, Darius showed Dana the formula he had received from Hermes and how to calculate the condition of a business. At first, Dana was amazed at how this worked, but then she began to frown. "Darius, lately your owner's claim has been decreasing rapidly. It has gone from $7,000 to $2,700 in only one month. Soon you will not be able to claim any of the wealth of the business. It will all go to the creditors!"

"Now you know why I am worried," he said. "I have no idea what is making my owner's claim decrease in such a way."

Dana looked at him for a long time and said, "Darius, you are a wonderful artist. That is what you do best. I will go home tonight and think more about the condition of your business. Together we can think of something." She smiled in the way that she saved just for Darius.

Early the next morning, when Dana entered the shop she went to Darius at his table and said, "I have an idea. We will carefully observe every business event that might affect the condition of your business. Then we will see which ones affect your owner's claim. We can use the good picture that you drew, with the three circles, to visualize the condition."

Darius looked at her with admiration and, for the first time, was surprised to see such a beautiful smile.

Transactions: Why The Picture Changes

For the next week, Darius and Dana watched as many business events as they could. To analyze an event, they wrote a description and drew a picture of the change in the condition of the business. Inside the circles, they showed only the particular item that was affected by the change. They analyzed the circles, one at a time.

The first event they observed was when the business used five gold coins to purchase some paint supplies.

First: did any *assets* change?
Yes (gold decreased by $5 and paint increased by $5; one asset was given up for another asset).

Second: did any *creditors' claims* change?
No (debts were not affected).

Third: did the *owner's claim* change?
No (the owner's claim was not affected because the total assets are the same and the total debts are the same).

Purchase $5 of paint supplies for $5 of gold

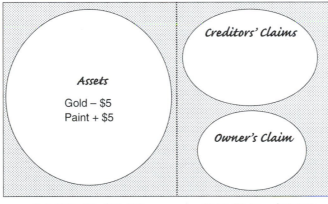

The picture showed them that there were more supplies than before—and less gold—but that was the only change in the condition of the business. None of the claims seemed to be affected at all by this event. Exchanging one asset for another asset only affected the assets.

In the next event that they observed, the business used $20 to pay Hela, a creditor.

Again, Darius and Dana wrote a description of what happened. Then they drew a picture of the business, showing the changes. One at a time, they analyzed each circle:

88

First: did any *assets* change?

Yes (gold decreased by $20 and this reduced total wealth to $10,380).

Second: did any *creditors' claims* change?

Yes (the creditors' claims also decreased, so the total claims on wealth decreased to $10,380).

Third: did the *owner's claim* change?

No. Although paying a debt reduced assets, it also reduced a creditor's claim on the assets; the owner's claim stayed the same. So Darius and Dana saw that paying a debt only had an effect on the creditors' claims, but not on the claim of the owner.

Pay $20 debt owing to Hela

Assets	Creditors' Claims
Gold – $20	Hela – $20
	Owner's Claim

Total Wealth: $10,380   Total Claims: $10,380

The next event occurred when Aulis visited the shop to tell Darius that he would be raising the price of many of the paints, beginning next month. When Aulis left, Darius and Dana talked about what happened. They decided that although this was a business event, it did not yet affect the financial condition of the business. The information did not change any part of the picture.

Darius and Dana continued watching the events. They even gave the events a special name. Any event that changed the picture of the condition of the business they called a "transaction."

What do you think?
Darius and Dana are developing a procedure to find out how each transaction makes a change in the condition of the business. What are the three questions they ask in the procedure?
1) **Assets:** did the transaction cause any assets to change?
2) **Creditors' claims:** did the transaction cause any creditors' claims (liabilities) to change?
3) **Owner's claim:** did the transaction cause the owner's claim (owner's equity) to change?

In the meantime, Darius watched as Somnus seemed to be attracting ever more customers. Two days later, in a moment of desperation, Darius decided to take all of his savings and invest them in the business. The business would then have money to purchase some special and rare paint colors. Darius went home and took $250—his entire savings—from a secret hiding place. He went back to town and placed the $250 in a metal box under the floor in his shop. The money now belonged to the business. With this new money, the business would buy the special paints and might take some customers back from Somnus.

Transactions That Affect the Owner's Claim

Fortunately, Darius told Dana what he had done. She said, "Darius, I think that this is a transaction, and an important one." As before, they wrote a description of the transaction, and drew a picture of the change in the condition.

Again, they analyzed the circles one at a time:

First: did any *assets* change?

Yes (the business now has $250 more gold; no other asset is affected).

Second: did any *creditors' claims* change?

No (the asset did not come from a creditor).

Third: did the *owner's claim* change?

Yes! The gold came entirely from the owner. This must be an increase in the owner's claim!

Darius invests $250 in his business

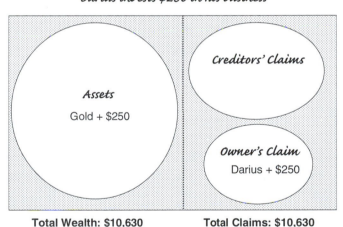

Total Wealth: $10,630 **Total Claims: $10,630**

Sure enough, when they drew the picture of the business, they could see the increase in assets and the increase in the owner's claim. Dana and Darius had discovered the first transaction that affected the owner's claim: the owner's investment in the business.

Then Dana began to think some more. "If an owner's investment increases the owner's claim, then would an owner's withdrawal of assets decrease it?" She asked, "Darius, did you withdraw gold from the business this month to pay any of your own personal debts?"

"Yes," he said. "This month I obtained the money to pay for your father's birthday party by withdrawing $80 from the business."

"Let us draw a picture of an owner's withdrawal of $80," Dana said. Before completing the picture, they first analyzed each circle, one at a time, as they did before:

First: did any *assets* change?
Yes (gold decreased by $80; the wealth is reduced to $10,550).

Second: did the *creditors' claims* change?
No (no debt was paid or changed).

Third: did the *owner's claim* change?
Yes! The owner's claim is only the excess of the assets over the debts. If the total assets decrease and the debts (creditors' claims) do not change, then the owner's claim must decrease.

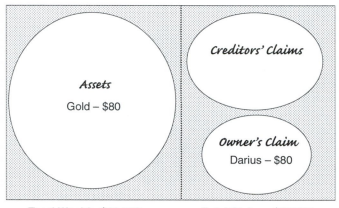

Darius withdraws $80 from his business

Total Wealth: $10,550   **Total Claims: $10,550**

Together they made their second discovery: when an owner withdraws assets, the decrease in assets also decreases the owner's claim. Now they had found two causes for changes in the owner's claim: investments and withdrawals. They hoped that these changes would explain the entire change in the owner's claim.

They would be disappointed. There were two more important changes to the owner's claim that they had not yet discovered.

At the End of the Month

When Darius prepared the calculation of the condition at the end of the current month, to his shock he saw the condition was even worse than before:

Assets	=	*Creditors' Claims*	+	*Owner's Claim*
$9,300		*$7,400*		*$1,900*

This time, Darius drew two pictures: a picture of the condition at the end of the prior month and a picture of the condition at the end of the current month. These pictures showed the total assets and the total claims after all the transactions were completed for each month.

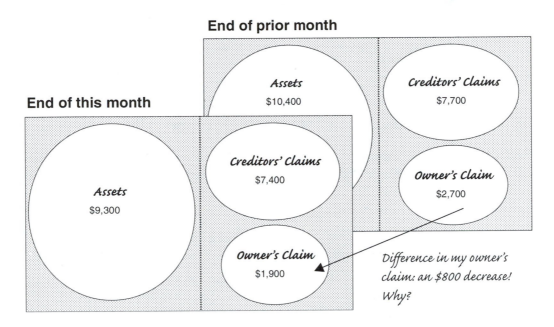

End of prior month

End of this month

Assets
$10,400

Creditors' Claims
$7,700

Creditors' Claims
$7,400

Owner's Claim
$2,700

Assets
$9,300

Owner's Claim
$1,900

Difference in my owner's claim: an $800 decrease! Why?

When Darius showed this to Dana, she looked concerned. "Your owner's claim is down another $800, Darius, and we still have not explained all the reasons why."

Then they wrote down how much of the change in the owner's claim they had been able to explain so far:

Owner's investment:	+ $250
Owner's withdrawal:	− 80
Net change identified:	+ 170

"Well, we certainly have more work to do," Dana said. "The total change in the owner's claim was a *decrease* of $800. So far, we have only identified the part of the change that is an *increase* of $170. There must be $970 of some other decrease hidden somewhere. We are still far from a complete answer! And at this rate of decrease, Darius, you will not have more than a few months left to operate your business."

92

What do you think?	

What are the two causes of the changes in the owner's claim that Darius and Dana have discovered so far? There are two more causes of change in the owner's claim that they have not yet discovered. Any guesses?

The Other Transactions That Affect the Owner's Claim

Darius made a suggestion. "I have an idea. I have no more money left to invest, so there will be no increases in my owner's claim for that reason. Next week, I will not withdraw any gold or other assets from the business, so there will be no changes caused by withdrawals …"

Dana finished his thought. "… so any change in your owner's claim will have to be caused by whatever is missing. Correct?"

"Yes, and this time, we will watch every transaction until we find what is missing," Darius answered.

Because they were alert and watching every transaction, it did not take them much time to find something interesting. The next afternoon, a customer came into the shop and Darius painted a small portrait of her. When she left, she paid Darius $25. Both Darius and Dana immediately saw that assets had increased by $25.

As before, they wrote a description of the transaction and drew a picture showing how the condition changed:

First: did *assets* change?
Yes (gold increased by $25 and this increased total assets to $9,325).

Second: did the *creditors' claims* change?
No (creditors were not involved; we did not borrow $25).

Third: …

Customer pays $25 portrait fee

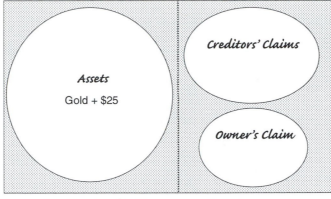

Total Wealth: $9,325   **Total Claims: $?**

"What do you think, Darius?" Dana asked. "What is the only thing left?"

Darius' eyes opened wide. "I think I understand! The owner operates the business and takes the risks. Therefore, the owner claims any increase in wealth that the business gets from customers. The assets increase because of the efforts of the owner, so the owner's claim also increases."

Dana said, "Yes, I agree. Fees do increase assets. So fees cause an increase in the owner's claim. I think we should give this kind of increase in the owner's claim a special name to show that it comes from making sales to customers."

Dana chose the word "revenue," which is derived from a word meaning "to return, or to come back home after being away." She finished drawing the picture:

Customer pays $25 portrait fee

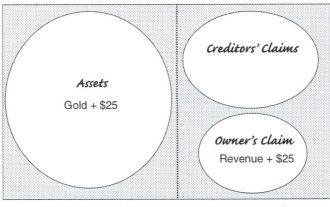

Total Wealth: $9,325   **Total Claims: $9,325**

Dana could see that Darius was thinking about something. "What is it?" she asked.

"Well, I think we are correct in what we just did," he said, "but now I am even more confused than I was before."

"Why is that?"

"Because my owner's claim has been decreasing, not increasing! This transaction we just found is an increase! So we still have not yet explained why my owner's claim has been decreasing so quickly."

Dana was quick to respond. "Darius, I have thought about this before when I watched you working. I think the answer has to do with what we have just seen. Tell me, do you think that customers give you money just because they want to be generous?"

"Of course not," he said. "I have to provide them with something they want— something valuable."

"Yes," she continued, "and are you able to do that at no cost to yourself? Do the gods just give you your supplies for free?"

"No, no. What are you saying? I buy supplies and tools, I pay employees, I use up paints and glazes, I use up candles and incense in the shop, I use up gold, I …" He stopped.

"Now do you see what I am saying?" she asked.

"Well …," he said, "I have to use up assets to operate the business. When assets are used up in my operations so I can create something to sell, there are less assets than before. My owner's claim is less!"

He continued, "So the 'operations' is almost like a race. Operations increase the owner's claim when I make a sale, but decrease the owner's claim when assets are used up."

Dana said, "I can look at your operations and see two examples of using up assets right now. First, how much paint did you use up for the portrait you just painted?"

"I am not exactly sure. I can guess it would be about $10."

"So, let us draw a diagram of that and see if it changed your owner's claim and the condition of your business."

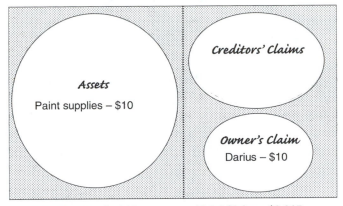

Use up $10 of paint and glaze to operate

Assets
Paint supplies – $10

Creditors' Claims

Owner's Claim
Darius – $10

Total Wealth: $9,315   **Total Claims: $9,315**

Darius and Dana thought in the same slow, careful way as before:

"I know that $10 of the asset supplies was used up," Darius reasoned. "There was no reduction in creditors' claims. Therefore, using up assets as part of business operations must cause a decrease to my owner's claim."

Dana said, "It is very clear to me now. Because of its operations, the business will receive the value of what it creates. That was $25: the fee you charged the customer. This increases the owner's claim."

She continued, "At the same time, to create something of value, the operations also consume assets: the $10 of paint supplies used up. This decreases the owner's claim."

Dana chose the word "expense" to mean the value of assets used up in operations to create a service or a product.

Just to be sure, they looked at another example of an expense. That morning, Darius had paid the rent to Opheron, the landlord. The monthly rent was $250 which Darius always paid on time. In this case, the asset used up was gold:

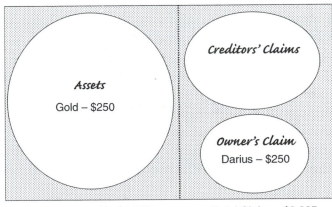

Use up $250 of gold to pay rent to operate

Assets
Gold – $250

Creditors' Claims

Owner's Claim
Darius – $250

Total Wealth: $9,065   **Total Claims: $9,065**

If the rent was not paid, there would be no shop to work in. The business needed a shop to operate and create value. So, paying rent was another example of using up assets as part of business operations, even though it did not involve a job for some particular customer.

All during the remainder of the week, Dana and Darius continued to carefully watch the transactions. They drew pictures of how the transactions changed the condition of the business. Except for operations, they were not able to discover anything else that increased or decreased the owner's claim. At the end of the week, they decided that it was business operations that caused the rest of the change in the owner's claim.

After thinking about the operations for several days, Darius asked, "Dana, do you think the business is using up assets in operations faster than it is receiving them from customers?"

"Yes, I think that is your problem," Dana suggested. "That would cause your owner's claim to decrease."

"But how can I be sure?"

"Darius, I do not know for certain. All I can suggest is that every day you keep a record of all the transactions. Then you can identify which ones are affecting your owner's claim the most. Whatever you find, you need to begin making changes soon."

"By the gods, that would be a great amount of effort! And I have never tried such a thing."

From far above, Hermes smiled as he watched the two mortals and thought to himself, "If Darius—poor mortal—thinks that business is difficult now, how quickly he will change his mind! I will soon favor him with a much bigger surprise."

Hermes' second trick would be of surpassing quality.

To be continued …

What do you think?

Darius and Dana spent much time searching for all the causes of change in the owner's claim (owner's equity). They discovered four kinds of events that affect the owner's claim—two cause increases and two cause decreases. Do you remember what the four kinds of transactions are?

The two increases: owner's investment and revenue.
The two decreases: owner's withdrawals and expenses.
Revenues and expenses are caused by business operations.

LEARNING GOAL 6
Analyze Individual Transactions

OVERVIEW

Introduction

In this learning goal, we will begin the most basic analysis of *changes* in the condition of a business. After some practice looking at changes, you will begin to see something pretty amazing: most of the events that change the condition of a business fall into typical patterns. Learning to analyze these patterns will give you a lot of confidence in your ability to understand the transactions of any business.

Fundamental principle

Because there are only three basic parts to the condition of any business, the effect of any change should be analyzed according to how it affects the three basic parts: $A = L + OE$. This is the essential idea for this learning goal.

"Double-entry" accounting

Using an equation approach to analyze and record transactions is called ***double-entry*** accounting. There are two basic requirements for double-entry accounting:

- Analyze every change by how it affects the three parts of the equation.
- The equation must always stay in balance.

    Reminder: Because we are forced to keep the equation in balance, every transaction always creates *at least two changes* within the equation. This is the only way to keep the equation in balance. That is why the method is called "double-entry"—at least two changes with every transaction.

What is "single-entry"?

Single-entry accounting is a simple, very old-fashioned system in which some items in the accounting equation are recorded, but there is no concept of describing a business by using an equation to describe all the changes.

For example, if you kept a record of the balance of your checking account and all the deposits and checks, but you did not keep a record of how the deposits and checks affected the other items in accounting equation, you would be doing single-entry accounting.

In Learning Goal 6, you will find:

▼ *Introduction to Transactions*

WHAT IS A TRANSACTION?

Definition   A *transaction* is any event that causes a change in the accounting equation. This means any event that will change the financial picture of the condition of a business.

"Well, boys, I'd say a 'transaction' is any event that causes a change in the accounting equation."

Examples of a transaction
- owner investment
- paying a debt
- borrowing money
- selling to a customer
- using up supplies
- buying more supplies

Not a transaction
- signing a contract (because the accounting equation is not affected)
- the bank offering to loan money (because nothing has happened yet)
- a proposed law affecting business (because nothing has changed yet)

Learning Goal 6: Analyze Individual Transactions

TYPES OF TRANSACTIONS

Two types: financial and organizing

Transactions can be conveniently classified as being either "financial transactions" or "organizing transactions."

Financial transactions

The most common and important kinds of transactions are financial. This is what you are going to study now.

Financial transactions are caused by *economic events*. An economic event is an event that can be measured in dollars.

Two kinds of financial transactions

There are two kinds of financial transactions:

● *External:* transactions between the company and some external entity or event
● *Internal:* transactions that occur entirely within the company

Organizing transactions

There is a second, less frequent, type of change that is an organizing transaction, rather than a financial transaction. This organizing transaction occurs not with any economic event, but rather as a way of reorganizing, reclassifying, or correcting the accounting information already recorded. We will study this later on. Organizing transactions are always internal.

Examples of both types

The table below compares examples of financial and organizing transactions.

	Financial	**Organizing**
External	● buying equipment ● selling land ● borrowing money ● investing by owner ● paying a bill ● providing service to a customer ● suffering a fire or other casualty loss	
Internal	● using up supplies ● wearing out equipment ● transferring between bank accounts	● correcting recording errors ● adjusting accounts ● closing accounts

TYPES OF TRANSACTIONS (continued)

Watch out for the owner's personal transactions. The owner's personal transactions are never part of the business activity, and are never recorded by the business (example: the owner buys a computer for use at home).

CHECK YOUR UNDERSTANDING

1) Briefly and accurately define the word "transaction" in the space below.

2) Briefly and accurately identify and explain the two kinds of financial transactions.

3) What does "double-entry" mean?

ANSWERS

1) A transaction is any event that causes a change in the accounting equation.

2) A) External transactions are economic events that occur between a business and some external entity or event.

B) Internal transactions are economic events that occur entirely within a business.

3) Keeping the accounting equation in balance requires that at least two items within the equation elements must change with each transaction. This is the only way the accounting equation can remain in balance. For example, if a business borrows $1,000, then the assets increase and so do the liabilities. Or, if a business uses $100 of cash to purchase supplies, then cash decreases by $100 and supplies increase by $100.

▼ *Transactions That Always Involve Assets*

EXAMPLES OF ANALYSIS AND PATTERNS

Overview

So far, you have learned that a transaction is any event that causes a change in the accounting equation. Now, we will begin our look at transactions by examining the kind of transactions that always affect assets. These are the most common kind of transactions.

Coming up ...

What follows is a series of typical transaction examples that all involve assets.

After the transaction is identified, there are three steps used to analyze the transaction. The effect that each step has on the accounting equation is shown by ↑ for increase and ↓ for decrease.

Below each analysis is a picture (a "snapshot") to help you visualize the effect on the basic financial condition.

> *Note:* Watch for events that do not qualify as transactions.

How to analyze each transaction

Go slowly and let yourself absorb the examples at a comfortable pace, being careful and methodical. You do not have to rush, because the analysis will become easier and easier as you practice. When you analyze each transaction, follow these three steps:

Step 1: Are *assets* affected?
Step 2: Are *liabilities* affected?
Step 3: Is *owner's equity* affected?

> *Note:* The imaginary business we are examining is an automotive repair business.

Owner investment

The owner invests $100,000 to begin a new automotive repair business. The business is a separate entity from the owner, so the owner is the *external* reason for the change.

> *Note:* At this point, there are no liabilities, so the owner can claim all the asset value.

EXAMPLES OF ANALYSIS AND PATTERNS (continued)

Analysis	Effect on Condition
Step 1: Are *assets* affected? Yes (Cash goes up by $100,000).	$\uparrow A = L +$ OE
Step 2: Are *liabilities* affected? No (no debt involved).	
Step 3: Is *owner's equity* affected? Yes (owner's equity increases by $100,000).	$\uparrow A = L + \uparrow OE$

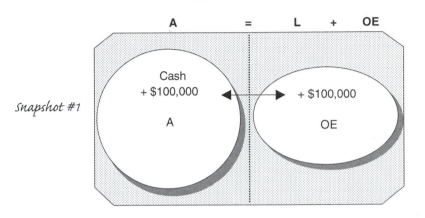

Snapshot #1

Use cash to purchase an asset

The business buys $500 of computer software for cash. The software supplier is the *external* party to the transaction. One asset is given up (Cash) for another asset (Computer Software), so total assets do not change.

Analysis	Effect on Condition
Step 1: Are *assets* affected? Yes (Cash decreases by $500; Software increases $500).	$\downarrow \uparrow A = L + OE$
Step 2: Are *liabilities* affected? No.	
Step 3: Is *owner's equity* affected? No.	

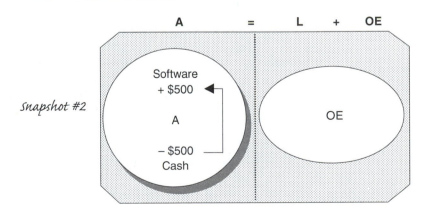

Snapshot #2

EXAMPLES OF ANALYSIS AND PATTERNS (continued)

Purchase asset on credit

The business buys $50,000 of testing equipment "on account." The supplier is the *external* party to the transaction. Total asset value increases, but now there is a creditor's claim because the equipment is not paid for.

Analysis	Effect on Condition
Step 1: Are *assets* affected? Yes (Equipment increases by $50,000).	$\uparrow A = \quad L + OE$
Step 2: Are *liabilities* affected? Yes (Accounts Payable increases by $50,000).	$\uparrow A = \uparrow L + OE$
Step 3: Is *owner's equity* affected? No.	

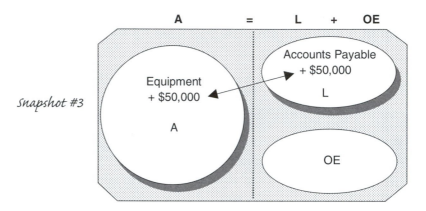

Snapshot #3

Borrow money

The business borrows $25,000 from a bank. The bank is the *external* party to the transaction. Total assets increase, but so do creditors' claims.

Analysis	Effect on Condition
Step 1: Are *assets* affected? Yes (Cash increases by $25,000).	$\uparrow A = \quad L + OE$
Step 2: Are *liabilities* affected? Yes (Loan Payable increases by $25,000).	$\uparrow A = \uparrow L + OE$
Step 3: Is *owner's equity* affected? No.	

EXAMPLES OF ANALYSIS AND PATTERNS (continued)

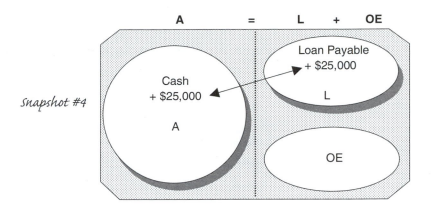

Snapshot #4

***Use up an asset
in the operations***

The business uses up $275 of supplies during operations. This event is completely within the business, so it is an *internal* transaction. This is an expense which decreases owner's equity because resources (in this case, supplies) are consumed in the process of operations to produce revenue.

Analysis	Effect on Condition
Step 1: Are *assets* affected? Yes (Supplies decrease by $275).	$\downarrow$ A = L + OE
Step 2: *Are liabilities* affected? No (nothing happens with creditors).	
Step 3: Is *owner's equity* affected? Yes (owner's equity decreases by $275).	$\downarrow$ A = L + $\downarrow$ OE

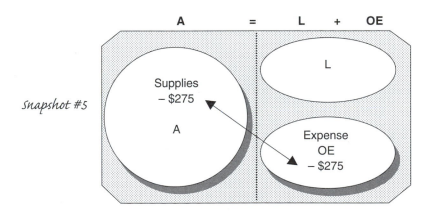

Snapshot #5

EXAMPLES OF ANALYSIS AND PATTERNS (continued)

Payment of a liability

The business uses $500 cash to pay the liability from the software purchase on account. The creditor (the supplier) is the *external* party to the transaction. Assets are used to reduce creditor claims.

Analysis	Effect on Condition
Step 1: Are *assets* affected? Yes (Cash decreases by $500).	$\downarrow A = \quad L + OE$
Step 2: Are *liabilities* affected? Yes (Account Payable decreases by $500).	$\downarrow A = \downarrow L + OE$
Step 3: Is *owner's equity* affected? No.	

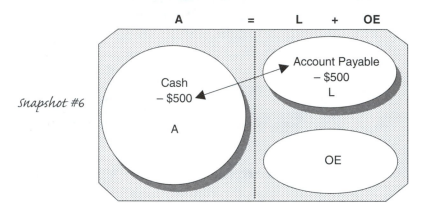

Snapshot #6

Perform services for customers

The business completes a diagnostic job for a customer, and receives $2,500 cash. The customer is the *external* party to the transaction. Providing services increases owner's equity because the new asset (Cash) was earned by the business. It did not come from creditors.

Analysis	Effect on Condition
Step 1: Are *assets* affected? Yes (Cash increases by $2,500).	$\uparrow A = L + \quad OE$
Step 2: Are *liabilities* affected? No.	
Step 3: Is *owner's equity* affected? Yes (owner's equity increases by $2,500).	$\uparrow A = L + \uparrow OE$

Learning Goal 6: Analyze Individual Transactions

EXAMPLES OF ANALYSIS AND PATTERNS (continued)

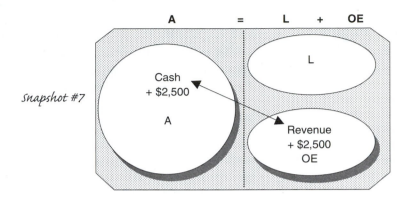

Snapshot #7

***Use cash to
purchase equipment***

The company spends $4,700 to purchase a new computer system. The seller (called a "vendor") is the *external* party to the transaction. Total assets do not change; they simply shift, as one asset decreases (Cash) and another asset increases (Computer Equipment).

Analysis	Effect on Condition
Step 1: Are *assets* affected? Yes (Cash decreases by $4,700; Computer Equipment increases by $4,700).	$\downarrow \uparrow A = L + OE$
Step 2: Are *liabilities* affected? No.	
Step 3: Is *owner's equity* affected? No.	

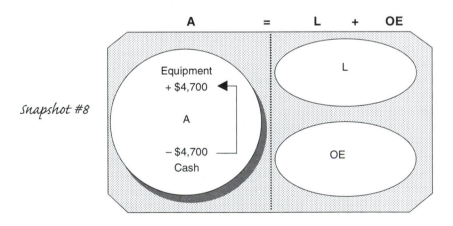

Snapshot #8

EXAMPLES OF ANALYSIS AND PATTERNS (continued)

Correcting an error

The accountant for the company corrects the records to reclassify an item into equipment that had been wrongly recorded as supplies. This is an *organizing* transaction, and organizing transactions are always *internal*. One asset (Equipment) increases and another asset (Supplies) decreases.

Analysis	Effect on Condition
Step 1: Are *assets* affected? Yes (Equipment increases; Supplies decrease).	↑ ↓ A = L + OE
Step 2: Are *liabilities* affected? No.	
Step 3: Is *owner's equity* affected? No.	

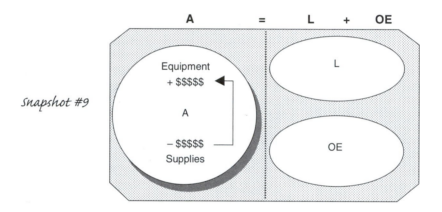

snapshot #9

Cash is used to pay for services consumed

The business uses up $150 cash to pay the telephone company for telephone service as soon as the bill is received. The telephone company is the *external* party to the transaction. This is an expense which decreases owner's equity because resources are consumed as part of operations to produce revenue.

Analysis	Effect on Condition
Step 1: Are *assets* affected? Yes (Cash decreases by $150).	↓ A = L +　OE
Step 2: Are *liabilities* affected? No.	
Step 3: Is *owner's equity* affected? Yes (owner's equity decreases by $150).	↓ A = L + ↓ OE

EXAMPLES OF ANALYSIS AND PATTERNS (continued)

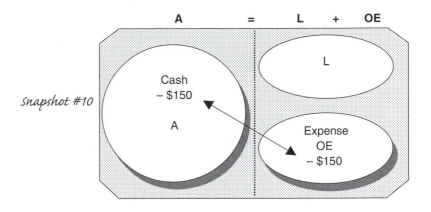

snapshot #10

Both creditor and owner provide cash

The business needs $20,000 cash. It borrows $15,000 from a bank and the owner invests an additional $5,000. The bank and the owner are the *external* parties to the transaction.

Note: There are *three* items affected by this transaction: Cash ($20,000), liabilities ($15,000), and owner's equity ($5,000). However, notice that the equation always stays in balance!

Analysis	Effect on Condition
Step 1: Are *assets* affected? Yes (Cash increases by $20,000).	$\uparrow A = \quad L + \quad OE$
Step 2: Are *liabilities* affected? Yes (liabilities increase by $15,000).	$\uparrow A = \uparrow L + \quad OE$
Step 3: *Is owner's equity* affected? Yes (owner's equity increases by $5,000).	$\uparrow A = \uparrow L + \uparrow OE$

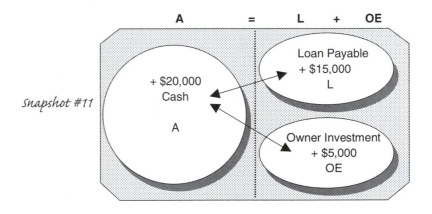

snapshot #11

EXAMPLES OF ANALYSIS AND PATTERNS (continued)

***Casualty loss: fire
destroys assets***

A fire destroys $10,000 of uninsured office equipment. The fire is the *external* agent of change in this event. Owner's equity decreases, because the owner of a business always assumes the risk of losses.

Analysis	Effect on Condition
Step 1: Are *assets* affected? Yes (Equipment decreases by $10,000).	$\downarrow A = L +$ OE
Step 2: Are *liabilities* affected? No.	
Step 3: *Is owner's equity* affected? Yes (owner's equity decreases by $10,000).	$\downarrow A = L + \downarrow OE$

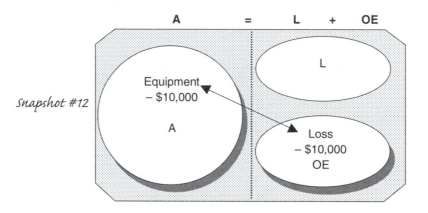

Snapshot #12

Signing a contract

The business signs a new contract with the employee labor union. This is a legal event. No economic event will happen until the employees are actually paid. There is no change to the condition of the business.

Analysis	Effect on Condition
Step 1: Are *assets* affected? No.	
Step 2: Are *liabilities* affected? No.	
Step 3: Is *owner's equity* affected? No.	

EXAMPLES OF ANALYSIS AND PATTERNS (continued)

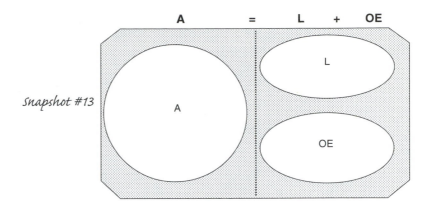

Snapshot #13

Unrecordable economic event

The bank notifies the company that interest rates will be higher on any new loans. This is an economic event, but it cannot be quantified in dollar terms until the company borrows money again.

Analysis	Effect on Condition
Step 1: Are *assets* affected? No.	
Step 2: Are *liabilities* affected? No.	
Step 3: Is *owner's equity* affected? No.	

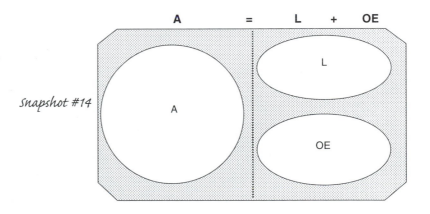

Snapshot #14

Owner withdraws assets from a business

The owner of the business needs some cash for personal expenses, so she draws out $2,000 cash from her business. The owner is a separate entity from the business, so the owner is the *external* party to the transaction. Assets are reduced, and not used to pay creditors, so owner's equity is the claim that decreases.

EXAMPLES OF ANALYSIS AND PATTERNS (continued)

Analysis	Effect on Condition
Step 1: Are *assets* affected? Yes (Cash decreases by $2,000).	$\downarrow A = L +$ OE
Step 2: Are *liabilities* affected? No.	
Step 3: Is *owner's equity* affected? Yes (owner's equity decreases by $2,000).	$\downarrow A = L + \downarrow OE$

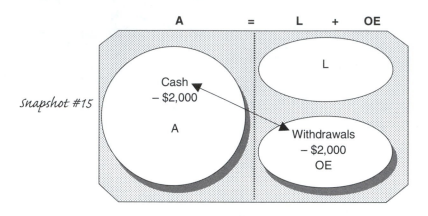

Snapshot #15

Owner's personal expenditure

The owner spends the $2,000 she withdrew from the business on the purchase of furniture for her home. This is not a transaction of the business, so the condition of the business is not affected.

Analysis	Effect on Condition
Step 1: Are *assets* affected? No.	
Step 2: Are *liabilities* affected? No.	
Step 3: Is *owner's equity* affected? No.	

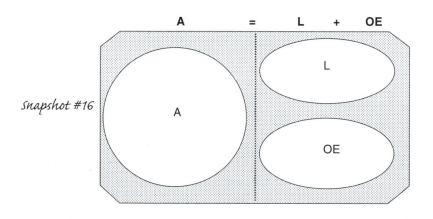

Snapshot #16

EXAMPLES OF ANALYSIS AND PATTERNS (continued)

Summary: three types of asset transactions

If you take a moment to review all the transactions that you have just analyzed, you will notice that every recordable transaction always involved an asset in some way. All of these transactions can be classified into three possible types of asset transactions:

Transactions between assets and liabilities

Transactions between assets and owner's equity

Transactions only within assets

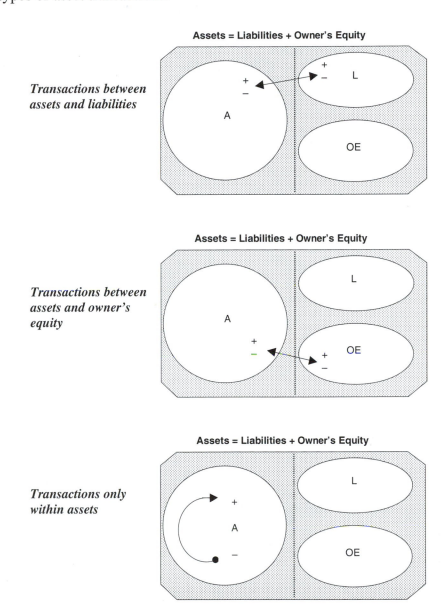

You can see that so far every transaction has involved an asset. Sometimes total assets did not change, sometimes total assets decreased, and sometimes total assets increased.

Learning Goal 6: Analyze Individual Transactions

CHECK YOUR UNDERSTANDING

For each of the transactions given to you, draw a diagram that illustrates the change in the condition of the business.

1) a purchase of $800 of supplies for cash
2) a $1,000 loan payment
3) a purchase of $200 of supplies on credit
4) using up $300 of supplies in operations
5) a $700 sale to a customer on credit
6) purchase $5,000 of equipment by paying $1,000 cash and signing a $4,000 note payable

ANSWERS

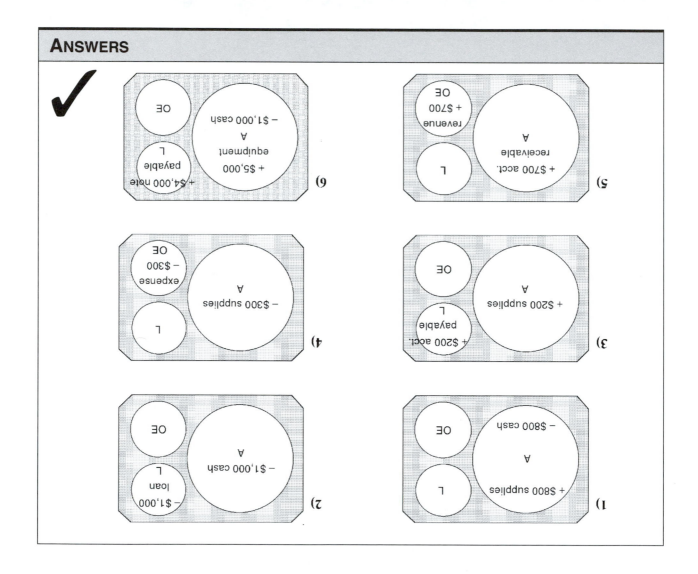

▼ *Expenses and Revenues Explained*

OVERVIEW

The need for precision	One of the most common errors that students make in basic accounting is the misinterpretation of the words "expense" and "revenue." It is vital that you have a clear understanding of these words for the following reasons: ● Expenses and revenues are the most powerful force of change on any business. ● You will always be dealing with expenses and revenues in your business classes and/or business practice. ● The next major topic shows how expenses and revenues affect the condition of a business in a new way.

EXPENSES

Review	On page 12, you saw "expense" described as the dollar cost of a resource used up in the operations that create a new resource. This is still true. However, we now understand how to describe the financial condition of a business more precisely, so let us use a definition for expense that is also more precise.
Definition of expense	An *expense* is a decrease in owner's equity that is caused by using up resources in operations. *Note:* The word "operations" still means that process which creates a new resource and sells it to customers.
Synonym	Operations is sometimes called "the revenue-earning process."
The amount of an expense	The *amount* of an expense is the dollar cost of the assets used up.
When does an expense happen?	An expense happens the moment a resource is consumed in operations. There are only two kinds of resources: property and services. Therefore, the moment property or services are consumed in operations, an expense has occurred.

EXPENSES (continued)

Using up resources always decreases assets

A business operates by consuming property resources and services resources. Using up these two resources always causes assets to decrease. Assets decrease like this in two possible ways:

- *Noncash asset used up:* Often, an asset itself is the resource (property) that is consumed in the operations. When the noncash asset is used up, total assets decrease (examples: using up supplies or wearing out equipment).
- *Cash used up:* The asset cash is used to pay for services consumed in the operations. When the services resource is consumed, total assets decrease because cash is used to pay for the services (examples: paying employees for their services or paying the telephone company for telephone service).

Examples of expenses

The table below shows some expenses. A property or services resource is consumed in operations. This causes total assets to decrease.

Description	Amount of expense	What resource used up?	What asset decreased?
Waterville Company used up supplies costing $400. The supplies would have cost $475 to replace.	$400	Supplies (property)	Supplies (the asset is also the resource used up)
Augusta Company received a telephone bill for $200 and immediately paid it.	$200	Telephone services	Cash (to pay for telephone services)
Bangor Enterprises completely wore out a machine that had cost $5,000.	$5,000	Machine (property)	Machine (the asset is also the resource used up)
Portland Company paid $7,500 for employee wages in the current month's production.	$7,500	Employee services	Cash (to pay for employee services)

EXPENSES (continued)

Why does owner's equity decrease?	When assets decrease as a result of the business operations, the owner's equity decreases. The accounting equation clarifies how the owner's claim decreases:
	If assets decrease, we know that part of the change in the condition of the business will show up like this: $\downarrow A = L + OE$
	To keep the equation in balance, what else must happen? *Owner's equity* also decreases: $\downarrow A = L + \downarrow OE$
	(The creditors are not going to let *their* claim be decreased!)

More examples of expenses

This expense …	would be called …	This expense …	would be called …
consuming office supplies	Office Supplies Expense	consuming repair services	Repairs Expense
wearing out equipment	Depreciation Expense	consuming advertising services	Advertising Expense
consuming gasoline	Fuel Expense	consuming municipal services	Property Tax Expense

Note: Each business decides what name to use for an expense, so there is always some variation in the exact names that are used.

Not expenses

All of the following transactions or items do not involve an expense. The missing quality is indicated to the right.

Transaction or Item	Missing Quality
A liability is paid.	Owner's equity is not affected, only creditors' equity.
Cash is used to purchase supplies.	Owner's equity is not affected. There is no decrease in resources—one asset is given up but another is obtained.
There is an uninsured fire loss.	The resource is not consumed as part of *operations* (a "loss" is an incidental decrease in owner's equity).
A liability	A liability is a creditor's claim; it is not a change in owner's equity.

EXPENSES (continued)

Remember that "expense" means a *change*—a decrease—in the owner's equity. When you think of expense, think of a *negative change in owner's equity*. If something similar confuses you, always test it for this feature:

You must see a **decrease** in the owner's equity resulting from **operations**.

Decrease in assets can be delayed

So far, in all the transactions that involve an expense, an asset immediately decreases when a resource is consumed (see Snapshot #5 on page 105 and Snapshot #10 on page 109). So an asset and the owner's equity both decrease.

However, if a service is the resource that is being consumed, it is often possible to delay payment. This is because service providers often allow up to 30 days (sometimes more) to pay a bill.

If payment is delayed, this will delay the need to decrease assets (cash). In the next major topic, we will see what this transaction looks like. If you want to study this right now, you can turn to page 124. Otherwise, let us next define the meaning of "revenue."

CHECK YOUR UNDERSTANDING

Fill in each blank space with the correct word. The answers are on page 119.

An expense is a(n) (increase/decrease) _____ in _____ _____ , caused by using up _____ in _____. The amount of the expense is the dollar _____ of the resources used up. Using up resources will always cause total _____ to decrease. This decrease (may/may not) _____ be delayed until later, after a payment is made.

*None of the items listed below are expenses. Explain why each item is **not** an expense.*

● payment of a debt

● a flood that destroys a warehouse

● using up cash to pay for supplies

ANSWERS

An expense is a decrease in owner's equity, caused by using up resources in operations. The amount of the expense is the dollar cost of the resources used up. Using up resources will always cause total assets to decrease. This decrease may be delayed until later, after a payment is made.

- A debt payment is not an expense because owner's equity is not affected. It is the creditor's equity that is being reduced.
- A casualty like a flood does reduce owner's equity, but this does not happen as part of the operations process. It is an incidental loss.
- Using cash to pay for supplies is not an expense because there is no overall using up of resources, so owner's equity does not decrease. One asset is simply exchanged for another.

REVENUES

Review	On page 17, you saw "revenue" described as the dollar value of a sale. However, we now understand how to describe the financial condition of a business more precisely, so let us use a definition for revenue that is also more precise.
Definition of revenue	A ***revenue*** is an increase in owner's equity that is caused by a sale of goods or services.
The amount of a revenue	The *amount* of a revenue is the dollar amount that the customer pays for the goods or services provided.
When does a revenue happen?	Generally, a revenue happens the moment that a customer receives the goods or services that were asked for. *Note:* At that time, the revenue is said to be "earned."

REVENUES (continued)

A revenue increases assets

When a business makes a sale to a customer, assets will increase. This is because the business will receive valuable property from the customer. Usually the kind of assets that a business receives will be:

● cash
● accounts receivable (a legal right to collect money)

> *Note:* Rarely, a business might receive some other kind of valuable resource, but this is quite unusual. I know of an attorney who was once paid in gold nuggets—mostly as a joke.

Examples of revenue

The table below shows various examples of revenue and how they all conform to the characteristics just described.

Description	Amount of revenue	What was sold?	What asset is increased?
Hutchinson Company provided $1,000 of advertising services and was paid immediately.	$1,000	Advertising (services)	Cash
Butler County Enterprises sold $25,000 of farm equipment to a customer on credit.	$25,000	Equipment (property)	Accounts Receivable
Casper Editing Company provided $10,000 of book editing services "on account."	$10,000	Editing (services)	Accounts Receivable
Sheridan Pizza Company sold $300 of pizza and was paid in cash.	$300	Pizza (property)	Cash

REVENUES (continued)

Not revenue

All of the following transactions or items do not involve a revenue. The missing quality is indicated to the right.

Transaction or Item	Missing Quality
Cash is received from a loan.	Owner's equity is not affected because there is no sale. The money must be paid back to the creditor, so only the creditors' equity is affected *(liability increase).*
Cash is collected from a customer's account receivable from a prior sale.	Owner's equity is not affected because there is no sale. The sale happened previously. *There is only an increase in one asset (cash) and a decrease in another (accounts receivable).*
A company wins a $100,000 lawsuit and collects the cash.	Although owner's equity increases, it does not happen because of a sale. *(This is called a "gain," which is an incidental increase in owner's equity.)*

Why does revenue increase owner's equity?

Sales made by the business means the business receives assets from customers, so total assets increase. The owner can claim this increase in assets. (The owner is certainly not going to let the creditors claim the new asset value!) The accounting equation can clarify how the owner's claim increases.

If total assets increase, then we know that part of the change in the condition of the business will show up like this: $\uparrow A = L + OE$

So, to keep the equation in balance, what else must happen? *Owner's equity also increases:* $\uparrow A = L + \uparrow OE$

REVENUES (continued)

Assets can also increase before the revenue is earned!

So far in our discussion of the transactions that involve a revenue, an asset is immediately increased at the moment revenue happens (see Snapshot #7 on page 107).

However, sometimes a customer will pay a business in advance, before the goods or services are provided. When this happens, the assets of a company will increase before the sale actually occurs. In the next major topic, you will see what this transaction looks like.

Remember that "revenue" means a *change*—an increase—in the owner's equity. When you think of revenue, think of a *positive change in owner's equity* caused by operations—making a sale. If something similar confuses you, always test it for this feature:

You must see an **increase** in the owner's equity resulting from **operations**.

REVIEW: AVOID THESE MISTAKES WITH EXPENSES AND REVENUES

Revenue does NOT always mean receiving cash

- Cash can come from loans and other sources such as owner investments. These have nothing to do with revenues.
- Revenue can cause *any* asset to increase (for example, accounts receivable). Usually, however, cash or accounts receivable are the assets that increase.

Expense does NOT always mean paying cash

- Cash can be paid for many different reasons that have nothing to do with expenses, such as paying back a loan.
- An expense can cause almost any asset to be used up, such as supplies. Using up supplies is an example of an expense *without cash being used*.

"Revenue" and "expense" are explanations, not things

Revenues and expenses are not "things" like assets.

The words "revenue" and "expense" are simply *explanations* of the causes of certain kinds of *changes in owner's equity* … changes caused by operations.

CHECK YOUR UNDERSTANDING

Fill in each blank space with the correct word. The answers are below.

A revenue is a(n) (increase/decrease) _____ in _____ _____ , caused by making a sale to a customer. The amount of the revenue is the dollar amount of the _____. A revenue will always cause total _____ to increase. This increase (may/may not) _____ be received before the revenue is actually earned.

*None of the items listed below are revenues. Explain why each item is **not** a revenue.*

- receipt of cash from a loan

- winning a lottery

- collecting cash from accounts receivable

ANSWERS

A revenue is an increase in owner's equity, caused by making a sale to a customer. The amount of the revenue is the dollar amount of the sale. A revenue will always cause total assets to increase. This increase may be received before the revenue is actually earned.

- Receiving cash from a loan is not a revenue because there is no sale to a customer, so owner's equity is not affected. Only the creditor's equity increases.
- Winning a lottery is not a revenue because there is no sale to a customer. (Winning a lottery would be a "gain," an incidental, nonoperational increase in owner's equity.)
- Collecting cash from accounts receivable is not revenue because there is no sale. (The sale has already happened at some previous time.) This is simply increasing cash and reducing accounts receivable—an exchange of assets.

▼ *Nonasset Transactions: Liabilities and Owner's Equity*

OVERVIEW

Introduction

Previously, all the individual transactions that you analyzed involved assets. Asset-related transactions are probably the most common types, so that is why we have looked at them first. However, another frequent kind of transaction is the kind that happens between liabilities and owner's equity. We will study those transactions here.

The two types

Transactions between liabilities and owner's equity can happen in two directions. In the illustration below, you can see that in one situation, owner's equity decreases and liabilities increase. In the other situation, liabilities decrease and owner's equity increases. We will look at each of these situations separately.

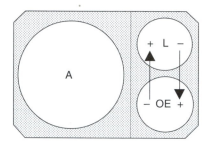

EXPENSES THAT INCREASE LIABILITIES

A delayed decrease in assets

In the prior discussion about expenses on page 116, you read that an expense will always cause assets to decrease. Often, assets decrease at the same time the expense happens. That is what you have studied up to now.

However, when a business has an expense because of services that were consumed, the company can often choose to pay later. Typically, a provider of services will allow 30 to 90 days for payment. There is a *delayed decrease in assets*, even though the expense has occurred when the resource (the service) was consumed.

EXPENSES THAT INCREASE LIABILITIES (continued)

Examples	• In March, Glendale Company receives a $500 utility bill for electrical services consumed during March. The company does not pay the bill until April; therefore, assets (cash) do not decrease until April, even though the expense was in March, and the expense should be recorded in March.

• Tsaile Corporation used $2,500 of computer programming services in October. The company did not pay the bill until November 15; therefore, assets (cash) do not decrease until November 15, even though the expense was in October, and the expense should be recorded in October.

• The last day of the December payroll for Tucson Company is December 31. However, the company does not actually pay the employees until January 3; therefore, assets (cash) do not decrease until January 3, even though the expense was in December, and the expense should be recorded in December.

How an expense can increase a liability

Whenever a business consumes a service and decides to pay for it later, liabilities increase because of the amount owed.

A new liability—a creditor's claim—is recorded against the value of the company assets. The liability is a legal obligation. The company is now legally obligated to use up assets to pay the new debt. Although total assets have not decreased yet, some assets (cash) are now as good as gone.

The accounting equation will show an increase in liabilities: $A = \uparrow L + OE$

What must happen to keep the equation in balance if the assets have not yet decreased? A decrease in *owner's equity:* $A = \uparrow L + \downarrow OE$

The owner has given up some of her claim on assets to the creditor.

When does the business condition change?

Condition changes at the time the expense occurs. This is when the service resource is consumed. A picture of the change looks like this:

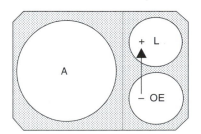

EXPENSES THAT INCREASE LIABILITIES (continued)

When do the assets actually decrease?

When the debt is paid a short time later, the assets will decrease. You can use the accounting equation to show this: $\downarrow A = \downarrow L + OE$

Notice that owner's equity is not affected. Why? Because there is no expense. The expense happened when the resource was consumed. That was when the company decided to delay payment, and liabilities increased. Later, assets must be used to pay the new liability.

Summary

The following table shows the stages of the condition of a company as these transactions happen:

Stage	Event	Accounting Equation
1	Business incurs an expense, but delays payment.	$A = \uparrow L + \downarrow OE$
2	Company pays the creditor who provided the service. Assets decrease when debt is paid.	$\downarrow A = \downarrow L + \quad OE$

Final result

The final result is:

- assets have decreased
- owner's equity has decreased
- the liability is gone—it was created and then paid

More examples

Starting on page 102, you saw 16 "snapshots" illustrating transactions. Now we will continue here with examples of expenses that increase liabilities, beginning with Snapshot #17.

Stage 1: bill received, but not paid immediately

Our business receives a $120 bill from the telephone company on July 10, but delays payment. The telephone company is the *external* party to the transaction. Because the bill is not paid, liabilities now increase and owner's equity decreases because the creditors take some of the owner's claim on assets.

EXPENSES THAT INCREASE LIABILITIES (continued)

Analysis	Effect on Condition
Step 1: Are *assets* affected? No (Assets are not used to pay the bill).	
Step 2: Are *liabilities* affected? Yes (Accounts Payable increase by $120).	A = ↑ L +　OE
Step 3: Is *owner's equity* affected? Yes (owner's equity decreases by $120).	A = ↑ L + ↓ OE

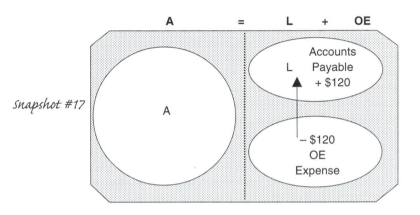

Snapshot #17

Stage 2: the liability is paid

The business in the example above pays the $120 telephone bill on August 2. As assets decrease, the creditor's claim also decreases. Owner's equity is unaffected by the payment to creditors.

Analysis	Effect on Condition
Step 1: Are *assets* affected? Yes (Assets decrease by $120).	↓ A =　L + OE
Step 2: Are *liabilities* affected? Yes (Accounts Payable decrease by $120).	↓ A = ↓ L + OE
Step 3: Is *owner's equity* affected? No.	

EXPENSES THAT INCREASE LIABILITIES (continued)

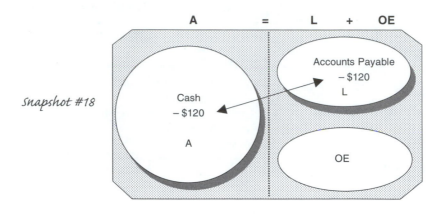

snapshot #18

Caution!

Remember that not every increase in a liability happens because of an expense. Expenses and liabilities only occur together when there are unpaid services consumed in operations.

For example, if a company borrows money or buys supplies on credit, no expense is involved. Can you use the equation (or draw the picture) to verify this?

Analysis	Effect on Condition
Step 1: Are *assets* affected? Yes (they increase).	$\uparrow A = \quad L + OE$
Step 2: Are *liabilities* affected? Yes (they increase).	$\uparrow A = \uparrow L + OE$
Step 3: Is *owner's equity* affected? No (no expense).	

Another caution!

Beginning students often confuse the word "liability" with the word "expense." I am not exactly sure why this happens; perhaps they both seem like negative or bad kinds of things, or because they sometimes occur together.

An expense can happen with or without a liability, and a liability can happen with or without an expense. The fact that they sometimes occur in the same transaction does not mean that they are the same thing.

A liability is not an expense, and an expense is not a liability.

"He thinks a 'liability' is the same thing as an 'expense.' "

• •

CHECK YOUR UNDERSTANDING

?

Fill in each blank space with the correct word. The answers are on page 130.

An asset is not always used up at the same time an expense occurs. Sometimes, there is a _____ decrease in assets. Instead of decreasing assets, _____ are increased. This only happens when a (property/service) _____ resource is consumed and not immediately _____.

Use up and/or down arrows (↑ ↓) in the accounting equation to show these transactions:

• Beebe Company used $5,000 of accounting services in June, but did not pay for them.

• In July, Beebe Company paid the amount owing for the accounting services.

REVENUES THAT DECREASE LIABILITIES

Assets increase in advance

On page 120, you read that a revenue will always cause assets to increase. Frequently, assets do increase at the same time a revenue is earned. That is what you have studied up to now.

However, sometimes a business receives an advance payment from a customer *before* goods or services are provided to the customer. When this happens, the business has increased its assets *before the revenue is earned*.

Examples

• Louisville Corporation receives a $2,000 advance payment from a customer one month before the merchandise is sold.
• Bowling Green Legal Services requires a $1,000 advance payment from a client before they begin doing the legal work.

The advance receipt creates a liability

Suppose that Blarney Advertising Company receives an advance payment of $800 from a customer in October. The advertising service is to begin in November. Assets increase when payment is received in October. However, no revenue is recorded. Why? Because no services have been provided yet!

Because Blarney Advertising Company received cash and has not yet performed services, *the company has a liability*. Until the services are provided, the company is obligated to return the money.

At this point, the accounting equation will show this: ↑ A = ↑ L + OE
$800 $800

REVENUES THAT DECREASE LIABILITIES (continued)

Earning the revenue decreases the liability	When Blarney Advertising Company provides the advertising service in November, it has earned the revenue. At this point, the liability will disappear because the service has been provided. Now owner's equity increases. The customer's claim on the cash payment has now shifted to the owner, because the business provided the service.

The accounting equation will now show this: $A = \downarrow L + \uparrow OE$
$$ \$800 \quad\quad \$800$$

Name of the liability	The name of the liability created by receiving an advance payment from a customer is ***unearned revenue***. It is also sometimes called ***deferred revenue***.

Summary	The following table shows the stages of the condition of a company as these transactions happen:

Stage	Event	Accounting Equation
1	Company receives advance payment.	$\uparrow A = \uparrow L + OE$
2	Company provides service or product and earns the revenue.	$A = \downarrow L + \uparrow OE$

Final result	The final result for Blarney Advertising Company is that cash increased by $800 and owner's equity increased by $800. The liability is gone.

Note: If the company had not performed the services, it would have to return the money. Both cash and liabilities would decrease by $800. |

More examples	Each of the following examples show how the condition of a business changes for businesses that receive advance payments from customers.

Stage 1: company receives advance payment	White-Knuckle Airlines receives $550 for a ticket. The flight will be in two weeks. The customer is the *external* party to the transaction. The customer is a creditor until the flight is provided. Notice that the airline cannot record an increase in owner's equity yet, because the service has not been provided.

Learning Goal 6: Analyze Individual Transactions

REVENUES THAT DECREASE LIABILITIES (continued)

Analysis	Effect on Condition
Step 1: Are *assets* affected? Yes (Cash increases by $550).	$\uparrow A = \quad L + OE$
Step 2: Are *liabilities* affected? Yes (liabilities increase by $550).	$\uparrow A = \uparrow L + OE$
Step 3: Is *owner's equity* affected? No.	

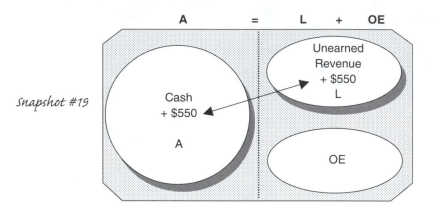

Snapshot #19

Stage 2: revenue is earned

Two weeks later, the customer uses the ticket and takes the flight. The customer is the *external* party to the transaction.

Analysis	Effect on Condition
Step 1: Are *assets* affected? No.	
Step 2: Are *liabilities* affected? Yes (liabilities decrease by $550).	$A = \downarrow L + \quad OE$
Step 3: Is *owner's equity* affected? Yes (owner's equity increases by $550).	$A = \downarrow L + \uparrow OE$

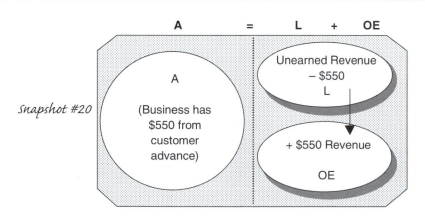

Snapshot #20

REVENUES THAT DECREASE LIABILITIES (continued)

Stage 2: different example

Last month, a lawyer received a $2,000 advance (called a "retainer") from a client. The lawyer now performs the services and earns the revenue.

Analysis	Effect on Condition
Step 1: Are *assets* affected? No.	
Step 2: Are *liabilities* affected? Yes (liabilities decrease by $2,000).	$A = \downarrow L +\quad OE$
Step 3: Is *owner's equity* affected? Yes (owner's equity increases by $2,000).	$A = \downarrow L + \uparrow OE$

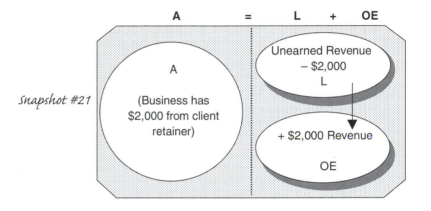

Snapshot #21

Naming revenues

To give decision-makers detailed information, each company will identify a revenue by the type of sale that is made.

Examples:
- "Consulting Fees" means consulting revenues increased the owner's equity.
- "Service Revenue" means that some kind of service activity revenue increased the owner's equity.
- "Product Sales" means sales of merchandise increased the owner's equity.

CHECK YOUR UNDERSTANDING

Fill in each blank space with the correct word. The answers are below.

Sometimes a business receives an advance payment from a customer. This creates (a/an) _____. When the business later provides the service or product to the customer, revenue is earned and the _____ will (increase/decrease) _____.

Comparing revenue types. The table below shows various transactions. For each transaction, place a mark in the correct box to show if the transaction is a revenue with an immediate increase in assets, a revenue with a decrease in liabilities, or is not a revenue.

Transaction	A revenue with a:		Not a Revenue
	Immediate Increase in Assets	Decrease in Liabilities	
1) A company receives a $300 cash advance payment from customer for repair services.			
2) A company provides service to a customer who had previously made a $300 advance payment.			
3) A customer pays a company $300 immediately upon completion of repair services.			
4) A business increases its cash when it borrows $4,000 from a bank.			
5) An accountant prepares a tax return and sends a bill to his client.			

ANSWERS

(continued on page 135)

Transaction	A revenue with a:		Not a Revenue
	Immediate Increase in Assets	Decrease in Liabilities	
1) A company receives a $300 cash advance payment from customer for repair services.			•

Sometimes a business receives an advance payment from a customer. This creates a liability. When the business later provides the service or product to the customer, revenue is earned and the liability will decrease.

Learning Goal 6: Analyze Individual Transactions

ANSWERS (CONTINUED)

(continued from page 134)

Transaction	A revenue with a:		
	Immediate Increase in Assets	Decrease in Liabilities	Not a Revenue
2) A company provides service to a customer who had previously made a $300 advance payment.		●	
3) A customer pays a company $300 immediately upon completion of repair services.	●		
4) A business increases its cash when it borrows $4,000 from a bank.			●
5) An accountant prepares a tax return and sends a bill to his client.	●		

*"How could I forget! A revenue can either
increase an asset or decrease a liability."*

● ● ●

Learning Goal 6: Analyze Individual Transactions

▼ *Nonasset Transactions: Other*

OVERVIEW

Well done!

You have already covered the most frequently occurring transactions in a business! Most business transactions you see will fall into one or a combination of these basic categories that you have studied.

The last two types

The only basic types of transactions that remain are the following:

- transactions only within the liabilities
- transactions only within the owner's equity

These transactions happen much less frequently than the others, so we will not spend much time on them.

TRANSACTIONS WITHIN LIABILITIES

Why they happen

These transactions happen when a company replaces old debts with new debts. For example, if a loan is coming due, a company can go to a new bank and obtain a new loan that pays off and replaces the old loan.

The accounting equation would show: A = ↓ ↑ L + OE

Picture example

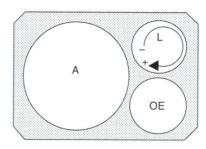

TRANSACTIONS WITHIN OWNER'S EQUITY

Why they happen

These types of transactions involve reorganizing the owner's equity accounts. The most important kind is called "closing the books," which is in Volume 2 of this series. The other transactions of this type involve certain partnership and corporation transactions that are beyond the scope of this book.

The accounting equation will show: A = L + ↓ ↑ OE

Picture example

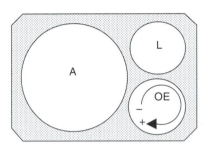

▼ *The Six Basic Patterns of Transactions*

A SUMMARY OF ALL TRANSACTION PATTERNS

Now you have seen them all

Congratulations! Now you know all the basic types of transactions that can happen to a business. Although there are thousands of possible different transactions that can occur, they all fall within six patterns as to how they change the condition of a business. You have now seen all six patterns. The last two types you will not see very often, so it is the first four that you need to practice the most. These are:

Type 1: transactions between assets and liabilities
Type 2: transactions between assets and owner's equity
Type 3: transactions within assets
Type 4: transactions between liabilities and owner's equity

A SUMMARY OF ALL TRANSACTION PATTERNS (continued)

ALL SIX TRANSACTION PATTERNS TOGETHER

Type 1: Assets and Liabilities (see Snapshots #3, #4, #6, #11 and #19)
Type 2: Assets and Owner's Equity (see Snapshots #1, #5, #7, #10, #11, #12 and #15)
Type 3: Within Assets (see Snapshots #2, #8, and #9)
Type 4: Liabilities and Owner's Equity (see Snapshots #17, #20 and #21)
Type 5: Within Liabilities
Type 6: Within Owner's Equity

Type 1: Assets and Liabilities 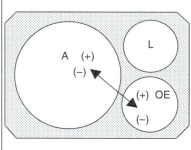 **EXAMPLES** • borrowing money (+) • buying on credit (+) • paying off debts (−)	**Type 4: Liabilities and Owner's Equity** 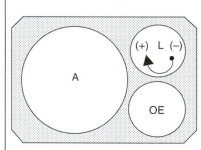 **EXAMPLES** • expenses: debts incurred while consuming services in operations (↑) • revenue: reducing debts as a result of selling goods and services (↓)
Type 2: Assets and Owner's Equity 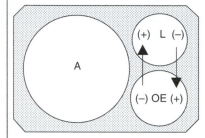 **EXAMPLES** • owner investment (+) • revenue: sales of goods and services (+) • owner drawing (−) • expenses: using up assets in operations (−)	**Type 5: Within Liabilities** 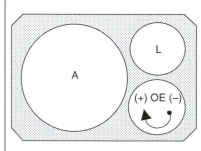 **EXAMPLE** Incurring new debts in order to pay off old debts. The old debt decreases, but a new debt takes its place.
Type 3: Within Assets 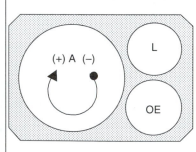 **EXAMPLES** • using cash to purchase another asset • collecting an account receivable	**Type 6: Within Owner's Equity** **EXAMPLES** • closing entries (see Volume 2) • certain transactions in corporations and partnerships that are beyond the scope of this book

***Note:* Practice the first four types as often as you can until you become comfortable with them.**

Learning Goal 6: Analyze Individual Transactions

A SUMMARY OF ALL TRANSACTION PATTERNS (continued)

Combinations are possible

Sometimes one transaction type can occur in combination with another. An example of this is Snapshot #11 on page 109. Snapshot #11 shows how both the assets and liabilities type as well as the assets and owners' equity type occur together in one event. However, this is not a new transaction; it is just a combination of what you already know.

VERY IMPORTANT RULE

DON'T JUST MEMORIZE—*ANALYZE!* Do not even think about memorizing all the possible individual transactions you will see. It is totally impossible. Instead, analyze each transaction by doing this:

Step 1: Are *assets* affected?
Step 2: Are *liabilities* affected?
Step 3: Is *owner's equity* affected?

When you are doing the analysis, use the accounting equation or the six basic pictures to visualize the change in the condition. You will be surprised at how easily you can train yourself. You will become confident that you can analyze how any transaction affects a business.

"Not 'sex,' you idiot! I said 'SIX'!
There are six basic transaction patterns!"

• • •

⌑QUICK REVIEW⌑

● A transaction is any event that changes the financial condition of a business. Transactions can be:

— internal or external events

— financial or organizing type changes

● Using A = L + OE to record the effects of each transaction is called "double-entry."

● *Always analyze* the effects of a transaction by either drawing a picture of the condition of a business or by using the accounting equation. Do this analysis:

— **Step 1:** Are *assets* affected?

— **Step 2:** Are *liabilities* affected?

— **Step 3:** Is *owner's equity* affected?

● When an expense occurs, an asset decreases or a liability increases. However, eventually the liability must be paid, and this will cause assets to decrease. Sooner or later, expenses always decrease total assets.

● When a revenue occurs, an asset increases or a liability decreases. However, the liability that decreases has previously caused assets to increase. Sooner or later, revenues always increase total assets.

● There are six basic types of transactions, of which only four types happen frequently. Every transaction will be one of the basic types, or sometimes a combination of types.

⌑VOCABULARY⌑

Deferred revenue: another name for unearned revenue (page 131)

Double-entry: a system of recording financial changes that requires at least two changes in the accounting equation, so it will stay in balance (page 97)

Expense: a decrease in owner's equity caused by using up resources in operations (page 115)

Revenue: an increase in owner's equity caused by making sales to customers (page 119)

Single-entry: an outdated method of recording transactions in which only a part of the change in the accounting equation is recorded (page 97)

Transaction: any event that causes a change in the accounting equation (page 99)

Unearned revenue: a liability created by receiving a payment from a customer before services are performed (page 131)

"Don't just memorize—analyze!"

• •

PRACTICE FOR LEARNING GOAL 6

SOLUTIONS FOR LEARNING GOAL 6 BEGIN ON PAGE 153.

Learning Goal 6 is about analyzing individual transactions. Use these questions and problems to practice what you have learned about analyzing individual transactions.

MULTIPLE CHOICE

On the line provided, enter the letter of the best answer for each question.

1) Which of these transactions would increase an asset and increase a liability? _____
   A) an owner's investment into a business
   B) borrowing money by signing a note payable
   C) purchasing supplies for cash
   D) performing services for a customer on account

2) Which of these transactions would increase an asset and decrease an asset? _____
   A) collecting an account receivable
   B) purchasing supplies for cash
   C) purchasing supplies on account
   D) both A and B

3) Which of these transactions would decrease an asset and decrease a liability? _____
   A) an owner's withdrawal of assets
   B) borrowing money by signing a note payable
   C) purchasing supplies on account
   D) paying a debt

4) Earning revenue by performing services on account would _____
   A) increase total assets and decrease total liabilities.
   B) decrease total assets and decrease total liabilities.
   C) increase total assets and increase owner's equity.
   D) decrease total assets and decrease owner's equity.

5) If San Jose Circuits Company bought $10,000 of equipment by paying $3,000 cash and signing a note payable for the balance, then _____
   A) total assets decrease and total liabilities increase.
   B) one asset increases and one liability increases.
   C) one asset increases, one asset decreases, and one liability increases.
   D) none of the above.

6) If $500 of supplies were used up in business operations, then _____
   A) total assets decrease and total liabilities increase.
   B) total assets increase and total liabilities decrease.
   C) total assets decrease and owner's equity decreases.
   D) total assets decrease and owner's equity increases.

7) The payment of an account payable would _____
   A) decrease total assets and increase total liabilities.
   B) increase total assets and increase total liabilities.
   C) decrease total assets and decrease total liabilities.
   D) not change total assets, total liabilities, or owner's equity.

8) Collection of an account receivable would _____
   A) increase total assets and increase owner's equity.
   B) increase total assets and increase total liabilities.
   C) decrease total assets and decrease total liabilities.
   D) not affect total assets or owner's equity.

PRACTICE FOR LEARNING GOAL 6

SOLUTIONS FOR LEARNING GOAL 6 BEGIN ON PAGE 153.

REINFORCEMENT PROBLEMS

1) **Give examples based on the information.** Give at least one example of a transaction that would cause the following changes to happen. Also identify any change described that cannot happen.

A) Assets increase and liabilities increase.

B) One asset decreases while another asset increases.

C) Owner's equity decreases and assets decrease.

D) Assets decrease and liabilities increase.

E) Owner's equity decreases and liabilities increase.

F) Assets decrease and liabilities decrease.

G) Liabilities decrease and owner's equity increases.

2) **Using the three steps to analyze a transaction.** In the table below, columns 2, 3, and 4 are for the three steps to use in analyzing each transaction. If any step results in a change in the condition of a business, write in the amount of the change with a ↑ to indicate an increase or a ↓ to indicate a decrease. Use the first item as an example.

Transaction	A =	L +	OE
	Step 1: Are assets affected?	Step 2: Are liabilities affected?	Step 3: Is owner's equity affected?
A) The owner of Ellisville Enterprises invests $10,000 in his business.	↑ $10,000	No	↑ $10,000
B) Senatobia Company borrowed $5,000.			
C) Youngstown Service Company earned $1,000 of revenue that had been prepaid by a customer.			
D) Canton Corporation used $5,000 of cash to purchase supplies.			
E) Brownsville Company provided $2,500 of consulting services to a customer on credit.			
F) Harlingen Partnership received a telephone bill and paid it at once.			
G) Chula Vista Corporation used $2,500 of consulting services and did not pay for them immediately.			
H) Redding Company purchased $10,000 of equipment by paying $2,000 cash and borrowing $8,000.			

Learning Goal 6: Analyze Individual Transactions

PRACTICE FOR LEARNING GOAL 6

SOLUTIONS FOR LEARNING GOAL 6 BEGIN ON PAGE 153.

3) **Explain the changes that are shown.** Write a brief, accurate explanation next to each of our "business photographs," describing the possible kind of transaction(s) that could have happened to the business in each snapshot.

A)

Business Photograph	Explanation
A $=$ L $+$ OE L (−) → (+) OE	

B)

Business Photograph	Explanation
A $=$ L $+$ OE (−) A (−) L OE	

C)

Business Photograph	Explanation
A $=$ L $+$ OE (−) A L (−) OE	(Assume that this happens as part of business operations.)

Learning Goal 6: Analyze Individual Transactions

PRACTICE FOR LEARNING GOAL 6

SOLUTIONS FOR LEARNING GOAL 6 BEGIN ON PAGE 153.

3) *continued*

D)

Business Photograph	Explanation
A = L + OE A (−) L (−) OE	(Assume that this transaction is not part of business operations.)

E)

Business Photograph	Explanation
A = L + OE (+) A (−) L OE	

F)

Business Photograph	Explanation
A = L + OE A L (+) (−) OE	

SOLUTIONS FOR LEARNING GOAL 6 BEGIN ON PAGE 153.

PRACTICE FOR LEARNING GOAL 6

3) *continued*

G)

Business Photograph	Explanation
A = L + OE A (+) L (+) OE	(Assume that this happens as part of business operations.)

H)

Business Photograph	Explanation
A = L + OE A (+) L (+) OE	(Assume that this transaction is not part of business operations.)

I)

Business Photograph	Explanation
A = L + OE A (+) (+) L OE	(Assume that this is not a prepayment by a customer.)

Learning Goal 6: Analyze Individual Transactions

PRACTICE FOR LEARNING GOAL 6

SOLUTIONS FOR LEARNING GOAL 6 BEGIN ON PAGE 153.

3) *continued*

J)

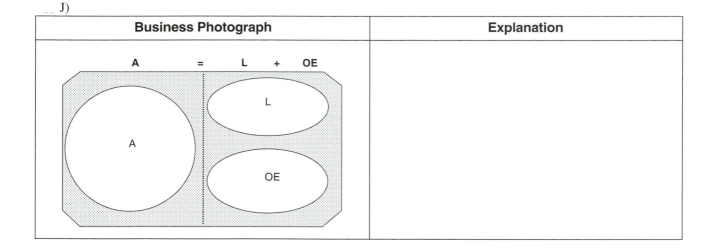

Business Photograph	Explanation
A = L + OE	

---

4) **What could have made the equation change?** Each situation below changes the prior balances and shows new balances in the three elements of the accounting equation. Assuming that just one transaction caused each new balance, write a brief, accurate explanation of what possible kind of business transaction it could be. There is at least one business transaction for each situation. The solution to the first situation is shown as an example.

	BALANCES			EXPLANATION
	Assets	= Liabilities	+ Owner's Equity	
	$5,000		$5,000	**Beginning Balances**
A)	$12,000	$7,000	$5,000	A) Business borrowed $7,000 or purchased $7,000 of assets on credit or received an advance of $7,000 from a customer.
B)	$17,000	$7,000	$10,000	B)
C)	$11,000	$1,000	$10,000	C)
D)	$11,000	–0–	$11,000	D)
E)	$8,000	–0–	$8,000	E)
F)	$8,000	–0–	$8,000	F)
G)	$8,000	$4,000	$4,000	G)

PRACTICE FOR LEARNING GOAL 6

SOLUTIONS FOR LEARNING GOAL 6 BEGIN ON PAGE 153.

5) **A comprehensive review for identifying and analyzing individual transactions.** Following is a problem consisting of different transactions. Complete each item as follows: Enter an "E" ("External") or an "I" ("Internal") for type of transaction, and complete the visualization box by drawing the circles, and indicating plus or minus, as needed, to show what assets or equities are affected by the transaction. Above the box, show the dollar *changes* in the accounting equation. Here is an example for the first transaction:

Example:

Transaction	Internal/ External (I or E?)	Assets $ _____	=	Liabilities $ _____	+	Owner's Equity $ _____
A) Mike Craven, an ex-firefighter but an interior decorator at heart, invests $15,000 in his new interior decorating service called "Hot Spots."	—					

Solution:

	Internal/ External (I or E?)	Assets + $15,000	=	Liabilities $ _____	+	Owner's Equity + $15,000
	E					

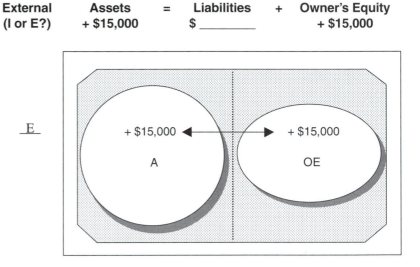

SOLUTIONS FOR LEARNING GOAL 6 BEGIN ON PAGE 153.

5) *continued*

Transaction	Internal/ External (I or E?)	Assets $ _____	=	Liabilities $ _____	+	Owner's Equity $ _____
B) The company purchases $1,000 of supplies for cash.	—					

Transaction	Internal/ External (I or E?)	Assets $ _____	=	Liabilities $ _____	+	Owner's Equity $ _____
C) The company purchases another $1,000 of supplies, but this time on credit.	—					

Transaction	Internal/ External (I or E?)	Assets $ _____	=	Liabilities $ _____	+	Owner's Equity $ _____
D) A large bank pays $5,000 to Hot Spots for decorating consulting services for its new corporate offices.	—					

Learning Goal 6: Analyze Individual Transactions

PRACTICE

PRACTICE FOR LEARNING GOAL 6

SOLUTIONS FOR LEARNING GOAL 6 BEGIN ON PAGE 153.

5) continued

Transaction	Internal/ External (I or E?)	Assets $ ____	=	Liabilities $ ____	+	Owner's Equity $ ____
E) The company pays the office help $1,200 in wages.	—					

Transaction	Internal/ External (I or E?)	Assets $ ____	=	Liabilities $ ____	+	Owner's Equity $ ____
F) The business pays $750 of the amount owing for the supplies.	—					

Transaction	Internal/ External (I or E?)	Assets $ ____	=	Liabilities $ ____	+	Owner's Equity $ ____
G) The company uses up $250 of supplies.	—					

Learning Goal 6: Analyze Individual Transactions

PRACTICE FOR LEARNING GOAL 6

SOLUTIONS FOR LEARNING GOAL 6 BEGIN ON PAGE 153.

5) *continued*

Transaction	Internal/External (I or E?)	Assets $ _____	=	Liabilities $ _____	+	Owner's Equity $ _____
H) The company receives a telephone bill showing $150 of telephone services. The bill is not paid immediately.	___					

Transaction	Internal/External (I or E?)	Assets $ _____	=	Liabilities $ _____	+	Owner's Equity $ _____
I) The company signs a contract with a new client. The client advances Hot Spots $1,200 before any services are performed.	___					

Transaction	Internal/External (I or E?)	Assets $ _____	=	Liabilities $ _____	+	Owner's Equity $ _____
J) Hot Spots fully performs all the work that was required according to the terms of the contract in the previous transaction.	___					

Learning Goal 6: Analyze Individual Transactions

PRACTICE FOR LEARNING GOAL 6

SOLUTIONS FOR LEARNING GOAL 6 BEGIN ON PAGE 153.

5) continued

P
R
A
C
T
I
C
E
.
P
R
A
C
T
I
C
E
.
P
R
A
C
T
I
C
E
.
P
R
A
C
T
I
C
E
.
P
R
A
C
T
I
C
E
.
P
R
A
C
T
I
C
E

Transaction	Internal/ External (I or E?)	Assets $ _____	=	Liabilities $ _____	+	Owner's Equity $ _____
K) Mike Craven withdraws $1,500 cash for his own personal use.	—					

Transaction	Internal/ External (I or E?)	Assets $ _____	=	Liabilities $ _____	+	Owner's Equity $ _____
L) Mike Craven uses the $1,500 that he withdrew to make an investment in land.	—					

Transaction	Internal/ External (I or E?)	Assets $ _____	=	Liabilities $ _____	+	Owner's Equity $ _____
M) Hot Spots purchases $3,500 of equipment by paying $1,000 cash and signing a note payable for $2,500.	—					

Learning Goal 6: Analyze Individual Transactions

SOLUTIONS FOR LEARNING GOAL 6

PRACTICE QUESTIONS FOR LEARNING GOAL 6 BEGIN ON PAGE 142.

MULTIPLE CHOICE

1) B $\quad \uparrow A = \uparrow L + OE$

2) D $\quad \downarrow \uparrow A = L + OE$

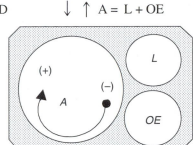

3) D $\quad \downarrow A = \downarrow L + OE$

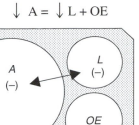

4) C $\quad \uparrow A = L + \uparrow OE$

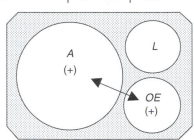

5) C $\quad \downarrow \uparrow A = \uparrow L + OE$

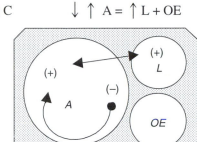

6) C $\quad \downarrow A = L + \downarrow OE$

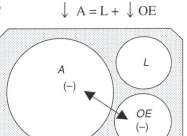

7) C $\quad \downarrow A = \downarrow L + OE$

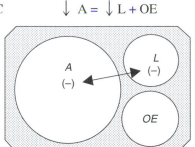

8) D $\quad \downarrow \uparrow A = L + OE$

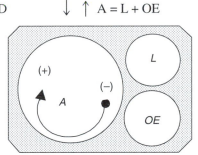

REINFORCEMENT PROBLEMS

1) A) Borrowing money; purchasing assets on credit; receiving a prepayment from a customer.
   B) Purchasing an asset for cash; using an asset to exchange for a different asset; collecting an account receivable.
   C) Expense: an asset is used up while operating the business, such as using up supplies; the owner withdraws cash or other assets.
   D) Not possible. (Notice that the accounting equation would not balance.)
   E) A bill for services is received but not immediately paid, such as telephone expense; wages are owed to employees.
   F) A bill is paid; a loan is repaid.
   G) The business performs services for a customer from whom it had previously received an advance payment.

Learning Goal 6: Analyze Individual Transactions

SOLUTIONS FOR LEARNING GOAL 6

PRACTICE QUESTIONS FOR LEARNING GOAL 6 BEGIN ON PAGE 142.

2)

Transaction	A	=	L	+	OE
	Step 1: Are assets affected?		Step 2: Are liabilities affected?		Step 3: Is owner's equity affected?
A) The owner of Ellisville Enterprises invests $10,000 in his business.	↑ $10,000		No		↑ $10,000
B) Senatobia Company borrowed $5,000.	↑ $5,000		↑ $5,000		No
C) Youngstown Service Company earned $1,000 of revenue that had been prepaid by a customer.	No		↓ $1,000		↑ $1,000
D) Canton Corporation used $5,000 of cash to purchase supplies.	↓ $5,000 ↑ $5,000		No		No
E) Brownsville Company provided $2,500 of consulting services to a customer on credit.	↑ $2,500		No		↑ $2,500
F) Harlingen Partnership received a telephone bill and paid it at once.	↓ $$$		No		↓ $$$
G) Chula Vista Corporation used $2,500 of consulting services and did not pay for them immediately.	No		↑ $2,500		↓ $2,500
H) Redding Company purchased $10,000 of equipment by paying $2,000 cash and borrowing $8,000.	↑ $10,000 ↓ $2,000		↑ $8,000		No

3) A)   The business performed services for a customer from whom it had previously received an advance payment.
   B)   The business paid a debt of some kind.
   C)   The business used up assets as part of operations—an expense.
   D)   The owner withdrew assets for personal use.
   E)   Cash was used to purchase an asset; one asset was exchanged for a different asset; an account receivable was collected.
   F)   A bill for services was received which was not immediately paid—an unpaid expense.
   G)   The business performed services for customers and received cash or accounts receivable, or any other asset.
   H)   The owner made an investment in the business.
   I)   The business borrowed money or purchased assets on credit.
   J)   If there was a transaction, it was one that had nothing to do with the business, so assets, liabilities, and owner's equity were all unaffected.

4) B)   Either the owner has invested $5,000 in the business, or the business has earned $5,000 of revenue and received cash or another asset.
   C) $6,000 of liabilities were paid, using up $6,000 of assets (probably cash).
   D)   The business provided services for a customer that had made an advance payment, thereby increasing the owner's equity and eliminating the obligation to the customer.
   E)   Assets are decreased either by being used up as part of business operations (an expense) or being withdrawn by the owner (a draw).
   F)   Given that there has to be at least one business transaction, then probably an asset was reduced while another was increased, such as using cash to buy supplies. This would keep the total assets unchanged at $8,000.
   G) $4,000 worth of services were consumed and not immediately paid for (example: wages owed to employees).

SOLUTIONS FOR LEARNING GOAL 6

PRACTICE QUESTIONS FOR LEARNING GOAL 6 BEGIN ON PAGE 142.

5)

B)

Assets	=	Liabilities	+	Owner's Equity
− $1,000				
+ $1,000		$ _____		$ _____

E

C)

Assets	=	Liabilities	+	Owner's Equity
+ $1,000		+ $1,000		$ _____

E

D)

Assets	=	Liabilities	+	Owner's Equity
+ $5,000		$ _____		+ $5000

E

E)

Assets	=	Liabilities	+	Owner's Equity
− $1,200		$ _____		− $1,200

E

F)

Assets	=	Liabilities	+	Owner's Equity
− $750		− $750		$ _____

E

G)

Assets	=	Liabilities	+	Owner's Equity
− $250		$ _____		− $250

I

Learning Goal 6: Analyze Individual Transactions

SOLUTIONS FOR LEARNING GOAL 6

PRACTICE QUESTIONS FOR LEARNING GOAL 6 BEGIN ON PAGE 142.

5) continued

H) **Assets = Liabilities + Owner's Equity**

$ _____   + $150   − $150

E ___

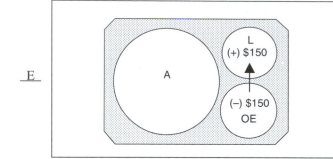

I) **Assets = Liabilities + Owner's Equity**

+ $1,200   + $1,200 $ _____

E ___

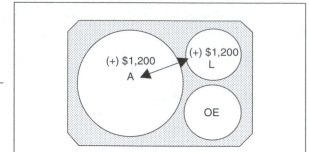

J) **Assets = Liabilities + Owner's Equity**

$ _____   − $1,200   + $1,200

E ___

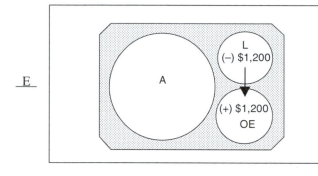

K) **Assets = Liabilities + Owner's Equity**

− $1,500 $ _____   − $1,500

E ___

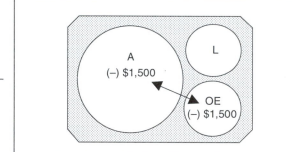

L) E.
Note:
This is
not a
Hot
Spots
trans-
action.
This is
a per-
sonal
expen-
diture.

Assets = Liabilities + Owner's Equity

$ _____ $ _____ $ _____

M) **Assets = Liabilities + Owner's Equity**
+ $3,500
− $1,000   + $2,500 $ _____

E ___

LEARNING GOAL 7
Analyze the Cumulative Effect of Transactions

OVERVIEW

Introduction

In Learning Goal 6, we carefully analyzed the effect of each *individual* transaction on the condition of a business. In this learning goal, we use the accounting equation to analyze the *cumulative effect* of many transactions. One simple but useful way to do this is to calculate the total change in assets, liabilities, and owner's equity balances. Doing this gives a basic overview of what has happened to a business over a period of time.

There are many ways to summarize and analyze the cumulative effects of transactions. It is a very important subject. You will return to it again in Section IV on page 269 when you study how financial statements are specialized summaries of the cumulative effects of transactions.

"Cumulative effect" defined

The "cumulative" effect of transactions means whatever total change in assets, liabilities, and owner's equity occurs over some period of time, and what balances are the result.

Examples

● On January 1, the beginning balance of total assets was $100,000 and on December 31, the ending balance was $90,000. The total assets decreased by $10,000.

● If the beginning balance of owner's equity on October 1 is $35,500 and the owner's equity increased by $4,000, then the ending balance on October 31 is $39,500.

● If the ending balance of liabilities on June 30 was $20,000 and liabilities increased by $5,000 during June, then the beginning balance on June 1 must have been $15,000.

Use the accounting equation for the analysis

It is most useful to analyze changes on all the parts that make up the entire condition of a company. For this reason, cumulative changes are usually expressed in the format of the accounting equation.

OVERVIEW (continued)

Example

If total liabilities of De Kalb Company last month increased by $50,000 and total owner's equity decreased by $12,000, what was the change in the total assets? Using the accounting equation:

Assets	**=**	**Liabilities**	**+**	**Owner's Equity**
?		+ $50,000		− $12,000

Notice that the equation now shows *changes* rather than balances. We can still use the equation, but now it will show changes. Because the right side increased by a total of $38,000 (+ 50,000 − 12,000), then the left side will also increase by the same amount. Assets must have increased by $38,000.

Note: Read the "Introduction to Algebra and Equations" section starting on page 639 if you need practice in calculating the missing item in an equation.

HOW TO SOLVE "CUMULATIVE EFFECT" PROBLEMS

Procedure

The following table shows how to use the accounting equation to solve "cumulative effect" problems.

IF the problem is about ...	THEN use ...
only calculating a *change*, and not a beginning or ending balance,	Format #1 (see below)
calculating a beginning or ending balance that involves cumulative changes,	Format #2 (see below)

Format #1

	A	=	L	+	OE
Cumulative Change					

Format #2

	A	=	L	+	OE
Beginning Balance					
Cumulative Change					
Ending Balance					

Learning Goal 7: Analyze the Cumulative Effect of Transactions

HOW TO SOLVE "CUMULATIVE EFFECT" PROBLEMS (continued)

Examples

Long Beach Luggage Company assets increased by $40,000 and owner's equity increased by $10,000. How much did liabilities change?

Solution: This problem only asks for how much liabilities changed. There is no information about beginning or ending balances (use Format #1).

	A	=	L	+	OE
Cumulative Change	+ $40,000		?		+ $10,000

Calculation: The left side changed by $40,000 so the right side must change by the same total. The change in liabilities is: $40,000 − $10,000 = $30,000.

Suppose the facts are the same for the Long Beach Luggage Company except that the owner's equity *decreased* by $10,000.

	A	=	L	+	OE
Cumulative Change	+ $40,000		?		− $10,000

Calculation: The left side changed by $40,000 so the right side must change by the same total. The change in liabilities is: $40,000 + $10,000 = $50,000.

HOW TO SOLVE "CUMULATIVE EFFECT" PROBLEMS (continued)

The Pyare Square Cleaning Service had assets of $100,000 and liabilities of $70,000. If assets decreased by $12,000 and liabilities decreased by $20,000, what is the new balance of owner's equity?

Solution: This problem has information about beginning and ending balances, and also wants to know an ending balance (use Format #2).

	A	=	L	+	OE
Beginning Balance	$100,000		$70,000		?
Cumulative Change	– $12,000		– $20,000		?
Ending Balance					?

First: Calculate the beginning balance of OE:
$100,000 – $70,000 = $30,000.

Second: Calculate the cumulative change in OE:
– $12,000 – (–$20,000) = $8,000.

Third: Calculate the ending balance of OE:
$30,000 + $8,000 = $38,000.

The filled-in table looks like this:

	A	=	L	+	OE
Beginning Balance	$100,000		$70,000		**$30,000**
Cumulative Change	– $12,000		– $20,000		**$8,000**
Ending Balance					**$38,000**

PRACTICE FOR LEARNING GOAL 7

SOLUTIONS FOR LEARNING GOAL 7 BEGIN ON PAGE 162.

Learning Goal 7 is about calculating the cumulative effect of transactions on the condition of a business. Use these questions and problems to practice what you have learned.

REINFORCEMENT PROBLEMS

1) The assets of Vermont Street Surf Shop increase by $5,000 and liabilities increase by $15,000. What is the change in owner's equity? Try to evaluate what has happened to the company.

2) The owner's equity of Gainesville Internet Services Shoppe increased by $20,000 and liabilities increased by $20,000. What is the change in total assets? Try to evaluate what has happened to the company.

3) Diablo Valley Consulting Enterprises had liabilities decrease by $9,000 and owner's equity increase by $25,000. What is the change in total assets? Try to evaluate what has happened to the company.

4) On December 31, 2001, Athens Computer Services had assets of $95,000 and liabilities of $25,000. During the year, assets increased by $12,000 and liabilities decreased by $15,000. What was the balance of owner's equity on January 1, 2001? Try to evaluate what happened to the company during 2001.

5) On June 1, Bucks County Enterprises had total assets of $90,000 and total owner's equity of $75,000. If assets increased by $12,000 and owner's equity decreased by $10,000, what is the total liabilities on June 30? Try to evaluate what happened to the company during June.

6) On January 1, Thieu Nguyen's company had total assets of $400,000 and total liabilities of $300,000. For each of the following *separate* situations, calculate the missing amount at December 31 year-end for his company:

A) If total assets increased by $25,000 and owner's equity increased by $25,000, what are the liabilities?

B) If total assets increased by $25,000 and total liabilities increased by $20,000, what is the owner's equity?

C) If total liabilities decreased by $25,000 and owner's equity increased by $20,000, what are the total assets?

D) If total assets increased by $25,000 and total liabilities decreased by $20,000, what is the owner's equity?

E) If total assets increased by $45,000 and owner's equity increased by $55,000, what are the total liabilities?

SOLUTIONS FOR LEARNING GOAL 7

PRACTICE QUESTIONS FOR LEARNING GOAL 7 BEGIN ON PAGE 161.

Note: **Bold** numbers mean a **calculated** amount.

REINFORCEMENT PROBLEMS

1)   **Assets**   **=**   **Liabilities**   **+**   **Owner's Equity**
Cumulative Change   + $5,000   + $15,000   **– $10,000**

   The company borrowed $15,000 in resources; during the same time, the combination of operations and owner's drawing decreased owner's equity by $10,000 (not a good business plan).

2)   **Assets**   **=**   **Liabilities**   **+**   **Owner's Equity**
Cumulative Change   **+ $40,000**   + $20,000   + $20,000

   The company borrowed $20,000 and also increased resources by $20,000 from operations and/or owner's investments.

3)   **Assets**   **=**   **Liabilities**   **+**   **Owner's Equity**
Cumulative Change   **+ $16,000**   – $9,000   + $25,000

   This company used $9,000 of resources to pay debts. These resources were more than replaced by a $25,000 combination of operations and/or owner investments. These are good changes.

4)   **Assets**   **=**   **Liabilities**   **+**   **Owner's Equity**
January 1   **$43,000**   (70,000 – 27,000)
Cumulative Change   + $12,000   – $ 15,000   **+ $27,000** [12,000 – (–15,000)]
December 31 $95,000 $25,000   **$70,000**   (95,000 – 25,000)

   This is similar to what happened to Diablo Valley Services in #3, above.

5)   **Assets**   **=**   **Liabilities**   **+**   **Owner's Equity**
June 1 $90,000   **$15,000** $75,000   (L = 90,000 – 75,000)
Cumulative Change   + $12,000   **+ $22,000**   – $10,000   [L = 12,000 – (–10,000)]
June 30   **$37,000**   (L = 15,000 + 22,000)

   This is similar to what happened to Vermont Street Surf Shop in #1, above.

6) First of all, calculate the January 1 equation and owner's equity: <u>(A) $400,000 = (L) $300,000 + (OE) $100,000</u>.
   A) Still $300,000 because assets and owner's equity have each gone up by the same amount.
   B) (OE) <u>$105,000</u>   C) (A) <u>$395,000</u>   D) (OE) <u>$145,000</u>   E) (L) <u>$290,00</u>

Your Questions?

It is *very* important to be aware of what you need to understand better. What do you need to understand better about this learning goal? Use this space to write the questions that you want to discuss with your classmates, instructor, or supervisor. Try to be very specific about what is bothering you, such as explanations that you do not fully understand.

LEARNING GOAL 8
Identify Common Assets and Liabilities

OVERVIEW

Introduction   We have defined the concept of assets, liabilities, and owner's equity. You also know how together they all describe the condition of any economic entity. Now you are ready to learn about some specific kinds of assets and liabilities that show up frequently in most businesses.

ASSET TYPES

Definitions and examples   The table below defines common kinds of assets and gives examples.

Kind of Asset	Examples
Cash: money	● currency that a business has on hand ● checking and savings accounts that can be withdrawn on demand
Supplies: materials that are frequently required for the daily operations of a business, and are used up relatively quickly	● office supplies (paper, copier toner, computer diskettes) ● cleaning supplies (soap, disinfectant) ● automotive supplies (oil, belts, hoses)
Accounts Receivable: a legal right to collect money, usually as the result of a sale and usually collectible in less than 90 days (the opposite of accounts payable)	● A sale is made to a customer "on account." The customer accepts the service or merchandise and therefore the seller has the right to require payment according to the credit terms of the sale.
Notes Receivable: a stronger legal right to collect money as the result of a borrower signing a *written promise* to pay, called a "promissory note." It normally involves receiving interest (the opposite of notes payable).	● Money is loaned to a borrower. The borrower signs a formal written promise to repay according to specified terms. ● A sale is made and the seller requires the buyer to sign a promissory note.

Comment: Receivables that are created *by sales to customers*—either accounts receivable *or* notes receivable—are called **trade receivables.**

ASSET TYPES (continued)

Kind of Asset	Examples
Interest Receivable: the amount of interest that is due and not yet received on a note receivable. Interest receivable is always recorded separately from the note receivable.	• The borrower must make regular payments to pay off the amount of a loan AND pay interest on the loan.
Prepaid Expense: an advance payment *paid* to a provider for goods or services, *before* the goods or services are received (usually for goods or services to be received in a year or less)	• The next 12 months of fire insurance is paid in advance (Prepaid Insurance). • The next three months of rent is paid in advance (Prepaid Rent). • Sometimes supplies are also referred to as a prepaid expense.
Inventory: the goods that a merchant has in stock for the purpose of selling to customers	• golf clubs in a sporting goods store • meat in a grocery store • video camera in an electronics store
Equipment: long-lived (more than a year) assets used in operations to produce goods or services	• a computer • a truck • an office building

Comment: The key difference between supplies and equipment is that supplies are used up quickly (in a year or less) while equipment is used up over a longer period of time. For example, "office supplies" (such as paper, pencils, computer diskettes, and binders) are used up relatively quickly, while "office equipment" (such as furniture, filing cabinets, and computers) provide their benefits over a period of years.

Intangible Assets: assets that have no physical substance—you cannot touch them! Intangible assets are usually legal rights.	• patent • trademark • franchise right—you can't open a MacDonald's hamburger operation without permission from the company. This permission is called a **franchise**, which gives you the legal right to operate someone else's business (in this case, MacDonald's) in a certain location. It costs a lot of money to buy one (if you can even get one).

LIABILITY TYPES

Definitions and examples

The table below defines common kinds of liabilities and gives examples.

Kind of Liability	Examples
Accounts Payable: a legal obligation to pay money, usually as the result of a purchase and usually requiring payment in less than 90 days (the opposite of accounts receivable).	• A sale is made to a customer "on account." The customer accepts the service or merchandise and is therefore obligated to pay according to the credit terms of the seller.
Comment: Accounts payable are promises to pay made using the general credit of a business, and are often referred to as made "on open account."	
Notes Payable: a stronger obligation to pay money as the result of a borrower signing a *written promise* to pay, called a "promissory note." It normally requires the payment of interest (the opposite of notes receivable).	• Money is loaned to a borrower. The borrower signs a formal written promise to repay according to specified terms. • A sale is made and the seller requires the buyer to sign a promissory note.
Interest Payable: the amount of interest that is due and unpaid on a note payable. It is always recorded separately from the amount of the note payable.	• The borrower must make regular payments to pay off the amount of a loan AND pay interest on the loan.
Unearned Revenue: an advance payment *received* from a customer *before* goods or services are provided to that customer (usually for goods or services to be provided in a year or less).	• An insurance company receives an advance payment for 12 months of fire insurance. • A landlord receives an advance payment for the next three months of office rent.
Comment about comparing unearned revenue and prepaid expense: Unearned revenue is a liability that is created because a business *receives cash* before a service or product is provided to the customer. Prepaid expense is an asset that is created because a business *pays cash* before a service or product is received.	

LIABILITY TYPES (continued)

Unearned revenue is *always* a liability. Unearned revenue is *always* a liability; it is *never* a revenue. Remember: any time you see the word "revenue" with the word "unearned" in front of it, it's a liability.

A creditor does not own the asset. Sometimes people think that a creditor's claim on assets is the same as the creditor actually owning the assets. This is not true. Remember that one part of the definition of an asset requires that it belong to a business. For example, even though your car is security for a bank loan, *you* still own the car—the bank doesn't own it—and you can use the car as you wish without asking the bank for permission. You can also sell the car, as long as you pay off the loan. You are the owner of the car, even though you owe money on it.

"Unearned revenues are … L I A B I L I T I E S !"

• •

SOLUTIONS FOR LEARNING GOAL 8 BEGIN ON PAGE 168.

Learning Goal 8 is about defining and identifying common assets and liabilities. Use these questions and problems to practice what you have learned.

REINFORCEMENT PROBLEMS

1) **Can you identify the assets and liabilities?** Write the name of the item in the space provided.

		Name of the Item
A)	A formal written promise by someone else to pay cash to our business	
B)	Amounts owing suppliers or service providers, usually due in 30-60 days	
C)	Items needed for the daily operation of a business and consumed in a year or less	
D)	Money that is collectible in addition to a note receivable	
E)	Currency on hand, plus amounts in checking and savings accounts	
F)	A formal written promise by our business to pay someone else	
G)	Amounts owed to us by our customers, usually due in 30-60 days	
H)	Money that is owed because of item F, above, but is not yet paid	
I)	A payment to a provider of services or goods before they are received	
J)	The receipt of a prepayment from a customer before providing goods or services to that customer	

2) **Explain the difference.** Briefly and accurately explain the difference between an account receivable, a note receivable, and interest receivable:

3) **Explain the difference.** Briefly and accurately explain the difference between office supplies and office equipment:

SOLUTIONS FOR LEARNING GOAL 8

PRACTICE QUESTIONS FOR LEARNING GOAL 8 BEGIN ON PAGE 167.

REINFORCEMENT PROBLEMS

1)

		Name of the Item
A)	A formal written promise by someone else to pay cash to our business	Note Receivable
B)	Amounts owing suppliers or service providers, usually due in 30-60 days	Accounts Payable
C)	Items needed for the daily operation of a business and consumed in a year or less	Supplies
D)	Money that is collectible in addition to a note receivable	Interest Receivable
E)	Currency on hand, plus amounts in checking and savings accounts	Cash
F)	A formal written promise by our business to pay someone else	Note Payable
G)	Amounts owed to us by our customers, usually due in 30-60 days	Accounts Receivable
H)	Money that is owed because of item F, above, but is not yet paid	Interest Payable
I)	A payment to a provider of services or goods before they are received	Prepaid Expense
J)	The receipt of a prepayment from a customer before providing goods or services to that customer	Unearned Revenue

2) An *account receivable* is money that is receivable from a customer as a result of making a sale, and is normally due in 30-60 days. A *note receivable* is a formal written promise to pay money to our business by someone else. A note receivable is normally due any time from several months to many years depending on the terms of the particular note. Interest is the cost of borrowing money. (You could think of it as the "rental" charge for money.) *Interest receivable* is the interest that the holder of the note is expecting to receive from the borrower for the use of the money for a particular period of time that has elapsed.

3) Office supplies are assets that are consumed quickly (in less than a year) in the normal course of business (such as paper, pens and pencils, paper clips, and copy machine toner). Office equipment is a category of assets that have a much longer useful life (greater than a year) and are used up slowly (such as desks, file cabinets, and computers).

Your Questions?

It is *very* important to be aware of what you need to understand better. What do you need to understand better about this learning goal? Use this space to write the questions that you want to discuss with your classmates, instructor, or supervisor. Try to be very specific about what is bothering you, such as explanations that you do not fully understand.

DO YOU LIKE A GOOD STORY?

It might help you to remember better	Sometimes people remember information better when the information is part of an interesting story. The story that continues on the next page is the third part of a three-part adventure, mystery, and romance story. If you have not read the first two parts of the story, you will probably want to go back to the beginning on page 27 or the second part which begins on page 82. If you think a story might help you remember better, of if you just want to have some fun, go ahead! The adventures of Darius continue.
Technical content	This part of the story contains the following technical content: • identifying all changes in owner's equity • summary statement: statement of owner's equity • identifying the operational changes in owner's equity • summary statement: income statement • business decision-making: using the income statement to analyze operations
You can skip the story	If you prefer to study the above technical content more quickly, you can skip the story and go directly to page 194 where the normal presentation and practice continue.

THE WEALTH OF DARIUS

PART III

Hermes' Second Trick

It was morning on the day of rest, and Darius was walking to Dana's house. He carried a basket of white roses and blue wildflowers that he had picked for her. Darius had decided that no matter what happened with his business, it was time to show Dana that he valued her special friendship. He smiled when he thought about seeing her again.

Hermes, however, had a surprise for Darius that day. Hermes had decided that Darius needed to fall in love, but not with Dana. To his regret, the god did not possess the power to make this happen by himself. Instead, Hermes had persuaded Aphrodite, the goddess of love and beauty, to help him make it happen in the way he wanted.

Aphrodite had a son named Cupid who could make people fall in love. Cupid was not a small baby with wings, but rather a beautiful youth, a young man, who himself yearned to be loved by a mortal woman. However, Cupid lived with a terrible curse. Cupid could never allow himself to be seen by any mortal. So great was Cupid's beauty that all who gazed upon him would become hypnotized by desire and lose the power to love, or to think, or even to live. Because of his beauty, Cupid forever lived without the love he wanted.

Even so, Cupid had the power to make others fall in love. He had a bow that shot invisible magic arrows. Cupid would wait until someone was looking at another person. At that moment, Cupid would shoot one of his arrows. Whoever was hit by one of Cupid's arrows would fall desperately, madly, hopelessly, and completely in love with the person he or she was gazing upon at that moment.

Cupid waited until Darius was walking on the road to the village. Cupid watched as Darius walked past a wealthy local trader walking with his family. As Darius went by them, he happened to see the trader's oldest daughter. She was a tall, graceful, black-haired woman named Lamia. In the next second, Darius felt himself overcome by admiration, love, and desire for this woman whom he had never seen before. Darius rushed up to her, introduced himself, and told her that she was the most beautiful woman he had ever seen. Then he anxiously asked her father for permission to visit the next day. Because Lamia was already past the age at which a woman was usually married, her father readily agreed to the visit.

Darius, who normally worked very hard, foolishly forgot his important business problems. He forgot that he was going to see Dana. Instead, Darius withdrew precious money from the business to buy rare eastern perfumes and silks as gifts for Lamia.

The next day Darius, holding the same flowers that he had intended for Dana, knocked on the door of Lamia's house and was shown into the main room to wait for her. As Darius walked into the room, he stopped in amazement. There, standing in the room and coldly staring back at him, was Somnus, who was also holding gifts and flowers.

The Test Is Revealed

Perhaps you have decided by now that it is best to never try to guess what the gods will do. That would be a wise decision, particularly with Hermes. The trickster Hermes had persuaded Aphrodite to ask her son Cupid to make Somnus fall in love with the same woman as Darius. Somnus, while he was in the market, also received one of Cupid's arrows.

Lamia, smiling a devious smile, entered the room with her father. If Darius and Somnus had not been so dumbstruck in their complete admiration of her, they would now have understood why no man had yet asked her to be his wife. Her devious greed soon became apparent as she spoke:

"Darius and Somnus, I am honored that you both seem to feel such strong love and admiration for me. Unfortunately, I cannot choose between you. My father and I have decided that it would be best to have a contest. Since you are both merchants and my family is a merchant family, we will have a contest of merchants. I will agree to marry whichever man that can demonstrate he is the most successful."

She continued. "The contest will be this: at the end of each month for six months, you will both visit me and my father to report the amount of your business wealth and debts. At the end of the six months, we will see which business could pay off all its debts and have the most wealth left over. The owner of that business will be the winner. You may not invest any money in your business. You must do this strictly by operating the business.

"One last requirement: the loser of this contest will agree to give up his entire business to my father. If you do not have the courage to agree to this, you cannot be in the contest, and you will never have my hand in marriage."

Of course, if Darius had been in his right mind he would never have agreed to such a ridiculous contest. Certainly, Lamia and her father wanted nothing more than to obtain the businesses of both men. In truth, Lamia cared little about any man, and like her father, was excited only by wealth and power. She would do what was necessary to obtain them.

Darius saw none of this, and as he and Somnus signed the document agreeing to the terms of the contest, Somnus turned and growled, "Darius, you are a boy trying to do a man's job." Lamia and her father smiled at this, but Darius did not see them. He was too much in love with Lamia to notice.

Darius Sees What the Contest Is Really About

Everyone in town thought Darius and Somnus were possibly the two greatest fools in the history of civilization, which even then was quite a while. There was much ridicule and laughter behind the backs of the two passionate competitors.

Darius was considered to be the greater of the two fools. Most people knew how much Dana cared for Darius. They knew that she was a sweet, intelligent, and faithful woman. This meant that Darius, instead of losing only his business, could lose the two most valuable prizes in his life.

Lamia had said that the winner would be the man whose business could pay off all its debts and have the most wealth remaining. That sounded familiar to Darius. Then, he remembered that the owner's claim was how much the value of assets exceeded the amount of the debts.

Darius then realized that this was really a contest about which man could increase his owner's claim the fastest! "Oh, by the gods," he thought, "this is the same problem that I was trying to fix before!" Darius decided to go to Dana, the only person he trusted to help him.

Dana, with great difficulty, had continued to work in the shop during the last two days, although she and Darius had not spoken. So strong was the power of Cupid's arrow on Darius, and so great was Darius' desire to win, that after work that day Darius asked Dana to help him.

He did not consider her pain when she learned what he had done. He did not consider how the laughter in the town had made her feel. He did not consider that she looked pale or that her eyes were red with dark circles under them. The same Darius, who had always been so generous to others, could now only think of himself … such is the power of Cupid's arrows.

Darius said, "Dana, when we spoke last week, you said it would be necessary to identify how each transaction changes the picture of the business. You said it would be necessary to identify which of the changes affected the owner's claim, and to keep a record of these items."

"Yes."

"Dana, I am not sure I can identify all the transactions that affect the owner's claim. Also, I do not know how to keep a record of all of them. It is very important to me now that I increase my owner's claim as fast as possible."

Dana looked down and waited a long time before she quietly spoke. To Darius, it seemed as if Dana was having difficulty speaking. Then she said, "I am sorry, Darius, but I do not feel well. Please forgive me, but I would rather not discuss this matter again with you."

Darius Creates a Plan

Darius, in his heart, still knew that Dana was a good person and that she had been good to him. He did not ask her anything more or try to speak to her again except for routine matters of the shop. But he had an idea: he remembered that fees from customers increase the owner's claim. Why not try to increase the fees by making more sales to more customers? Also, Darius felt that it would be much easier to only keep a record of sales transactions rather than all the transactions.

Darius had several ideas for increasing sales. He decided to purchase brighter and more long-lasting paints. He would purchase some new and unusual colors and paint more pottery. This was more costly but he would have more customers. He would hire another employee to help him with the complicated designs of large wall paintings. Yes, making more sales to customers was the key thing!

The day of the first month's comparison with Somnus approached, and Darius was hopeful.

After the first month passed, Darius completed his record of the fees earned. He was very proud of his work. It showed each type of fee and looked like this:

Revenue	Month 1
Portrait fees	$ 500
Wall and fresco fees	900
Pottery fees	400
Total fees earned	$1,800

The following day, Darius would meet with Lamia and her father. This was the day that Darius and Somnus were going to show their progress after the first month. Darius felt the excitement of seeing Lamia again, and he felt especially good because he felt that his fees had been increasing. Darius excitedly began to prepare the statement of condition of his business.

Darius calculated the condition of his business and could not believe what he saw. He calculated the condition a second time. Then he compared the statement of condition at the end of last month to the statement of condition he had just completed. This is what Darius saw:

End of this month
Assets = Creditors' Claims + Owner's Claim
$8,800 = $7,500 $1,300

End of last month
Assets = Creditors' Claims + Owner's Claim
$9,300 = $7,400 $1,900

Darius sat in amazement. What had happened? How could his owner's claim have decreased by another $600? He went to bed that night with one hope: that Somnus had a worse month.

The next day, Darius was disappointed. As they were instructed, Darius and Somnus each presented a statement of the wealth and debts of their businesses. Somnus began to smile when he saw that he was winning.

Darius	
Total Wealth	**$8,800**
Gold	300
Due from customers	1,450
Supplies	1,700
Equipment	5,350
Total Debts	**$7,500**

Somnus	
Total Wealth	**$25,300**
Gold	4,300
Due from customers	950
Supplies	4,700
Equipment	15,350
Total Debts	**$7,400**

Darius tried to keep his wits. He noticed that neither Somnus nor Lamia nor Lamia's father knew how to calculate the condition of a business in the way that Darius knew how. They simply compared the wealth and the debts. When Darius saw this, he remembered something that he had learned from Hermes.

Immediately, Darius pointed out that Somnus had included his personal clothing and household furniture as part of the equipment of the business. Lamia and her father had to agree that this was incorrect. They reduced Somnus' business assets by the amount of the items that were personal. Somnus clenched his fists and glared at Darius.

Then Darius showed that Somnus had also included his shop as part of the equipment. Somnus, like Darius, rented his shop, so the shop did not belong to Somnus' business either. After this was subtracted, the wealth of the two businesses was almost equal. Lamia and her father smiled at Somnus' rage. They really did not care who won. They knew that both businesses would soon be under their control.

The Second Month

Darius knew he had been lucky this time. Somnus would be more careful the next time. Darius tried harder than before for more fees. He and his assistant worked longer, used better paints, and painted better pottery. At the end of the second month, Darius calculated the total fees, and saw they were $940 greater than the first month:

Revenue	Month 1	Month 2
Portrait fees	$ 500	$ 840
Wall and fresco fees	900	1,100
Pottery fees	400	800
Total fees earned	$1,800	$2,740

Darius felt momentary relief, but when he prepared his statement of condition, this is what he got:

End of Month 2
Assets = Creditors' Claims + Owner's Claim
$8,500 = $7,250 $1,250

The owner's claim and the assets had decreased again. The owner's claim was $50 less than the first month of the contest. At the two-month comparison, Darius watched Somnus smile with glee when the comparisons were made. Somnus did not make the same mistakes that he had made the last time.

Darius looked closely. Although Somnus did not think about calculating an owner's claim, Darius mentally calculated Somnus' owner's claim by subtracting $3,500 from $12,900. Somnus had a claim of $9,400. Then Darius anxiously looked back at his own claim again: only $1,250!

Darius	
Total Wealth	**$8,500**
Gold	250
Due from customers	350
Supplies	2,550
Equipment	5,350
Total Debts	**$7,250**

Somnus	
Total Wealth	**$12,900**
Gold	4,100
Due from customers	1,100
Supplies	2,150
Equipment	5,550
Total Debts	**$3,500**

When he returned to his shop, Darius knew that he had been much too confident in his plan. It was not working. The problem was that he had not yet fully explained the operational change in his owner's claim. He had not done what Dana had suggested when they had worked together.

Darius had not bothered to keep a record of the assets used up in operations. Because it was easier, he had only been recording the operational increases caused by the fees. Only four months to go!

To get control, Darius knew now that he also needed to identify the decreases caused by operations. Darius was not sure that he could identify all the operational decreases, but now he had to try. He had no choice.

The Third Month

Darius discovered that keeping a record of all the operational decreases in his owner's claim was a great amount of extra work. There were so many of them! Even the name "assets used up in operations" was too long and too difficult to say. He started using the name "expenses" because assets were being expended … that is, used up.

To keep a record of expenses, Darius worked hard and his days were long. It was not easy to know exactly when there was an expense. It was clear to Darius when the business used up paints or canvas—that was an expense (it helped to create value). It was clear to him that when the business used up gold to pay an employee—that was an expense. It was less clear when he paid the rent, but then he remembered he could not do his work for customers without a shop to work in. So, paying the rent was an expense.

Paying the creditors puzzled Darius. After much thought, he decided that paying debts was not an expense, because this was only benefiting the creditors, not the customers. Paying debts did not use up assets as part of the process of creating something valuable for customers. The purpose of paying debts was to reduce a creditor's claim. With practice, Darius became better at identifying expenses.

At the end of the third month, Darius summarized the fees and the expenses with a new table:

Revenue	Month 2	Month 3
Portrait fees	$ 840	$ 850
Wall and fresco fees	1,100	1,500
Pottery fees	800	1,900
Total fees earned	$2,740	4,250
Expenses		4,500
Operational decrease in owner's claim		$ – 250

Darius now began to sense what was wrong. When he looked at the results of Month 3, he could see that his owner's claim was decreasing mostly because of operations. The operations used up assets as expenses faster than the operations received assets (the fees earned) from customers. For Month 3, operations used up $250 more in the value of the assets than was received from customers, which reduced the wealth of the business, and the owner's claim.

Then Darius calculated the condition of his business and compared it to the condition at the end of last month. *Worse!* His owner's claim was down again!

End of Month 3
Assets = Creditors' Claims + Owner's Claim
$9,050 = $8,100 $950

End of Month 2
Assets = Creditors' Claims + Owner's Claim
$8,500 = $7,250 $1,250

Darius again looked at the owner's claim. The difference between $950 and $1,250 was a $300 decrease, not $250. Why the extra $50 decrease?

Darius felt his neck tighten and his head ache. He sensed that he could not try much harder. He already had worked very, very hard. He had kept a record of all sales. He had kept a record of all expenses. All this plus doing all his usual painting and design work! "Perhaps I am just too stupid to compete against Somnus," he thought. A feeling of sadness overcame him as he remembered all his wonderful dreams of a life together with beautiful and graceful Lamia.

Next day, the meeting confirmed his fears. Again, Somnus was further ahead. Somnus' business had even paid off all its debts! Somnus loudly suggested that Darius quit the contest so he would not embarrass himself anymore. Lamia laughed and seemed not to notice Darius at all.

Darius	
Total Wealth	$9,050
Gold	100
Due from customers	1,550
Supplies	2,050
Equipment	5,350
Total Debts	$8,100

Somnus	
Total Wealth	$14,900
Gold	4,000
Due from customers	1,200
Supplies	2,700
Equipment	7,000
Total Debts	$0

The Fourth Month

Darius did not go to the shop the next day. Instead, he walked in the meadows around his house. He began to think about the real possibility of losing his business.

Darius did not go to work for the next two days. On the fourth day, when he returned to his shop, he had not shaved. Darius did not work on any new designs, and he did not do the thing that he loved the most: his painting.

Darius gave up recording the sales and the expenses. Although Darius had always liked to talk with his employees and customers, he seldom spoke now. For more than a week, he did no painting. He did nothing. Customers became angry waiting for their work. Two creditors, Aulis and Hela, came to Darius and told him that they were tired of waiting to be paid. They would not supply any more materials unless the business paid them more quickly.

All the employees, of course, observed this. Among them, Dana worried the most. Darius' foolish behavior had not stopped Dana from caring about what happened to him. Even though she had given up all hope for Darius' love, her noble character would not let him continue to suffer.

One day, she came to him in the shop and said, "Darius, I have not seen you do much painting lately. Are you thinking about new designs?"

"No," he said, "I am finished with that and I am finished with painting."

"Why is that?"

"Because I have discovered that I am probably too stupid to be any good at what I am trying to do. I think that my painting is poor and my ideas are poor. Even if I were a good painter, I am unable to be a businessman. It has taken me all this time to finally understand how operations decreased my owner's claim, and now I am too stupid to do anything more with this knowledge."

This shocked Dana. Darius had been a wonderful artist since he had been a small child and loved painting more than anything in life. Dana decided to be bold. "Darius, I know all about this contest with Somnus. Everyone knows that one of you will lose his business." Darius opened his eyes wide when he heard her say this.

"I understand how taken you are with Lamia. But I know you well, Darius. There is something that you love even more than Lamia, and that is the joy you feel when you paint. Are you willing to give up painting because of her? Is her approval that important to you? Is she going to take your life away?" Darius stared at her with his mouth open.

"As for being stupid ... well, Darius, do you not realize what you have just done? By identifying the fees earned and the expenses, you have explained the operational changes to your owner's claim! This is powerful knowledge. Use it to change whatever is wrong! You are acting ridiculous, Darius. I will not watch you give up everything. Would you like me to help?"

"Help?" Darius mumbled. "Me? Now?"

"Darius," Dana said, putting her hand on his shoulder, "it is time to take what you have learned and really use it. We will figure out a way to make your owner's claim grow and then you can beat Somnus. But first help me put all this information together so we can understand what has happened." With more encouragement, Darius began to think about his business again.

Over the next several hours, Dana and Darius designed a statement that explained all the changes in the owner's claim that they had found. (Their creation was so good that a similar statement is still used today.)

As a starting point, they wrote down the beginning and ending balances of the owner's claim for Month 3. This is what it looked like:

Statement of All Changes in Owner's Claim for Month 3		*Total decrease is $300!*
Prior balance, end of **Month 2**	$1,250	←
Current balance, end of **Month 3**	$ 950	←

Next, they prepared the statement showing the operational changes in the owner's claim because of fees and expenses. This was similar to what Darius had already prepared.

Statement of Operational Changes for Month 3	
Fees Earned	
Portraits	$ 850
Walls and frescoes	1,500
Pottery	1,900
Total fees earned	4,250
Total Expenses	4,500
Operational decrease	($250)

Then, in the statement of owner's claim, they entered the $250 operational decrease. Dana used brackets ( ) to show a minus amount, because it was easier to see than a minus sign of "–". Next, Dana wrote a "?" to show that a change was still unidentified.

Statement of All Changes in Owner's Claim for Month 3	
Prior balance, end of **Month 2**	$1,250
Less: Operational decrease	(250)
???	?
Current balance, end of **Month 3**	$950

Statement of Operational Changes for Month 3	
Fees Earned	
Portraits	$ 850
Walls and frescoes	1,500
Pottery	1,900
Total fees earned	4,250
Total Expenses	4,500
Operational decrease	($250)

Finally, Dana asked if there were any changes caused by investments and withdrawals. Darius had made no investments, but remembered that he had taken out $50 in withdrawals. This was the missing $50 dollar decrease! This completed all the changes in the owner's claim!

Statement of All Changes in Owner's Claim for Month 3	
Prior balance, end of **Month 2**	$1,250
Add: Owner's investments	–0–
Less: Operational decrease	(250)
Less: Owner's withdrawals	(50)
Current balance, end of **Month 3**	$950

Statement of Operational Changes for Month 3	
Fees Earned	
Portraits	$850
Walls and frescoes	1,500
Pottery	1,900
Total fees earned	4,250
Total Expenses	4,500
Operational decrease	($250)

The Mystery Is Solved

When they had finished, Dana clapped her hands. "Darius, look at what we have done! We have completely explained the entire change in your owner's claim with these two beautiful statements! The $300 decrease in your owner's claim was caused by just two kinds of increases and two kinds of decreases! Your investments and the fees from customers are the two increases. Withdrawals and expenses are the two decreases. The fees and expenses are from operations. We have solved the mystery!"

"This must be what Hermes had wanted," Darius said.

"Now comes the matter of beating Somnus," Dana answered. "Darius, I think I see what you need to do and it is rather important."

"What is that?" he asked.

"The expenses," she said. "Your troubles, I think, are caused by the operational decrease in your owner's claim. The expenses seem to be reducing your owner's claim faster than the fees from customers are increasing it."

"Yes, I think I understand that now."

"Good. But Darius, you have not yet detailed all the expenses as you have done with the fees. If you knew how much each of the individual expenses were, you could make decisions about changing or reducing them. I think we need to start keeping a record of *each kind* of expense. I can help you do this."

This is how Darius and Dana began keeping detailed records of the business operations. They began with the sales and expenses from the beginning of Month 4, and they continued recording for the remainder of the month. For Month 4, they had a much more detailed explanation of the operational change in the owner's claim. It looked like this:

Revenue	Month 3	Month 4
Portrait fees	$ 850	$ 1,200
Wall and fresco fees	1,500	2,750
Pottery fees	1,900	3,450
Total fees earned	4,250	7,400
Expenses	4,500	
Portrait materials and supplies		200
Walls/frescoes materials and supplies		1,250
Pottery materials and supplies		6,450
Rent		250
Other expenses		100
Operational decrease in owner's claim	$ (250)	$ (850)

The size of the decrease shocked Darius. He prepared the statement of condition at the end of Month 4. He could not believe what he saw.

End of Month 4		
Assets =	Creditors' Claims +	Owner's Claim
$8,250 =	$8,200	$50

Next, he prepared the statement that explained all the changes in his owner's claim.

Statement of All Changes in Owner's Claim for Month 4	
Prior balance, end of **Month 3**	$950
Less: Operational decrease	(850)
Less: Withdrawals	(50)
Current balance, end of **Month 4**	$50

Statement of Operational Changes for Month 4	
Fees Earned	
Portraits	$1,200
Walls and frescoes	2,750
Pottery	3,450
Total fees earned	7,400
Expenses	
Portrait materials/supplies	200
Walls/frescoes materials/supplies	1,250
Pottery materials/supplies	6,450
Rent	250
Other expenses	100
Total expenses	8,250
Operational decrease	($850)

As usual, Darius had not made any investments, so they omitted the line for investments.

"By the gods, I have only $50 of owner's claim left! I am practically finished!"

"No, you are not," Dana replied. "I think that now is your best opportunity. Tomorrow I will show you why I believe this, after you finish your meeting with Somnus and Lamia. Stay strong, Darius."

When Darius presented his wealth and debts at the end of the fourth month, he endured even more humiliation than usual. Somnus asked, "Darius, why do you not stop the contest to avoid further humiliation? You can leave town quietly." Both Somnus and Lamia burst into laughter when they saw Darius' presentation of wealth and debts. Darius remained silent as he clenched his jaw.

What do you think?

- *What amount caused an increase in owner's claim? Where do you find it?*
- *What two amounts caused a decrease in owner's claim? Where do you find them?*
- *What business or financial advice would you offer to Darius now?*

Total revenues of $7,400 caused the increase in owner's claim. It is on the Statement of Operational Changes. (An owner's investment would also have increased owner's claim, but Darius did not do this.)

Expenses of $8,250 decreased the owner's claim. Expenses are on the Statement of Operational Changes. A withdrawal of $50 also decreased the owner's claim. This is shown separately on the Statement of All Changes in Owner's Claim, because it is not part of operations.

The Fifth Month—Important Business Decisions

When Darius returned from the monthly meeting more angry and upset than usual, Dana immediately said, "All right, Darius, now is our time."

"I am ready to try anything," he said. "What was the opportunity that you spoke of yesterday?"

"Darius, you now have something very special—something that neither Somnus nor anyone else understands. You possess detailed information that tells you all the reasons why operations have decreased your owner's claim. To increase your claim, all you need to do now is use this information so you can make decisions that change the way you operate. Are you ready?"

"For anything."

"Good. I am certain that the answers you need are hiding in the two parts of operations—expenses and fees. There is one question for each part. First, the expenses: look closely at the total amount of each expense. Is the expense justified for the amount of value it creates? Second, the fees: are you charging the right price for each kind of work that you do?"

"I will need some time to think," he replied.

"Then think about these questions carefully tonight. We will discuss this again tomorrow."

Darius stayed in his shop that night. He lit many candles to keep his shop bright, and then thought intently about the two questions. One at a time, he thought about each expense that he saw on the statement of operations. For each expense, he asked himself, "*Is the expense justified* by the amount of value—that is, the fees—it helps my business get?"

The expenses of the pottery work amazed him, and as he began to think more about it, Darius realized that the special paints and glazes for pottery had always been the most expensive of all the supplies. Also, the waste was significant because pottery often baked improperly in the ovens and had to be thrown away.

The second question was, "Am I charging the right price for each kind of work?" For months, Darius had been charging less than Somnus for everything: the portraits, the walls and frescoes, and the pottery. Darius had hoped that selling for less would attract more customers, but this did not seem to attract many new customers except for pottery painting.

After giving all of this much thought, Darius then made three business decisions:

First, he decided to increase some of his prices. He would charge the same as Somnus for walls and frescoes. Then, Darius decided to double his prices for portraits because they took so much time, and because he was a much better portrait painter than Somnus.

Second, Darius decided that he would try to reduce the cost of the wall and fresco designs.

Darius enjoyed his third decision most of all. Except for a few special customers, Darius decided to completely stop all the pottery painting!

Why? Darius realized that it would be impossible for pottery painting to be profitable. The pottery painting was slow and much more costly than he had ever realized. What was worse, he could never raise prices for pottery painting! Most customers refused to pay very much for the pottery painting because eventually the pottery would break and need to be replaced. Except for a small number of wealthy customers, painting pottery would always cause large losses.

When he looked at the statement of operational changes for Month 4, Darius saw that pottery painting was the single biggest cause of his problems with the business. The pottery expenses of $6,450 were much greater than the pottery fees of $3,450. The pottery expenses simply could never create enough value!

The Perfect Trick

Then Darius had a wonderful idea, a trick that was worthy of Hermes himself! Darius decided to tell everyone that he was giving up pottery painting because Somnus was so much better. If the plan worked, then arrogant Somnus would eagerly take all of Darius' old pottery customers. In this way, Somnus would soon have all the same pottery expenses and begin to destroy his own business.

Darius realized that Somnus did not understand about the complete calculation of the condition of a business. He certainly had no idea about calculating the operational changes in the owner's claim. So, it would be a long, long time—if ever—before Somnus would find out what was wrong. The perfect trick!

Next morning, when Darius and Dana discussed the decisions about increasing prices and trying to reduce the cost of wall and fresco designs, she agreed. She had reached those conclusions herself. And when Dana heard Darius' reasons for letting Somnus take over all the pottery painting in the village, she bubbled with excitement. "Why Darius, you are as clever as Hermes himself!" and she laughed so long that she had to sit on a bench as tears streamed from her eyes. Darius could not restrain his own smile.

On the second day of the fifth month of the contest, Darius raised his prices. He also began telling most of his customers that he would no longer paint pottery for them because Somnus was too good. Somnus fell right into the trap. Soon he was working long hours for all his new pottery customers. He had to buy new equipment and hire an extra employee.

Darius could hardly wait until the end of the month.

It had started out as a difficult month, but it seemed to become easier to pay the creditors as the month progressed. Darius had high hopes as the time came to calculate the monthly statement of condition. Before he did this, Darius summarized his fees and expenses and compared them to Month 4.

Revenue	Month 4	Month 5	
Portrait fees	$ 1,200	$ 2,200	
Wall and fresco fees	2,750	3,250	
Pottery fees	3,450	–0–	←
Total fees earned	7,400	5,450	
Expenses			
Portrait materials and supplies	200	250	
Walls/frescoes materials and supplies	1,250	1,150	
Pottery materials and supplies	6,450	–0–	←
Rent	250	250	
Other expenses	100	100	
Operational change in owner's claim	$ (850)	$ 3,700	

When Darius saw the results of Month 5, satisfaction filled him like nourishment to a starving man. The operations had increased owner's equity by $3,700! The plan was beginning to work.

Next, he prepared the three necessary statements: the basic statement of condition, and the two statements explaining the changes in the owner's claim.

End of Month 5		
Assets =	Creditors' Claims +	Owner's Claim
$10,850 =	$7,200	$3,650

Statement of All Changes in Owner's Claim for Month 5	
Prior balance, end of **Month 4**	$50
Add: Investments	–0–
Add: Operational increase	3,700
Less: Withdrawals	(100)
Current balance, end of **Month 5**	$3,650

Statement of Operational Changes in Owner's Claim for Month 5	
Fees Earned	
Portraits	$2,200
Walls and frescoes	3,250
Pottery	–0–
Total fees earned	5,450
Expenses	
Portrait materials/supplies	250
Walls/frescoes materials/supplies	1,150
Pottery materials/supplies	–0–
Rent	250
Other expenses	100
Total expenses	1,750
Operational increase	$3,700

In the meeting at the end of the fifth month, Darius watched a different Somnus review wealth and debts for Lamia and her father. Somnus' assets had decreased and his debts had increased.

Darius	
Total Wealth	$10,850
Gold	1,900
Due from customers	1,550
Supplies	2,050
Equipment	5,350
Total Debts	$7,200

Somnus	
Total Wealth	$13,500
Gold	2,750
Due from customers	1,200
Supplies	2,550
Equipment	7,000
Total Debts	$3,900

Somnus kept staring at the paper and taking quick little breaths, which made him stammer. "Do not wor … wor … worry, Lamia, it is jus … jus … just … one mm … mm … month."

It was true that Somnus still had more wealth and fewer debts than Darius. It was also true that if this had been the last month of the contest, Somnus would win, because after paying all his debts Somnus would have $9,600 of wealth left over. Darius only had an owner's claim of $3,650. However, it was not yet the last month of the contest. There was still one more month to go, and Darius was catching up.

The Final Month

As Month 6 began, Darius felt his determination surge like a rising river. Now he could chuckle to himself as he saw Somnus toiling at his shop every day, seldom resting, trying to complete all of his pottery painting work. Moreover, because Somnus now spent so much time on pottery painting, he began to lose some wall and fresco painting customers to Darius. Darius' decision now looked even better than before.

Dana also noticed the difference. Darius had both higher prices and new wall painting customers. Meanwhile Somnus, by painting so much pottery, was sinking into a hole that he was digging for himself. Dana felt that Darius had a chance to win when Lamia made the last comparison.

Dana was happy that Darius had a chance to save his business and that he was painting again. Every day she prayed for him to win. But Dana also knew that if Darius won, she would soon be out of his life. Lamia would see to that. The moment that Lamia selected Darius, Lamia would throw Dana out. Dana promised herself that no matter what, she would always be a friend to Darius; she would always give Darius the best advice that she knew. Her special smile would always belong to him.

The last day of the sixth month arrived. Darius calculated the fees and expenses for the sixth month, and compared them to Month 5.

Revenue	Month 5	Month 6
Portrait fees	$2,200	$2,100
Wall and fresco fees	3,250	3,400
Pottery fees	–0–	–0–
Total fees earned	5,450	5,500
Expenses		
Portrait materials and supplies	250	300
Walls/frescoes materials and supplies	1,150	600
Pottery materials and supplies	–0–	–0–
Rent	250	250
Other expenses	100	50
Operational increase in owner's claim	$3,700	$4,300

Nervously, Darius calculated the condition of his owner's claim:

End of Month 6		
Assets =	Creditors' Claims +	Owner's Claim
$14,900 =	$7,000	$7,900

Darius and Dana again prepared the statements explaining the changes in the owner's claim. However, what Darius really worried about now was the final balance of his owner's claim. It was the end of the six months and Darius' balance was $7,900. At the end of the previous month, Somnus had shown $9,600. Darius could only hope that the pottery losses were enough to bring Somnus down below $7,900.

That night, Darius slept restlessly, tossing and turning. He dreamed of Ammon, and Darius felt his old fears of losing the business. He dreamed of the old woman dressed in black, and of the frightening visits by Hermes. He dreamed about his friends, the birthdays, and the wonderful feasts and good times. He dreamed about the beautiful Lamia and her father. In his dream they became great spiders, and he could hear their spider fangs clicking together and their spider feet brushing the ground as they hungrily approached him … Darius awoke with a scream.

The day's first light illuminated the silver dew on every tree and flower, and soon changed the silver into millions of glowing rainbow drops. As the minutes brightened, birds began sharing their melodies in a joyful chorus that proclaimed the fresh day. Darius made his final decision.

He bathed, ate a small breakfast, and into a pocket he put the paper on which he had written the business wealth and debts for Lamia and her father to examine.

He went directly to Dana's house. Ammon answered the door, and Darius said, "Ammon, I apologize if I am too early this morning. However, may I speak to your daughter?"

"Yes, Darius, one moment."

In a few minutes, Dana appeared. Darius looked at her directly and then said, "Dana, as you know, I am meeting with Lamia, her father, and Somnus this morning. I would like you to be there with me."

She stared at him. "Darius, you love Lamia. How can you ask me to do this?"

"Dana, trust me and be my friend one last time, please."

She was a true friend and, despite her uncertainty, she left with Darius. In another moment, Darius and Dana were walking on the road together. In less than an hour, they arrived at the home of Lamia and her father. Somnus arrived at almost the same time. Sullen and dark, he glared at them and said, "Now Darius, it is at last time for you to see who is the better man. It is time for you to disappear."

They were shown into the house, where Lamia and her father were waiting, smiling. Lamia's eyebrows arched and her eyes showed surprise when she saw Dana.

"Well, Dana, this is truly an unexpected pleasure. Did you come here to say good-bye?" Lamia and her father smiled hungrily. Lamia continued. "This is the moment, dear Darius and dear Somnus, I know you both have been eagerly awaiting. Now show me the statements you have prepared and the winner will be my husband."

Darius handed his statement to Lamia. Somnus turned and glowered at Darius, to which Darius responded with a smile and a wink. Choking down his fury, Somnus shoved his statement into Lamia's outstretched hand.

"Gentlemen, gentlemen," she said, "let us now see which one of you shall enjoy the blessings of my companionship for the rest of your life." With that, she placed the two statements on a table so all could see:

Darius	
Total Wealth	$14,900
Gold	4,550
Due from customers	3,500
Supplies	1,500
Equipment	5,350
Total Debts	$ 7,000

Somnus	
Total Wealth	$15,500
Gold	1,100
Due from customers	2,700
Supplies	3,800
Equipment	7,900
Total Debts	$ 7,800

Lamia seemed to hesitate and consulted with her father. She turned and faced the three people in front of her. "Somnus, if we subtract the debts from the wealth, your business would have $7,700 of wealth remaining, if it were to pay off all its debts today. Darius, I am surprised to say that your business would have $7,900 of wealth remaining if it were to do the same. Darius, you appear to be the winner."

Shaking, Somnus snarled, "Fraud!"

"No," Darius said, "you may check and verify everything, as I am sure Lamia will do."

Lamia now ignored Somnus and smiled directly at Darius. "Oh Darius, you are much the better man. You know, I never once doubted you. You have truly won my heart and you will at last be my husband." Then Lamia turned to a servant and said, "Show Dana the door. It is time for her to leave."

At the same moment, Somnus exploded into a rage, shrieking, "Fraud, fraud, you are a *fraud!*" Madly shaking, raving, Somnus screamed, "I … YOU … I challenge you, Darius, to a duel! … to the death … *the death!* … now, at this instant!"

Quick as cats, two of Lamia's servants were upon Somnus and forced him into a chair. After several minutes, Somnus began to calm and Darius spoke.

"First, Somnus, I regretfully decline your offer of a duel. It is not my intention to demonstrate your unworthiness twice in one day, and at the cost of your life."

Then Darius turned to Lamia. "Lamia, I have indeed won the contest. Regrettably, I must inform you that I decline your offer as well. You will not be my wife. However, as the winner, I will choose to keep my business for myself. I suggest that you and Somnus will be excellent for each other."

Darius reached over to Dana, and brought her nearest hand to his lips. "As for me, I have already won my prize, long before today."

Epilogue

And so that is what happened when the gods decided to let mankind learn about the condition of a business. Darius came to realize that despite all his troubles, he had received two wonderful gifts for which he always thanked the gods:

The first great gift was the ability to explain the condition of a business and why the condition changes, especially the change in the owner's claim. Darius, always generous, decided to share this knowledge with other merchants—yes, even with Somnus, who years later came to hold Darius in high esteem as his one true friend.

Darius told the other merchants that three statements are necessary: the first one is the basic statement of condition and is like a picture drawn at a point in time. The other two statements explain change, so they show what happened over a period of time. Darius made a list:

STATEMENT OF CONDITION
- *a picture of the business at any point in time*

STATEMENT OF CHANGES IN OWNER'S CLAIM
- *summarizes all the changes in the owner's claim*

STATEMENT OF OPERATIONAL CHANGES IN OWNER'S CLAIM
- *explains in detail the changes in the owner's claim caused by operations, which have the most powerful effect on the owner's claim*

Darius, always the artist, drew a diagram as an example for the other merchants to show them the three kinds of statements. In the diagram, Darius showed the condition of his business at the end of Month 3, Month 4, and Month 5 of the contest. Then he drew the two statements that showed change, explaining the changes in the owner's claim for Months 4 and 5.

192

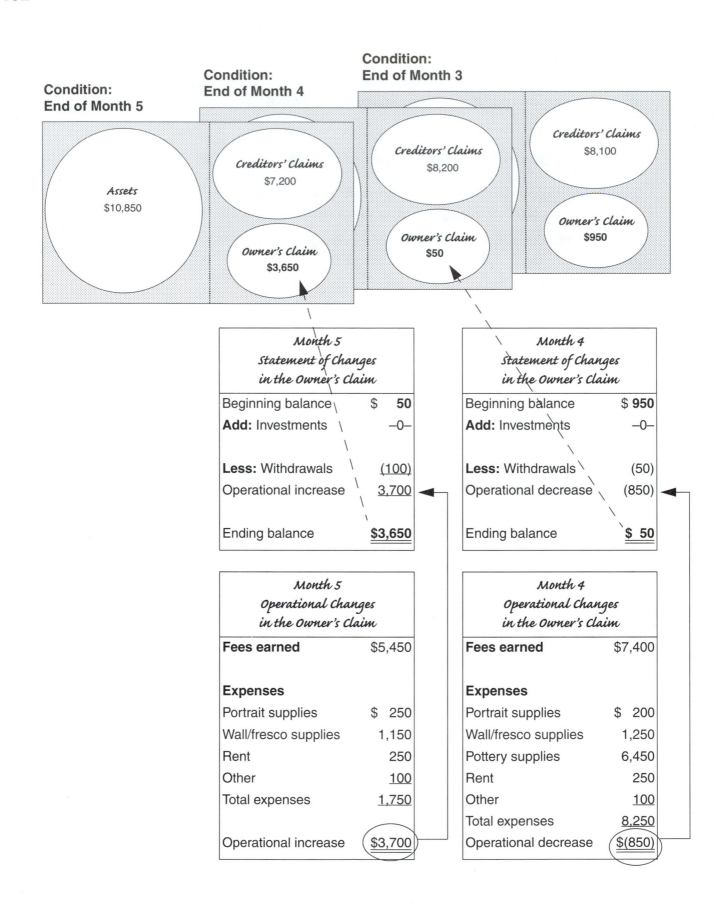

Condition: End of Month 5

Assets $10,850

Condition: End of Month 4

Creditors' Claims $7,200

Owner's Claim $3,650

Condition: End of Month 3

Creditors' Claims $8,200

Owner's Claim $50

Creditors' Claims $8,100

Owner's Claim $950

Month 5 Statement of Changes in the Owner's Claim	
Beginning balance	$ 50
Add: Investments	–0–
Less: Withdrawals	(100)
Operational increase	3,700
Ending balance	**$3,650**

Month 4 Statement of Changes in the Owner's Claim	
Beginning balance	$ 950
Add: Investments	–0–
Less: Withdrawals	(50)
Operational decrease	(850)
Ending balance	**$ 50**

Month 5 Operational Changes in the Owner's Claim	
Fees earned	$5,450
Expenses	
Portrait supplies	$ 250
Wall/fresco supplies	1,150
Rent	250
Other	100
Total expenses	1,750
Operational increase	$3,700

Month 4 Operational Changes in the Owner's Claim	
Fees earned	$7,400
Expenses	
Portrait supplies	$ 200
Wall/fresco supplies	1,250
Pottery supplies	6,450
Rent	250
Other	100
Total expenses	8,250
Operational decrease	$(850)

This knowledge was passed from generation to generation throughout history, and to this very day, the condition of a business is still shown in the same way! Moreover, people in business today still use two statements to show the four changes to their owner's claim in the same way, except that now the two statements are called the "statement of owner's equity" and the "income statement."

The second great gift was even more valuable. Darius learned the real meaning of love, a power that turned out to be stronger than Cupid's arrows. Darius also shared this gift with all the people that he met, and of course with Dana, his wife. Unfortunately, this gift has been more difficult for mankind to understand. However, 2,500 years later, a famous poet and writer who understood all about accepting people as they are, wrote these timeless words so everyone could remember:

The quality of mercy is not strained,
It falls as gentle as the rain.

"And what happened to Hermes?" you're asking. He decided not to reveal any more secrets to Darius. Instead, Hermes became involved in other amusements and diversions, such as creating the false science of alchemy (a belief that any metal could be turned into gold), which wasted many lives. On a later whim, he caused the famous Dutch tulip speculation, which resulted in the great panic of 1636.

Then, 2,970 years after our story, Hermes, in a moment of diabolical merriment, decided that it was now time to reveal the statement of cash flows to mankind. A frantic businessman desperately needed to explain all the changes in his cash balance … well, I suppose that is a story we should save for another day.

What do you think?

● *Darius had special business knowledge that Somnus did not have. As a result of this knowledge, what was the most important thing that Darius could do better than Somnus? Why did this matter?*

● *Darius had a special advantage because he prepared business data so he could use it effectively. How did Darius prepare the data?*

Answers are on page 206.

LEARNING GOAL 9

Explain the Four Basic Changes in Owner's Equity

OVERVIEW

Introduction

Because there are several different reasons for the changes in owner's equity, students who are just beginning their study of business and accounting often forget or become confused by some of these changes. Owner's equity is so important—it is the owner's claim on business wealth—that its essential features are summarized for you in this learning goal.

There are four basic changes in owner's equity.

•   •

In Learning Goal 9, you will find:

Learning Goal 9: Explain the Four Basic Changes in Owner's Equity

▼ *The Features of Owner's Equity*

ESSENTIAL FEATURES OF OWNER'S EQUITY

It is a secondary claim on asset value	Owner's equity is the owner's claim on the value of the business assets. However, when you are the owner, your owner's claim is secondary to the claim of the creditors. The owner's claim is calculated like this: $$\text{Assets} - \text{Liabilities} = \text{Owner's Equity}$$
The name to use in a specific business	For any business (except a corporation), the owner's equity is identified by the word "capital" and the owner's name. For each individual business, the name of the owner of that business is written before the word "capital" to show whose claim it is.
Example	If your name is John Elton, then the owner's equity for your particular business would be called "John Elton, Capital."
Synonyms	Owner's equity is sometimes called ***net worth*** or ***net assets***.

"What do you mean …
'My claim is secondary'?"

• • •

Learning Goal 9: Explain the Four Basic Changes in Owner's Equity

▼ *The Changes in Owner's Equity*

ALL THE CHANGES IN OWNER'S EQUITY

The causes of change

There is actually a total of six causes of increase or decrease in the owner's equity:

Cause	Increase or Decrease	Example
OWNER'S DIRECT ACTIONS		
● Investments	Increase	You invest $5,000 of your own cash into your business.
● Withdrawals	Decrease	You remove $5,000 cash from your business and use it personally.
OPERATIONAL CHANGES		
● Revenues	Increase	The business sells $500 of services to a client.
● Expenses	Decrease	The business uses up $100 of supplies.
OTHER CHANGES INCIDENTAL TO BEING IN BUSINESS		
● Gains	Increase	The business sold some old equipment for $2,000 more than it cost.
● Losses	Decrease	A fire burned down the warehouse.

The first four changes

The first four items—investments, withdrawals, revenues, and expenses—are by far the most important. These occur regularly in every business. These are the changes you will continue to study in this book.

The last two changes

The last two items—gains and losses—are incidental occurrences that happen much less often than revenues and expenses. However, they have the same effect on owner's equity as revenues and expenses. For this reason, gains and losses will not be part of the discussion of owner's equity in the rest of this book.

Learning Goal 9: Explain the Four Basic Changes in Owner's Equity

ALL THE CHANGES IN OWNER'S EQUITY (continued)

Illustration

The four basic causes of change in the owner's capital balance is illustrated below for an imaginary business in the years 1999 and 2000.

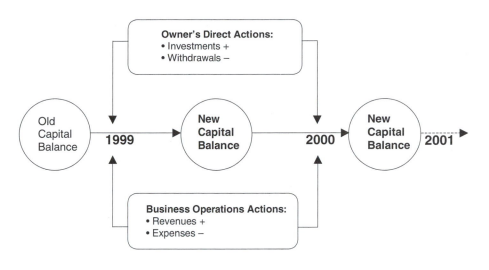

THE FOUR BASIC CHANGES

Owner's investment

Owners investment is an *increase* in owner's capital caused by the owner contributing cash or other personal wealth into the business. These items become assets of the business, so this causes the total assets in the business to increase. As a result, the owner's equity increases. Using the equation:

$$A \uparrow = L + OE \uparrow$$

Note: Rarely, an owner may pay the debts of the business with his/her own personal funds. This is an owner investment that would make liabilities decrease instead of assets increase.

Owner's withdrawals

Withdrawals (also called *drawing*) is a *decrease* in the owner's capital caused by the owner's withdrawal of cash or other assets out of the business for personal use. This causes the total assets to decrease, so the owner's claim decreases. Using the equation:

$$A \downarrow = L + OE \downarrow$$

Learning Goal 9: Explain the Four Basic Changes in Owner's Equity

THE FOUR BASIC CHANGES (continued)

Revenue

Revenue is an *increase* in the owner's capital that results from making a sale of goods or services. The amount of the revenue is whatever the customer pays for the product or service. Owner's capital increases because the sale will always cause either assets to increase or liabilities to decrease. Using the equation:

$$A \uparrow = L \quad + OE \uparrow \text{, or}$$

$$A \quad = L \downarrow + OE \uparrow$$

Expense

An expense is a *decrease* in the owner's capital caused by the business operations consuming resources. The amount of the expense is the cost of the asset or services consumed. The owner's capital decreases because an expense will always cause either assets to decrease or liabilities to increase. Using the equation:

$$A \downarrow = L \quad + OE \downarrow \text{, or}$$

$$A \quad = L \uparrow + OE \downarrow$$

Summary of the four basic changes

The table below summarizes the features of the four basic changes.

Increases or Decreases	Owner's Direct Actions	Operational Activity	Effect on Assets and Liabilities
Increases in Owner's Equity	Owner Investments	Revenues	Assets $\uparrow$ **or** Liabilities $\downarrow$
Decreases in Owner's Equity	Owner Withdrawals	Expenses	Assets $\downarrow$ **or** Liabilities $\uparrow$

Changes in a corporation

For a corporation, the changes are practically identical, except owners' direct actions in a corporation are called "paid-in capital" (or "contributed capital") for owner investments, and "dividends" for owner withdrawals.

☞*QUICK REVIEW*☜

- For any business (except a corporation), use the owner's name followed by the word "capital" to describe the ownership claim.
- There are four basic changes in owner's equity:
    - *changes caused by operations:* revenues and expenses
    - *changes caused by the owner directly:* investments and withdrawals
- Revenues and investments are increases.
- Expenses and withdrawals are decreases.

☞*VOCABULARY*☜

Net assets: another name for owner's equity (page 195)

Net worth: another name for owner's equity (page 195)

Withdrawals: a decrease in the owner's capital caused by the owner's withdrawal of cash or other assets out of the business for personal use (page 197)

PRACTICE FOR LEARNING GOAL 9

SOLUTIONS FOR LEARNING GOAL 9 BEGIN ON PAGE 206.

Learning Goal 9 is about explaining the four basic causes of change in the owner's equity. Use these questions and problems to practice what you have learned.

REINFORCEMENT PROBLEMS

1) **Is it an expense?** Is the transaction of *paying a liability* an expense? Give a brief, accurate answer in the space below.

_____

2) **A review of different items.** Use this question to review all the specific kinds of assets, liabilities, and owner's equity items. Place the letter of an item from the list into the correct description below:

A)	Cash	H)	Unearned Revenue
B)	Supplies	I)	Revenue
C)	Accounts Receivable	J)	Equipment
D)	Note Receivable	K)	Withdrawal
E)	Prepaid Expense	L)	Owner Investment
F)	Account Payable	M)	Expense
G)	Note Payable	N)	Dividends

1) An increase in owner's equity caused by either an increase in assets or a decrease in liabilities as a result of performing services or selling products is called _____.
2) An item such as paper, diskettes, binders, staples, solvents, and paper towels is called _____.
3) An asset created when a sale is made to a customer "on account" (that is, no cash is received at the time of sale) is _____.
4) A liability that is created on the books of the seller when a customer prepays before the service or product is provided to the customer is called _____.
5) An asset that is created for the lender when a formal written promise to pay a certain amount is signed is called (a/an) _____.
6) A liability that is created for the payor when a formal written promise to pay a certain amount is prepared and signed is called (a/an)_____.
7) The owner transferring personal assets into a business is called _____.
8) A decrease in owner's equity caused by a decrease in assets or an increase in liabilities resulting from the process of operating the business is (a/an) _____.
9) An obligation to pay money (normally in 30–60 days) to a supplier is (a/an) _____.
10) Currency that a business has on hand and the amounts in the checking and savings accounts that can be withdrawn on demand is called _____.
11) A short-term asset created when a business pays for goods or services before it receives them or uses them up is (a/an) _____.
12) The owner's withdrawal of assets from the business for his own personal use is called (a/an) _____.

3) **Practice with revenues affecting assets and liabilities.** Revenues always increase the owner's equity. The revenue transaction either causes an increase in assets or a decrease in liabilities. The purpose of this exercise is to have you identify whether a revenue is causing an increase in assets or a decrease in liabilities. (Just for fun, we've also included some examples that are not revenues. This is to remind you that not *all* increases in assets or decreases in liabilities are caused by revenues!)

Learning Goal 9: Explain the Four Basic Changes in Owner's Equity

SOLUTIONS FOR LEARNING GOAL 9 BEGIN ON PAGE 206.

3) *continued*

Fill in the table below with the correct answers. Also draw an arrow indicating which part of the accounting equation is increasing and/or decreasing. Use the first two transactions as examples.

Transaction	Assets increased or liabilities decreased?	Revenue?	Why is it a revenue or not a revenue?	A	=	L	+	OE
A) An accountant performs $2,000 of accounting services and is paid in cash.	Yes (the asset Cash increases)	Yes	Assets increase because services are performed for a customer, so it is a revenue transaction.	↑				↑
B) The accountant borrows $2,000 from her bank.	Yes (the asset Cash increases)	No	Assets increase because of a loan, so it is not a revenue transaction.	↑		↑		
C) An accountant receives a $2,000 cash advance from a client as a prepayment for future services.								
D) The accountant fully performs all the services for the client who prepaid her in Example C, above.								
E) The accountant invests an additional $5,000 in her business.								
F) In September, the accountant performs $2,500 of services "on account."								
G) The accountant collects $2,000 cash from the accounts receivable.								
H) A magazine publisher mails magazines to its subscribers who prepaid subscriptions.								
I) A computer consultant is paid $1,000 immediately after finishing a job.								

Learning Goal 9: Explain the Four Basic Changes in Owner's Equity

PRACTICE FOR LEARNING GOAL 9

SOLUTIONS FOR LEARNING GOAL 9 BEGIN ON PAGE 206.

4) **Why isn't it a revenue?** A revenue will increase assets or decrease liabilities. All of the following transactions either increase assets or decrease liabilities, but *none* of them are revenues. What critical attribute are they all missing that causes them *not* to be revenues?

- A business receives a $1,000 cash advance from a customer (the asset Cash increases).
- Supplies are purchased on account (the asset Supplies increases).
- Cash is collected from accounts receivable (the asset Cash increases).
- Accounts payable are paid (the liability Accounts Payable decreases).
- Owner invests $10,000 in the business (the asset Cash increases).

5) **Why isn't it an expense?** An expense will decrease assets or increase liabilities. All the following transactions either decrease assets or increase liabilities, but *none* of them are expenses. What critical attribute are they all missing that causes them *not* to be expenses?

- The owner withdraws $1,000 cash from the business (the asset Cash decreases).
- The business pays off a $200 account payable (the asset Cash decreases).
- The business borrows $10,000 from a bank (the liability Notes Payable increases).
- The business purchases $500 of supplies for cash (the asset Cash decreases).
- The business buys supplies on credit (the liability Accounts Payable increases).

6) **Practice with expenses affecting assets or liabilities.** Expenses always decrease the owner's capital, and this can involve either a decrease in assets or an increase in liabilities. The purpose of this exercise is to have you identify whether an expense is causing a decrease in assets or an increase in liabilities. (For more fun, some items are not expenses.)

Fill in the table below with the correct answers. Also draw an arrow indicating which part of the accounting equation is increasing and/or decreasing. Use the first two transactions as examples.

Transaction	Assets decreased or liabilities increased?	Expense?	Why is it an expense or not an expense?	A	=	L	+	OE
A) The business pays off a loan of $10,000.	Yes (the asset Cash decreases)	No	Only creditors' equity is affected, not the owner's.	↓		↓		
B) $1,500 of supplies are used up.	Yes (the asset Supplies is used up)	Yes	A direct using up of resources in operations.	↓				↓
C) A business pays off an account payable of $1,500.								
D) A business pays employees $1,500 in wages as soon as they are earned.								

PRACTICE FOR LEARNING GOAL 9

SOLUTIONS FOR LEARNING GOAL 9 BEGIN ON PAGE 206.

6) *continued*

	Transaction	Assets decreased or liabilities increased?	Expense?	Why is it an expense or not an expense?	A	=	L	+	OE
E)	A business receives a $750 repair bill for this month's computer repair services. The bill is not paid immediately.								
F)	The owner pays himself a "salary" and withdraws $1,000 in cash.								
G)	A business pays this month's telephone bill of $300 as soon as it is received.								
H)	A business owes its employees $15,000 in wages but will not pay them until next Monday.								
I)	Next Monday, the business pays the wages to the employees.								

7) **Sometimes liabilities and expenses go together and sometimes they don't.** The purpose of this exercise is to help remind you that when liabilities are created, sometimes this involves an expense, and sometimes not. What matters is *why* the liability is being created. From the description of the transaction, indicate if there is an expense, and the reason for your answer. Use the first transaction as an example.

	Transaction	Expense?	Liabilities increased?	Did event happen as part of revenue-earning operations?
A)	The business borrows $10,000 and records a liability to Fifth National Bank.	No	Yes (the liability Notes Payable increases)	No (borrowing money is not part of revenue-earning operations)
B)	The business owes its employees $8,500 for this week's wages and records it as a new liability by classifying it as Wages Payable.			
C)	The business receives a bill for this month's utilities.			
D)	The business receives a bill for this month's accounting services.			
E)	The business purchases $700 of supplies "on account."			
F)	The $700 of supplies is consumed.			

Learning Goal 9: Explain the Four Basic Changes in Owner's Equity

PRACTICE FOR LEARNING GOAL 9

SOLUTIONS FOR LEARNING GOAL 9 BEGIN ON PAGE 206.

7) *continued*

Transaction	Expense?	Liabilities increased?	Did event happen as part of revenue-earning operations?
G) The business purchases $4,000 of equipment on account.			
H) The business receives a $1,000 bill for this month's computer repair services.			
I) The business receives a $500 prepayment from a customer for services to be performed next month.			

8) **Practice with the four kinds of changes to owner's equity.** Revenues and expenses and investments and withdrawals are the four basic kinds of changes in owner's equity, and they are always accompanied by changes in either the assets or the liabilities. In the following exercise, *all the transactions affect owner's equity.* In each transaction, indicate the type of change to owner's equity that is occurring, if the change is an increase or decrease, if an asset or a liability is affected, and whether that is an increase or decrease. Use the first transaction as an example.

Transaction affecting owner's equity	Type of change to owner's quity	Owner's equity increase or decrease?	Asset or liability affected?	Increase or decrease?
A) An accountant prepares a tax return and collects $500 from a client.	Revenue	Increase	Asset (Cash)	Increase
B) An owner invests $10,000 cash in her business.				
C) Office supplies are used up.				
D) A business receives a bill for consulting services payable on account.				
E) The same accountant as in Example A, above, prepares another tax return for $400 and sends the bill to the client.				
F) A real estate company receives and pays its current bill for advertising.				
G) A law firm receives its current bill from the telephone company but doesn't immediately pay it.				
H) An owner withdraws $500 worth of supplies from his business.				
I) An airline company provides a flight to a customer who purchased the ticket three months ago.				

Learning Goal 9: Explain the Four Basic Changes in Owner's Equity

SOLUTIONS FOR LEARNING GOAL 9 BEGIN ON PAGE 206.

8) *continued*

Transaction affecting owner's equity	Type of change to owner's quity	Owner's equity increase or decrease?	Asset or liability affected?	Increase or decrease?
J) The accountant receives a $950 bill for computer repair services for this month.				
K) An owner pays a debt of his business by writing a check on his personal checking account (not a good business practice).				

9) **Practice with transactions that don't affect owner's equity.** For each of the five transactions below, briefly and accurately write in the space provided the reason why they *don't* affect owner's equity.

A) Supplies are purchased on account.

B) A business receives a prepayment from a customer before services are provided.

C) A business pays an account payable.

D) A business borrows money.

E) A business collects cash from an account receivable.

Learning Goal 9: Explain the Four Basic Changes in Owner's Equity

"WHAT DO YOU THINK" SOLUTION

"WHAT DO YOU THINK" QUESTIONS BEGIN ON PAGE 193.

● Darius was able to make better *decisions*. These decisions improved the way Darius operated his business. This would not have been possible without improved information.
● The special way Darius had to learn to prepare business data consisted of two things:
  — Once he learned how to analyze transactions, he kept a cumulative record of all the transactions.
  — He then prepared *statements that summarized* the cumulative record. These summaries were the statements that:
    1) showed the condition of the business; and 2) analyzed the changes in the owner's claim.
  These are the essentials of the financial statements that we will study in Section IV.

SOLUTIONS FOR LEARNING GOAL 9

PRACTICE QUESTIONS FOR LEARNING GOAL 9 BEGIN ON PAGE 200.

REINFORCEMENT PROBLEMS

1) No. Paying a liability reduces a creditor's claim, never the owner's claim. An expense is a reduction in the owner's claim because of the operations. It has nothing to do with paying liabilities.

2) 1) An increase in owner's equity caused by either an increase in assets or a decrease in liabilities as a result of performing services or selling products is called (I) <u>Revenue</u>.
    2) An item such as paper, diskettes, binders, staples, solvents, and paper towels is called (B) <u>Supplies</u>.
    3) An asset created when a sale is made to a customer "on account" (that is, no cash is received at the time of sale) is (C) <u>Accounts Receivable</u>.
    4) A liability that is created on the books of the seller when a customer prepays before the service or product is provided to the customer is called (H) <u>Unearned Revenue</u>.
    5) An asset that is created for the recipient when a formal written promise to pay a certain amount is signed is called a (D) <u>Note Receivable</u>.
    6) A liability that is created for the payor when a formal written promise to pay a certain amount is prepared and signed is called a (G) <u>Note Payable</u>.
    7) The owner transferring personal assets into a business is called (L) <u>Owner Investment</u>.
    8) A decrease in owner's equity caused by a decrease in assets or an increase in liabilities resulting from the process of operating the business is an (M) <u>Expense</u>.
    9) An obligation to pay money (normally in 30–60 days) to a supplier is an (F) <u>Account Payable</u>.
    10) Currency that a business has on hand and the amounts in the checking and savings accounts that can be withdrawn on demand is called (A) <u>Cash</u>.
    11) A short-term asset created when a business pays for goods or services before it receives them or uses them up is a (E) <u>Prepaid Expense</u>.
    12) The owner's withdrawal of assets from the business for their own personal use is called a (K) <u>Withdrawal</u>.

SOLUTIONS FOR LEARNING GOAL 9

PRACTICE QUESTIONS FOR LEARNING GOAL 9 BEGIN ON PAGE 200.

3)

	Transaction	Assets increased or liabilities decreased?	Revenue?	Why is it a revenue or not a revenue?	A	=	L	+	OE
A)	An accountant performs $2,000 of accounting services and is paid in cash.	Yes (the asset Cash increases)	Yes	Assets increase because services are performed for a customer, so it is a revenue transaction.	↑				↑
B)	The accountant borrows $2,000 from her bank.	Yes (the asset Cash increases)	No	Assets increase because of a loan, so it is not a revenue transaction.	↑		↑		
C)	An accountant receives a $2,000 cash advance from a client as a prepayment for future services.	Yes (the asset Cash increases)	No	Assets increase as a result of a liability, so it is not a revenue (revenue not earned yet).	↑		↑		
D)	The accountant fully performs all the services for the client who prepaid her in Example C, above.	Yes (the liability Unearned Revenue decreases)	Yes	Services were performed so revenue was earned.			↓		↑
E)	The accountant invests an additional $5,000 in her business.	Yes (the asset Cash increases)	No	Owner's equity increases, but not because of a sale of services or goods. Investment is not revenue.	↑				↑
F)	In September, the accountant performs $2,500 of services "on account."	Yes (the asset Accounts Receivable increases)	Yes	Accounting services were performed.	↑				↑
G)	The accountant collects $2,000 cash from the accounts receivable.	No (the asset Cash increases and the asset Accounts Receivable decreases)	No	Simply an exchange of one kind of asset for another kind of asset.	↓ ↑				
H)	A magazine publisher mails magazines to its subscribers who prepaid subscriptions.	Yes (the liability Unearned Revenue decreases)	Yes	Service is being performed when the magazines are mailed out to customers.			↓		↑
I)	A computer consultant is paid $1,000 immediately after finishing a job.	Yes (the asset Cash increases)	Yes	Assets increased because services were performed.	↑				↑

Learning Goal 9: Explain the Four Basic Changes in Owner's Equity

SOLUTIONS FOR LEARNING GOAL 9

PRACTICE QUESTIONS FOR LEARNING GOAL 9 BEGIN ON PAGE 200.

4) **No sale has been made.** A revenue must meet two requirements: it is an *increase in owner's equity* caused by making a sale of services or goods. None of the examples meet both requirements. Except for owner's investment, none of the transactions affect owner's equity. The investment increases owner's equity, but not because of a sale being made.

5) **None of the transactions involve operations.** An expense must meet two requirements: it a *decrease in owner's equity* caused by *operations*. None of the examples meet both requirements. Except for owner's drawing, none of the transactions affect owner's equity. The withdrawal does decrease owner's equity, but not because of operations.

6)

	Transaction	Assets decreased or liabilities increased?	Expense?	Why is it an expense or not an expense?	A	=	L	+	OE
A)	The business pays off a loan of $10,000.	Yes (the asset Cash decreases)	No	Only creditors' equity is affected, not the owner's.	↓		↓		
B)	$1,500 of supplies are used up.	Yes (the asset Supplies is used up)	Yes	A direct using up of resources in operations.	↓				↓
C)	A business pays off an account payable of $1,500.	Yes (the asset Cash decreases)	No	Paying a liability is never an expense; it affects the creditor's equity, not the owner's	↓		↓		
D)	A business pays employees $1,500 in wages as soon as they are earned.	Yes (the asset Cash decreases)	Yes	Asset used up in operations.	↓				↓
E)	A business receives a $750 repair bill for this month's computer repair services. The bill is not paid immediately.	Yes (the liability Accounts Payable increases)	Yes	A new claim is placed on existing assets because of a service consumed and not paid for.			↑		↓
F)	The owner pays himself a "salary" and withdraws $1,000 in cash.	Yes (the asset Cash decreases)	No	Drawing is never an expense; it is not part of business operations.	↓				↓
G)	A business pays this month's telephone bill of $300 as soon as it is received.	Yes (the asset Cash decreases)	Yes	Cash decreases immediately as a result of operations.	↓				↓
H)	A business owes its employees $15,000 in wages but will not pay them until next Monday.	Yes (the liability Wages Payable increases)	Yes	A new claim is placed on existing assets because of a service consumed and not paid for.			↑		↓
I)	Next Monday, the business pays the wages owing to the employees.	Yes (the asset Cash decreases)	No	Payment of debt is never an expense.	↓		↓		

PRACTICE QUESTIONS FOR LEARNING GOAL 9 BEGIN ON PAGE 200.

7)

	Transaction	Expense?	Liabilities increased?	Did event happen as part of revenue-earning operations?
A)	The business borrows $10,000 and records a liability to 5th National Bank.	No	Yes (the liability Notes Payable increases)	No (borrowing money is not part of revenue-earning operations)
B)	The business owes its employees $8,500 for this week's wages and records it as a new liability by classifying it as wages payable.	Yes	Yes (the liability Wages Payable increases)	Yes (employee services were used)
C)	The business receives a bill for this month's utilities.	Yes	Yes (the liability Accounts Payable increases)	Yes (utility services were consumed)
D)	The business receives a bill for this month's accounting services.	Yes	Yes (the liability Accounts Payable increases)	Yes (accounting services were consumed)
E)	The business purchases $700 of supplies "on account."	No	Yes (the liability Accounts Payable increases)	No (a resource has not been consumed in operations)
F)	The $700 of supplies is consumed.	Yes	No (liabilities are not affected)	Yes (this is to remind you that the expense occurs when the supplies are consumed, even though the $700 liability for the purchase of the supplies happened in Example F).
G)	The business purchases $4,000 of equipment on account.	No	Yes (the liability Accounts Payable increases)	No (a resource has not been consumed in operations)
H)	The business receives a $1,000 bill for this month's computer repair services.	Yes	Yes (the liability Accounts Payable increases)	Yes (repair services were consumed)
I)	The business receives a $500 prepayment from a customer for services to be performed next month.	No	Yes (the liability Unearned Revenue increases)	No (a resource has not been consumed in operations)

SOLUTIONS FOR LEARNING GOAL 9

PRACTICE QUESTIONS FOR LEARNING GOAL 9 BEGIN ON PAGE 200.

8)

	Transaction affecting owner's equity	Type of change to owner's equity	Owner's equity increase or decrease?	Asset or liability affected?	Increase or decrease?
A)	An accountant prepares a tax return and collects $500 from a client.	Revenue	Increase	Asset (Cash)	Increase
B)	An owner invests $10,000 cash in her business.	Owner's investment	Increase	Asset (Cash)	Increase
C)	Office supplies are used up.	Expense	Decrease	Asset (Supplies)	Decrease
D)	A business receives a bill for consulting services payable on account.	Expense	Decrease	Liability (Accounts Payable)	Increase
E)	The same accountant as in Example A, above, prepares another tax return for $400 and sends the bill to the client.	Revenue	Increase	Asset (Accounts Receivable)	Increase
F)	A real estate company receives and pays its current bill for advertising.	Expense	Decrease	Asset (Cash)	Decrease
G)	A law firm receives its current bill from the telephone company but does not immediately pay it.	Expense	Decrease	Liability (Accounts Payable)	Increase
H)	An owner withdraws $500 worth of supplies from his business.	Owner's drawing	Decrease	Asset (Supplies)	Decrease
I)	An airline company provides a flight to a customer who purchased the ticket three months ago.	Revenue	Increase	Liability (Unearned Revenue)	Decrease
J)	The accountant receives a bill for computer repair services for this month for $950.	Expense	Decrease	Liability (Accounts Payable)	Increase
K)	An owner pays a debt of his business by writing a check on his personal checking account (not a good business practice).	Owner's investment	Increase	Liability	Decrease

9) A) Assets increase, but not as a result of revenue-earning operations. Only creditors' equity is affected.
   B) The advance payment is not the result of a sale, so owner's equity is not affected.
   C) Again, only creditors' equity is affected. Paying a debt is never an expense.
   D) Assets increase, but not as a result of revenue-earning operations or owner's investment. Only creditors' equity is affected.
   E) There is no change in total assets. Cash increases but accounts receivable decrease. Collection of a receivable is not part of revenue-earning operations. (The revenue was earned previously, when the receivable was created.)

Your Questions?

It is *very* important to be aware of what you need to understand better. What do you need to understand better about this learning goal? Use this space to write the questions that you want to discuss with your classmates, instructor, or supervisor. Try to be very specific about what is bothering you, such as explanations that you do not fully understand.

CUMULATIVE VOCABULARY REVIEW

This is a vocabulary review for Learning Goals 1 through 9. Match each description with the term that it describes. Enter the letter of the correct description in the space provided on the left next to each term. The answer for each term is in the right column.

	Term	Description	Answers
_____	1) Accounts payable	A) A system of accounting which always maintains the equality of assets and claims on assets.	1E
_____	2) Accounting equation	B) The removal of business assets for personal use by the owner.	2S
_____	3) Net income	C) A business with one owner.	3T
_____	4) Asset	D) A seller of goods or services.	4L
_____	5) Vendor	E) Short-term debts to suppliers of goods and services.	5D
_____	6) Equity	F) An advance payment from a customer.	6Q
_____	7) Personal liability	G) Revenue earned from a loan, but not yet received.	7P
_____	8) Bookkeeping	H) The owner's claim on the asset value in a business.	8O
_____	9) Partnership	I) The term for a particular owner's claim on assets.	9R
_____	10) Double-entry accounting	J) The increase in owner's equity as a result of operations.	10A
_____	11) Leasing	K) A debt.	11U
_____	12) Owner's capital, such as "Bill Jones, Capital"	L) A future economic benefit that is owned or controlled by the business as a result of measurable past events.	12I
_____	13) Liability	M) A payment of an expense in advance.	13K
_____	14) Expense	N) Another name for owner's equity.	14V
_____	15) Revenue	O) The part of the accounting process that is primarily concerned with identifying and recording transactions.	15J
_____	16) Drawing	P) The condition of personal assets being subject to creditors' claims for business debts.	16B
_____	17) Owner's equity	Q) A general term meaning a claim on asset value.	17H
_____	18) Notes receivable	R) A business that is not a corporation and that is owned by two or more people.	18Y
_____	19) Interest receivable	S) A = L + OE	19G
_____	20) Unearned revenue	T) When revenues are greater than expenses.	20F
_____	21) Paid-in capital	U) The act of renting property.	21X
_____	22) Accounts receivable	V) The decrease in owner's equity caused by using up resources in operations.	22W
_____	23) Add value	W) Money owed to a business by its customers.	23Z
_____	24) Prepaid expense	X) The stockholders' investment in a corporation.	24M
_____	25) Proprietorship	Y) Money receivable recorded by a written promise.	25C
_____	26) Net worth or net assets	Z) Use resources to create something people will want.	26N

CUMULATIVE TEST: LEARNING GOALS 1 THROUGH 9

CUMULATIVE TEST SOLUTIONS BEGIN ON PAGE 216.

TIME LIMIT: 55 MINUTES

INSTRUCTIONS

*In the space provided, enter the best answer to each question. Do **not** look back in the book when taking the test. (If you need to do this, you are not ready.) After you finish the test, refer to the answers and circle the number of each question that you missed. Then go to the **Help Table** (on page 218) to identify your strong and weak knowledge areas by individual learning goal.*

MULTIPLE CHOICE

On the line provided, enter the letter of the best answer for each question.

1) An asset _____
   A) is a future economic benefit.
   B) always must belong to and be controlled by a business.
   C) cannot be contingent upon future events.
   D) all of the above.

2) How many categories of claims on the total assets of business can there be? _____
   A) one (just for the owner)
   B) two (the owner and the creditors)
   C) three (the owner, the creditors, and the investors)
   D) more than three in any combination

3) Which of the following is a correct presentation of the accounting equation? _____
   A) $A = L + OE$
   B) $A - L - OE = 0$
   C) $A - OE = L$
   D) all of the above

4) The only business type in which the owner(s) do (does) not have personal liability for business debts is a ___
   A) general partnership.
   B) corporation.
   C) proprietorship.
   D) any of the above.

5) A business is _____
   A) an organized group of activities that uses up resources.
   B) an organized group of activities that creates and sells resources.
   C) organized with the intention of making the owner richer.
   D) all the above.

6) If $50,000 of land is purchased by paying $30,000 cash and signing a $20,000 note payable for the remainder, _____
   A) total owner's equity increases.
   B) total assets increase.
   C) total assets decrease.
   D) total owner's equity decreases.

7) Money that is owed to suppliers and service providers, but not yet paid, is called _____
   A) accounts payable.
   B) unearned revenue.
   C) notes payable.
   D) accounts receivable.

8) The two changes that are increases in the owner's equity are _____
   A) owner investments and withdrawals.
   B) expenses and revenues.
   C) owner investments and revenues.
   D) withdrawals and expenses.

CUMULATIVE TEST SOLUTIONS BEGIN ON PAGE 216.

9) A revenue is _____
   A) a sale of a service or product causing an increase in owner's equity.
   B) an increase in business cash.
   C) any increase in owner's equity.
   D) any combination of an increase in assets and/or decrease in liabilities.

10) Money that is advanced to a business by a customer before services are performed is called _____
   A) accounts payable.
   B) unearned revenue.
   C) notes payable.
   D) interest payable.

11) The following event (transaction) takes place for Santa Clara Company: liabilities decrease by $1,000. Therefore, _____
   A) owner's equity will decrease by $1,000.
   B) total assets could decrease by $1,000 or owner's equity could decrease by $1,000.
   C) total assets could increase by $1,000 or owner's equity could decrease by $1,000.
   D) total assets could decrease by $1,000 or owner's equity could increase by $1,000.

12) Butte Dry Cleaners spends $50,000 to renovate its lobby and storefront. _____
   A) This will probably add more than $50,000 value to its services.
   B) Exactly $50,000 of value will be added.
   C) It is difficult to say how much value is added until revenues are added up.
   D) This cannot add value.

13) Which of the following probably does not add value? _____
   A) throwing away parts damaged in production
   B) consuming resources in order to create economic resources
   C) spending money for janitorial services
   D) spending money on advertising

14) The accounting equation describes _____
   A) the condition of a business over a period of time.
   B) the condition of a business at one point in time.
   C) the condition of any economic entity at one point in time.
   D) none of the above.

15) If a business incurs an expense, then the owner's equity will decrease because the expense _____
   A) caused either liabilities to increase or assets to decrease.
   B) caused either assets to increase or liabilities to increase.
   C) caused either assets to decrease or liabilities to decrease.
   D) caused both assets and liabilities to decrease.

16) Which of the following is not an asset? _____
   A) a sculpture purchased for the front office
   B) a prepayment of rent for three months
   C) the owner's equity
   D) a 15-year-old company truck that is occasionally used for deliveries

17) Select the one item which is an asset. _____
   A) accounts receivable
   B) company employees
   C) suggestions by employees that will increase efficiency
   D) the owner's capital

18) Yorrick's bookstore is going out of business. Who has first claim on the assets? _____
   A) the creditors
   B) the owner
   C) both creditors and owner equally
   D) both creditors and owner proportionately

CUMULATIVE TEST SOLUTIONS BEGIN ON PAGE 216.

19) At the start of the month, Travis Company has total debt of $10,000 and Travis Patterson, Capital is $40,000. During the month, total assets increased by $10,000 and total liabilities increased by $3,000. What is the balance of owner's equity at the end of the month? _____
   A) $40,000
   B) $50,000
   C) $47,000
   D) $37,000

20) Which of the following is not true about a proprietorship? _____
   A) It is the most common form of business organization in the United States.
   B) It is simpler and easier to start than a partnership or corporation.
   C) The assets and debts of the proprietorship should be combined with the personal assets and debts of the owner.
   D) A proprietorship is not a separate legal entity from the owner.

21) Tuxedo Road Costume Center has $40,000 in liabilities and $50,000 in owner's equity. At the start of the month, it had $40,000 in liabilities and $40,000 in owner's equity. How much did assets change during the month? _____
   A) $20,000
   B) $90,000
   C) $70,000
   D) none of the above

22) The only form(s) of business in which payments for owner services can be a wage expense is _____
   A) a corporation.
   B) a partnership.
   C) both A and B.
   D) a proprietorship.

23) If Willamette Company uses up $10,000 cash to pay off an account payable, then _____
   A) total assets will decrease and total claims will decrease.
   B) owner's equity will increase and total liabilities will decrease.
   C) total assets will decrease and owner's equity will decrease.
   D total liabilities will decrease and owner's equity will decrease.

24) A basic assumption that any individual economic unit or operation must identify and keep a record of its own transactions if it is to provide meaningful financial information is called _____
   A) the monetary assumption.
   B) the time period assumption.
   C) the going-concern concept.
   D) the entity assumption.

25) At the end of the month, Ojo Caliente Bottle Shop has $70,000 of assets and $22,000 of owner's equity. If owner's equity decreased by $10,000 during the month and total assets increased by $5,000 during the month, what was the amount of liabilities at the beginning of the month? _____
   A) $12,000
   B) $32,00
   C) $33,000
   D) none of the above

26) If total assets decrease and total liabilities decrease, then what transaction is probably happening? _____
   A) The owner is withdrawing money from the business.
   B) The owner is investing money in the business.
   C) The business is borrowing money.
   D) The business is paying back a loan.

27) When a business pays for a service before the service is actually used, for the business making the payment this is called _____
   A) unearned revenue.
   B) prepaid expense.
   C) accounts payable.
   D) notes receivable.

CUMULATIVE TEST SOLUTIONS BEGIN ON PAGE 216.

28) A payment of a liability is not an expense because _____
   A) it causes cash to be decreased.
   B) an expense would reduce the owner's claim instead of the creditor's.
   C) payment of a liability is a using-up of business resources as part of operations.
   D) it causes owner's capital to be decreased.

29) All of the following are liabilities except _____
   A) accounts payable.
   B) wages owed to the employees.
   C) withdrawals by the owner.
   D) unearned revenues.

30) It is discovered that the supplies owned by a business have increased in value by approximately $1,000. Why is the increase in value not an asset or added to the value of the asset? _____
   A) not a probable future economic benefit
   B) not something owned by the business
   C) not a result of measurable past events
   D) none of the above

31) If total liabilities are subtracted from total assets, the result is sometimes called _____
   A) equity or net investment.
   B) net worth or net assets.
   C) working capital.
   D) net liability.

32) Daisy Company has assets of cash of $150,0000, supplies of $1,000, and some equipment. It has liabilities of $20,000 and owner's equity of $148,000. The amount of equipment is _____
   A) $168,000.
   B) $131,000.
   C) $18,000.
   D) none of the above.

33) If Brooklyn Avenue Golf Shop collects $10,000 from an account receivable, then _____
   A) total assets are being decreased and owner's equity is being increased.
   B) total assets are being increased and owner's equity is being increased.
   C) total assets are being decreased and owner's equity is being decreased.
   D) there is no increase or decrease in the total assets or the total claims on assets.

34) Humbolt Square Bakery has total debt of $25,000 and owner's equity of $50,000. If assets increase by $20,000 and liabilities increase by $15,000, what is the final balance of the owner's equity? _____
   A) $50,000
   B) $40,000
   C) $55,000
   D) none of the above

35) In a transaction by Tasha Company, assets decrease and owner's equity decreases. What could have happened? _____
   A) either the purchase of an asset or an expense
   B) either an expense or an owner's drawing
   C) either payment of a liability or an expense
   D) none of the above

36) What transaction will cause one asset to decrease, one asset to increase, and one liability to increase? _____
   A) the payment of liability
   B) purchasing supplies on account
   C) purchasing equipment by paying cash and signing a note payable
   D) none of the above

CUMULATIVE TEST: LEARNING GOALS 1 THROUGH 9

37) If the total liabilities of Los Altos Company are $37,000 and the owner's equity is $22,000, then total assets must be ____
   A) $15,000.
   B) $22,000.
   C) $59,000.
   D) $37,000.

CUMULATIVE TEST SOLUTIONS: LEARNING GOALS 1 THROUGH 9

CUMULATIVE TEST QUESTIONS BEGIN ON PAGE 212.

MULTIPLE CHOICE

1) D.
2) B.
3) D. These are just variations on the same equation.
4) B.
5) D.
6) B. Total assets increase because a $50,000 asset (land) is received and a $30,000 asset (cash) is given up.
7) A.
8) C.
9) A.
10) B.
11) D. It will probably help to visualize this by drawing the diagram of a business with the circles, or by using the accounting equation with up and down arrows.
12) C.
13) A.
14) C. The accounting equation applies to any economic entity or unit (business, government, nonprofit, etc.).
15) A. Visualize by drawing a diagram or by using the equation with up and down arrows.
16) C. The owner's equity is a claim on assets.
17) A.
18) A.
19) C (figures in bold are calculated).

	Assets	**= Liabilities**	**+ Owner's Equity**
Beginning Balance	**$50,000**	$10,000	$40,000
Change	+ 10,000	+ 3,000	
Ending Balance	**60,000**	**13,000**	**47,000**

20) C (a proprietorship is always a separate financial and economic entity, even if it may not be a separate legal entity).
21) D. Assets increased by $10,000 (figures in bold are calculated).

	Assets	**= Liabilities**	**+ Owner's Equity**
Beginning Balance	**$80,000**	$40,000	$40,000
Change	**+ 10,000**		
Ending Balance	**90,000**	40,000	50,000

22) A.
23) A. Payment of debt never affects owner's equity, only creditor's equity.

24) D. Remember, an "entity" can be any business, a division of a business, an individual, or any other economic operation or unit for which financial reporting is wanted.

CUMULATIVE TEST QUESTIONS BEGIN ON PAGE 212.

25) C (figures in bold are calculated).

	Assets	=	Liabilities	+	Owner's Equity
Beginning Balance	**$65,000**		**$33,000**		**$32,000**
Change	+ 5,000				– 10,000
Ending Balance	70,000				22,000

26) D (visualize with a circle diagram of condition or use the accounting equation with arrows).
27) B.
28) B.
29) C.
30) C. An increase in value is always a subjective estimate and is not considered to be a measurable past event. There is no objective evidence such as a sale that confirms value. For now, it's a matter of opinion.
31) B. Of course, it is also called owner's equity.
32) D. Total equities of $168,000 minus the known assets of $151,000 = $17,000 of equipment.
33) D. One asset (accounts receivable) is given up in exchange for another asset (cash) of equal amount.
34) C (figures in bold are calculated).

	Assets	=	Liabilities	+	Owner's Equity
Beginning Balance	**$75,000**		$25,000		$50,000
Change	+ 20,000		+ 15,000		
Ending Balance	95,000		40,000		55,000

35) B (draw the diagram of a business with the circles or use the accounting equation with up and down arrows).
36) C. Equipment increases, cash decreases, and notes payable increases (visualize using the diagram or accounting equation).
37) C (because A = L + OE, so A = 37,000 + 22,000).

HELP TABLE

Identify Your Strengths and Weaknesses

The questions in this test cover the nine learning goals of Sections I and II. After you have circled the number of each question that you missed, look at the table below.

Go to the first learning goal category in the table: "Explain What a Business Is and What It Does." The second column in the table shows which questions on the test covered this learning goal. Look on the test to see if you circled numbers 5, 12, or 13. How many did you miss? Write this number in the "How Many Missed?" column. Repeat this process for each of the remaining learning goal categories in the table.

If you *miss two or more questions* for any learning goal, you are too weak in that learning goal and you need to *review*. The last column shows you where to read and practice so you can improve your score.

Some learning goal categories have more questions because you need to be especially well prepared in these areas. More questions means your performance must be better.

Learning Goal	Questions	How many missed?	Material begins on …
SECTION I			
1) Explain What a Business Is and What It Does	5, 12, 13		page 3
2) Define and Identify Assets	1, 16, 17, 30		page 36
3) Define and Identify the Two Claims on Assets	2, 18, 29, 31		page 51
4) Use the Accounting Equation to Show the Condition	3, 14, 32, 37		page 61
5) Define "Entity" and Identify Different Types	4, 20, 22, 24		page 67
SECTION II			
6) Analyze Individual Transactions	6, 11, 23, 26, 33, 35, 36		page 97
7) Analyze the Cumulative Effect of Transactions	19, 21, 25, 34		page 157
8) Identify Common Assets and Liabilities	7, 10, 27		page 163
9) Explain the Four Basic Changes in Owner's Equity	8, 9, 15, 28		page 194

SECTION III

Transactions—
Basic Recording Concepts

Overview: what this section does	This section gives you an overview of what accounting does, and gives you practice that makes it easier to learn debits and credits without using confusing terminology.
Use this section if ...	... you want a quick overview of the accounting process. ... you want special practice that will make it easier for you to understand and use debits and credits later on.
Do NOT use this section if ...	... you already understand how to analyze transactions, AND now you feel ready to learn about debits and credits in a real accounting system (see Section V on page 364). ... you do not understand what a "transaction" is, or how to analyze the effects of transactions on the accounting equation (see Section II on page 80).

LEARNING GOAL 10

Explain the Accounting Process

In Learning Goal 10, you will find:

▼ *What Is Accounting and How Does It Work?*

ACCOUNTING

Overview	So far, you have spent a great deal of time learning the first step—analyzing transactions. Now you are ready to start practicing the last two steps in the accounting process: • processing transaction information • communicating financial information in reports First, we will define "accounting."
Definition	Actually, there is no single, precise definition of accounting. However, one useful definition of accounting is as follows: ***Accounting*** is a system of activities which analyzes, processes, communicates, and interprets financial data about a business or other entity. The objective of accounting is to provide financial information that is useful for decision-making.

ACCOUNTING (continued)

Examples	• the information system used by a college to record tuition payments and operating expenses
	• the work done by all of the people in the accounting department of a business
	• the system used by a church to record contributions and expenditures

▼ *The Accounting System*

THREE-STAGE PROCESS

Overview	An accounting system functions by a process of sequential steps. The process begins each time there is an event that could potentially affect the financial condition of a business. If an event does affect the financial condition, then the financial information from that event continues through each stage in the process that you see illustrated on page 222.
Process illustrated	The illustration on page 222 shows the sequential stages of the accounting system as a process. The process begins with analysis of a business event. This analysis is done to identify any event that is a transaction. If the event does qualify as a transaction, then the data concerning that event will pass through Stage 2 and Stage 3.

THREE-STAGE PROCESS (continued)

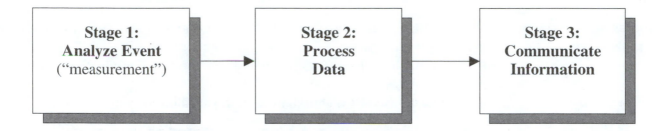

Stage 1: **Analyze Event** ("measurement")	Stage 2: **Process Data**	Stage 3: **Communicate Information**

What Happens

Test the event:
• Is there a change
  in the accounting
  equation?

If yes, go to Stage 2.
If no, stop.

What Happens

• *record* transactions

• *classify* data (sort it)

• *summarize* data

What Happens

• prepare *financial
  reports* and
  interpret them

***Example of Stage 1:
analyzing***

On May 19, Ohlone Company purchases office supplies and pays $250 cash.

This is how to analyze the event in order to identify it as a transaction (or not a transaction):

● *Items:* What items in the accounting equation are affected?
● *Amount:* How much are each of the items affected?
● *Date:* When did the event happen?

In this example, the items that are affected in the accounting equation are office supplies (an asset increases) and cash (another asset decreases). The amount of the change to each item is $250. The date of the event is May 19.

Note: This analysis process is also referred to as ***measurement***.

THREE-STAGE PROCESS (continued)

Stage 2: processing

After the event is analyzed and determined to be a transaction, the processing stage begins by recording the event. To record the event, the transaction is first carefully visualized to verify the exact changes, which are then recorded into permanent accounting records using certain specific methods. Later on, these data are further classified and summarized.

You will begin to learn the processing procedures in this learning goal and continue learning them in subsequent learning goals in this book. Processing functions are often called ***bookkeeping***.

Stage 3: reporting and interpreting

Accounting information must be reported clearly in order to be useful. Without the reports, the record-keeping serves little purpose. Generally, at least four all-purpose reports are prepared. You will learn much more about these reports in Learning Goal 12 (starting on page 270) through Learning Goal 17 in Section IV.

Note: Accountants also prepare graphs, ratios, notes, charts, and tables to help users of financial statements understand and interpret the meaning of the information contained in the reports.

Who uses the reports?

The paragraph above states that, "Accounting information must be reported clearly in order to be useful." Useful to whom?

People and organizations that use accounting information are sometimes called ***stakeholders*** because, directly or indirectly, they have a stake in the condition and success or failure of the business. There are many kinds of stakeholders who rely upon accounting information—more than you might think. They can be categorized into two groups:

● *Internal users* are those who manage and operate a business (such as officers and managers of a company).
● *External users* are those outside of a business who do not manage or work in the business (such as investors, creditors, suppliers, customers, and government agencies).

CHECK YOUR UNDERSTANDING

Fill in each blank space with the correct word. The answers are below.

Accounting uses a three-step process to provide information to the decision-makers who want it. The first step is to _____ events in order to _____ transactions. The second step is to _____ transaction data, and the third step is to _____ financial information by preparing _____. Accountants also help _____ the information they provide.

Processing accounting information is called _____. People and organizations that use accounting information are sometimes called _____.

ANSWERS

✓

Accounting uses a three-step process to provide information to the decision-makers who want it. The first step is to analyze events in order to identify transactions. The second step is to process transaction data, and the third step is to communicate financial information by preparing reports. Accountants also help interpret the information they provide.

Processing accounting information is called bookkeeping. People and organizations that use accounting information are sometimes called stakeholders.

⌐VOCABULARY⌐

Accounting: a system of activities that has the objective of providing financial information which is useful for decision-making (page 220)

Bookkeeping: another name for the processing functions in the accounting process (page 223)

Measurement: another name for the analysis step in the accounting process (page 222)

Stakeholders: people and organizations that use accounting information (page 223)

LEARNING GOAL 11
Begin to Record

OVERVIEW

Introduction

Until now, you looked at the individual items in each transaction in order to analyze their effects on the total condition of a business. For example, if you saw cash decrease and accounts payable decrease, you could conclude that total assets decreased and total liabilities decreased because a debt was paid. This analysis is important, and you will continue to practice it.

But analysis is of little use unless a permanent record is kept of the transactions. Now you will begin to record the individual items in a transaction when you are finished analyzing them.

BEGIN TO RECORD TRANSACTIONS

Get a job!

Because you have progressed this far, I have decided that it is time for you to get a job. I want you to meet a friend of mine. His name is Jack "Flash" Davis, a professional guitar player who performs in his own band called "Flash." To supplement his performance income, Jack is opening a small guitar school in June, where he will give guitar lessons at all levels from beginner to master class. He needs accounting help and I have recommended you as the accountant for his guitar school.

To help you get started, I suggest that you keep a permanent record of all the increases and decreases for each item in the accounting equation. This can be done by setting up one column for each separate asset, liability, and owner's equity item. The increases and decreases are then shown in each column with a "+" or a "–." Using some imaginary transactions, such an approach would look like the table on page 226.

BEGIN TO RECORD TRANSACTIONS (continued)

Transaction	Assets			= Liabilities + Owner's Equity	
	Cash	Accounts Receivable	Supplies	Accounts Payable	Jack Davis, Capital
Owner's investment of cash	(+) $10,000				(+) $10,000
Purchase supplies	(–) 500		(+) 500		
Balance	9,500		500		10,000
Earned revenue "on account"		(+) 750			(+) 750
Balance	9,500	750	500		10,750
Collect receivable	(+) 750	(–) 750			
Balance	10,250	-0-	500		10,750
Withdraw cash	(–) 1,000				(–) 1,000
Balance	9,250		500		9,750
Use up supplies			(–) 100		(–) 100
Balance	9,250		400		9,650

… and so on, with each new transaction being added to or subtracted from the applicable columns, such that the equation always remains in balance.

SEPARATE COLUMNS FOR INCREASES AND DECREASES

One column for increase and one column for decrease

Another good way of recording the changes in each of the equation items is to have separate increase columns and decrease columns for each item. The advantage of this is that all the increases and decreases are easier to locate. What's more, this method is the method that is used in practice and that you will later learn when studying accounts. Using the same transactions, the recording would look like the table on page 227.

SEPARATE COLUMNS FOR INCREASES AND DECREASES (continued)

Transaction	Cash		Accounts Receivable		Supplies		Accounts Payable		Jack Davis, Capital	
	Increase	Decrease	Increase	Decrease	Increase	Decrease	Decrease	Increase	Decrease	Increase
Owner's investment of cash	$10,000									$10,000
Purchase supplies		500			500					
Balance	9,500				500					10,000
Earned revenue "on account"			750							750
Balance	9,500		750		500					10,750
Collect receivable	750			750						
Balance	10,250		-0-		500					10,750
Withdraw cash		1,000							1,000	
Balance	9,250				500					9,750
Use up supplies						100			100	
Balance	9,250				400					9,650

Same balances as before

We get exactly the same balances as before, except that now all the increases and decreases are easier to locate. We will use the two-column approach here so that you can get used to it. In this way, the increases and decreases for each item are split out into separate columns.

Use accounting customs

The custom in accounting is that "increase" columns for items on the left side of the equation (assets) are always placed to the left of each item name, and that "increase" columns for items on the right side of the equation are always placed to the right of each item name.

It is also the custom to show balances on the increase side, because balances are positive numbers, just like increases. We will use these customary patterns. This will become clear as you follow the events.

Start your job and enjoy …

Relax, take your time, and watch what happens to Jack.

In analysis, it might also help you to visualize each transaction as explained in Section II. You can draw a picture or use the accounting equation.

Learning Goal 11: Begin to Record

SEPARATE COLUMNS FOR INCREASES AND DECREASES (continued)

Here are the transactions for Jack's school for June, the first month of business:

A) **Owner investment.** Jack deposits $12,000 cash from personal funds into a business checking account.

Assets	=
$12,000	

Cash		
Increase	**Decrease**	
$12,000		

B) **Equipment purchased for cash.** The business purchases some sound amplifiers and digital electronic equipment for $5,500 cash. (Notice that total assets don't change.)

Assets	=
$12,000	

Cash				Equipment	
Increase	**Decrease**			**Increase**	**Decrease**
A $12,000					
B	$5,500			$5,500	
Balance $6,500				$5,500	

C) **Purchase supplies on credit.** The business purchases $200 of office supplies "on account." (Notice that total assets increase by $200, but so do creditors' claims.)

Assets	=
$12,200	

Cash			Supplies		Equipment	
Increase	**Decrease**		**Increase**	**Decrease**	**Increase**	**Decrease**
A $12,000						
B	$5,500				$5,500	
C			$200			
Balance $6,500			$200		$5,500	

Notice that the custom is to always place balances on the "increase" side for each item, because an increase means a positive number. The natural balance of any item is always a positive number, so it makes sense to put a balance on the increase—the positive—side. For example, after two transactions, Cash has a balance of $6,500. Of course, this $6,500 balance is a positive number, so we place it on the positive side.

Learning Goal 11: Begin to Record

SEPARATE COLUMNS FOR INCREASES AND DECREASES (continued)

Liabilities + Owner's Equity

$12,000

	Jack Davis, Capital		Operational Change in Owner's Equity	
	Decrease	Increase	Expense	Revenue
		$12,000		

Liabilities + Owner's Equity

$12,000

	Jack Davis, Capital		Operational Change in Owner's Equity	
	Decrease	Increase	Expense	Revenue
A		$12,000		
B				
Balance		$12,000		

Liabilities + Owner's Equity

$12,200

	Accounts Payable			Jack Davis, Capital		Operational Change in Owner's Equity	
	Decrease	Increase		Decrease	Increase	Expense	Revenue
A					$12,000		
B							
C		$200					
		$200			$12,000		

SEPARATE COLUMNS FOR INCREASES AND DECREASES (continued)

D) **Revenue earned.** Jack teaches a beginners' class and receives $350 in cash from his students. (Notice that the revenue is an operational increase in owner's equity.)

Assets   =

$12,550

	Cash			Supplies		Equipment	
	Increase	Decrease		Increase	Decrease	Increase	Decrease
A	$12,000						
B		$5,500				$5,500	
C				$200			
D	$350						
Balance $6,850				$200		$5,500	

E) **Revenue earned.** Jack teaches a blues weekend master class at the university and receives $2,000 on account, plus $500 in cash. (Notice that three items are affected with this transaction.)

Assets   =

$15,050

	Cash		Accounts Receivable		Supplies		Equipment	
	Increase	Decrease	Increase	Decrease	Increase	Decrease	Increase	Decrease
A	$12,000							
B		$5,500					$5,500	
C					$200			
D	$350							
E	$500		$2,000					
Balance $7,350			$2,000		$200		$5,500	

You are in Jack's office and the door opens with a rush. Jack walks in with an angry look on his face. "Can you explain this to me?" he asks, his face red and his eyebrows menacingly tight. "I have only been in this business a few weeks and already I have lost almost $5,000!" You ask him how he found that out. "I invested $12,000 of my hard-earned money, and now the bank statement shows that I only have $7,350 left. That's how I know! That's almost a $5,000 loss in just a few weeks! You're the accountant. How did I have this loss and what happened to my money?" What do you think you should say to Jack?

SEPARATE COLUMNS FOR INCREASES AND DECREASES (continued)

Liabilities + Owner's Equity

$12,550

Accounts Payable			Jack Davis, Capital			Operational Change in Owner's Equity	
Decrease	Increase		Decrease	Increase		Expense	Revenue
A				$12,000			
B							
C	$200						
D				$350			$350
	$200			$12,350			

Liabilities + Owner's Equity

$15,050

Accounts Payable			Jack Davis, Capital			Operational Change in Owner's Equity	
Decrease	Increase		Decrease	Increase		Expense	Revenue
A				$12,000			
B							
C	$200						
D				$350			$350
E				$2,500			$2,500
	$200			$14,850			

SEPARATE COLUMNS FOR INCREASES AND DECREASES (continued)

First, you're silent for a moment, reflecting on Jack's questions. Then you open the lower desk drawer and pull out the manila folder which contains the accounting papers that you have been using to record the changes in Jack's business. You see that Jack is right about the cash; your records do show a balance of $7,350.

The first thing that you say is, "OK, I've got all the data right here for you. Let's look at the cash." You show Jack that there have been four cash transactions: (item A) a $12,000 increase from his investment; (item B) a $5,500 decrease spent on equipment; (item D) a $350 increase from the revenue for the beginner's class that he taught; and (item E) a $500 increase from the master blues class revenue.

Jack says, "Well, OK, at least I can see what has happened to the cash, but how could I have had a loss so quickly?"

"Jack," you say, "I have some good news for you, pal. You do not have a loss. You actually have net income—you know, a profit."

"How's that?"

You say, "How much did you invest?"

He answers, "$12,000."

"Jack, look at these records. They show that you have $15,050 in assets: $7,350 in cash, $2,000 in an accounts receivable, $200 in supplies, and $5,500 in equipment. If you subtract the $200 you owe on the account payable, that leaves you with $14,850 in owner's equity—you know, assets that you could claim. That's $2,850 more than you invested!"

Jack is quiet for a little while and then you hear him say, "Ah ... aaaaah, I think I see! When I have a profit or loss, that doesn't necessarily mean that it will all be just in cash. I have to count everything!"

You smile politely.

CHECK YOUR UNDERSTANDING

Fill in each blank space with the correct word. The answers are below.

For any item that normally appears on the left side of the equation, the custom in accounting is to place the "increase" column to the (left/right) _____ of the name of that item. For any item that normally appears on the right side of the equation, the custom is to place the "increase" column to the (left/right) _____ of the name of that item. A decrease column is then simply opposite from the _____ column.

Because balances are positive amounts, balances are shown in the _____ column of each item.

ANSWERS

For any item that normally appears on the left side of the equation, the custom in accounting is to place the "increase" column to the <u>left</u> of the name of that item. For any item that normally appears on the right side of the equation, the custom is to place the "increase" column to the <u>right</u> of the name of that item. A decrease column is then simply opposite from the <u>increase</u> column.

Because balances are positive amounts, balances are shown in the <u>increase</u> column of each item.

"When I count my wealth, it isn't always just in cash. I have to count everything."

• • •

SEPARATE COLUMNS FOR INCREASES AND DECREASES (continued)

F) **Expenses incurred on credit.** The school receives a utility bill for $100 and a telephone bill for $70 which are not paid immediately.

Assets   **=**

$15,050

	Cash		Accounts Receivable		Supplies		Equipment	
	Increase	Decrease	Increase	Decrease	Increase	Decrease	Increase	Decrease
A	$12,000							
B		$5,500					$5,500	
C					$200			
D	$350							
E	$500		$2,000					
F								
Balance $7,350			$2,000		$200		$5,500	

G) **Payment of a liability.** Jack pays the $200 account payable owing on the supplies. (Notice that paying a liability only affects the creditors' equity, not the owner's.)

Assets   **=**

$14,850

	Cash		Accounts Receivable		Supplies		Equipment	
	Increase	Decrease	Increase	Decrease	Increase	Decrease	Increase	Decrease
A	$12,000							
B		$5,500					$5,500	
C					$200			
D	$350							
E	$500		$2,000					
F								
G		$200						
Balance $7,150			$2,000		$200		$5,500	

SEPARATE COLUMNS FOR INCREASES AND DECREASES (continued)

Liabilities + Owner's Equity

$15,050

	Accounts Payable			Jack Davis, Capital			Operational Change in Owner's Equity	
	Decrease	Increase		Decrease	Increase		Expense	Revenue
A					$12,000			
B								
C	$200							
D					$350			$350
E					$2,500			$2,500
F	**$170**			**$170**			**$170**	
		$370			**$14,680**			

Liabilities + Owner's Equity

$14,850

	Accounts Payable			Jack Davis, Capital			Operational Change in Owner's Equity	
	Decrease	Increase		Decrease	Increase		Expense	Revenue
A					$12,000			
B								
C		$200						
D					$350			$350
E					$2,500			$2,500
F		$170		$170			$170	
G	$200							
		$170			**$14,680**			

SEPARATE COLUMNS FOR INCREASES AND DECREASES (continued)

H) **Incur expense from consuming asset.** You check the supplies cabinet to find that only $50 of supplies remain ($150 has been used).

	Assets							=
			$14,700					
	Cash		Accounts Receivable		Supplies		Equipment	
	Increase	Decrease	Increase	Decrease	Increase	Decrease	Increase	Decrease
A	$12,000							
B		$5,500					$5,500	
C					$200			
D	$350							
E	$500		$2,000					
F								
G		$200						
H						$150		
Balance $7,150			$2,000		$50		$5,500	

I) **Incur expense from consuming asset.** The school pays $800 for rent expense for the month.

	Assets							=
			$13,900					
	Cash		Accounts Receivable		Supplies		Equipment	
	Increase	Decrease	Increase	Decrease	Increase	Decrease	Increase	Decrease
A	$12,000							
B		$5,500					$5,500	
C					$200			
D	$350							
E	$500		$2,000					
F								
G		$200						
H						$150		
I		$800						
Balance $6,350			$2,000		$50		$5,500	

Learning Goal 11: Begin to Record

SEPARATE COLUMNS FOR INCREASES AND DECREASES (continued)

One day, you meet Jack walking into your office. He is in a great mood, because Flash has just signed for a three-week gig to play in a big Los Angeles club. Jack happily pulls a $15,000 check from his pocket and asks you to deposit it for him in the business checking account. What's your comment?

Liabilities + Owner's Equity

$14,700

	Accounts Payable			Jack Davis, Capital			Operational Change in Owner's Equity	
	Decrease	Increase		Decrease	Increase		Expense	Revenue
A					$12,000			
B								
C		$200						
D					$350			$350
E					$2,500			$2,500
F	$170			$170			$170	
G	$200							
H				$150			$150	
		$170			$14,530			

Liabilities + Owner's Equity

$13,900

	Accounts Payable			Jack Davis, Capital			Operational Change in Owner's Equity	
	Decrease	Increase		Decrease	Increase		Expense	Revenue
A					$12,000			
B								
C		$200						
D					$350			$350
E					$2,500			$2,500
F	$170			$170			$170	
G	$200							
H				$150			$150	
I				$800			$800	
		$170			$13,730			

Learning Goal 11: Begin to Record

SEPARATE COLUMNS FOR INCREASES AND DECREASES (continued)

You say, "Well, look—it's probably a lot better if you just hold the check until you can deposit it in your own personal account." Jack looks at you in a funny way, but says nothing, so you continue. "You see, 'Flash' is a separate business—it's your band—and is not part of the guitar school. There is something in accounting called the 'entity assumption' … well, never mind, Jack. Just remember not to mix up the income between the guitar school and the band, OK?"

J) **Collecting accounts receivable.** The music school collects $750 of the open account receivable from the university. (Total assets don't change; neither do liabilities or owner's equity.)

	Assets							=
	$13,900							
	Cash		**Accounts Receivable**		**Supplies**		**Equipment**	
	Increase	Decrease	Increase	Decrease	Increase	Decrease	Increase	Decrease
A	$12,000							
B		$5,500					$5,500	
C						$200		
D	$350							
E	$500		$2,000					
F								
G		$200						
H						$150		
I		$800						
J	$750			$750				
Balance $7,100			$1,250		$50		$5,500	

SEPARATE COLUMNS FOR INCREASES AND DECREASES (continued)

Jack looks at you as though all accountants are very peculiar and says, "OK, no problem. I would never have thought of anything like that myself." With the $15,000 check in his pocket, he strolls off to his one o'clock appointment at the school.

Liabilities + Owner's Equity

$13,900

	Accounts Payable			Jack Davis, Capital			Operational Change in Owner's Equity	
	Decrease	Increase		Decrease	Increase		Expense	Revenue
A					$12,000			
B								
C		$200						
D					$350			$350
E					$2,500			$2,500
F	$170			$170			$170	
G	$200							
H				$150			$150	
I				$800			$800	
J								
		$170			$13,730			

SEPARATE COLUMNS FOR INCREASES AND DECREASES (continued)

K) **Jack withdraws $1,000 cash** out of the business for his own personal use. He calls it a "salary." (Notice that if Jack "pays" himself a "salary," it's still really just a withdrawal—a capital reduction—not an expense of the business, no matter what he wants to call it.)

Assets   **=**

$12,900

	Cash		Accounts Receivable		Supplies		Equipment	
	Increase	Decrease	Increase	Decrease	Increase	Decrease	Increase	Decrease
A	$12,000							
B		$5,500					$5,500	
C					$200			
D	$350							
E	$500		$2,000					
F								
G		$200						
H						$150		
I		$800						
J	$750			$750				
K		**$1,000**						
Balance	$6,100		$1,250		$50		$5,500	

SEPARATE COLUMNS FOR INCREASES AND DECREASES (continued)

Liabilities + Owner's Equity

$12,900

	Accounts Payable			Jack Davis, Capital			Operational Change in Owner's Equity	
	Decrease	Increase		Decrease	Increase		Expense	Revenue
A					$12,000			
B								
C		$200						
D					$350			$350
E					$2,500			$2,500
F		$170		$170			$170	
G	$200							
H				$150			$150	
I				$800			$800	
J								
K				**$1,000**				
		$170			**$12,730**			

SEPARATE COLUMNS FOR INCREASES AND DECREASES (continued)

L) Unearned revenue. A student's parent pays an advance to the school in the amount of $250 cash for six weeks of lessons. (Receiving a customer advance payment creates a liability called "unearned revenue." No service has been provided yet, so there is an obligation to return the money until the revenue is actually earned.)

Assets   **=**

$13,150

| | Cash | | Accounts Receivable | | Supplies | | Equipment | |
	Increase	Decrease	Increase	Decrease	Increase	Decrease	Increase	Decrease
A	$12,000							
B		$5,500					$5,500	
C					$200			
D	$350							
E	$500		$2,000					
F								
G		$200						
H						$150		
I		$800						
J	$750			$750				
K		$1,000						
L	$250							
Balance	**$6,350**		**$1,250**		**$50**		**$5,500**	

The day after you meet Jack in the parking lot with his $15,000 check, he walks into your office and says, "You know, now that things are going well, I have a loan application here that I'm working on to see if we can get some additional funds to expand our teaching facilities. The bank wants to see the financial statements of the business and I need to show the best situation possible on the loan application. I want to make sure that we get that loan. I have an idea that I want you to use on the financial statements for me.

"When we get paid for lessons in advance, you have been showing the money we receive as a liability called 'unearned revenue.' This does not show up as revenue until later, when the lesson is given. I don't like this! After all, sooner or later we are going to give the lessons and earn the revenue anyway.

"I want you to show these receipts as revenue as soon as we get the money. I do not want you to show it as a liability. We will have a big advance coming in soon and this is a real good way to show a big increase in our profits right away."

SEPARATE COLUMNS FOR INCREASES AND DECREASES (continued)

He looks you straight in the eye and says, "You know, this bank loan is going to be very important to both of us … to both of our jobs … do you understand what I mean?"

How do you respond to Jack? Is his proposal ethical?

Liabilities + Owner's Equity

<u>$13,150</u>

	Accounts Payable		Unearned Revenue		Jack Davis, Capital		Operational Change in Owner's Equity	
	Decrease	Increase	Decrease	Increase	Decrease	Increase	Expense	Revenue
A						$12,000		
B								
C		$200						
D						$350		$350
E						$2,500		$2,500
F	$170				$170		$170	
G	$200							
H					$150		$150	
I					$800		$800	
J								
K					$1,000			
L				$250				
		$170		$250		$12,730		

Jack is assuming that accounting rules can be changed to satisfy his own purposes, and that he can force you to do what he wants. He is asking you to change an accounting method that you know is correct to one that is incorrect, for the sole purpose of misleading the bank by making the business look more profitable.

You really have only one safe and ethical course of action open to you. First, you need to explain to Jack that there is a set of accounting principles that you are obligated to follow. One of them requires that revenue can only be shown after it is fully earned, and not before. The purpose of this is to provide reliable financial statements that do not make the business seem more profitable than it really is. You should also tell Jack that he will be much better off in the long run if the banker learns that Jack's financial statements are always accurate, and Jack becomes known as an ethical and trusted customer of the bank.

SEPARATE COLUMNS FOR INCREASES AND DECREASES (continued)

Right now, Jack is not acting in an ethical way either to the bank or to you. To make you do as he wishes, Jack is putting you in a no-win situation, because he is implying that if you don't cooperate, he will fire you. On the other hand, if you do cooperate, you are putting your own reputation and career at risk.

If Jack completely refuses to listen to you, you have no alternative but to respectfully and politely quit. As an accountant, your ethical conduct must set a standard for others, and the financial statements you prepare must be reliable, because so many people depend upon them. However difficult leaving may seem at the time, it is far better than developing a relationship in which Jack knows that he can always manipulate you. In a situation like this, your career and life will inevitably suffer as his demands become greater and greater every month.

This situation should be viewed as one of the occasional causes of job turnover in a field in which ethical requirements are unusually high.

M) Unearned revenue is earned. Jack gives a $50 lesson to the student whose parents previously advanced the $250 for lessons. (Notice that when the revenue is earned, the liability is reduced. By performing $50 worth of services, Jack removed $50 of the liability and increased his own claim on the assets by $50.)

	Cash		Accounts Receivable		Supplies		Equipment	
	Increase	Decrease	Increase	Decrease	Increase	Decrease	Increase	Decrease
A	$12,000							
B		$5,500					$5,500	
C					$200			
D	$350							
E	$500		$2,000					
F								
G		$200						
H						$150		
I		$800						
J	$750			$750				
K		$1,000						
L	$250							
M								
Balance	$6,350		$1,250		$50		$5,500	

Assets = **$13,150**

SEPARATE COLUMNS FOR INCREASES AND DECREASES (continued)

SUMMARY

What the Processing Has Accomplished So Far

- You have recorded all transactions in an organized way.
- You now have a permanent record of:
  — the individual transactions
  — the current balance of each item in the accounting equation

---

Notice that the "operational change in owner's equity" includes only revenues and expenses. The investment of $12,000 and the withdrawal of $1,000 did affect owner's equity, but they were not part of the business operations. By separately identifying the operational changes, we can now see that the business operations increased the owner's equity, and therefore the owner's wealth, by $2,900 – $1,120 = $1,780. This means that the business was profitable—it has a "net income" of $1,780.

Liabilities + Owner's Equity

$13,150

	Accounts Payable		Unearned Revenue		Jack Davis, Capital		Operational Change in Owner's Equity	
	Decrease	Increase	Decrease	Increase	Decrease	Increase	Expense	Revenue
A						$12,000		
B								
C		$200						
D						$350		$350
E						$2,500		$2,500
F		$170			$170		$170	
G	$200							
H					$150		$150	
I					$800		$800	
J								
K					$1,000			
L				$250				
M			$50			$50		$50
		$170		$200		$12,780	$1,120	$2,900

PRACTICE FOR LEARNING GOAL 11

SOLUTIONS FOR LEARNING GOAL 11 BEGIN ON PAGE 258.

Learning Goal 11 is about beginning to record transactions. Use these questions and problems to practice what you have learned.

REINFORCEMENT PROBLEMS

1) Following is a schedule showing the balances **(Bal)** of the assets and equities of Sugar Eclair's Gym and Aerobics Club at the end of August. Record the September transactions as they happen. Space has been provided to add new assets or equities to the schedule. After you record each transaction, retotal the assets and equities, carry the new balances down, and then enter the totals of the assets and equities at the top of the next section to prove that the equation still balances. You may omit $ signs.

If any transaction involves an expense or a revenue, keep a separate record of expenses and revenues after you record their effects on owner's equity. Calculate the net income or loss for the period of September.

A) *Example:* Supplies of $100 are purchased for cash.

Assets   =

$40,020

	Cash		Accounts Receivable				Gym Supplies		Gym Equipment	
	Increase	Decrease	Increase	Decrease			Increase	Decrease	Increase	Decrease
(Bal)	10,300		4,100				620		25,000	
A)		100					100			
(New Bal.)	10,200		4,100				720		25,000	

B) The club collects $2,000 cash from the accounts receivable.

Assets   =

$40,020

	Cash		Accounts Receivable				Gym Supplies		Gym Equipment	
	Increase	Decrease	Increase	Decrease			Increase	Decrease	Increase	Decrease
(Bal)	10,200		4,100				720		25,000	
B)										
(New Bal.)										

PRACTICE FOR LEARNING GOAL 11

SOLUTIONS FOR LEARNING GOAL 11 BEGIN ON PAGE 258.

Liabilities + Owner's Equity

$40,020

Accounts Payable						Sugar Eclair, Capital			Exp.	Rev.
Decrease	Increase					Decrease	Increase			
	200						39,820			
	200						39,820			

Liabilities + Owner's Equity

$40,020

Accounts Payable						Sugar Eclair, Capital			Exp.	Rev.
Decrease	Increase					Decrease	Increase			
	200						39,820			

PRACTICE FOR LEARNING GOAL 11

SOLUTIONS FOR LEARNING GOAL 11 BEGIN ON PAGE 258.

1) *continued*

C) The club prepays a nine-month fire insurance policy for $1,500.

Assets   **=**

$_____

	Cash		Accounts Receivable				Gym Supplies		Gym Equipment	
	Increase	Decrease	Increase	Decrease			Increase	Decrease	Increase	Decrease
(Bal)										
C)										
(New Bal.)										

D) The club receives member dues of $5,300.

Assets   **=**

$_____

	Cash		Accounts Receivable				Gym Supplies		Gym Equipment	
	Increase	Decrease	Increase	Decrease			Increase	Decrease	Increase	Decrease
(Bal)										
D)										
(New Bal.)										

E) The club sends out bills to members for dues of $2,900.

Assets   **=**

$_____

	Cash		Accounts Receivable				Gym Supplies		Gym Equipment	
	Increase	Decrease	Increase	Decrease			Increase	Decrease	Increase	Decrease
(Bal)										
E)										
(New Bal.)										

SOLUTIONS FOR LEARNING GOAL 11 BEGIN ON PAGE 258.

Liabilities + Owner's Equity

$_____

Accounts Payable					Sugar Eclair, Capital			Exp.	Rev.
Decrease	Increase				Decrease	Increase			

Liabilities + Owner's Equity

$_____

Accounts Payable					Sugar Eclair, Capital			Exp.	Rev.
Decrease	Increase				Decrease	Increase			

Liabilities + Owner's Equity

$_____

Accounts Payable					Sugar Eclair, Capital			Exp.	Rev.
Decrease	Increase				Decrease	Increase			

Learning Goal 11: Begin to Record

PRACTICE FOR LEARNING GOAL 11

SOLUTIONS FOR LEARNING GOAL 11 BEGIN ON PAGE 258.

1) *continued*

F) The club receives and pays the utilities bill of $550.

	Cash		Accounts Receivable				Gym Supplies		Gym Equipment	
	Increase	Decrease	Increase	Decrease			Increase	Decrease	Increase	Decrease
(Bal)										
F)										
(New Bal.)										

Assets = $_____

G) The club receives but does not pay the telephone bill of $185.

	Cash		Accounts Receivable				Gym Supplies		Gym Equipment	
	Increase	Decrease	Increase	Decrease			Increase	Decrease	Increase	Decrease
(Bal)										
G)										
(New Bal.)										

Assets = $_____

H) The club pays $200 of the accounts payable.

	Cash		Accounts Receivable				Gym Supplies		Gym Equipment	
	Increase	Decrease	Increase	Decrease			Increase	Decrease	Increase	Decrease
(Bal)										
H)										
(New Bal.)										

Assets = $_____

PRACTICE FOR LEARNING GOAL 11

SOLUTIONS FOR LEARNING GOAL 11 BEGIN ON PAGE 258.

Liabilities + Owner's Equity

$\$_____$

Accounts Payable						Sugar Eclair, Capital			Exp.	Rev.
Decrease	Increase					Decrease	Increase			

Liabilities + Owner's Equity

$\$_____$

Accounts Payable						Sugar Eclair, Capital			Exp.	Rev.
Decrease	Increase					Decrease	Increase			

Liabilities + Owner's Equity

$\$_____$

Accounts Payable						Sugar Eclair, Capital			Exp.	Rev.
Decrease	Increase					Decrease	Increase			

PRACTICE FOR LEARNING GOAL 11

SOLUTIONS FOR LEARNING GOAL 11 BEGIN ON PAGE 258.

1) *continued*

I) The club borrows $50,000 from the 5th National Bank and signs a 15-year note.

Assets =

$_____

	Cash		Accounts Receivable				Gym Supplies		Gym Equipment	
	Increase	Decrease	Increase	Decrease			Increase	Decrease	Increase	Decrease
(Bal)										
I)										
(New Bal.)										

J) Cash of $590 is received from members who prepay next month's dues.

Assets =

$_____

	Cash		Accounts Receivable				Gym Supplies		Gym Equipment	
	Increase	Decrease	Increase	Decrease			Increase	Decrease	Increase	Decrease
(Bal)										
J)										
(New Bal.)										

K) Sugar withdraws $2,000 from the business for personal living expenses.

Assets =

$_____

	Cash		Accounts Receivable				Gym Supplies		Gym Equipment	
	Increase	Decrease	Increase	Decrease			Increase	Decrease	Increase	Decrease
(Bal)										
K)										
(New Bal.)										

Learning Goal 11: Begin to Record

PRACTICE FOR LEARNING GOAL 11

SOLUTIONS FOR LEARNING GOAL 11 BEGIN ON PAGE 258.

Liabilities + Owner's Equity

$_____

Accounts Payable						Sugar Eclair, Capital			Exp.	Rev.
Decrease	**Increase**					**Decrease**	**Increase**			

Liabilities + Owner's Equity

$_____

Accounts Payable						Sugar Eclair, Capital			Exp.	Rev.
Decrease	**Increase**					**Decrease**	**Increase**			

Liabilities + Owner's Equity

$_____

Accounts Payable						Sugar Eclair, Capital			Exp.	Rev.
Decrease	**Increase**					**Decrease**	**Increase**			

PRACTICE FOR LEARNING GOAL 11

SOLUTIONS FOR LEARNING GOAL 11 BEGIN ON PAGE 258.

1) *continued*

   L)   The business purchases $500 of supplies and $1,000 of equipment on credit.

Assets   **=**

$_____

	Cash		Accounts Receivable				Gym Supplies		Gym Equipment	
	Increase	Decrease	Increase	Decrease			Increase	Decrease	Increase	Decrease
(Bal)										
M)										
(New Bal.)										

   M) Air conditioning repairs are required for $900. The bill will be paid later.

Assets   **=**

$_____

	Cash		Accounts Receivable				Gym Supplies		Gym Equipment	
	Increase	Decrease	Increase	Decrease			Increase	Decrease	Increase	Decrease
(Bal)										
N)										
(New Bal.)										

   N) Sugar spends the $2,000 she withdrew for new furniture for her home.

Assets   **=**

$_____

	Cash		Accounts Receivable				Gym Supplies		Gym Equipment	
	Increase	Decrease	Increase	Decrease			Increase	Decrease	Increase	Decrease
(Bal)										
O)										
(New Bal.)										

- What are the total revenues that the club received during September? _____
- What are the total expenses of the club during September? _____
- Calculate the club's net income or loss during September. _____

Learning Goal 11: Begin to Record

PRACTICE FOR LEARNING GOAL 11

SOLUTIONS FOR LEARNING GOAL 11 BEGIN ON PAGE 258.

Liabilities + Owner's Equity

$_____

Accounts Payable						Sugar Eclair, Capital			Exp.	Rev.
Decrease	Increase					Decrease	Increase			

Liabilities + Owner's Equity

$_____

Accounts Payable						Sugar Eclair, Capital			Exp.	Rev.
Decrease	Increase					Decrease	Increase			

Liabilities + Owner's Equity

$_____

Accounts Payable						Sugar Eclair, Capital			Exp.	Rev.
Decrease	Increase					Decrease	Increase			

PRACTICE FOR LEARNING GOAL 11

SOLUTIONS FOR LEARNING GOAL 11 BEGIN ON PAGE 258.

2) Use the information for items A through N, below, to record which specific items increase or decrease as a result of each event. Write in the name of the item affected in the "increase" or "decrease" columns below. Use the first item as an example.

	Assets		=	Liabilities	+	Owner's Equity	
	Increase	Decrease	Decrease	Increase	Decrease	Increase
A) A business collects $1,000 of accounts receivable from a customer.	Cash	Accts. Rec.				
B) A business pays a bill to a vendor.						
C) A business purchases supplies on account.						
D) A business makes a sale on account.						
E) A business uses up some supplies.						
F) A business buys a $5,000 computer, pays $1,000 cash, and signs a note.						
G) A business receives an advance payment from a customer.						
H) The owner removes some cash and supplies from her business.						
I) A business prepays rent for three months in the amount of $1,500.						
J) The owner buys a new car for herself.						
K) A business pays the wages to its employees.						
L) One month has passed since the rent was prepaid in item I, above.						
M) A business receives a bill from the telephone company.						
N) The business performs services for the customer who prepaid in item G, above.						

"Darling, of course I'll learn accounting!"

• •

SOLUTIONS FOR LEARNING GOAL 11

PRACTICE QUESTIONS FOR LEARNING GOAL 11 BEGIN ON PAGE 246.

1) Sugar Eclair's Gym September transactions.
   A) *Example:* Supplies of $100 are purchased for cash.

Assets   **=**

$40,020

	Cash		Accounts Receivable				Gym Supplies		Gym Equipment	
	Increase	Decrease	Increase	Decrease			Increase	Decrease	Increase	Decrease
(Bal)	10,300		4,100				620		25,000	
A)		100					100			
(New Bal.)	10,200		4,100				720		25,000	

B) The club collects $2,000 cash from the accounts receivable.

Assets   **=**

$40,020

	Cash		Accounts Receivable				Gym Supplies		Gym Equipment	
	Increase	Decrease	Increase	Decrease			Increase	Decrease	Increase	Decrease
(Bal)	10,200		4,100				720		25,000	
B)	2,000			2,000						
(New Bal.)	12,200		2,100				720		25,000	

C) The club prepays a nine-month fire insurance policy for $1,500.

Assets   **=**

$40,020

	Cash		Accounts Receivable		Prepaid Insurance		Gym Supplies		Gym Equipment	
	Increase	Decrease	Increase	Decrease	Increase	Decrease	Increase	Decrease	Increase	Decrease
(Bal)	12,200		2,100				720		25,000	
C)		1,500			1,500					
(New Bal.)	10,700		2,100		1,500		720		25,000	

SOLUTIONS FOR LEARNING GOAL 11

PRACTICE QUESTIONS FOR LEARNING GOAL 11 BEGIN ON PAGE 246.

Liabilities + Owner's Equity

$40,020

Accounts Payable						Sugar Eclair, Capital			Exp.	Rev.
Decrease	Increase					Decrease	Increase			
	200						39,820			
	200						39,820			

Liabilities + Owner's Equity

$40,020

Accounts Payable						Sugar Eclair, Capital			Exp.	Rev.
Decrease	Increase					Decrease	Increase			
	200						39,820			
	200						39,820			

Liabilities + Owner's Equity

$40,020

Accounts Payable						Sugar Eclair, Capital			Exp.	Rev.
Decrease	Increase					Decrease	Increase			
	200						39,820			
	200						39,820			

PRACTICE QUESTIONS FOR LEARNING GOAL 11 BEGIN ON PAGE 246.

1) *continued*

D) The club receives member dues of $5,300.

Assets =

$45,320

	Cash		Accounts Receivable		Prepaid Insurance		Gym Supplies		Gym Equipment	
	Increase	Decrease	Increase	Decrease	Increase	Decrease	Increase	Decrease	Increase	Decrease
(Bal)	10,700		2,100		1,500		720		25,000	
D)	5,300									
(New Bal.)	16,000		2,100		1,500		720		25,000	

E) The club sends out bills to members for dues for $2,900.

Assets =

$48,220

	Cash		Accounts Receivable		Prepaid Insurance		Gym Supplies		Gym Equipment	
	Increase	Decrease	Increase	Decrease	Increase	Decrease	Increase	Decrease	Increase	Decrease
(Bal)	16,000		2,100		1,500		720		25,000	
E)			2,900							
(New Bal.)	16,000		5,000		1,500		720		25,000	

F) The club receives and pays the utilities bill of $550.

Assets =

$47,670

	Cash		Accounts Receivable		Prepaid Insurance		Gym Supplies		Gym Equipment	
	Increase	Decrease	Increase	Decrease	Increase	Decrease	Increase	Decrease	Increase	Decrease
(Bal)	16,000		5,000		1,500		720		25,000	
F)		550								
(New Bal.)	15,450		5,000		1,500		720		25,000	

SOLUTIONS FOR LEARNING GOAL 11

PRACTICE QUESTIONS FOR LEARNING GOAL 11 BEGIN ON PAGE 246.

Liabilities + Owner's Equity

$45,320

Accounts Payable						Sugar Eclair, Capital			Exp.	Rev.
Decrease	Increase					Decrease	Increase		Exp.	Rev.
	200						39,820			
							5,300			5,300
	200						45,120			5,300

Liabilities + Owner's Equity

$48,220

Accounts Payable						Sugar Eclair, Capital			Exp.	Rev.
Decrease	Increase					Decrease	Increase		Exp.	Rev.
	200						45,120			5,300
							2,900			2,900
	200						48,020			8,200

Liabilities + Owner's Equity

$47,670

Accounts Payable						Sugar Eclair, Capital			Exp.	Rev.
Decrease	Increase					Decrease	Increase		Exp.	Rev.
	200						48,020			8,200
						550			550	
	200						47,470			550	8,200

SOLUTIONS FOR LEARNING GOAL 11

PRACTICE QUESTIONS FOR LEARNING GOAL 11 BEGIN ON PAGE 246.

1) *continued*

G) The club receives but does not pay the telephone bill of $185.

Assets   =

$47,670

	Cash		Accounts Receivable		Prepaid Insurance		Gym Supplies		Gym Equipment	
	Increase	Decrease	Increase	Decrease	Increase	Decrease	Increase	Decrease	Increase	Decrease
(Bal)	15,450		5,000		1,500		720		25,000	
G)										
(New Bal.)	15,450		5,000		1,500		720		25,000	

H) The club pays $200 of the accounts payable.

Assets   =

$47,470

	Cash		Accounts Receivable		Prepaid Insurance		Gym Supplies		Gym Equipment	
	Increase	Decrease	Increase	Decrease	Increase	Decrease	Increase	Decrease	Increase	Decrease
(Bal)	15,450		5,000		1,500		720		25,000	
H)		200								
(New Bal.)	15,250		5,000		1,500		720		25,000	

I) The club borrows $50,000 from the 5th National Bank and signs a 15-year note.

Assets   =

$97,470

	Cash		Accounts Receivable		Prepaid Insurance		Gym Supplies		Gym Equipment	
	Increase	Decrease	Increase	Decrease	Increase	Decrease	Increase	Decrease	Increase	Decrease
(Bal)	15,250		5,000		1,500		720		25,000	
I)	50,000									
(New Bal.)	65,250		5,000		1,500		720		25,000	

SOLUTIONS FOR LEARNING GOAL 11

PRACTICE QUESTIONS FOR LEARNING GOAL 11 BEGIN ON PAGE 246.

Liabilities + Owner's Equity

$47,670

Accounts Payable						Sugar Eclair, Capital			Exp.	Rev.
Decrease	Increase					Decrease	Increase		Exp.	Rev.
	200						47,470		550	8,200
	185					185			185	
	385						47,285		735	8,200

Liabilities + Owner's Equity

$47,470

Accounts Payable						Sugar Eclair, Capital			Exp.	Rev.
Decrease	Increase					Decrease	Increase		Exp.	Rev.
	385						47,285		735	8,200
200										
	185						47,285		735	8,200

Liabilities + Owner's Equity

$97,470

Accounts Payable		Notes Payable				Sugar Eclair, Capital			Exp.	Rev.
Decrease	Increase	Decrease	Increase			Decrease	Increase		Exp.	Rev.
	185						47,285		735	8,200
			50,000							
	185		50,000				47,285		735	8,200

SOLUTIONS FOR LEARNING GOAL 11

PRACTICE QUESTIONS FOR LEARNING GOAL 11 BEGIN ON PAGE 246.

1) *continued*

J)   Cash of $590 is received from members who prepay next month's dues.

Assets =

$98,060

	Cash		Accounts Receivable		Prepaid Insurance		Gym Supplies		Gym Equipment	
	Increase	Decrease	Increase	Decrease	Increase	Decrease	Increase	Decrease	Increase	Decrease
(Bal)	65,250		5,000		1,500		720		25,000	
J)	590									
(New Bal.)	65,840		5,000		1,500		720		25,000	

K)   Sugar withdraws $2,000 from the business for personal living expense.

Assets =

$96,060

	Cash		Accounts Receivable		Prepaid Insurance		Gym Supplies		Gym Equipment	
	Increase	Decrease	Increase	Decrease	Increase	Decrease	Increase	Decrease	Increase	Decrease
(Bal)	65,840		5,000		1,500		720		25,000	
K)		2,000								
(New Bal.)	63,840		5,000		1,500		720		25,000	

L)   The business purchases $500 of supplies and $1,000 of equipment on credit.

Assets =

$97,560

	Cash		Accounts Receivable		Prepaid Insurance		Gym Supplies		Gym Equipment	
	Increase	Decrease	Increase	Decrease	Increase	Decrease	Increase	Decrease	Increase	Decrease
(Bal)	63,840		5,000		1,500		720		25,000	
L)							500		1,000	
(New Bal.)	63,840		5,000		1,500		1,220		26,000	

SOLUTIONS FOR LEARNING GOAL 11

PRACTICE QUESTIONS FOR LEARNING GOAL 11 BEGIN ON PAGE 246.

Liabilities + Owner's Equity
$98,060

Accounts Payable		Notes Payable		Unearned Revenue		Sugar Eclair, Capital			Exp.	Rev.
Decrease	Increase	Decrease	Increase	Decrease	Increase	Decrease	Increase		Exp.	Rev.
	185		50,000				47,285		735	8,200
					590					
	185		50,000		590		47,285		735	8,200

Liabilities + Owner's Equity
$96,060

Accounts Payable		Notes Payable		Unearned Revenue		Sugar Eclair, Capital			Exp.	Rev.
Decrease	Increase	Decrease	Increase	Decrease	Increase	Decrease	Increase		Exp.	Rev.
	185		50,000		590		47,285		735	8,200
						2,000				
	185		50,000		590		45,285		735	8,200

Liabilities + Owner's Equity
$97,560

Accounts Payable		Notes Payable		Unearned Revenue		Sugar Eclair, Capital			Exp.	Rev.
Decrease	Increase	Decrease	Increase	Decrease	Increase	Decrease	Increase		Exp.	Rev.
	185		50,000		590		45,285		735	8,200
	1,500									
	1,685		50,000		590		45,285		735	8,200

SOLUTIONS FOR LEARNING GOAL 11

PRACTICE QUESTIONS FOR LEARNING GOAL 11 BEGIN ON PAGE 246.

1) *continued*

M) Air conditioning repairs are required for $900. The bill will be paid later.

Assets =

$97,560

	Cash Increase	Cash Decrease	Accounts Receivable Increase	Accounts Receivable Decrease	Prepaid Insurance Increase	Prepaid Insurance Decrease	Gym Supplies Increase	Gym Supplies Decrease	Gym Equipment Increase	Gym Equipment Decrease
(Bal)	63,840		5,000		1,500		1,220		26,000	
M)										
(New Bal.)	63,840		5,000		1,500		1,220		26,000	

N) Sugar spends the $2,000 she withdrew for new furniture for her home.

Assets =

$97,560

	Cash Increase	Cash Decrease	Accounts Receivable Increase	Accounts Receivable Decrease	Prepaid Insurance Increase	Prepaid Insurance Decrease	Gym Supplies Increase	Gym Supplies Decrease	Gym Equipment Increase	Gym Equipment Decrease
(Bal)	63,840		5,000		1,500		1,220		26,000	
N)										
(New Bal.)	63,840		5,000		1,500		1,220		26,000	

This is a personal transaction of the owner. It is not recorded by the business!

SOLUTIONS FOR LEARNING GOAL 11

PRACTICE QUESTIONS FOR LEARNING GOAL 11 BEGIN ON PAGE 246.

Liabilities + Owner's Equity

$97,560

Accounts Payable		Notes Payable		Unearned Revenue		Sugar Eclair, Capital			Exp.	Rev.
Decrease	Increase	Decrease	Increase	Decrease	Increase	Decrease	Increase			
	1,685		50,000		590		45,285		735	8,200
	900					900			900	
	2,585		50,000		590		44,385		1,635	8,200

Liabilities + Owner's Equity

$97,560

Accounts Payable		Notes Payable		Unearned Revenue		Sugar Eclair, Capital			Exp.	Rev.
Decrease	Increase	Decrease	Increase	Decrease	Increase	Decrease	Increase			
	2,585		50,000		590		44,385		1,635	8,200
	2,585		50,000		590		44,385		1,635	8,200

- What are the total revenues that the club received during September? $8,200

- What are the total expenses of the club during September? $1,635

- Calculate the club's net income or loss during September. $8,200 – 1,635 = $6,565 net income

SOLUTIONS FOR LEARNING GOAL 11

PRACTICE QUESTIONS FOR LEARNING GOAL 11 BEGIN ON PAGE 246.

2)

		Assets		=	Liabilities	+	Owner's Equity	
		Increase	Decrease	Decrease	Increase		Decrease	Increase
A)	A business collects $1,000 of accounts receivable from a customer.	Cash	Accts. Rec.					
B)	A business pays a bill to a vendor.		Cash	Accts. Pay.				
C)	A business purchases supplies on account.	Supplies			Accts. Pay.			
D)	A business makes a sale on account.	Accts. Rec.						Revenue
E)	A business uses up some supplies.		Supplies				Supp. Exp.	
F)	A business buys a $5,000 computer, pays $1,000 cash, and signs a note.	Office Equip. $5,000	Cash $1,000		Notes Pay. $4,000			
G)	A business receives an advance payment from a customer.	Cash			Unearned Revenue			
H)	The owner removes some cash and supplies from her business.		Cash Supplies				Withdrawals (or drawing)	
I)	A business prepays rent for 3 months in the amount of $1,500.	Prepaid Rent $1,500	Cash $1,500					
J)	The owner buys a new car for herself.	Not a business transaction.						
K)	A business pays the wages to its employees.		Cash				Wages Exp.	
L)	One month has passed since the rent was prepaid in item I, above.		Prepaid Rent $500				Rent Exp. $500	
M)	A business receives a bill from the telephone company.				Accts. Pay.		Telephone Exp.	
N)	The business performs services for the customer who prepaid in item G, above.			Unearned Revenue				Fees Revenue

Your Questions?

It is *very* important to be aware of what you need to understand better. What do you need to understand better about this learning goal? Use this space to write the questions that you want to discuss with your classmates, instructor, or supervisor. Try to be very specific about what is bothering you, such as explanations that you do not fully understand.

Preparing and Interpreting Financial Statements

Overview: what this section does	This section explains the four basic financial statements, and shows you how they are prepared.
Use this section if ...	... you want to understand the purpose of the balance sheet, income statement, statement of owner's equity, and statement of cash flows. ... you want to learn how to prepare all of these statements, except for the statement of cash flows, and you want to learn how they are connected.
Do NOT use this section if ...	... you already understand the meaning of the financial statements and how to prepare them, or ... you have studied Section III, and now you want to study debits and credits (see Section V starting on page 364).

LEARNING GOAL 12
Describe the Financial Statements

REVIEW AND PREVIEW

Review

In the prior learning goal, you practiced Stages 1 and 2 of the accounting process: you analyzed events and, if the events qualified as transactions, you recorded them.

In this learning goal ...

This learning goal introduces you to Stage 3 in the accounting process: communicating what has happened to a business. Communication in accounting is done by summarizing what has been recorded into financial statements.

In Learning Goal 12, you will find:

▼ *Financial Statements and What They Do*

FINANCIAL STATEMENTS ARE SUMMARIES

What are financial statements?	Financial statements are well-organized summaries of all the transactions that have already been recorded.
What financial statements do	Because financial statements are well-organized summaries, they can *communicate* important financial information about a business to the people and organizations (the stakeholders) who make decisions concerning the business. This clarified overview would be impossible by only looking at individual transactions one at a time.

"So ... tell me all about financial statements."

● ● ●

Learning Goal 12: Describe the Financial Statements

THE TYPES OF FINANCIAL STATEMENTS

Four general-purpose financial statements

There are four general-purpose financial statements that are normally prepared to provide information to stakeholders:

- the balance sheet (the basic statement of financial condition)
- the income statement (explains certain changes in the balance sheet)
- the statement of owner's equity (explains certain changes in the balance sheet)
- the statement of cash flows (explains certain changes in the balance sheet)

These statements are called "general purpose" because they are prepared for general use by any stakeholder. This could be an owner, a manager, an investor, a lender, or anyone else.

> *Note:* An individual financial statement is sometimes called a "report."

Special-purpose financial statements

Accountants can also prepare special-purpose reports. These reports usually focus on the business operations in great detail, and are intended only for owners and managers for use within the business. This kind of work is called *managerial accounting*. This is a topic you will study in other accounting classes.

The annual report

Large companies present the four general-purpose reports at the end of each year's operations in a single document called the *annual report*.

FEATURES OF THE ANNUAL REPORT

Frequency

Annual.

Financial statements

The four general-purpose financial statements are in the annual report: balance sheet, income statement, statement of owner's equity, and statement of cash flows.

FEATURES OF THE ANNUAL REPORT (continued)

Supplementary information	Annual reports contain very detailed footnotes, graphs, charts, and tables that help to explain the financial statements.
Audited	The financial statements in the annual report are audited by Certified Public Accountants.
MD & A	Annual reports also contain management's analysis of the financial statements, and management's opinion about the past and future performance of the company. This is called "management discussion and analysis," or simply *MD & A*.

▼ *The Qualities of Information*

HOW GOOD IS INFORMATION IN THE FINANCIAL STATEMENTS?

It must be useful!	If you wanted to use a financial report so you could make a decision next week, would you want to use numbers that were only guesses? Would you want information about the cost of eggs in Boston in 1909? Would you want information that was calculated using one method one month and a different method the next month? Of course not—none of this would be useful to you. The highest authority in accounting, the Financial Accounting Standards Board, has stated that the most important quality of the information on financial statements is that it must be *useful*.
Various qualities required	If you were to study more advanced accounting, you would discover a surprising number of separate qualities that are needed to make financial information useful. The most essential of these important qualities is shown on page 274.

FOUR IMPORTANT QUALITIES

The two most important qualities   The table below shows the two most important qualities of financial information:

Quality Name	What It Means	Example	Nonexample
• *Reliability*	Information must be free of material error. It can be verified.	The balance sheet shows that the cash balance of Kline Company is $15,500. Auditors verified this by examining the bank account, which showed $15,501.32.	The Kline Company president reports that the value of some company land is $500,000 because that is what she thinks is correct. She feels the land has this value because it might contain oil.
• *Relevance*	The information would be important enough to make a difference in a decision, if the information were not available.	The loan officer at the bank discovers that the liabilities of Lin Company are $250,000, twice the amount of last year. The loan officer changes her mind about approving a loan.	On one occasion, Lin Company was late making a payment to a creditor. The amount was $100. This information has no effect on the loan officer's decision.

Two other qualities

• *Consistency:* The information on the financial statements should be determined by using the same method of accounting, consistently applied.

• *Comparability:* The information on the financial statements should be comparable both over time and between different companies.

☞QUICK REVIEW☜

- Financial statements are well-organized summarizations of information already recorded. Financial statements (reports) communicate important information to stakeholders.

- There are four general-purpose reports:
    — balance sheet
    — income statement
    — statement of owner's equity
    — statement of cash flows

- Annual reports are prepared by large companies and contain financial reports, footnotes, and "MD & A."

- The most important quality of financial statements is that they must be useful. To be useful, financial statements must have the essential qualities of reliability, relevance, consistency, and comparability.

☞VOCABULARY☜

Annual report: a document, usually prepared by a large corporation, that contains audited financial statements, footnotes, and management discussion and analysis (page 272)

Comparability: the quality of information that makes it comparable between companies and over time (page 274)

Consistency: the quality of information that is prepared using the same methods and procedures (page 274)

Managerial accounting: a kind of accounting that focuses on the detailed information needs of a specific company, rather than on the general public (page 272)

MD & A: "Management discussion and analysis" found in annual reports (page 273)

Relevance: the quality of information that makes it significant or important (page 274)

Reliability: the quality of information that makes it free from material error or bias (page 274)

LEARNING GOAL 13
Identify and Prepare an Income Statement

OVERVIEW

Preparation sequence

When all the financial statements are being prepared, the income statement is normally prepared first. This and the next three learning goals explain each of the financial statements in the same order in which they are normally prepared: income statement (Learning Goal 13), statement of owner's equity (Learning Goal 14), balance sheet (Learning Goal 15), and statement of cash flows (Learning Goal 16).

INTRODUCTION

What the income statement shows

The *income statement* shows the change in owner's equity that was caused by the business operations. *Remember:* "Operations" means the process of creating and selling desired resources.

> *Note:* Activities that are incidental to, but not directly part of, operations are also shown. They usually appear under the title "other."

The income statement formula

The basic formula for the income statement is: $R - E = NI$ (or NL), where:

- "R" means total revenues
- "E" means total expenses
- "NI" and "NL" mean net income and net loss.

Reason for the income statement

Revenues and expenses are the *most powerful* force of change on the condition of the business.

All the efforts that go into operating the business show up in the amount of revenues and expenses. There is great interest in revenues and expenses among all users of financial statements. Financial statement users want to identify and analyze the individual amounts of revenues and expenses. To provide this detail, the revenues and expenses are identified individually on a separate statement—the income statement.

In Learning Goal 13, you will find:

▼ *What It Is and the Four Steps to Prepare It*

FEATURES OF THE INCOME STATEMENT

Time period	Unlike the balance sheet, the income statement is for a *period of time*.
Why a period of time?	The date of an income statement shows a period of time because the income statement shows change, and *change happens over time*. This could be a month, a quarter, a year, etc. Notice in the example below for Jack's Guitar School that the date is "for the *month ended* June 30, 2000." Therefore, this is the operational change in owner's equity that happened during June.
Individual sections	There is a separate section for revenues and another section for expenses.
Synonyms	Other names for the income statement are: • *statement of earnings* • *operating statement/statement of operations* • *profit and loss statement* • *P & L statement*

FEATURES OF THE INCOME STATEMENT (continued)

Example

Jack's Guitar School Income Statement For the Month Ended June 30, 2000		
Revenues		
Instruction fees		$2,900
Expenses		
Rent expense	$800	
Supplies expense	150	
Utilities expense	100	
Telephone expense	70	
Total expenses		1,120
Net income		$1,780

CHECK YOUR UNDERSTANDING

?

Fill in each blank space with the correct word. The answers are below.

The date of an income statement is for a _____ of _____, because the income statement shows _____. This is different than a balance sheet, which shows the condition of the business at a _____ in time.

What the income statement explains is the _____ _____in owner's equity. This is caused by _____ and _____.

ANSWERS

The date of an income statement is for a period of time, because the income statement shows change. This is different than a balance sheet, which shows the condition of the business at a point in time.

What the income statement explains is the operational change in owner's equity. This is caused by revenues and expenses.

FOUR STEPS IN PREPARING AN INCOME STATEMENT

Summary of steps

The following pages show you how to prepare an income statement in four basic steps. Here is a summary of the steps:

1) Write the title.
2) List the revenues (type and amount).
3) List the expenses (type and amount).
4) Calculate and enter net income (or loss) and enter it on the statement.

STEP 1	
Action	**Rule**
Write the title.	The title is always prepared in the following order: 1) name of company 2) name of statement 3) time period

Example

Jack's Guitar School **Income Statement** **For the Month Ended June 30, 2000**

STEP 2	
Action	**Rule**
List the revenues (type and amount).	● If there are separate types of revenues, the total of each type is always shown. ● If there is more than one type, show the largest total first. ● The total of all revenues is always shown above the expenses.

Source of the numbers

The numbers for this income statement come from the totals of the revenue and expense transactions that are recorded for Jack's Guitar School (see page 245).

FOUR STEPS IN PREPARING AN INCOME STATEMENT (continued)

STEP 3	
Action	**Rule**
List the expenses (type and amount).	• If there are separate types of expenses, the total of each type is always shown (examples are wages expense, supplies expense, etc.). • The total of all expenses is always shown below the revenues.

Note: There are different ways to list expenses, but we will put the *largest expenses first.* Listing expenses this way makes it easy to quickly see the expenses that reduced the net income the most.

Example of Steps 2 and 3

Jack's Guitar School
Income Statement
For the Month Ended June 30, 2000

Revenues		
Instruction fees		$2,900
Expenses		
Rent expense	$800	
Supplies expense	150	
Utilities expense	100	
Telephone expense	70	
Total expenses		1,120

STEP 4	
Action	**Rule**
Calculate and enter net income (or loss).	• *Net income* or *net loss* is always calculated by subtracting total expenses from total revenues. (The completed statement is on page 278.)

Rule for dollar signs

A dollar sign ($) is placed next to the top number in any column of numbers. A dollar sign is also placed next to the final total—the number above the double line.

Learning Goal 13: Identify and Prepare an Income Statement

Quick Review

The income statement Also called: • operating statement • P & L statement • profit and loss statement • statement of earnings • statement of operations			
explains ...			
the *operational* changes in *owner's equity*			
and contains ...			
• revenues • expenses			

Vocabulary

Income statement: a report that explains the operational changes in owner's equity for a specific period of time (page 276)

Net income: when revenues exceed expenses (page 280)

Net loss: when expenses exceed revenues (page 280)

Operating statement: another name for the income statement (page 277)

P & L statement: another name for the income statement (page 277)

Profit and loss statement: another name for the income statement (page 277)

Statement of earnings: another name for the income statement (page 277)

Statement of operations: another name for the income statement (page 277)

PRACTICE FOR LEARNING GOAL 13

SOLUTIONS FOR LEARNING GOAL 13 BEGIN ON PAGE 301.

Learning Goal 13 concerns the identification and preparation of the income statement. Use these three problems to practice the material you just read.

REINFORCEMENT PROBLEMS

1) **Prepare an income statement.** On July 1, 2001, David Running-Elk begins his new orthopedic medical practice with an investment of $37,000 which he has borrowed from his friends and relatives. As of the end of the first month of operation, the bookkeeper has determined the balances for the items you see below. On a separate sheet of paper, use the correct items to prepare an income statement for David Running-Elk, M.D., for the month of July.

Accounts Payable	$ 1,100	Fees Earned	$ 4,250
Unearned Revenue	$ 500	Equipment	$35,000
Supplies	$ 700	Utilities Expense	$ 150
Cash	$ 8,500	Note Payable	$ 9,000
Wages Expense	$ 850	Accounts Receivable	$ 3,100
Rent Expense	$ 1,500	Interest Expense	$ 300
Drawings	$ 1,000	Prepaid Insurance	$ 750

2) **Missing information—prepare an income statement.** An analysis of the owner's equity of the De Anza Operating Company shows the following items for the year ended December 31, 2000.

Rent Expense	$12,000	Supplies Expense	?	Owner Withdrawals	$5,000
Service Revenue Earned	?	Wages Expense	$7,500	Utilities Expense	$2,000
Advertising Expense	$3,000				

Other information: The net income for the year was $10,000. On January 1, the company had $3,000 of supplies and on December 31, the company had $5,000 of supplies. During the year, the company purchased $4,000 of supplies.

Required: On a separate sheet of paper, prepare an income statement for the De Anza Operating Company. Show calculations separately and in good form.

3) **Business operations.** You know that the income statement explains the effect of business operations on the owner's equity. Operations affect the owner's equity in two ways. What are the two ways?

A)

B)

LEARNING GOAL 14
Identify and Prepare a Statement of Owner's Equity

REVIEW

What it shows

The *statement of owner's equity* explains *all* the changes in owner's equity for a specific period of time. The statement of owner's equity combines the *operational* change in owner's equity from the income statement *with the rest of the changes* in owner's equity. The rest of the changes are:

1) owner's investments; and
2) owner's withdrawals.

The owner's equity statement formula

The formula for the statement of owner's equity consists of three parts: beginning balance + (current changes) = ending balance.

There are three possible current changes:

1) net income or net loss (+/–)
2) owner's investment (+)
3) owner's withdrawals (–)

Net income combines two effects

Question: We previously said that there are four major changes that can affect owner's equity: revenues, expenses, investments, and withdrawals. So why do we see only three current changes on the statement of owner's equity?

Answer: Two of the changes—revenues and expenses—are combined into one number—net income (or net loss)—from the income statement.

In Learning Goal 14, you will find:

▼ *What It Is and the Four Steps to Prepare It*

▼ *What It Is and the Four Steps to Prepare It*

FEATURES OF THE STATEMENT OF OWNER'S EQUITY

Date	Like the income statement, the statement of owner's equity is for a *period of time*, because it is a statement that shows change.
Same final balance as shown on the balance sheet	The final balance on the statement of owner's equity is the same balance of owner's equity as on the balance sheet. The statement of owner's equity is simply itemizing the current changes to arrive at the final balance of owner's equity.
Synonym	The statement of owner's equity is sometimes called the **capital statement**.
Example	*Note:* Beginning balance is zero because this is a new business.

Jack's Guitar School
Statement of Owner's Equity
For the Month Ended June 30, 2000

Jack Davis, Capital, June 1		$ 0
Add: Owner investment		12,000
	Net income	1,780
		13,780
Less: Drawings		1,000
Jack Davis, Capital, June 30		$12,780

CHECK YOUR UNDERSTANDING

?

Fill in each blank space with the correct word. The answers are on page 285.

The statement of owner's equity is for a _____ of time and summarizes _____ the changes in owner's equity. The statement has three parts: 1) the _____ balance of owner's equity; 2) the _____ _____; and 3) the _____ balance. The ending balance of owner's equity must be the same number as the owner's equity that appears on the _____ _____.

ANSWERS
The statement of owner's equity is for a period of time and summarizes all the changes in owner's equity. The statement has three parts: 1) the beginning balance of owner's equity; 2) the current changes; and 3) the ending balance. The ending balance of owner's equity must be the same number as the owner's equity that appears on the balance sheet.

FOUR STEPS IN PREPARING THE STATEMENT OF OWNER'S EQUITY

Summary of steps

The following pages show you how to prepare a statement of owner's equity in four basic steps. Here is a summary of the steps:

1) Write the title.
2) Enter the beginning balance (with description).
3) Enter the current changes (with descriptions).
4) Calculate the ending balance (with description) and verify it.

STEP 1	
Action	**Rule**
Write the title.	The title is always prepared in the following order: 1) name of company 2) name of statement 3) time period

Example

> **Jack's Guitar School**
> **Statement of Owner's Equity**
> **For the Month Ended June 30, 2000**

STEP 2	
Action	**Rule**
Enter the beginning balance (with description).	The beginning balance is always: • the ending balance from the *prior* statement of owner's equity or balance sheet, or • for a new business, the beginning balance of owner's equity is zero.

Learning Goal 14: Identify and Prepare a Statement of Owner's Equity

FOUR STEPS IN PREPARING THE STATEMENT OF OWNER'S EQUITY (continued)

STEP 3	
Action	**Rule**
Enter the current changes (with descriptions).	The possible current changes are: • net income (or loss) from the income statement • owner investments • owner withdrawals

Example

The beginning balance and current changes for Jack's Guitar School are shown below.

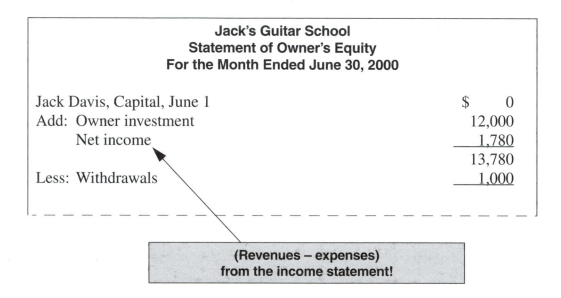

Jack's Guitar School
Statement of Owner's Equity
For the Month Ended June 30, 2000

Jack Davis, Capital, June 1	$ 0
Add: Owner investment	12,000
Net income	1,780
	13,780
Less: Withdrawals	1,000

(Revenues – expenses)
from the income statement!

STEP 4	
Action	**Rule**
Calculate the ending balance (with description) and, verify it.	• The ending balance is calculated by adding/subtracting the three possible current changes to the beginning balance. • The ending balance is verified by checking that it is the same amount as the owner's equity showing on the balance sheet.

Example

An example of the completed statement of owner's equity for Jack's Guitar School is on page 284.

☙QUICK REVIEW☙

The income statement	The statement of owner's equity		
Also called: • operating statement • P & L statement • profit and loss statement • statement of earnings • statement of operations	Also called: • capital statement		
explains ...	**explains ...**		
the *operational* changes in *owner's equity*	*all* the changes in *owner's equity*		
and contains ...	**and contains ...**		
• revenues • expenses	• net income (loss) • investments • withdrawals		

☙VOCABULARY☙

Capital statement: another name for the statement of owner's equity (page 284)

Statement of owner's equity: the financial statement that explains all the changes in owner's equity (page 283)

PRACTICE FOR LEARNING GOAL 14

SOLUTIONS FOR LEARNING GOAL 14 BEGIN ON PAGE 302.

Learning Goal 14 concerns the identification and preparation of the statement of owner's equity. Use these two problems to practice the material you just read.

REINFORCEMENT PROBLEMS

1) **Prepare a statement of owner's equity.** On July 1, 2001, David Running-Elk began his new orthopedic medical practice with an investment of $37,000 which he has borrowed from his friends and relatives. As of the end of the first month of operation, the bookkeeper has determined the balances for the items you see below. On a separate sheet of paper, use the correct items to prepare a statement of owner's equity for David Running-Elk, M.D., for the month of July. Remember that you can use the information on the income statement that you already prepared in the Practice section for Learning Goal 13 (see page 282, Reinforcement Problem #1).

Accounts Payable	$ 1,100	Fees Earned	$ 4,250
Unearned Revenue	$ 500	Equipment	$35,000
Supplies	$ 700	Utilities Expense	$ 150
Cash	$ 8,500	Note Payable	$ 9,000
Wages Expense	$ 850	Accounts Receivable	$ 3,100
Rent Expense	$ 1,500	Interest Expense	$ 300
Drawings	$ 1,000	Prepaid Insurance	$ 750

2) **Missing information—prepare a statement of owner's equity.** Lucy Palangian, the owner of West Valley Company, wants you (her assistant) to prepare a statement of owner's equity and to determine the net income or loss for the year ended December 31, 2000. Unfortunately, there is no detailed information that shows individual revenue or expense transactions.

Luckily, the owner does remember that she invested $15,000 in the business this year and withdrew $5,300 for personal expenses. The balance of owner's equity on January 1, 2000 was $3,800. On December 31, total assets are $41,000 and total liabilities are $37,000.

Required: On a separate sheet of paper, prepare a statement of owner's equity. Then tell the owner the net income or loss for the year. Show any calculations clearly and in good form.

LEARNING GOAL 15

Identify and Prepare a Balance Sheet

In Learning Goal 15, you will find:

▼ *What It Is and the Four Steps to Prepare It*

▼ *What It Is and the Four Steps to Prepare It*

FEATURES OF THE BALANCE SHEET

Date	The *balance sheet* is like a flash picture—it shows assets and claims on assets at a point in time. Notice that in the example on page 290 for Jack's Guitar School, the date is a point in time—June 30—meaning at the end of the business day on June 30. The date is not for a period of time, like "the month of June."
It balances	The total claims on assets equal the total assets. In the example, the total assets are $13,150. The creditors' claims of $370 + the owner's claim of $12,780 = $13,150.
Individual sections	The assets, liabilities, and owner's equity are each presented in their own sections, and the total is calculated for each section.
Format: report form and account form	The side-by-side presentation of assets and equities in the example is called the *account form* of the balance sheet. Sometimes the form of the balance sheet varies slightly, with all assets shown at the top of a page, and the liabilities and owner's equity shown underneath the assets. Such a format is called the *report form*.

FEATURES OF THE BALANCE SHEET (continued)

Synonym	The balance sheet is sometimes called the ***statement of position*** or the ***statement of condition***.
Source of the information	The asset and liability amounts come from the ending balances of the individual accounting equation items for Jack's Guitar School (see pages 244 and 245). The owner's equity is the ending balance that was calculated in the statement of owner's equity.

See it as a photograph. Try to remember the balance sheet as a "flash photograph" of the business at a moment in time.

Example: completed balance sheet (account form)

Jack's Guitar School
Balance Sheet
June 30, 2000

Assets		Liabilities	
Cash	$6,350	Accounts payable	$ 170
Accounts receivable	1,250	Unearned revenues	200
Supplies	50	Total liabilities	370
Equipment	5,500		
		Owner's Equity	
		Jack Davis, Capital	12,780
Total assets	$13,150	Total liabilities and owner's equity	$13,150

This must also be the ending balance on the statement of owner's equity on page 284.

CHECK YOUR UNDERSTANDING

Fill in each blank space with the correct word. The answers are on page 291.

The balance sheet is also called the statement of _____ or the statement of _____.
The balance sheet is like a flash _____ of a business. The source of information for a balance sheet is the _____ balances of the individual accounting equation items.

Learning Goal 15: Identify and Prepare a Balance Sheet

ANSWERS

The balance sheet is also called the statement of position or the statement of condition. The balance sheet is like a flash picture of a business. The source of information for a balance sheet is the ending balances of the individual accounting equation items.

FOUR STEPS IN PREPARING A BALANCE SHEET

Summary of steps

The following pages show you how to prepare a balance sheet in four basic steps. Here is a summary of the steps:

1) Write the title.
2) Enter the asset and liability names, and amounts.
3) Enter the owner's equity and verify it.
4) Total the assets, and then total the liabilities and owner's equity.

STEP 1	
Action	**Rule**
Write the title.	The title is always prepared in the following order: 1) name of company 2) name of statement 3) date *(NOT a time period)*

Jack's Guitar School
Balance Sheet
June 30, 2000

FOUR STEPS IN PREPARING A BALANCE SHEET (continued)

STEP 2	
Action	**Rule**
Enter the asset and liability names, and amounts.	**Assets:** • Assets are listed in order of liquidity. ***Liquidity*** means how quickly an asset can be turned into cash. The most liquid asset is cash, so it is written first. The next most liquid asset is accounts receivable, and so on. This takes a little practice, but after working some problems, you will soon be doing it perfectly. • Assets must be totaled. A <u>double line</u> indicates a total. **Liabilities:** • Liabilities are listed in the order in which they will probably require payment. There is no exact order here, but often accounts payable are written first. • Liabilities must be totaled. A line is not necessary.

Jack's Guitar School
Balance Sheet
June 30, 2000

Assets		Liabilities	
Cash	$ 6,350	Accounts payable	$170
Accounts receivable	1,250	Unearned revenues	200
Supplies	50	Total liabilities	370
Equipment	5,500		
		Owner's Equity	
Total assets	$13,150		

STEP 3	
Action	**Rule**
Enter the owner's equity and verify it.	• Use the ending balance on the statement of owner's equity to find the amount of owner's equity. • Owner's equity must be labeled by writing the owner's name followed by the word "capital." • Owner's equity is *verified* by subtracting total liabilities from total assets.

Learning Goal 15: Identify and Prepare a Balance Sheet

FOUR STEPS IN PREPARING A BALANCE SHEET (continued)

STEP 4	
Action	**Rule**
Total the assets, and then total the liabilities and owner's equity.	• The total of the liabilities and the owner's equity is always shown. It must be equal to the total assets.

Example

The completed balance sheet for Jack's Guitar School is on page 290. Notice that total assets of $13,150 minus total liabilities of $370 verify owner's equity of $12,780.

Rule for dollar signs ($)

A dollar sign ($) is placed next to the top number in any column of numbers. A dollar sign is also placed next to the final total—the number above the double line.

> *Note:* Some preparers of financial statements omit dollar signs entirely, because they believe that it is understood that all amounts are in U.S. dollars. (Do not do this without checking with your instructor or supervisor.)

☞ QUICK REVIEW ☜

The income statement	The statement of owner's equity	The balance sheet	
Also called: • operating statement • P & L statement • profit and loss statement • statement of earnings • statement of operations	**Also called:** • capital statement	**Also called:** • statement of position • statement of condition	
explains ...	explains ...	shows ...	
the *operational* changes in *owner's equity*	*all* the changes in *owner's equity*	the condition of a business at a point in time	
and contains ...	and contains ...	and contains ...	
• revenues • expenses	• net income (loss) • investments • withdrawals	• assets • liabilities • owner's equity	

☞ VOCABULARY ☜

Account form: a balance sheet format in which assets are placed on the left side of page, and liabilities and owner's equity are placed on the right side (page 289)

Balance sheet: a report that shows the assets and claims on assets as of a specific date (page 289)

Liquidity: how quickly an asset can be turned into cash (page 292)

Report form: a balance sheet format in which assets are placed at the top of a page, and liabilities and owner's equity are placed underneath the assets (page 289)

Statement of condition: another name for the balance sheet (page 290)

Statement of position: another name for the balance sheet (page 290)

SOLUTIONS FOR LEARNING GOAL 15 BEGIN ON PAGE 304.

Learning Goal 15 concerns the identification and preparation of the balance sheet. Use these two problems to practice the material you just read.

REINFORCEMENT PROBLEMS

1) **Prepare a balance sheet.** On July 1, 2001, David Running-Elk began his new orthopedic medical practice with an investment of $37,000 which he has borrowed from his friends and relatives. As of the end of the first month of operation, the bookkeeper has determined the balances for the items you see below. On a separate sheet of paper, use the correct items to prepare an account form balance sheet for David Running-Elk, M.D., as of July 31. Remember that you can use the information from the financial statement you prepared for this company in the Practice section for Learning Goal 14 (see page 288, Reinforcement Problem #1).

Accounts Payable	$ 1,100	Fees Earned	$ 4,250
Unearned Revenue	$ 500	Equipment	$35,000
Supplies	$ 700	Utilities Expense	$ 150
Cash	$ 8,500	Note Payable	$ 9,000
Wages Expense	$ 850	Accounts Receivable	$ 3,100
Rent Expense	$ 1,500	Interest Expense	$ 300
Drawings	$ 1,000	Prepaid Insurance	$ 750

2) **Missing information—prepare a balance sheet.** The Fulton Avenue Company shows the balances of the following balance sheet items as of April 30, 2001:

Cash:	$25,000	Accounts Receivable:	$?	Don Chen, Capital:	?
Supplies:	$?	Accounts Payable:	$12,000	Equipment:	$10,000

Other information: On the March 31 balance sheet, the balance of supplies was $1,000. During April, Fulton Avenue Company purchased $7,000 of supplies and used $4,000 of supplies. On April 30, the total liabilities and owner's equity are $41,000.

Required: On a separate sheet of paper, prepare the Fulton Avenue Company balance sheet as of April 30. Show any calculations clearly and in good form.

LEARNING GOAL 16
Identify the Statement of Cash Flows

OVERVIEW

Why it is important	Like a plant without water, a business will soon die without enough cash. Owners and managers always want to know exactly why business cash is increasing or decreasing.
What it does	The *statement of cash flows* is a report that explains the change in a company's cash balance during a specific period of time—the same period of time that corresponds to the income statement and the statement of owner's equity. The change that is explained is the difference between the total cash showing on one balance sheet and the total cash appearing on the next balance sheet.
Three types of change in cash	The change in the cash balance is explained by categorizing the cash transactions into three possible categories. Each category is a major activity in which there can be inflows or outflows of cash. The three categories are: 1) operating activities 2) investing activities 3) financing activities

OPERATING ACTIVITIES

Definition	*Operating activities* are the inflows and outflows of cash that are caused by regular business operations.
Examples	• cash paid to employees • cash paid to vendors of materials used in operations • cash received from customers • cash received from interest earned • cash paid for interest expense
Nonexamples	See the examples for investing and financing activities on page 297.

INVESTING ACTIVITIES

Definition	***Investing activities*** are the inflows and outflows of cash that are caused by acquiring and disposing of assets which are generally long-term in nature, or are owned only as investments.

Examples	• cash paid to buy equipment • cash paid to invest in stocks • cash paid to make a loan • cash paid to buy computers • cash received from selling equipment • cash received from an investment

Nonexamples	See the examples for operating and financing activities.

FINANCING ACTIVITIES

Definition	***Financing activities*** are the inflows and outflows of cash that are caused by borrowing, and by the investments and withdrawals of the owner(s).

Examples	• cash received from a loan • cash received from the owner(s) investment • loan paid to a lender • cash paid to an owner

EXAMPLE OF A STATEMENT OF CASH FLOWS

The net cash flow	The statement of cash flows for Jack's Guitar School is shown on page 298. The ***net cash flow*** (the net change in cash) for June was a net increase of $6,350.

EXAMPLE OF A STATEMENT OF CASH FLOWS (continued)

The ending cash balance ties to the balance sheet	Because this is a new business, the beginning cash balance was zero, so the ending cash balance is also $6,350. If you look again at the June 30 balance sheet on page 290, you will see that *this balance exactly corresponds to the amount of cash showing on the balance sheet.*
Example	What you see below is a simple statement of cash flows.

Jack's Guitar School
Statement of Cash Flows
For the Month Ended June 30, 2000

Cash flows from **operating** activities:		
Receipts:		
Cash collections from customers		$ 1,850
Payments:		
Cash payments for expenses		1,000
Net cash provided by operating activities		850
Cash flows from **investing** activities:		
Purchase of equipment		(5,500)
Cash flows from **financing** activities:		
Investment by owner	$12,000	
Withdrawal by owner	(1,000)	
Net cash provided by financing activities		11,000
Net increase in cash		6,350
Cash balance June 1, 2000		–0–
Cash balance June 30, 2000		$ 6,350

USING THE STATEMENT FOR ANALYSIS

Examine each activity

The idea behind the statement of cash flows is to *explain* why cash changed. Therefore, you must examine each activity that appears on the statement.

- Operating activities caused a net inflow of cash of $850. Operating activities are the most important part of the statement. Operations are the recurring and regular sources and uses of cash. Operations should generally be a dependable source of cash flow.
- The investing activities used up $5,500 of cash (outflow) with purchases of equipment.
- Finally, the financing activities show that the owner invested $12,000 and later withdrew $1,000 for a net inflow from financing activities of $11,000. There was no borrowing or payments to lenders.

CHECK YOUR UNDERSTANDING

?

Fill in each blank space with the correct word. The answers are below.

The statement of cash flows is prepared in order to show the change in the _____ balance that occurred during the same period of time as the _____ statement and the statement of _____ _____.

There are three types of activities that can affect the cash. The first type, called _____ activities, explains the change in cash caused by operations. Second, _____ activities explain the change caused by acquiring and selling assets. Finally, _____ activities explain the change resulting from borrowing and the owner's actions.

ANSWERS

The statement of cash flows is prepared in order to show the change in the cash balance that occurred during the same period of time as the income statement and the statement of owner's equity.

There are three types of activities that can affect the cash. The first type, called operating activities, explains the change in cash caused by operations. Second, investing activities explain the change caused by acquiring and selling assets. Finally, financing activities explain the change resulting from borrowing and the owner's actions.

ᔢ QUICK REVIEW ᔢ

The income statement	The statement of owner's equity	The balance sheet	The statement of cash flows
Also called: • operating statement • P & L statement • profit and loss statement • statement of earnings • statement of operations	Also called: • capital statement	Also called: • statement of position • statement of condition	
explains ...	explains ...	shows ...	explains ...
the *operational* changes in *owner's equity*	*all* the changes in *owner's equity*	the condition of a business at a point in time	all the changes in the cash balance
and contains ...	and contains ...	and contains ...	and contains ...
• revenues • expenses	• net income (loss) • investments • withdrawals	• assets • liabilities • owner's equity	• operating activities • investing activities • financing activities

ᔢ VOCABULARY ᔢ

Financing activities: inflows and outflows of cash that are caused by borrowing, and by owner's investments and withdrawals (page 297)

Investing activities: inflows and outflows of cash that are caused by acquiring and disposing of assets (page 297)

Net cash flow: the net change in cash during any specified time period (page 297)

Operating activities: inflows and outflows of cash that are caused by regular business operations (page 296)

Statement of cash flows: a report that explains the change in the cash balance during a specific period of time (page 296)

SOLUTIONS FOR LEARNING GOAL 13

PRACTICE QUESTIONS FOR LEARNING GOAL 13 BEGIN ON PAGE 282.

1) Income statement:

David Running-Elk, M.D.
Income Statement
For the Month Ended July 31, 2001

Revenues		
Fees earned		$4,250
Expenses		
Rent expense	$1,500	
Wages expense	850	
Interest expense	300	
Utilities expense	150	
Total expenses		2,800
Net income		$1,450

2) There are two good ways to find the missing information for a financial statement problem:
   A) One good way to is to actually prepare the statement using the amounts available, and then fill in or calculate the amounts you identified as missing. This helps you visually identify what you need to do.
   B) A second, and faster, way is simply to use the relationships that exist on the income statement. This is always: Revenues – expenses = net income.

Using the first method:

De Anza Operating Company
Income Statement
For the Year Ended December 31, 2000

Revenues		
Service revenue earned		$?
Expenses		
Rent expense	$12,000	
Wages expense	7,500	
Advertising expense	3,000	
Utilities expense	2,000	
Supplies expense	?	
Total expenses		
Net income		$10,000

Supplies Expense is the supplies used up: $3,000 (balance on January 1) + $4,000 purchased – X used up = $5,000 (balance on December 31). Therefore, $7,000 – X = $5,000. The supplies used up is $2,000.

Service Revenue Earned is the sum of net income plus the total expenses. Now that you know Supplies Expense, you can calculate the total expenses as $26,500. Therefore, total revenue is $10,000 + $26,500 = $36,500.

If you use the second method: R – (12,000 + 7,500 + 3,000 + 2,000 + S) = 10,000. After you calculate Supplies Expense, you have: R – 26,500 = 10,000. Therefore, revenue is $36,500.

Whichever method you use, you can now complete the income statement.

Learning Goal 16: Identify the Statement of Cash Flows

SOLUTIONS FOR LEARNING GOAL 13

PRACTICE QUESTIONS FOR LEARNING GOAL 13 BEGIN ON PAGE 282.

2B) *continued*

De Anza Operating Company Income Statement For the Year Ended December 31, 2000		
Revenues		
Service revenue earned		$36,500
Expenses		
Rent expense	$12,000	
Wages expense	7,500	
Advertising expense	3,000	
Utilities expense	2,000	
Supplies expense	2,000	
Total expenses		26,500
Net income		$10,000

3) The owner's equity is changed by the operational effects of A) revenues and B) expenses.

SOLUTIONS FOR LEARNING GOAL 14

PRACTICE QUESTIONS FOR LEARNING GOAL 14 BEGIN ON PAGE 288.

1) Statement of Owner's Equity:

David Running-Elk, M.D. Statement of Owner's Equity For the Month Ended July 31, 2001		
David Running-Elk, Capital, July 1, 1999		$ –0–
Add: Initial investment by owner	$37,000	
Net income	1,450	
Subtotal		38,450
Less: Withdrawals		(1,000)
David Running-Elk, Capital, July 31, 1999		$37,450

(The statement of owner's equity explains the David Running-Elk, Capital, balance of $37,450 on the balance sheet.)

2) As before, with any "missing information" financial statement problem, there are two good ways to set up the problem and identify what you need to do. You can either:
   A) Prepare a statement using the amounts available, so you can identify what is missing; or
   B) You can use the formula relationship that the statement is based on.

SOLUTIONS FOR LEARNING GOAL 14

PRACTICE QUESTIONS FOR LEARNING GOAL 14 BEGIN ON PAGE 288.

2) *continued*

Method A) A statement using the amounts available:

West Valley Company
Statement of Owner's Equity
For the Year Ended December 31, 2000

Lucy Palangian, Capital, January 1, 2000		$ 3,800
Add: Investment by owner	$15,000	
Net income/loss	?	
Subtotal		
Less: Withdrawals		(5,300)
Lucy Palangian, Capital, December 31, 2000		$?

Method B) Use the formula that the statement is based on: Beginning balance + (net income/(loss) + investments – withdrawals) = ending balance. Filling in what you know: $3,800 + net income/(loss) + $15,000 – $5,300 = ending balance.

Reviewing the information, you see that you know total assets and total liabilities on December 31, so therefore you can calculate the balance of owner's capital as A – L = OE, or $41,000 – $37,000 = $4,000 on December 31.

Once you know the ending balance, you can complete the statement by filling in the difference as a net loss on the statement, or by calculating it in the formula as: $3,800 + X +$15,000 – $5,300 = $4,000. Therefore, X = – 9,500 (a net loss).

West Valley Company
Statement of Owner's Equity
For the Year Ended December 31, 2000

Lucy Palangian, Capital, January 1, 2000		$ 3,800
Add: Investment by owner		15,000
Less: Withdrawals	(5,300)	
Net (Loss)	(9,500)	
Subtotal		(14,800)
Lucy Palangian, Capital, December 31, 2000		$ 4,000

Learning Goal 16: Identify the Statement of Cash Flows

SOLUTIONS FOR LEARNING GOAL 15

PRACTICE QUESTIONS FOR LEARNING GOAL 15 BEGIN ON PAGE 295.

1)

David Running-Elk, M.D.
Balance Sheet
July 31, 2001

Assets		Liabilities	
Cash	$ 8,500	Accounts payable	$ 1,100
Accounts receivable	3,100	Unearned fees revenue	500
Supplies	700	Note payable	9,000
Prepaid insurance	750	Total liabilities	10,600
Equipment	35,000		
		Owner's Equity	
		David Running-Elk, Capital	37,450
Total assets	$48,050	Total liabilities and owner's equity	$48,050

NOTES

- Owner's equity is calculated as $48,050 total assets – $10,600 total liabilities = $37,450.
- $ signs are generally used at the top of a column and at the total of the column.
- Always double-check that the title is correctly written, and especially that the date is proper.

2) To prepare this balance sheet, you have to calculate the following:

Supplies: This is $1,000 (March 31 balance) + $7,000 purchased – $4,000 used = $4,000 (April 30 balance).

Accounts Receivable: To calculate this, we need to know the total assets. Because the balance sheet is based on the accounting equation A = L + OE, we know that total assets equal the total liabilities and owner's equity of $41,000. If total assets are $41,000, we can subtract $25,000 of this for cash, $4,000 for supplies, and $10,000 for equipment. What is left must be accounts receivable of $2,000.

Don Chen, Capital: If total liabilities and owner's equity equal $41,000, and we know the only liability is accounts payable of $12,000, then Don Chen, Capital must be $41,000 – $12,000 = $29,000.

Fulton Avenue Company
Balance Sheet
April 30, 2001

Assets		Liabilities	
Cash	$25,000	Accounts payable	$12,000
Accounts receivable	2,000		
Supplies	4,000	**Owner's Equity**	
Equipment	10,000	Don Chen, Capital	29,000
Total assets	$41,000	Total liabilities and owner's equity	$41,000

Format note: Because there is only one liability, we do not have to write "total liabilities" and repeat the number.

Learning Goal 16: Identify the Statement of Cash Flows

LEARNING GOAL 17
Compare, Contrast, and Connect All the Financial Statements

In Learning Goal 17, you will find:

▼ *Comparing the Four Financial Statements*

▼ *Comparing the Four Financial Statements*

REVIEW

Four statements

There are four general-purpose financial statements:

- income statement
- statement of owner's equity
- balance sheet
- statement of cash flows

THE FOUR GENERAL-PURPOSE FINANCIAL STATEMENTS

One condition statement and three change statements compared

The table below compares the features and functions of the condition statement (balance sheet) and the three change statements.

The Condition Statement is ...	The Change Statements are ...		
The balance sheet Also called: • statement of position • statement of condition	**The income statement** Also called: • operating statement • P & L statement • profit and loss statement • statement of earnings • statement of operations	**The statement of owner's equity** Also called: • capital statement	**The statement of cash flows**
shows ...	**explains ...**	**explains ...**	**explains ...**
the condition of a business at a point in time	the *operational* changes in *owner's equity*	*all* the changes in *owner's equity*	all the changes in the cash balance
and contains ...	**and contains ...**	**and contains ...**	**and contains ...**
• assets • liabilities • owner's equity	• revenues • expenses	• net income (loss) • investments • withdrawals	• operating activities • investing activities • financing activities
and is structured ...	**and is structured ...**	**and is structured ...**	**and is structured ...**
A = L + OE	R – E = Net Income (or Loss)	beginning balance + net income (loss) + investments – drawings = ending balance	beginning balance + operating activities + investing activities + financing activities = ending balance

WHAT ARE THE CONNECTIONS BETWEEN THE STATEMENTS?

Each balance sheet is linked to the next one

As you can see in the above table, each change statement explains changes in certain key parts of the balance sheet—the owner's equity and the cash balances. You could say that the change statements form "links" between one balance sheet and the next.

Learning Goal 17: Compare, Contrast, and Connect All the Financial Statements

WHAT ARE THE CONNECTIONS BETWEEN THE STATEMENTS? (continued)

Example: two balance sheets

Suppose that you prepared the balance sheet for a company as of June 30 and later prepared another balance sheet for that company as of July 31:

Explain the changes in the owner's equity and cash

- You want to explain why the owner's equity is different on the July 31 balance sheet from the June 30 balance sheet.
- You also want to explain why the cash balance on the July 31 balance sheet is different than on the June 30 balance sheet. How can the changes in these items be explained? By preparing statements that show change!

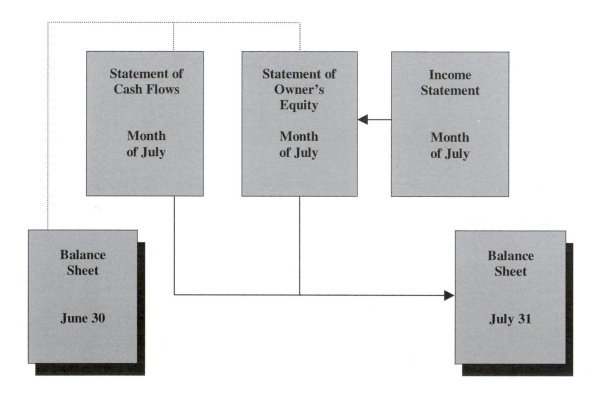

WHAT ARE THE CONNECTIONS BETWEEN THE STATEMENTS? (continued)

Prior balance sheet provides the beginning balances	The line from the June 30 balance sheet (see page 307) to the statement of cash flows and the statement of owner's equity means the following: ● The July 1 beginning cash balance on the statement of cash flows, before any July transactions, comes from the June 30 balance sheet. ● The July 1 beginning owner's equity balance on the statement of owner's equity, before any July transactions, also comes from the June 30 balance sheet.
Current period transactions complete the links	The link to the July 31 balance sheet by each change statement is completed like this: ● All the current period July transactions that affect cash are summarized on the statement of cash flows, which shows the ending cash balance as of July 31. ● All the current period July transactions that affect owner's equity are summarized on the statement of owner's equity and the income statement. The statement of owner's equity shows the ending balance as of July 31. The ending balances showing on the statement of cash flows and the statement of owner's equity correspond exactly to the same balances on the July 31 balance sheet. The statement of cash flows and the statement of owner's equity now link the June 30 and the July 31 balance sheet balances in cash and owner's equity.
Articulation	Whenever any change statement is connected to another financial statement, this connection is called "articulation."

EXAMPLES OF THE CONNECTIONS

Jack's Guitar School July results	Imagine that you have also recorded the July transactions and prepared the July financial statements for Jack's Guitar School, for which you followed the June transactions in Learning Goal 11. Without actually looking at any specific July transactions, assume that an overview of the results is what you see on page 309, with the cash and owner's equity balances shown to you.

EXAMPLES OF THE CONNECTIONS (continued)

	Prior Balance Sheet June 30			(July changes) Transactions		Current Balance Sheet July 31		
	Assets		**Liabilities**			**Assets**		**Liabilities**
Cash	$6,350	xxx	$$$$		Cash	$22,300	xxx	$$$$
xxx	$$$$	xxx	$$$$	⟶	xxx	$$$$	xxx	$$$$
xxx	$$$$	xxx	$$$$		xxx	$$$$	xxx	$$$$
xxx	$$$$	Owner's Equity	$12,780	⟶	xxx	$$$$	Owner's Equity	$17,420
Totals	**$13,150**		**$13,150**	⟶		**$32,520**		**$32,520**

July changes

You can see that the July transactions are the reasons for changes in the balance sheet amounts. The new balance sheet as of July 31 is clearly different than the previous one. Specifically, we are most interested in the changes in cash and owner's equity.

The cash balance has changed from $6,350 on June 30 to $22,300 on July 31. The owner's equity balance has changed from $12,780 on June 30 to $17,420 on July 31.

Page 311 shows an illustration of the July 31 balance sheet, along with the three change statements *that explain the changes* in cash and owner's equity balances *during July*. These change statements are the "links" between the June 30 and July 31 balance sheet totals of cash and owner's equity.

Cash transaction examples

Suppose that during July:

● the business spends $500 cash to purchase supplies. This transaction will change the cash balance on the balance sheet, and will be included as part of the "Operating activities" explanation on the July statement of cash flows.
● the business spends $4,200 to buy equipment. This transaction will change the cash balance on the balance sheet, and will be explained as "Investing activities" on the July statement of cash flows.

EXAMPLES OF THE CONNECTIONS (continued)

***Owner's equity
transaction examples***

Suppose that during July:

• the business sells $1,500 of teaching services to a customer on account. This transaction will increase the owner's equity on the balance sheet (as well as accounts receivable), and will be explained on the the July income statement as "Revenue."

• the business uses up $200 of supplies in the operations. This transaction will decrease the owner's equity on the balance sheet, and will be explained on the July income statement as "Expense."

• the total revenues exceed the total expenses by $2,940. This net income increases the owner's equity on the balance sheet, and will be detailed on the July income statement and also appear on the July statement of owner's equity.

***More than one
change statement***

Sometimes a transaction may affect both cash and owner's equity.

Examples:

• An owner's cash investment will increase both cash and owner's equity on the balance sheet. Therefore, the transaction will be explained on both the statement of owner's equity and the statement of cash flows.

• Paying cash for an expense item will decrease both owner's equity and cash on the balance sheet. Therefore, this will be part of the income statement and the statement of cash flows.

EXAMPLES OF THE CONNECTIONS (continued)

July Statement of Cash Flows
(The July Changes in Cash)

Operating activities:	
Collections from customers	$33,000
Less: Expense payments	(14,550)
Net cash from operating activities	$18,450
Investing activities:	
Purchase of equipment	(4,200)
Financing activities:	
Owner investments less drawing	1,700
Net change in cash	15,950
Beginning cash balance **July 1, 2000**	6,350
Ending cash balance **July 31, 2000**	**$22,300**

Balance Sheet: July 31

Assets		**Liabilities**	
Cash	$22,300		$$$$
	$$$$		$$$$
	$$$$		$$$$
	$$$$	**Owner's Equity**	$17,420
	$$$$		
Total	$32,520	Total	$32,520

July Statement of Owner's Equity
(All the July Changes in Owner's Equity)

Beginning balance: **July 1**, 2000		$12,780
July transactions:		
Add: Net income	$2,940	
Owner's investments	5,000	
Subtotal		7,940
Less: Owner's drawings		(3,300)
Ending balance: **July 31**, 2000		**$17,420**

July Income Statement
(The July Operational Changes in Owner's Equity)

Revenues		
Instruction fees		$27,390
Expenses		
Wages expense	$12,100	
Advertising expense	11,730	
Supplies expense	300	
Utilities expense	200	
Telephone expense	120	
Total expenses		24,450
Net income		**$ 2,940**

MORE EXAMPLES OF OWNER'S EQUITY CONNECTIONS

Transactions highlighted

So that you can have a good picture of how owner's equity transactions connect the statements, we will look at a very simplified balance sheet of an imaginary company called Uncle Billy's Courier Service. To focus on the idea of how statements are connected, we will look at transactions that happen over the course of one day, December 23. For this example, you will see the changes recorded directly onto the financial statements, so that you can see how the statements are connected by the owner's equity-type transactions.

Note: Individual transactions are not normally recorded directly onto financial statements. We are doing it here just for illustration. Also, to save space, descriptions are abbreviated.

MORE EXAMPLES OF OWNER'S EQUITY CONNECTIONS (continued)

December 23: Here are the beginning balances for Uncle Billy's Courier Service on the morning of December 23, before business begins for the day. The $15,000 cash and capital balances on the balance sheet are the *ending balances from the prior day* (December 22). There are no other assets or liabilities.

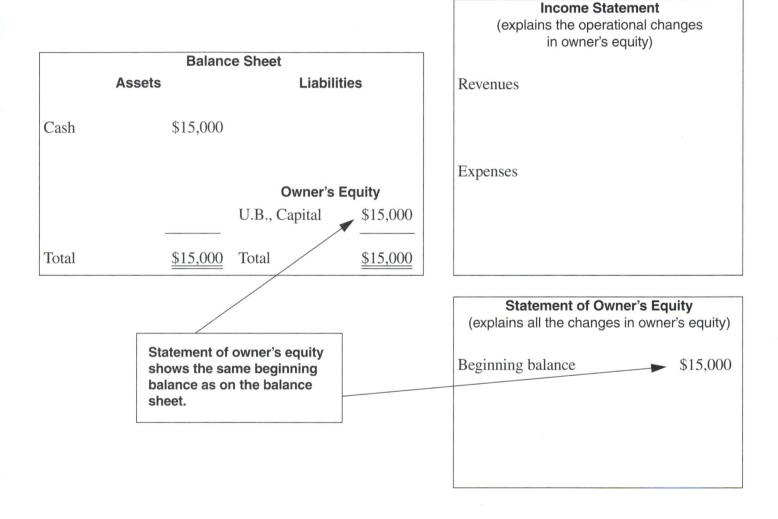

MORE EXAMPLES OF OWNER'S EQUITY CONNECTIONS (continued)

For the first transaction of the day, the business delivers some high-priority documents to the Bedford Falls National Bank. The fee for this service is $3,000. The bank will pay for this service next week, so a $3,000 account receivable is recorded. This is a revenue transaction, so it appears on the income statement. Accounts Receivable increases on the balance sheet and revenue increases on the income statement.

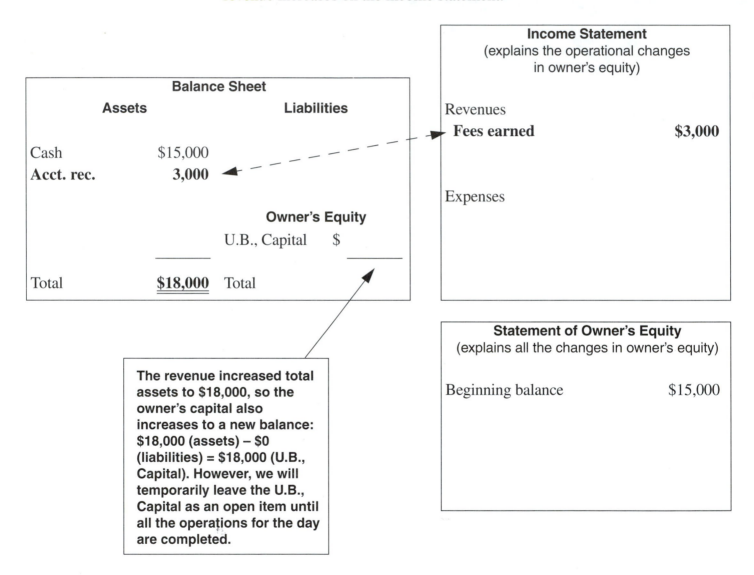

Income Statement
(explains the operational changes in owner's equity)

Revenues
Fees earned   **$3,000**

Expenses

Balance Sheet

Assets		Liabilities
Cash	$15,000	
Acct. rec.	**3,000**	

Owner's Equity

U.B., Capital $ _____

| Total | **$18,000** | Total |

The revenue increased total assets to $18,000, so the owner's capital also increases to a new balance: $18,000 (assets) – $0 (liabilities) = $18,000 (U.B., Capital). However, we will temporarily leave the U.B., Capital as an open item until all the operations for the day are completed.

Statement of Owner's Equity
(explains all the changes in owner's equity)

Beginning balance $15,000

MORE EXAMPLES OF OWNER'S EQUITY CONNECTIONS (continued)

For the next operational transaction of the day, the business pays the landlord $2,000 rent for office space. This changes the balance sheet again, as cash resources are used up to operate the business, and cash decreases to $13,000. This appears as rent expense on the income statement. On the balance sheet, the expense decreased total assets, so the owner's capital also decreases to a new balance: $16,000 (assets) – $0 (liabilities) = $16,000 (U.B., Capital).

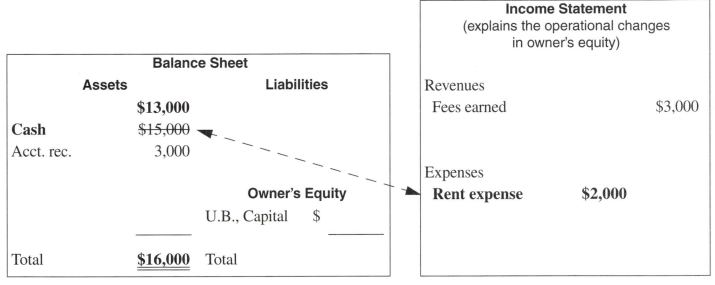

Balance Sheet

Assets		Liabilities
	$13,000	
Cash	$~~15,000~~	
Acct. rec.	3,000	
		Owner's Equity
		U.B., Capital $
Total	**$16,000**	Total

Income Statement
(explains the operational changes in owner's equity)

Revenues	
Fees earned	$3,000
Expenses	
Rent expense	**$2,000**

Statement of Owner's Equity
(explains all the changes in owner's equity)

Beginning balance	$15,000

MORE EXAMPLES OF OWNER'S EQUITY CONNECTIONS (continued)

The final operational transaction of the day occurs when the business uses a consulting firm to help improve efficiency, after the business had a problem with a delivery. The consulting firm sends a bill for $1,500 which will be paid next week. This expense does not affect assets, but it does cause liabilities to increase, so again the owner's capital decreases to a new balance: $16,000 (assets) − $1,500 (liabilities) = $14,500 (U.B., Capital).

Balance Sheet

Assets		**Liabilities**	
Cash	$13,000	**Acct. pay.**	**$1,500**
Acct. rec.	3,000		
		Owner's Equity	
		U.B., Capital	$
Total	$16,000	Total	

Income Statement
(explains the operational changes in owner's equity)

Revenues		
Fees earned		$3,000
Expenses		
Rent expense	$2,000	
Consulting expense	**1,500**	

Statement of Owner's Equity
(explains all the changes in owner's equity)

Beginning balance	$15,000

Learning Goal 17: Compare, Contrast, and Connect All the Financial Statements

MORE EXAMPLES OF OWNER'S EQUITY CONNECTIONS (continued)

Because the day's operations are done, we can now total the income statement. You saw how each income statement transaction changed an asset or a liability on the balance sheet, and effectively connected the income statement with the balance sheet.

The net result of the income statement transactions is a *$500 net loss that is also recorded on the statement of owner's equity*, which reduced the owner's equity to $14,500. This can be verified by subtracting the new liability balance from the new asset balance on the balance sheet ($16,000 − $1,500 = $14,500).

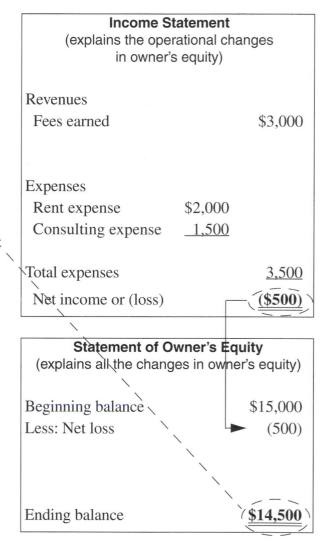

MORE EXAMPLES OF OWNER'S EQUITY CONNECTIONS (continued)

There are also transactions that directly affect both the balance sheet and the statement of owner's equity, but not the income statement. These are owner's direct actions of investments and drawing.

First, suppose that on the morning of December 23, Uncle Billy made a $5,000 investment. That increases cash by $5,000 on the balance sheet. This owner's equity transaction also directly affects the statement of owner's equity.

Income Statement
(explains the operational changes in owner's equity)

Revenues		
Fees earned		$3,000
Expenses		
Rent expense	$2,000	
Consulting expense	1,500	
Total expenses		3,500
Net income or (loss)		($500)

Balance Sheet

Assets		Liabilities	
	18,000		
Cash	$13,000	Acct. pay.	$1,500
Acct. rec.	3,000		
		Owner's Equity	
		U.B., Capital $	
Total	$21,000	Total	

Statement of Owner's Equity
(explains all the changes in owner's equity)

Beginning balance	$15,000
Add: Investment	**5,000**
Less: Net loss	(500)
Ending balance	$

MORE EXAMPLES OF OWNER'S EQUITY CONNECTIONS (continued)

Finally, suppose that in the afternoon (quite a busy day), Uncle Billy decides that he needs $1,000 for personal reasons, and withdraws the money from his business. You can see that this transaction causes cash to decrease on the balance sheet, and is also a reduction of owner's equity on the statement of owner's equity.

If we now total the owner's equity on the statement of owner's equity, and total the balance sheet, we again can see how the owner's direct transactions have connected the statements.

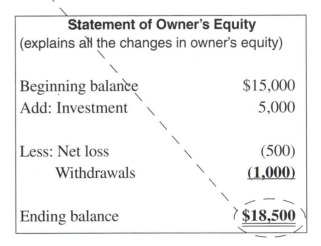

Balance Sheet

Assets		Liabilities	
	$17,000		
Cash	~~$18,000~~	Acct. pay.	$1,500
Acct. rec.	3,000		
		Owner's Equity	
		U.B., Capital	**18,500**
Total	$20,000	Total	$20,000

Income Statement
(explains the operational changes in owner's equity)

Revenues		
Fees earned		$3,000
Expenses		
Rent expense	$2,000	
Consulting expense	1,500	
Total expenses		3,500
Net income or (loss)		($500)

Statement of Owner's Equity
(explains all the changes in owner's equity)

Beginning balance	$15,000
Add: Investment	5,000
Less: Net loss	(500)
Withdrawals	**(1,000)**
Ending balance	**$18,500**

Learning Goal 17: Compare, Contrast, and Connect All the Financial Statements

MORE EXAMPLES OF OWNER'S EQUITY CONNECTIONS (continued)

Summary

What you have seen are accurate, but simplified, examples of how individual owner's equity transactions connect three financial statements. But keep in mind that in "real life":

● Individual transaction data are never entered directly onto financial statements, like we did here. Instead, the data are first recorded and classified in special accounting records over a period of time. Then the data are summarized, and the summary totals are placed on the financial statements. In the next section, you will begin to do this for yourself.

● Financial statements are never prepared "moment by moment" for each individual transaction. This would be impossible and totally unnecessary (actually, crazy). Financial statements are normally prepared at useful intervals such as monthly, quarterly, or annually.

However, you would be perfectly correct to say that the summary totals used on financial statements consist of many individual transactions, many of which are owner's equity transactions that form connections between the statements, as you have seen here.

MORE EXAMPLES OF OWNER'S EQUITY CONNECTIONS (continued)

Owner's Equity Summary   The following table summarizes how owner's equity transactions shown on the change statements also affect the balances on the balance sheet.

Change in Owner's Equity	Change Statement		Condition Statement	
	Income Statement	Statement of Owner's Equity	Effect on Balance Sheet	Examples
			WHEN OWNER'S EQUITY IS INCREASED	
Increase in Owner's Equity	Revenue	Owner Investment	Assets ↑ or Liabilities ↓	• Cash or A/R received when services are performed (Revenue) • Owner invests cash in the business (Owner Investment) • Unearned revenue decreases when services are performed (Revenue) • Owner personally pays business debts (Owner Investment)
			WHEN OWNER'S EQUITY IS DECREASED	
Decrease in Owner's Equity	Expense	Owner Drawing	Assets ↓ or Liabilities ↑	• Cash is used to pay for repairs when done (Expense) • Owner takes cash from the business (Owner Drawing) • Repairs are done, but bill will be paid later (Expense) • Business incurs debt, but owner keeps the money (rare)

Could other change statements be created?   Sure! You could explain the changes in more than just owner's equity and cash. You could design a statement that explains the change in anything else on the balance sheet. For example, a statement of change in accounts receivable could explain all the changes in accounts receivable; a statement of change in notes payable could explain all the changes in notes payable, etc.

In fact, many companies keep informal records analyzing the changes in many balance sheet items (for example, accounts receivable and inventory). However, these records are not prepared as formal financial statements because of time, cost, and other considerations.

Learning Goal 17: Compare, Contrast, and Connect All the Financial Statements

MORE EXAMPLES OF OWNER'S EQUITY CONNECTIONS (continued)

Which statement should you prepare first? It is best to prepare the financial statements in the following order:

1) *Income statement* because net income is used in the statement of owner's equity.
2) *Statement of owner's equity* because the ending balance of owner's equity is the owner's equity on the balance sheet.
3) *Balance sheet* because balance sheets are needed to prepare the statement of cash flows.
4) *Statement of cash flows*.

⤙ QUICK REVIEW ⤚

- There are four general-purpose financial statements:
  — income statement
  — statement of owner's equity
  — balance sheet
  — statement of cash flows

- The balance sheet is a statement of condition at a point in time. The other statements are all "change" statements—they summarize the kinds of transactions that caused changes in either the cash balance or the owner's equity balance on the balance sheet.

- Because the change statements explain the differences between two balance sheets, the change statements can be viewed as the "links" between one balance sheet and the next.

- The connection between a change statement and any other financial statement is called "articulation."

- The kinds of transactions that create connections from one owner's capital balance to the next are:
  — revenues
  — expenses
  — investments
  — withdrawals

PRACTICE FOR LEARNING GOAL 17

SOLUTIONS FOR LEARNING GOAL 17 BEGIN ON PAGE 331.

Learning Goal 17 is about comparing, contrasting, and connecting financial statements. Use these questions and problems to practice what you have learned.

MULTIPLE CHOICE

On the line provided, enter the letter of the best answer for each question.

1) If revenue of $1,000 is earned and received in cash, then _____
   A) assets will increase and revenue will appear on the statement of owner's equity.
   B) assets will decrease and revenue will appear on the statement of owner's equity.
   C) assets will decrease and expense will appear on the statement of owner's equity.
   D) assets will increase and revenue will appear on the income statement.

2) If the owner withdraws $1,000 in cash, then _____
   A) assets will decrease and expense will appear on the statement of owner's equity.
   B) assets will decrease and revenue will appear on the statement of owner's equity.
   C) assets will decrease and drawing will appear on the statement of owner's equity.
   D) assets will decrease and drawing will appear on the income statement.

3) An income statement _____
   A) details all the changes in owner's equity.
   B) shows total assets, liabilities, and owner's equity.
   C) shows the revenues and expenses at a specific date.
   D) none of the above.

4) If a telephone expense of $500 appears on the income statement, then _____
   A) assets have decreased and expenses will appear on the statement of owner's equity.
   B) either assets have increased and/or liabilities have decreased.
   C) either assets have decreased and/or liabilities have increased.
   D) none of the above.

5) If Service Fees Earned of $10,000 appears on the income statement, then _____
   A) assets have increased and expenses will decrease on the income statement.
   B) either assets have increased and/or liabilities have decreased because of this.
   C) either assets have decreased and/or liabilities have increased because of this.
   D) none of the above.

6) Four kinds of transactions affect owner's equity, but the statement of owner's equity only shows three change items: 1) net income/(loss); 2) owner's investments; and 3) owner's drawings. This is because _____
   A) owner's drawings need to be considered as an expense.
   B) owner's investments are never counted as a change.
   C) showing four changes would be an overstatement.
   D) the revenues and expenses are combined into one number.

7) If accounts receivable have increased by $1,500, then most likely _____
   A) the owner has invested in the business.
   B) revenue has been earned.
   C) expenses have been incurred.
   D) none of the above.

PRACTICE FOR LEARNING GOAL 17

SOLUTIONS FOR LEARNING GOAL 17 BEGIN ON PAGE 331.

8) One balance sheet prepared on March 31 is linked by the other financial statements to the next balance sheet prepared on April 30 because _____
   A) the statement of cash flows for April explains the difference between the two cash balances.
   B) revenues and expenses on the April income statement affect the owner's equity on the balance sheet.
   C) the drawings and owner investments on the April statement of owner's equity affect the owner's equity on the balance sheet.
   D) all of the above.

9) The Mikado Tea Shop income statement for the month of October 2001 shows a net loss of $14,000. There were no withdrawals or investments. Which of the following is not true?
   A) The statement of owner's equity will show a decrease of $14,000.
   B) Total assets on the balance sheet have decreased and/or total liabilities will have increased.
   C) Expenses have exceeded revenues.
   D) The change in the cash balance can be determined from this information.

10) The statement of cash flows is primarily _____
   A) a statement of condition.
   B) a statement of equity.
   C) a statement of change.
   D) none of the above.

11) The three types of activities that change the cash balance are _____
   A) operating, investing, and withdrawing.
   B) operating, recording, and financing.
   C) operating, investing, and financing.
   D) none of the above.

12) You are interested in investing in a company. Which financial statement(s) would you use to analyze the profitability of the company?
   A) statement of owner's equity or statement of cash flows
   B) statement of owner's equity and income statement
   C) income statement
   D) balance sheet

13) You are a supplier of auto parts. Kansas City Company wants to make a large purchase from you on account, with payment in 30 days. Which financial statement(s) would you use to find out how much debt Kansas City Company already has coming due in the near future, and how much available cash it has?
   A) statement of cash flows
   B) statement of owner's equity and income statement
   C) income statement
   D) balance sheet

14) Financial statements are usually prepared in the following order:
   A) balance sheet, income statement, statement of cash flows, owner's equity statement
   B) income statement, balance sheet, statement of cash flows, owner's equity statement
   C) income statement, owner's equity statement, balance sheet, statement of cash flows
   D) the order varies among accountants.

15) On an income statement, the net loss is $7,000 and total expenses are $50,000. Total revenue _____
   A) is $43,000.
   B) is $57,000.
   C) is greater than $57,000.
   D) cannot be determined with this information.

SOLUTIONS FOR LEARNING GOAL 17 BEGIN ON PAGE 331.

16) On the statement of owner's equity for Pettigrew Company, the ending balance of owner's equity is $90,000, the net loss was $10,000, owner's drawings were $12,000, and the owner's investment was $5,000. What is the beginning balance of owner's equity?
   A) $107,000
   B) $100,000
   C) $73,000
   D) none of the above

17) During the month of October, total assets of Macon Company increased by $50,000 and total liabilities increased by $30,000. If the owner had invested $5,000 but did not withdraw anything, then the income statement will show ____
   A) a net income of $15,000.
   B) a net income of $20,000.
   C) a net loss of $20,000.
   D) a net income of $80,000.

18) A balance sheet is often called by the name ____
   A) statement of cash flows.
   B) P & L statement.
   C) statement of position.
   D) operating statement.

19) The financial statements which show change in a business are ____
   A) the balance sheet, the income statement, and the statement of owner's equity.
   B) the balance sheet, the income statement, and the statement of cash flows.
   C) the income statement, statement of owner's equity, and the statement of cash flows.
   D) the income statement and the balance sheet.

20) Which financial statement is similar to a "flash photograph" of a business?
   A) the balance sheet
   B) the income statement
   C) the statement of cash flows
   D) the statement of owner's equity

PRACTICE FOR LEARNING GOAL 17

SOLUTIONS FOR LEARNING GOAL 17 BEGIN ON PAGE 331.

REINFORCEMENT PROBLEMS

1) **Which statement is it on?** The following table shows items that occur in the four financial statements. Place an "✗" in the correct space to identify which financial statement the item appears on. The financial statements are for the month ending May 31 and the condition as of May 31 of the Bill Jones Company. Use the first item as an example.

Item	Balance Sheet	Income Statement	Statement of Owner's Equity	Statement of Cash Flows
Office Supplies	✗			
Service Revenue				
Accounts Payable				
Net Loss				
Withdrawals (Drawing)				
Financing Activities				
Bill Jones, Capital—May 31				
Wages Expense				
Net Income				
Accounts Receivable				
Operating Activities				
Investing Activities				
Rent Expense				
Bill Jones, Capital—May 1				
Unearned Revenue				
Wages Payable				
Cash				
Prepaid Rent Expense				

SOLUTIONS FOR LEARNING GOAL 17 BEGIN ON PAGE 331.

2) **Identifying where items appear on the financial statements.** Place an "**✗**" in the correct box to indicate which part of either the income statement or the balance sheet an item appears on. Use the first item as an example.

	Income Statement		Balance Sheet		
	Revenue	**Expense**	**Asset**	**Liability**	**Capital**
A) Cash			✗		
B) Accounts Payable					
C) Interest Revenue					
D) Interest Receivable					
E) Fees Earned					
F) Unearned Revenue					
G) Notes Receivable					
H) Wages Payable					
I) Office Supplies					
J) Office Equipment					
K) Office Supplies Expense					
L) Prepaid Insurance Expense					
M) Dee Markowitz, Capital					

3) **Review: identify which transactions affect owner's equity.** In the table below, indicate whether each transaction increases owner's equity (**+**), decreases owner's equity (**–**), or has no effect on owner's equity (**NE**). Use the first transaction as an example.

Transaction	Effect
A) The owner invests $7,500 in his business.	**+**
B) The business earns service revenue and receives $500 cash.	
C) The business buys $100 of office supplies on account.	
D) The business buys $2,000 of equipment for cash.	
E) The business pays rent expense of $1,500.	
F) The business earns service revenue for $1,000 on account (accounts receivable).	
G) The business pays the $100 account payable for the purchases of supplies.	
H) The owner withdraws $200 cash.	
I) The business collects $1,000 cash from the account receivable.	

PRACTICE FOR LEARNING GOAL 17

SOLUTIONS FOR LEARNING GOAL 17 BEGIN ON PAGE 331.

4) **You be the teacher—grade the financial statements!** You have just given a weekly quiz and asked the students to prepare financial statements for the month of November 2001. Here is a paper from one of your students who has just taken the quiz. Each mistake is minus one point. The three statements together are worth 30 points. Grade the exam. What score would you give? (Mistakes are from actual exams.)

Moorpark Repair Services
Balance Sheet
November 30, 2001

Assets		Debts	
Cash	$10,900	Accounts payable	$ 2,000
Equipment	$15,440	Wages payable	$540
Supplies	$95	Total	$ 2,540
Accounts receivable	$1,050		
		Owner's Equity	
		Diane Smith, Capitol	$24,485
Total	$27,385	Total liabilities and owner's equity	$27,385

Moorpark Repair Services
Income Statement
November 30, 2001

Revenues		
Service revenues	$44,200	
Unearned revenues	3,500	
Total revenues		47,700
Expenses		
Wages expense	$24,100	
Rent expense	4,950	
Prepaid expenses	4,100	
Telephone expenses	290	
Total expenses		33,440
Profit		$14,260

Moorpark Repair Services
Statement of Owner's Equity
For the Period Ending November 30, 2001

Diane Smith, Capital, November 1		$ 6,325
Add: Owner investment	$ 5,000	
Net income	14,620	
		19,620
Less: Withdrawals		1,000
Diane Smith, Capital, November 30		$24,945

Learning Goal 17: Compare, Contrast, and Connect All the Financial Statements

PRACTICE FOR LEARNING GOAL 17

SOLUTIONS FOR LEARNING GOAL 17 BEGIN ON PAGE 331.

5) **Calculate missing financial statement balances using information from other financial statements.** For each of the four separate businesses below, fill in the missing amounts for 2001.

	Mheta Tarsal Medical School	Lynne Guinni Cooking College	Pop Flies Baseball Clinic	Manuel Dexterity Acting Academy
JANUARY 1, 2001				
Assets	$ 75,000	$100,000	G _____	$120,000
Liabilities	$ 15,000	$ 20,000	$ 15,000	J _____
Owner's Equity	A _____	D _____	H _____	K _____
DECEMBER 31, 2001				
Assets	$120,000	$112,000	$ 51,000	L _____
Liabilities	$ 40,000	E _____	$ 1,000	$ 50,000
Owner's Equity	B _____	F _____	I _____	$ 22,000
CHANGE IN OWNER'S EQUITY DURING 2001				
Owner Investment	C _____	$ 12,000	$ -0-	$ 10,000
Revenues	$ 52,000	$ 82,000	$ 49,000	$ 98,000
Expenses	$ 35,000	$ 71,000	$ 22,000	$178,000
Withdrawals	$ 5,000	$ 3,000	$ 8,000	$ -0-

6) **Prepare financial statements—use them for a decision.** Robert Jimenez started his real estate sales business on January 1, 2000 with an investment of $10,000. At year-end on December 31, 2000, Robert gives you a listing of the assets and liabilities as well as the revenues and expenses for the year. Robert withdrew $17,000 during the year. On a separate piece of paper, prepare an income statement and statement of owner's equity for the year ended December 31, 2000, and a balance sheet as of December 31, 2000 in good form.

Robert wants to take the financial statements to his bank in order to apply for a business loan, but he isn't sure what the loan officer will think of them. Based on the information in the financial statements, do you think that Robert's business would be able to borrow money? How much do you think you would lend Robert if you were the banker?

Cash	$38,000	Unearned Fees	$3,800
Notes Payable	10,000	Travel Expense	2,050
Accounts Receivable	12,000	Accounts Payable	1,150
Fees Earned	84,000	Utilities Expense	1,000
Prepaid Insurance Expense	2,500	Insurance Expense	3,000
Rent Expense	18,400	Equipment	15,000

P
R
A
C
T
I
C
E

P
R
A
C
T
I
C
E

P
R
A
C
T
I
C
E

P
R
A
C
T
I
C
E

P
R
A
C
T
I
C
E

P
R
A
C
T
I
C
E

PRACTICE FOR LEARNING GOAL 17

SOLUTIONS FOR LEARNING GOAL 17 BEGIN ON PAGE 331.

7) **Prepare financial statements and determine missing item on the statement of owner's equity.** Listed below are amounts of various financial statement items for the Sanderson Ecology Services Company. From the amounts listed, prepare an income statement and a statement of owner's equity for the year ended December 31, 2000, and a balance sheet as of year-end. Dave Sanderson opened the firm with an investment of $250,000 on January 1. He cannot remember the amount of his drawings. Please tell him.

Service Fees	$122,500	Cash	$199,300
Wages Expense	104,300	Accounts Receivable	43,080
Rent Expense	16,500	Supplies	3,800
Utilities Expense	1,400	Office Equipment	25,600
Supplies Expense	750	Prepaid Insurance	1,500
Advertising Expense	3,300	Accounts Payable	23,750
Travel Expense	8,150	Unearned Service Fees	12,300

8) **Calculate missing information and determine the owner's equity.** When the Traverse City Company had a fire in its office, some of the information on its December 31,1999 and December 2000 balance sheets was destroyed. The bookkeeper summarized all the information like this:

December 31, 1999	
Cash	$25,000
Accounts Receivable	$12,000
Supplies	$4,000
Equipment	$40,000
Accounts Payable	$5,000
J. Dunfield, Capital	?

December 31, 2000	
Cash	$39,000
Accounts Receivable	?
Supplies	$5,000
Equipment	$41,000
Accounts Payable	$20,000
J. Dunfield, Capital	?

The income statements were destroyed, but the owner remembered that the net income for 1999 had been $15,000, and for 2000 it had been $17,000. There were no other changes to owner's equity. The owner hopes that you can fill in the missing information. Can you help the owner?

SOLUTIONS FOR LEARNING GOAL 17

PRACTICE QUESTIONS FOR LEARNING GOAL 17 BEGIN ON PAGE 323.

MULTIPLE CHOICE

1) D.
2) C.
3) D. Choice C is incorrect because it says: "… at a specific date." Revenues and expenses are over a period of time.
4) C. An expense either decreases an asset or increases a liability (see Learning Goal 6 on page 97).
5) B. A revenue either increases an asset or decreases a liability (see Learning Goal 6 on page 97).
6) D. Revenues and expenses are combined as the net income or net loss taken from the income statement.
7) B.
8) D.
9) D.
10) C.
11) C.
12) C.
13) D. You could also find out the cash balance from the statement of cash flows.
14) C.
15) A, because Revenues – Expenses = Net Income. So, R – 50,000 = (7,000). R = 43,000.
16) A, because Beginning Balance + (–10,000 – 12,000 + 5,000) = 90,000. So, Beginning Balance = 107,000.
17) A. Total owner's equity increased by $20,000. There are three possible changes on the statement of owner's equity (net income/(loss), investments, and drawing), but there was no drawing. Therefore, net income is the $20,000 increase minus the increase caused by the investment of $5,000 = $15,000.
18) C.
19) C.
20) A.

SOLUTIONS FOR LEARNING GOAL 17

PRACTICE QUESTIONS FOR LEARNING GOAL 17 BEGIN ON PAGE 323.

REINFORCEMENT PROBLEMS

1)

Item	Balance Sheet	Income Statement	Statement of Owner's Equity	Statement of Cash Flows
Office Supplies	✗			
Service Revenue		✗		
Accounts Payable	✗			
Net Loss		✗	✗	
Withdrawals (Drawing)			✗	
Financing Activities				✗
Bill Jones, Capital—May 31	✗		✗	
Wages Expense		✗		
Net Income		✗	✗	depends on method
Accounts Receivable	✗			
Operating Activities				✗
Investing Activities				✗
Rent Expense		✗		
Bill Jones, Capital—May 1			✗	
Unearned Revenue	✗			
Wages Payable	✗			
Cash	✗			✗
Prepaid Rent Expense	✗			

2)

	Income Statement		Balance Sheet		
	Revenue	Expense	Asset	Liability	Capital
A) Cash			✗		
B) Accounts Payable				✗	
C) Interest Revenue	✗				
D) Interest Receivable			✗		
E) Fees Earned	✗				
F) Unearned Revenue				✗	
G) Notes Receivable			✗		
H) Wages Payable				✗	
I) Office Supplies			✗		
J) Office Equipment			✗		
K) Office Supplies Expense		✗			
L) Prepaid Insurance Expense			✗		
M) Dee Markowitz, Capital					✗

SOLUTIONS FOR LEARNING GOAL 17

PRACTICE QUESTIONS FOR LEARNING GOAL 17 BEGIN ON PAGE 323.

3)

Transaction	Effect
A) The owner invests $7,500 in his business.	+
B) The business earns service revenue and receives $500 cash.	+
C) The business buys $100 of office supplies on account.	NE
D) The business buys $2,000 of equipment for cash.	NE
E) The business pays rent expense of $1,500.	–
F) The business earns service revenue for $1,000 on account (accounts receivable).	+
G) The business pays the $100 account payable for the purchases of supplies.	NE
H) The owner withdraws $200 cash.	–
I) The business collects $1,000 cash from the account receivable.	NE

4)

Balance Sheet Errors	Income Statement Errors	Statement of Owner's Equity Errors
● Assets are in the wrong order. Accounts receivable and supplies should come after cash. ● Addition error. Total assets are actually $27,485. ● The correct terminology to use for a financial statement is "liabilities," not "debts." ● "Total" is used instead of "Total Assets." ● "Capital" is misspelled with an "o." ● The owner's equity cannot be $24,485 if the balance sheet balances but the assets were added incorrectly. ● Dollar signs should only be used for the first number in a column and a final total in a column.	● Date is incorrect. The income statement is for a period, and the date should read "For the Month Ending November 30, 2001." (Making a mistake in the title does not look good!) ● Unearned revenues is a liability, not a revenue. The $3,500 should be part of the liabilities on the balance sheet. ● Prepaid expenses are an asset, not an expense. The $4,100 should be an asset on the balance sheet. ● "Profit" is not the correct terminology for an income statement. The correct term is "Net Income."	● The date is wrong again! The "period ending …" is not correct because a period can be any length of time, and this statement is for a month. It should read "For the month ending …" ● Net income of $14,620 is not the same number as the net income on the income statement. The difference is $360. ● The ending capital balance of $24,945 is not the same balance as the amount of $24,485 on the balance sheet. These numbers must be the same.

Why all these "detail" corrections?
● People must have total confidence in the complete reliability of financial statements.
● Financial statements must be useful and as easy as possible to read. This includes every detail, such as making sure that terminology and format are accurate, clear, and consistent. This takes practice, and now is a good time to begin with the basics.

   Final score? I count 14 mistakes! 30 possible – 14 wrong = *a final score of 16.*

SOLUTIONS FOR LEARNING GOAL 17

PRACTICE QUESTIONS FOR LEARNING GOAL 17 BEGIN ON PAGE 323.

5)

	Mheta Tarsal Medical School	Lynne Guinni Cooking College	Pop Flies Baseball Clinic	Manuel Dexterity Acting Academy
JANUARY 1, 2001				
Assets	$ 75,000	$100,000	G $ 46,000	$120,000
Liabilities	$ 15,000	$ 20,000	$ 15,000	J $ 28,000
Owner's Equity	A $ 60,000	D $ 80,000	H $ 31,000	K $ 92,000
DECEMBER 31, 2001				
Assets	$120,000	$112,000	$ 51,000	L $ 72,000
Liabilities	$ 40,000	E $ 12,000	$ 1,000	$ 50,000
Owner's Equity	B $ 80,000	F $100,000	I $ 50,000	$ 22,000
CHANGE IN OWNER'S EQUITY DURING 2001				
Owner Investment	C $ 68,000	$ 12,000	$ –0–	$ 10,000
Revenues	$ 52,000	$ 82,000	$ 49,000	$ 98,000
Expenses	$ 35,000	$ 71,000	$ 22,000	$178,000
Withdrawals	$ 5,000	$ 3,000	$ 8,000	$ –0–

6)

Robert Jimenez Company
Income Statement
For the Year Ended December 31, 2000

Revenue		
Fees earned		$84,000
Expenses		
Rent expense	$18,400	
Travel expense	2,050	
Utilities expense	1,000	
Insurance expense	3,000	
Total expenses		24,450
Net income		$59,550

Robert Jimenez Company
Balance Sheet
December 31, 2000

Assets		Liabilities	
Cash	$38,000	Accounts payable	$ 1,150
Accounts receivable	12,000	Notes payable	10,000
Prepaid insurance expense	2,500	Unearned fees revenue	3,800
Equipment	15,000	Total liabilities	14,950
		Owner's Equity	
		Robert Jimenez, Capital	52,550
Total assets	$67,500	Total liabilities and owner's equity	$67,500

NOTES

- Owner's equity is calculated as $67,500 – $14,950 = $52,550.
- $ signs are generally used at the top of a column and at the total of the column.
- Always double-check that the title is correctly written, and especially that the date is proper.

Learning Goal 17: Compare, Contrast, and Connect All the Financial Statements

PRACTICE QUESTIONS FOR LEARNING GOAL 17 BEGIN ON PAGE 323.

6) *continued*

Robert Jimenez Company **Statement of Owner's Equity** **For the Year Ended December 31, 2000**		
R. Jimenez, Capital, January 1, 2000		$ –0–
Add: Initial investment by R. Jimenez	$ 10,000	
Net income	59,550	
Subtotal		$69,550
Less: Withdrawals		(17,000)
R. Jimenez, Capital, December 31, 2000		$52,550

Robert could probably get a loan from a bank. The balance sheet shows about $50,000 of cash or items that will quickly turn into cash ($38,000 + $12,000), while there is a need for cash of only about $11,150 assuming that the note payable is due in the near future. Also, the business is very profitable ($84,000 revenues and only $24,450 of expense) which indicates a reliable, continuing business in the future. A bank would probably loan Robert something in the range of 50% of his excess cash.

7)

Sanderson Ecology Services Company **Income Statement** **For the Year Ended December 31, 2000**		
Revenue		
Fees earned		$ 122,500
Expenses		
Wages expense	$104,300	
Rent expense	16,500	
Travel expense	8,150	
Advertising expense	3,300	
Utilities expense	1,400	
Supplies expense	750	
Total expenses		134,400
(Net loss)		$(11,900)

SOLUTIONS FOR LEARNING GOAL 17

PRACTICE QUESTIONS FOR LEARNING GOAL 17 BEGIN ON PAGE 323.

7) *continued*

Sanderson Ecology Services Company **Balance Sheet** **December 31, 2000**				
Assets			**Liabilities**	
Cash	$199,300		Accounts payable	$23,750
Accounts receivable	43,080		Unearned fees revenue	12,300
Supplies	3,800		Total liabilities	36,050
Prepaid insurance	1,500			
Office equipment	25,600			
			Owner's Equity	
			Dave Sanderson, Capital	237,230
Total assets	$273,280		Total liabilities and owner's equity	$273,280

NOTE

● Owner's equity has to be calculated as assets minus liabilities, because no other information is available.

Sanderson Ecology Services Company **Statement of Owner's Equity** **For the Year Ended December 31, 2000**		
Dave Sanderson, Capital, January 1, 2000	**(no prior balance)**	$ –0–
Add: Initial investment by Dave Sanderson	**(fill in)**	250,000
Less: Withdrawals	**(calculate as last number)**	(870)
Net (loss)	**(fill in)**	(11,900)
Subtotal		(12,770)
Dave Sanderson, Capital, December 31, 2000	**(calculate from b/s totals)**	$237,230

Withdrawals can be calculated by filling in the items on the statement of owner's equity and then using the ending owner's equity on the balance sheet for the ending owner's equity on the statement of owner's equity. (Of course, you must remember that information is missing here—otherwise, the statements would be prepared independently and be used to verify each other.)

The amount of the draws can now be determined by calculating the difference between the $250,000 and the ending owner's equity balance of $237,230 less the loss of 11,900. Or, you can make the statement of owner's equity into the form of an equation:

$$\$0 + \$250,000 - X - \$11,900 = \$237,230$$
$$-X = \$870$$
$$X = -\$870.$$

PRACTICE QUESTIONS FOR LEARNING GOAL 17 BEGIN ON PAGE 323.

8)

December 31, 1999	
Cash	$25,000
Accounts Receivable	$12,000
Supplies	$4,000
Equipment	$40,000
Accounts Payable	$5,000
J. Dunfield, Capital	**$76,000**

December 31, 2000	
Cash	$39,000
Accounts Receivable	**$28,000**
Supplies	$5,000
Equipment	$41,000
Accounts Payable	$20,000
J. Dunfield, Capital	**$93,000**

1999 owner's equity: Total assets of $81,000 – total liabilities of $5,000 = $76,000 owner's equity.

2000 owner's equity: 1999 owner's equity of $76,000 + year 2000 income of $17,000 = $93,000. 1999 income is not relevant, because it was already part of the December 31, 1999 owner's equity.

2000 Accounts Receivable: Total liabilities and owner's equity = $20,000 + $93,000 = $113,000. Therefore, total assets must also be $113,000. A/R = $113,000 – $39,000 – $5,000 – $41,000 = $28,000.

Your Questions?

It is *very* important to be aware of what you need to understand better. What do you need to understand better about this learning goal? Use this space to write the questions that you want to discuss with your classmates, instructor, or supervisor. Try to be very specific about what is bothering you, such as explanations that you do not fully understand.

LEARNING GOAL 18
Describe the Conceptual Framework of Accounting

OVERVIEW

Important note	**If you are using this book as a study guide for an accounting class, check with your instructor. Some instructors prefer to cover much of this material at a later time.**
Purpose of this learning goal	The purpose of this learning goal is to give you an overview, or "big picture," of the basic theory and principles of financial accounting. This will give you an understanding of why things are done the way they are in accounting.

In Learning Goal 18, you will find:

▼ *The Conceptual Framework and Its Components*

THE CONCEPTUAL FRAMEWORK

Definition of conceptual framework	The ***conceptual framework*** of accounting is the organized reasoning that explains the basic nature of accounting. The framework justifies why things are done in a certain way, and gives guidance to accountants. It includes the goals of financial reporting.
Examples of conceptual frameworks	To perform any activity well, it is always necessary to precisely set a goal. After that is done, you must understand the basic operation and conditions of the activity. Finally, with experience, you develop rules and principles to follow.
Examples	Here are some examples of "conceptual frameworks" for everyday activities:

Activity	Set Goal(s)	Understand the Activity	Develop Rules and Principles
kick a soccer ball	• score a goal	• force and spin on ball • angles of kicking • effect of other players • weather conditions	• attempt goal when … • pass the ball when …
mow a lawn	• short grass • healthy lawn • attractive lawn	• how mowers work • how lawns grow • different types of grass • what people like to see	• set mower at certain height … • do not mow when wet …
study accounting	• grade of "A" • prepare for job	• the way I learn things • how much time I need • asking questions • priorities	• write notes when … • study schedule of …. • write questions when …

Learning Goal 18: Describe the Conceptual Framework of Accounting

THE CONCEPTUAL FRAMEWORK (continued)

The accounting conceptual framework	The accounting conceptual framework has the same basic parts: **Set goal(s)** ● "Objectives of financial reporting" **Understand the activity** ● "Qualitative characteristics" ● "Elements of financial statements" **Develop rules and principles** ● "Operating Guidelines"

OBJECTIVES OF FINANCIAL REPORTING

Three objectives	What is accounting trying to do? The objectives are shown below. However, the first objective is by far the most important and all-inclusive. The objectives of financial accounting are to provide information that: ● is useful in making financial decisions ● helps you understand cash flows ● identifies assets and claims on assets, and the causes of changes in them

QUALITATIVE CHARACTERISTICS

Overview	Accounting creates financial information. This information has many different features, or "qualities." This is a subject that is mostly beyond the scope of this book; however, two important qualities of accounting information are shown on page 341.

QUALITATIVE CHARACTERISTICS (continued)

Examples of qualitative characteristics	• *Reliability:* How reliable is the information? How is it verified? • *Relevance:* Is all information equally important? What should be excluded? There are numerous other important characteristics, but the two mentioned above are the most important. In more advanced classes, you will study the qualitative characteristics of financial information.

ELEMENTS OF FINANCIAL STATEMENTS

Definition	***Elements of financial statements*** are the items that appear on the financial statements.
Why they are important	You have already learned many of these. The elements of financial statements are important because if people do not understand them, then the financial statements are unusable.
Examples	• *Balance sheet elements:* assets, liabilities, and owner's equity • *Income statement elements:* revenues and expenses

OPERATING GUIDELINES

Definition	***Operating guidelines*** are the rules, assumptions, and limitations that accountants must use for guidance when deciding how to do something.

OPERATING GUIDELINES (continued)

Various (and confusing) names used	The operating guidelines consist of three basic parts. Unfortunately, the guidelines are frequently referred to by different names by different people. This can be really confusing.
	For example, sometimes the word "concepts" is used to mean all of the different individual parts of operating guidelines. At other times, "concepts" is used to refer to basic assumptions. Sometimes the words "concepts" and "principles" are used interchangeably. Even though the ideas are consistent, the words can be very confusing.
Our labels	We will use the most common labels here. However, if you are reading another accounting book and find a different name, don't panic. Just take a moment to compare it to what you see below, and it will be clear.
	Described below are some simple, accurate, and easy-to-use definitions of the three operating guidelines.
Principles	"Principles" are rules or methods to be followed when doing accounting work. Principles say: "how to … ." In accounting, these are called ***Generally Accepted Accounting Principles***, or just simply ***GAAP*** (pronounced *gap*).
Underlying assumptions	"Underlying assumptions" are the basic conditions that must exist in order for the principles to be applied.
Constraints	"Constraints" are limitations on the way in which principles are used, so that improper or ridiculous outcomes do not result even when the correct principles are applied.

▼ *Components of the Operating Guidelines*

GAAP (GENERALLY ACCEPTED ACCOUNTING PRINCIPLES)

What is GAAP?

In the United States, GAAP is a set of rules and standards that guide accountants as to when and how to properly record transactions, and how to prepare proper financial statements. GAAP is not like the laws of physics. GAAP is designed to meet the needs of society. GAAP is always evolving as the economic environment changes. Also, GAAP only refers to rules of accounting in the United States. Different countries have different rules for different purposes.

Broad GAAP

There are a few broad GAAP principles that provide general guidance and that apply to all types of transactions. These are fundamental accounting rules. These are like general traffic laws. Some of these are discussed below.

Specific GAAP

Specific GAAP rules offer specific direction for important kinds of specific situations. As you continue your study of accounting and learn how to record specific types of transactions, you will be learning specific GAAP rules.

Examples of some specific GAAP rules are:

- how uncollectible accounts receivable should be recorded
- acceptable methods for calculating inventory cost
- how interest should be calculated on certain kinds of debt

GAAP (GENERALLY ACCEPTED ACCOUNTING PRINCIPLES) (continued)

Where does GAAP come from?

There is no single source or listing of GAAP! There are a number of different sources, some more important than others.

● *Official Pronouncements:* An official pronouncement is a formal and authoritative document issued by the *Financial Accounting Standards Board (FASB)*, which is the highest standard-setting authority in accounting. The FASB is an independent organization that derives its authority from the Federal Securities and Exchange Commission and the fact that all state licensing boards for accountants accept the FASB pronouncements as highest authority.

The pronouncements of the FASB are called *Statements of Financial Accounting Standards (SFAS)*. An SFAS prescribes how certain kinds of transactions must be recorded and presented. It is the highest authoritative directive.

● *FASB Technical Guides:* The next level below an SFAS is a technical guide, usually dealing with narrow or very specific subject matter.

Examples:
— FASB Technical Bulletins
— AICPA (American Institute of CPAs) Audit and Accounting Guides
— EITF (Emerging Issues Task Force) Positions and Recommendations

● *Industry Practice:* Industry practice is a source of GAAP. Historically, some industry practices have achieved wide acceptance over many years. Sometimes this has created conflict and a lack of consistency within GAAP, because the practices serve the purposes of different groups. This process continues today, to a diminished degree.

● *Other Accounting Literature:* Research publications by educators, journal articles, textbooks, professional association publications, and AICPA technical practice aids are examples of this source of GAAP. These are the least authoritative GAAP sources.

FOUR IMPORTANT BROAD GAAP RULES

Reliability principle

You now know that an important qualitative characteristic of information is that it must be reliable.

In order for this to happen, accountants must follow the reliability principle. This principle requires that accountants record only that information into the accounting system which can be verified by objective evidence.

Examples of objective evidence are documents such as receipts, invoices, canceled checks, bank statements, and verified measurements such as supervised counts of merchandise.

Sometimes in the accounting process, estimates may be required in some situations. This is an especially tricky and difficult problem. To conform to the reliability principle in these situations, the accountant must take extra effort to demonstrate that the estimate is free of bias, was made by a qualified and completely independent person, and conforms as closely as possible to known objective evidence. You will see some examples of accounting estimates later on when you study adjusting entries (Volume 2 in this series).

Cost principle

The "cost principle" is also called the "historical cost principle."

The cost principle requires that all transactions be recorded at original (historical) cost. They must also be stored in the records and presented on the financial statements at historical cost. Historical cost is what was paid or charged for something.

> *Example:* Supplies are purchased for $100, which is $50 less than the price available anywhere else. One week later, the supplies go up in value and could be sold for $180. The cost principle requires that the supplies be recorded at $100, be maintained in the records at $100, and be shown on the balance sheet at $100, even though they are now worth $180.

Why use cost? Because it is reliable. Cost is always verifiable.

MANY PEOPLE DO NOT UNDERSTAND THAT THE BALANCE SHEET DOES NOT NORMALLY SHOW CURRENT MARKET VALUE.

Learning Goal 18: Describe the Conceptual Framework of Accounting

FOUR IMPORTANT BROAD GAAP RULES (continued)

It is important to observe that the balance sheet reports dollar amounts at historical cost, not at current market value. For example, land purchased for $50,000 10 years ago and worth $1,000,000 today is shown on the balance sheet at a cost of $50,000.

Exceptions to historical cost

Note: There are some exceptions to always using only the cost principle. You will learn these later on as you study more accounting.

Revenue recognition principle

The "revenue recognition principle" requires that accountants only record revenue *when it is earned*. As a general rule, revenue from the sale of goods or services is considered earned when all three of the following conditions are satisfied:

• The seller has delivered the correct service or product.
• The amount of revenue is measurable.
• The buyer can reasonably be expected to pay.

The revenue recognition principle is particularly important because many businesses are often too eager to prematurely record revenues in order to show net income at a higher number. The revenue recognition principle is the accountant's guideline when confronting these situations.

You will learn more about this when you study adjusting entries in Volume 2 of this series.

Matching principle

Revenues happen because a business is willing to incur expenses. The "matching principle" requires accountants to identify which expenses have helped to generate which revenues, and then "match" the expenses against those particular revenues. "Match" means subtract the expenses from the revenues.

You will learn more about this when you study adjusting entries in Volume 2 of this series.

FOUR IMPORTANT BROAD GAAP RULES (continued)

Don't confuse "cost" with "expense." The word "cost" means the expenditure of money or other resources to acquire an asset. For example, if a business spends $3,500 to purchase supplies, it has expended money and the cost is $3,500. If the cost is used up in the process of generating business revenues, then the cost becomes an "expense." So, if $500 worth of the supplies is used up, then $500 of the cost becomes $500 of "Supplies Expense."

In practice, the words "cost" and "expense" are often used interchangeably, and you have to be careful about their intended meanings.

UNDERLYING ASSUMPTIONS

Basic conditions

Underlying assumptions are the most basic conditions that *must exist* before GAAP can be applied. If these conditions do not exist, accounting as we know it cannot be used. Underlying assumptions are the "foundation" of the operating guidelines.

The essential underlying assumptions are defined in the illustration on page 349.

MODIFYING CONSTRAINTS

They constrain results

Modifying constraints are rules that are used to make sure that GAAP rules are applied sensibly, and not in some arbitrary way that would result in ridiculous distinctions or foolish outcomes.

- **Materiality:** Strict adherence to GAAP is not required for items not important enough to make a difference to a decision-maker.
- **Conservatism:** When two alternatives equally satisfy GAAP requirements, select the least favorable alternative.
- **Cost/benefit:** The cost of providing specific information should not exceed the benefits to the users of it.

MODIFYING CONSTRAINTS (continued)

Example

The GAAP matching principle requires expenses to be recorded when resources are used up in order to produce revenues.

Suppose that Mega Corporation purchased a $20 wastebasket that would last about 10 years. Literally and technically, GAAP would require the business to record a separate expense of $2 per year for 10 years.

The modifying constraint of *materiality* would say: "Are you kidding? This is so small (not material) that you can record the entire $20 expense when the item is purchased."

ILLUSTRATION OF THE CONCEPTUAL FRAMEWORK OF ACCOUNTING

Overview of all elements

The illustration on page 349 gives you an overview of the conceptual framework of accounting. Notice how operating guidelines work together to achieve reliable and relevant financial statements used for decision-making.

ILLUSTRATION OF THE CONCEPTUAL FRAMEWORK OF ACCOUNTING (continued)

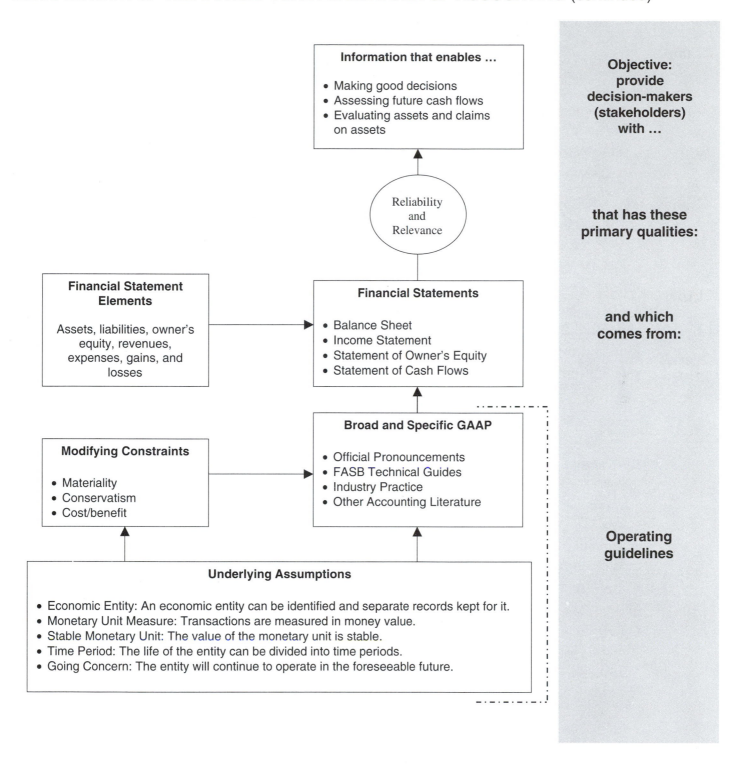

Information that enables ...

- Making good decisions
- Assessing future cash flows
- Evaluating assets and claims on assets

Reliability and Relevance

Financial Statement Elements

Assets, liabilities, owner's equity, revenues, expenses, gains, and losses

Financial Statements

- Balance Sheet
- Income Statement
- Statement of Owner's Equity
- Statement of Cash Flows

Modifying Constraints

- Materiality
- Conservatism
- Cost/benefit

Broad and Specific GAAP

- Official Pronouncements
- FASB Technical Guides
- Industry Practice
- Other Accounting Literature

Underlying Assumptions

- Economic Entity: An economic entity can be identified and separate records kept for it.
- Monetary Unit Measure: Transactions are measured in money value.
- Stable Monetary Unit: The value of the monetary unit is stable.
- Time Period: The life of the entity can be divided into time periods.
- Going Concern: The entity will continue to operate in the foreseeable future.

Objective: provide decision-makers (stakeholders) with ...

that has these primary qualities:

and which comes from:

Operating guidelines

⌐QUICK REVIEW⌐

- The conceptual framework of accounting is the organized reasoning that explains the basic nature of accounting.
- The conceptual framework consists of:
  — objectives of financial reporting
  — qualitative characteristics
  — financial statements and their elements
  — operating guidelines
- GAAP (Generally Accepted Accounting Principles) are the rules that accountants must follow. It is the part of the operating guidelines that you will encounter most frequently.
- GAAP comes from several sources, but the most important authority is the FASB (Financial Accounting Standards Board).
- In addition to GAAP, the other two parts of the operating guidelines are assumptions and constraints.

⌐VOCABULARY⌐

Conceptual framework: the organized reasoning that explains the basic nature of accounting (page 339)

Elements of financial statements: the basic components of financial statements (page 341)

Financial Accounting Standards Board (FASB): the highest standard-setting authority in accounting (page 344)

Generally Accepted Accounting Principles (GAAP): the rules and methods that accountants must follow (page 342)

Operating guidelines: the principles, constraints, and assumptions part of the conceptual framework that gives guidance to accountants (page 341)

Statements of Financial Accounting Standards (SFAS): the official pronouncements of the Financial Accounting Standards Board (page 344)

PRACTICE FOR LEARNING GOAL 18

SOLUTIONS FOR LEARNING GOAL 18 BEGIN ON PAGE 353.

Learning Goal 18 is about the conceptual framework of accounting. Use these questions and problems to practice what you have learned.

MULTIPLE CHOICE
On the line provided, enter the letter of the best answer for each question.

1) GAAP refers to ____
   A) all of accounting theory that is called "generally accepted accounting principles."
   B) basic conditions that must be satisfied for accounting to function correctly.
   C) "generally accepted auditing procedures."
   D) rules or standards that must be followed by accountants when they perform their work, called "generally accepted accounting principles."
2) Which of the following is not a source of GAAP? ____
   A) general industry practice over time
   B) the Internal Revenue Service
   C) the FASB
   D) Emerging Issues Task Force (EITF)
3) When determining the total current value of a business, this information can be found on ____
   A) the balance sheet.
   B) the income statement.
   C) the statement of owner's equity.
   D) none of the above.
4) It would be a good idea to use the balance sheet to ____
   A) determine the current value of the assets.
   B) determine the reasons for the change in the cash balance.
   C) identify the historical costs of assets and the claims against them.
   D) determine the current net income or net loss.
5) Which of the following is true? ____
   A) Historical cost is reliable but is not a good indicator of value.
   B) Historical cost is reliable and is a good indicator of value.
   C) Historical cost is not reliable and is not a good indicator of value.
   D) Historical cost misstates expenses on the income statement.
6) The purpose of the matching principle is ____
   A) to make sure that revenues are matched against the correct expenses of a period.
   B) to make sure that assets are matched against the liability claims on them.
   C) to make sure that expenses are matched against the revenues they helped to create.
   D) none of the above.
7) In July, an architect prepares drawings for a new patio and charges the client $750. The client pays the architect in August. Using the correct method of revenue recognition, ____
   A) the revenue should be recorded in July, because that is when it was earned.
   B) the revenue should be recorded in August, because that is when it was paid.
   C) the revenue is recorded in either July or August because it was earned in July and cash received in August.
   D) the revenue should not be recorded until the expenses related to it are recognized.
8) The historical cost principle ____
   A) requires that all transactions be recorded at original cost.
   B) requires that assets be reported on the balance sheet at original cost.
   C) both A and B.
   D) none of the above.

PRACTICE FOR LEARNING GOAL 18

SOLUTIONS FOR LEARNING GOAL 18 BEGIN ON PAGE 353.

9) Paseo Rancho Castilla Company owns several stores that all together cost $800,000. A buyer calls the company and offers $1,000,000 for the three stores. The company hires an appraiser who says the stores are worth $1,300,000. Based on this information, the company ____
   A) should make no changes to its balance sheet.
   B) should change the assets to $1,300,000.
   C) should change the assets to $1,000,000.
   D) none of the above.

10) Which of the following qualitative characteristics are essential to financial statements? ____
   A) relevance
   B) reliability
   C) both A and B
   D) none of the above

11) "Underlying Assumptions" refers to ____
   A) the specific GAAP rules that accounts use in their daily practice of accounting.
   B) limitations in the way GAAP is properly applied.
   C) the annual decisions by the FASB.
   D) the conditions that must exist in any enterprise if GAAP accounting is to be applied.

12) An American company and a French company both show approximately $1,000,000 of net income. ____
   A) The true increase in the owners' wealth would be the same for both companies.
   B) The net income of the French company is probably incorrect.
   C) The net income of the French company probably cannot be measured according to GAAP rules.
   D) GAAP rules probably apply to both companies.

13) A cost is ____
   A) the amount of money spent on something.
   B) the amount of resources given up to acquire something.
   C) an expense.
   D) a decrease in owner's equity.

14) FASB refers to ____
   A) the Financial Assets Securities Board.
   B) the Financial Accounting Standards Board.
   C) the Financial Auditing Standards Board.
   D) none of the above.

15) An example of a stakeholder would be ____
   A) the owner.
   B) the customer.
   C) the financial analyst.
   D) all of the above.

16) "Operating guidelines" refers to ____
   A) broad GAAP and specific GAAP.
   B) assumptions, constraints, and GAAP.
   C) when to identify and record expenses.
   D) all of the above.

17) A generally accepted accounting principle is ____
   A) a standard or rule that guides accountants on how to do something.
   B) a required condition that must exist for accounting to function.
   C) an objective of financial reporting.
   D) a limitation on the way certain rules can be applied.

SOLUTIONS FOR LEARNING GOAL 18

PRACTICE QUESTIONS FOR LEARNING GOAL 18 BEGIN ON PAGE 351.

MULTIPLE CHOICE

1) D.
2) B. The Internal Revenue Service has rules, but they are about determining the correct amount of tax. This is not an objective of financial reporting.
3) D. Remember the historical cost rule. An appraiser would have to restate the balance sheet. Even this is quite subjective.
4) C.
5) A.
6) C.
7) A. The general rule for recording revenue is when it is earned. This is usually considered to be when a valid sale of a service or product is made.
8) C.
9) A, because the historical cost principle requires that original cost be used.
10) C.
11) D.
12) C.
13) B.
14) B.
15) D.
16) B.
17) A.

Your Questions?

It is *very* important to be aware of what you need to understand better. What do you need to understand better about this learning goal? Use this space to write the questions that you want to discuss with your classmates, instructor, or supervisor. Try to be very specific about what is bothering you, such as explanations that you do not fully understand.

CUMULATIVE VOCABULARY REVIEW

Match each description with the term that it describes. Enter the letter of the correct description in the space provided next to each term on the left. The answer for each term is in the right column.

	Term		Description	Answers
____	1) GAAP	A)	A report, issued annually by publicly held companies, that contains audited financial statements for the current and prior years, as well as a management discussion and analysis of the financial statements.	1P
____	2) Balance sheet	B)	Private organization that conducts accounting research and establishes generally accepted accounting principles.	2H
____	3) Articulation	C)	GAAP, constraints, and underlying assumptions.	3D
____	4) Revenue recognition principle	D)	The connection between the financial statements, such that a change in one statement also causes a related change in another statement.	4J
____	5) Financing activities	E)	A category on the statement of cash flows for transactions involving borrowing and owner's equity.	5E
____	6) Bookkeeping	F)	The financial statement that summarizes the changes in cash over a specific time period.	6S
____	7) Income statement	G)	A GAAP rule that requires that assets be recorded and maintained in the accounting records at their actual (historical) cost.	7K
____	8) Statement of owner's equity	H)	The financial statement that summarizes the amount of assets, liabilities, and owner's equity at a specific date.	8R
____	9) The accounting process	I)	A category on the statement of cash flows for transactions involving investing and long-term assets.	9T
____	10) Matching principle	J)	A GAAP rule that determines when revenues are to be recorded, by requiring that they be recorded in the same time period in which they are earned.	10N
____	11) Operating activities	K)	The financial statement that reports the changes to owner's equity over a specific period of time as a result of revenues and expenses.	11O
____	12) Underlying assumption	L)	Any person or organization that requires financial information about the financial condition or performance of a company.	12Q
____	13) Stakeholder	M)	A phrase referring to a transaction in which a promise to pay is given instead of paying cash immediately.	13L
____	14) FASB	N)	A GAAP rule that determines when expenses are to be recorded, by requiring that expenses be recorded in the same time period as the revenues which the expenses had helped to create.	14B
____	15) Operating guidelines	O)	A category on the statement of cash flows for any cash transactions which occur as part of the revenue-earning operations of a business.	15C
____	16) Investing activities	P)	Authoritative rules and standards that accountants must follow, and that are called "Generally Accepted Accounting Principles."	16I
____	17) Recognize	Q)	Basic conditions which must exist in order for GAAP accounting to be used.	17U
____	18) Statement of cash flows	R)	The financial statement that summarizes all the changes in owner's equity over a specific time period.	18F
____	19) Annual report	S)	The act of processing or recording accounting information.	19A
____	20) Historical cost principle	T)	Analyze, process, communicate.	20G
____	21) "On account"	U)	Meaning to record in the accounting records.	21M

CUMULATIVE TEST SOLUTIONS BEGIN ON PAGE 361.

TIME LIMIT: 55 MINUTES

INSTRUCTIONS

In the space provided, enter the best answer to each question. Do **not** *look back in the book when taking the test. (If you need to do this, you are not ready.) After you finish the test, refer to the answers and circle the number of each question that you missed. Then go to the* **Help Table** *(on page 363) to identify your strong and weak knowledge areas by individual learning goal.*

MULTIPLE CHOICE

On the line provided, enter the letter of the best answer for each question.

1) The accounting process meets the information needs of stakeholders. A stakeholder is _____
   A) either an investor or a creditor.
   B) either an owner or a creditor.
   C) any person or organization who needs financial information about a company.
   D) none of the above.

2) The Mission Advertising Agency recorded purchases of $3,000 of art supplies on account. This transaction would have the following effect: _____
   A) supplies increase by $3,000 and cash decreases by $3,000
   B) cash increases by $3,000 and supplies decreases by $3,000
   C) supplies decrease by $3,000 and accounts payable increases by $3,000
   D) none of the above

3) Information in financial statements must have these two essential important qualities: _____
   A) relevance and timeliness
   B) reliability and accuracy
   C) relevance and reliability
   D) ease of use and accuracy

4) If a balance sheet is presented in such a way that the assets are shown at the top of the page, and liabilities and owner's equity are shown underneath them, then _____
   A) this would be called the report form.
   B) this would be called the account form.
   C) this would be incorrect.
   D) the balance sheet would not balance.

5) On the income statement of Bridgeport Company, net loss is $10,000 and total expenses are $15,000. Total revenue must have been _____
   A) $5,000.
   B) $25,000.
   C) $10,000.
   D) some other amount.

CUMULATIVE TEST SOLUTIONS BEGIN ON PAGE 361.

5) *continued*

Sue Collette started Salem Graphic Arts Services in January 2000. Below are the comparative balance sheet figures for the business as of December 31, 2000 and December 31, 2001. Use these figures to help you answer the multiple choice questions 6) and 7) that follow.

Assets	2000	2001
Cash	$20,200	$ 7,900
Accounts receivable	7,300	4,300
Supplies	900	250
Office equipment	12,500	12,500
Total assets	$40,900	$ 24,950
Liabilities and owner's capital		
Accounts payable	$ 4,100	$ 2,500
Notes payable	5,000	12,450
Sue Collette, Capital	31,800	10,000
Total liabilities and owner's capital	$40,900	$24,950

6) The statement of cash flows for Salem Graphic Arts Services will show how much net change in cash for 2000? ____
   A) $20,200 increase in cash
   B) $21,800 decrease in cash
   C) $12,300 increase in cash
   D) $12,300 decrease in cash

7) If Sue made no investments during 2001, and withdrew $15,000 cash, then the statement of owner's equity for Salem Graphics Arts Services will show how much net income or loss for 2001? ____
   A) $15,950 net income
   B) $950 net loss
   C) $6,800 net loss
   D) $36,800 net income

8) The same item of information appears on what two financial statements? ____
   A) the balance sheet and statement of owner's equity
   B) the income statement and statement of owner's equity
   C) the balance sheet and statement of cash flows
   D) all of the above

9) "Generally Accepted Accounting Principles (GAAP)" refers to ____
   A) the conceptual framework of accounting.
   B) the operating guidelines defined by the FASB.
   C) basic assumptions that must be met by every economic entity.
   D) rules and standards that accountants must follow when doing their work.

10) A business owner has his business appraised. As a result, he increases the value of the assets by $50,000. This is a violation of which principle? ____
   A) the matching principle
   B) the historical cost principle
   C) the reliability principle
   D) the revenue recognition principle

CUMULATIVE TEST: LEARNING GOALS 10 THROUGH 18

CUMULATIVE TEST SOLUTIONS BEGIN ON PAGE 361.

11) If the Guadalupe Street Design partnership earns $1,500 of fees, which of the following is true? _____
   A) Assets will increase or liabilities will decrease on the balance sheet, and revenues will increase on the income statement.
   B) Assets will decrease or liabilities will increase on the balance sheet, and expenses will increase on the income statement.
   C) Owner withdrawals will increase on the statement of owner's equity.
   D) None of the above.

12) The Alexandria Company received $75,000 cash when it sold some equipment. On the statement of cash flows, the change in cash would be classified as part of _____
   A) net income.
   B) investing activities.
   C) financing activities.
   D) operating activities.

13) The owner's capital balance at the end of an accounting period is equal to _____
   A) net income.
   B) the balance at the beginning of the period plus net income minus withdrawals.
   C) the balance at the beginning of the period plus net income plus investments minus withdrawals.
   D) the balance at the beginning of the period plus net income minus liabilities.

14) The income statement is also called the _____
   A) operating statement, profit and loss statement, or P & L statement.
   B) position statement or statement of condition.
   C) operating statement, P & L statement, or position statement.
   D) capital statement.

15) The balance sheet shows _____
   A) assets, expenses, and liabilities.
   B) assets, revenues, and liabilities.
   C) assets, expenses, and owner's equity.
   D) none of the above.

16) If investors were researching a certain large company and needed to obtain financial information from audited financial statements that conformed to generally accepted accounting principles, as well as management's discussion and analysis of the statements, _____
   A) they should review the tax returns of the company before making the investment decision.
   B) they should review the current income statement before making the investment decision.
   C) they should review the annual report before making the investment decision.
   D) they should review *Wall Street Journal* articles before making the investment decision.

17) The recording and processing aspect of the accounting process is called _____
   A) bookkeeping.
   B) accounting.
   C) GAAP.
   D) transaction analysis.

18) The accountant of Harper Insurance Agency sees that $100 of supplies was used up. How should this be recorded? _____
   A) Decrease supplies and increase expenses by $100, thereby decreasing Linda Harper, Capital.
   B) Increase supplies and increase expenses by $100, thereby increasing Linda Harper, Capital.
   C) Decrease cash by $100 and increase expenses by $100, thereby decreasing Linda Harper, Capital.
   D) There would be no change to the owner's capital.

19) The final step in the accounting process is _____
   A) analyzing transactions.
   B) communicating information.
   C) processing transactional information.
   D) auditing financial statements.

CUMULATIVE TEST SOLUTIONS BEGIN ON PAGE 361.

20) Marla and Grace are both taking an accounting class, and are practicing recording transactions.

Marla has recorded cash transactions like this:		Grace has recorded cash transactions like this:		
	Cash		Cash	
			Increase	Decrease
Balance, November 1	?	Balance, November 1	?	
Owner withdrawal	− 1,000	Owner withdrawal		1,000
Collect accounts receivable	+ 2,500	Collect accounts receivable	2,500	
Purchase supplies	− 350	Purchase supplies		350
Service to customer	+ 2,100	Service to customer	2,100	
Balance, November 8	$11,200	Balance, November 8	$11,200	

Because they kept a record of transactions, we can know that the correct November 1 cash balance was _____
A) $14,450 for Marla and $7,950 for Grace.
B) $14,450 for Marla and $14,450 for Grace.
C) $7,950 for Marla and $7,950 for Grace.
D) $7,950 for Marla and $14,450 for Grace.

21) The bookkeeper of Luzerne Company recorded that $3.77 of pencil erasers had been used up during the last year. The bookkeeper has the receipts. This is an example of information quality that is _____
A) reliable but not relevant.
B) relevant but not reliable.
C) relevant and reliable.
D) relevant and reliable, but not timely.

22) The balance sheet is based upon the following relationship: _____
A) Revenues – Expenses = Net Income
B) Beginning balance + (operating, investing, and financing activities) = ending balance
C) Beginning balance + (net income or loss + investments – withdrawals) = ending balance
D) Assets = Liabilities + Owner's Equity

23) Bundsen's Village Coffee Shop has the following balances: Cash $1,000; Meal Revenue $7,000; Utility Expense $850; Wages Expense $2,000; Unearned Revenue $1,500; Prepaid Insurance Expense $700; Rent Expense $2,500; Total liabilities $3,500. The income statement will show net income of _____
A) $1,950.
B) $3,150.
C) $1,650.
D) none of the above.

24) On the statement of owner's equity for Quan Company, the balance of Eric Quan, Capital, on January 1, 1999 is $12,500. On January 31, 1999, it is $10,000. Eric's drawings were $1,000 and his investments were $2,000 during January. Both the statement of owner's equity as well as the income statement show _____
A) net income of $2,500.
B) net loss of $3,500.
C) net income of $500.
D) net loss of $2,500.

25) The financial statement that explains all the sources of cash and all the uses of cash during any accounting period is the _____
A) operating statement.
B) statement of position.
C) capital statement.
D) statement of cash flows.

CUMULATIVE TEST SOLUTIONS BEGIN ON PAGE 361.

26) If the total assets on the balance sheet of Al's Barber Shop increased by $10,000 at the end of the year, with no change in the total liabilities, and if the barber shop was profitable, then _____
   A) the income statement will show net income of $10,000.
   B) if there was no drawing, the statement of owner's equity will show an investment of $10,000.
   C) if there was no drawing, the income statement and the statement of owner's equity will show some combination of net income and owner's investment, totaling $10,000.
   D) none of the above.

27) After a transaction is analyzed, the recording process requires that _____
   A) every item in the accounting equation must show some change.
   B) every item affected by the transaction must show either an increase or decrease.
   C) every item affected by the transaction must show either an increase or decrease, and a new balance.
   D) none of the above.

28) Which of the following is true? _____
   A) The financial information in the balance sheet, income statement, and statement of owner's equity is for a specific period of time, and explains changes.
   B) The financial information in the balance sheet, income statement, and statement of owner's equity is for a specific point in time, and shows condition.
   C) The financial information in the balance sheet is for a specific date, and the information in the income statement and statement of owner's equity is for a specific period of time.
   D) The financial information in the income statement is for a specific date, and the information in the balance sheet and statement of owner's equity is for a specific period of time.

29) The revenue recognition principle _____
   A) requires that revenue be recorded only when it is earned.
   B) requires that revenue must be recorded as soon as the cash is received.
   C) is an example of a narrow or specific GAAP principle, rather than a broad one.
   D) is an example of articulation between financial statements.

30) The ultimate objective described by the conceptual framework is to _____
   A) simplify financial statements.
   B) provide useful information that improves decision-making and analysis.
   C) increase the reliability of audits.
   D) minimize taxes that are paid by businesses.

31) The balance sheet of Lehigh Company included the following balances:

   Cash ?   Accounts Receivable $3,000
   Accounts Payable $18,000   Land $35,000
   Supplies $1,000   Robert Fair, Capital ?
   Unearned Revenue $4,000

   If the balance of Robert Fair, Capital was $55,000 then what was the balance of cash? _____
   A) $34,000
   B) $16,000
   C) $55,000
   D) none of the above

32) Which of the following items does not belong on the income statement? _____
   A) Insurance Expense
   B) Service Revenue Earned
   C) Miscellaneous Expense
   D) Accounts Payable

CUMULATIVE TEST SOLUTIONS BEGIN ON PAGE 361.

33) Which of the following items does not belong on the statement of owner's equity? _____
   A) Net Income
   B) Net Loss
   C) Service Revenue Earned
   D) Prior period ending balance of owner's equity

34) Gillis Company had these balances at the dates indicated:

   Cash (March 1) $?   Cash (March 31) $10,000
   Accounts Receivable (March 1) $5,000   Accounts Receivable (March 31) $3,000
   Supplies (March 1) $1,000   Supplies (March 31) $1,500
   Accounts Payable (March 1) $2,000   Accounts Payable (March 31) $2,500
   Richard Gillis, Capital (March 1) $?   Richard Gillis, Capital (March 31) $?

   Gillis Company had a net loss of $5,000 during March, and there were no withdrawals, but the owner invested $2,000 during March. The correct owner's equity balances for March 1 and March 31 are _____
   A) March 1: $6,000   March 31: $14,500
   B) March 1: $12,000   March 31: $15,000
   C) March 1: $9,000   March 31: $12,000
   D) March 1: $15,000   March 31: $12,000

35) Which financial statement shows the liabilities?
   A) income statement
   B) balance sheet
   C) both A and B
   D) statement of owner's equity

CUMULATIVE TEST SOLUTIONS: LEARNING GOALS 10 THROUGH 18

CUMULATIVE TEST QUESTIONS BEGIN ON PAGE 355.

MULTIPLE CHOICE

1) C.
2) D. Supplies increase by $3,000 and Accounts Payable increase by $3,000.
3) C. These are the two most important qualitative characteristics that make information useful, although there are other characteristics as well.
4) A.
5) A. Using the income statement formula: Revenues – Expenses = Net income/(loss): Revenues – 15,000 = – 10,000. Therefore, Revenues = 5,000.
6) D. ($20,200 – $7,900 = $12,300 decrease)
7) C. Using the formula for the statement of owner's equity, which explains all the changes in the capital balance: beginning balance + net income/(loss) + investments – withdrawals = ending balance. Therefore: 31,800 + **X** + 0 – 15,000 = 10,000. X = –6,800 (a net loss).
8) D. For "A," the item is the ending balance of owner's equity; for "B," the item is net income/(loss); for "C," the item is the ending cash balance.
9) D.
10) B.
11) A.
12) B.
13) C.
14) A.
15) D. The balance sheet shows assets, liabilities, and owner's equity.
16) C. "D" is also a good idea; "A" would be nice, but tax returns would be difficult to obtain.
17) A.
18) A. Using up assets in operations is an expense, and this decreases the owner's claim.
19) B.
20) C. Same transactions and ending balances—the beginning balances must be the same! For any item you can always use the formula: beginning balance + increases — decreases = ending balance, and then solve for whatever the missing item is. Beginning balance + 4,600 – 1,350 = 11,200.   Beginning balance = 7,950.
21) A.
22) D.
23) C. Cash is an asset and would be on the balance sheet. *Unearned* revenue is a liability and would be on the balance sheet. *Prepaid* insurance expense is an asset and would be on the balance sheet. Liabilities would be on the balance sheet.
24) B. You can visualize the statement of owner's equity or you can use the formula for the statement of owner's equity, which is faster. To visualize: beginning balance: $12,500 *plus* owner's investments of $2,000 *plus* net income of ? (or minus net loss of ?) *less* owner's drawing of $1,000 equals the ending balance of $10,000. Putting the data into a familiar format may be easier for you, like this:

Beginning balance	$12,500
Add: Owner's investment	2,000
Net income (or loss)	?
Less: Owner's drawing	1,000
Ending balance	$10,000

Or, you can use a formula: $12,500 + $2,000 + **X** – $1,000 = $10,000.
X = – $3,500 (a net loss).

CUMULATIVE TEST QUESTIONS BEGIN ON PAGE 355.

25) D.

26) C. If total assets increase but total liabilities do not change, then owner's equity must have gone up. There are only three possible items on the statement of owner's equity to explain the change: net income/(loss), investments, and drawing. Loss and drawing did not occur.

27) C.

28) C.

29) A.

30) B.

31) D. Total equities are: $55,000 + $4,000 + $18,000 = $77,000. Therefore, $77,000 – $1,000 –$3,000 – $35,000 = $38,000 cash balance.

32) D.

33) C.

34) D. First, determine the March 31 owner's capital and then use the formula for the statement of owner's equity, which explains all the changes in owner's equity, to work back to the beginning balance. This question should remind you that both the income statement and statement of owner's equity link the owner's equity balances between balance sheets. March 31: Total assets $14,500 – $2,500 liabilities = $12,000 owner's equity. Using the formula in the statement of owner's equity: X – $5,000 + $2,000 = $12,000. X = $15,000 beginning balance of owner's equity.

35) B.

HELP TABLE

Identify Your Strengths and Weaknesses

The questions in this test cover the nine learning goals of Sections III and IV. After you have circled the number of each question that you missed, look at the table below.

Go to the first learning goal category in the table: "Explain the Accounting Process." The second column in the table shows which questions on the test covered this learning goal. Look on the test to see if you circled numbers 1, 17, or 19. How many did you miss? Write this number in the "How Many Missed?" column. Repeat this process for each of the remaining learning goal categories in the table.

If you *miss **two** or more questions* for any learning goal, you are too weak in that learning goal and you need to *review*. The last column shows you where to read and practice so you can improve your score.

Some learning goal categories have more questions because you need to be especially well prepared in these areas. More questions means your performance must be better.

Learning Goal	Questions	How many missed?	Material begins on ...
SECTION III			
10) Explain the Accounting Process	1, 17, 19		page 220
11) Begin to Record	2, 18, 20, 27		page 225
SECTION IV			
12) Describe the Financial Statements	3, 16, 21		page 270
13) Identify and Prepare an Income Statement*	5, 14, 23, 32		page 276
14) Identify and Prepare a Statement of Owner's Equity*	7, 13, 24, 33		page 283
15) Identify and Prepare a Balance Sheet*	4, 15, 22, 31		page 289
16) Identify the Statement of Cash Flows	6, 12, 25		page 296
17) Compare, Contrast, and Connect All the Financial Statements	8, 11, 26, 28, 34, 35		page 305
18) Describe the Conceptual Framework of Accounting	9, 10, 29, 30		page 338

* For Learning Goals 13, 14 and 15, you should also practice preparing a balance sheet, an income statement, and a statement of owner's equity on a blank piece of paper. Use problems in any book for which you also have a solution. (You do not have to prepare a statement of cash flows, but you should be able to identify one and understand what it does.)

Transactions—
Recording in an Accounting System

Overview	This section shows you how to use a traditional accounting system.
Use this section if ...	... you want to learn about a traditional accounting system. This includes debits and credits, journals, ledgers, trial balance, and the accounting cycle.
Do NOT use this section if ...	... you are not clear about how to analyze a transaction (see Section II starting on page 80), or ... debits and credits have already given you a lot of trouble. Study Section III first (starting on page 219), and then return to this section.

LEARNING GOAL 19
Explain the Five Kinds of Information

OVERVIEW

Introduction

In this section, you are introduced to a traditional, general-purpose accounting system. The ultimate purpose of every accounting system is to provide useful information to decision-makers. To do this, five particular kinds of information arrangements are always necessary.

These five kinds of information arrangements are what every general-purpose accounting system must supply to users. Everything that you learn in the rest of this book is a part of these five information arrangements. Learning Goal 19 introduces you to these five arrangements.

Note: If you are reading Section V as a continuation of Section I through Section IV, all the principles that you have learned will continue to apply and will help you here.

In Learning Goal 19, you will find:

▼ *Review of Section I through Section III*

REVIEW

Visualizing the financial condition of a business

In Section I through Section III, you learned how to see the basic financial condition of all businesses. The condition of any business can be shown as a picture that is based on the accounting equation. This equation is: Assets = Liabilities + Owner's Equity. The financial picture of any business looks like this:

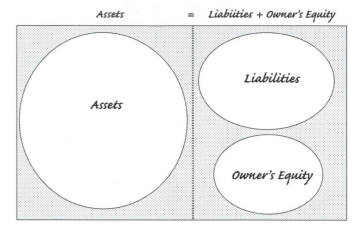

What the picture and the equation both show is that the value of the assets, which is the wealth of a business, is claimed first by creditors and then by the owner.

In Section III, you learned how to record changes in the picture. You learned that we can show the *changes*, called "transactions," in the condition of the business directly in the picture. For example, if we wanted to show the business buying $5,000 of equipment by paying $1,000 cash and signing a $4,000 promissory note, we could show:

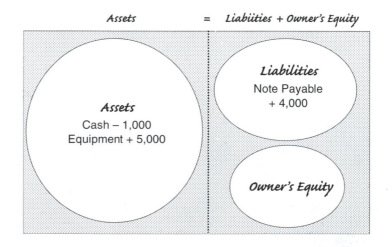

Learning Goal 19: Explain the Five Kinds of Information

REVIEW (continued)

Use a table to show changes	However, a more efficient way to show the changes (transactions) is to use the accounting equation to create a table. We use the table to record all the changes in the individual items in the equation. We can create separate columns for all the items in the accounting equation and record the changes directly in the columns. For example, suppose the Nevada Company has recorded all its transactions in this way for the week beginning May 2. You can prepare a table like this:

Week of May 2	Assets				=	Liabilities + Owner's Equity	
	Cash	Accounts Receivable	Supplies	Equipment		Note Payable	C. Goldman, Capital
5/2 Balance	17,300	4,500	900	12,000		10,000	24,700
5/4 Collection	+ 800	– 800					
5/5 Revenue		+ 1,000					+ 1,000
5/7 Buy supplies	– 400		+ 400				
5/7 Revenue	+ 2,000						+ 2,000

On May 8, the Nevada Company recorded the purchase of $5,000 of equipment by paying $1,000 cash and signing a $4,000 note payable. It would look like this:

Week of May 2	Assets				=	Liabilities + Owner's Equity	
	Cash	Accounts Receivable	Supplies	Equipment		Note Payable	C. Goldman, Capital
5/2 Balance	17,300	4,500	900	12,000		10,000	24,700
5/4 Collection	+ 800	– 800					
5/5 Revenue		+ 1,000					+ 1,000
5/7 Buy supplies	– 400		+ 400				
5/7 Revenue	+ 2,000						+ 2,000
5/8 Buy equipment	– 1,000			+ 5,000		+ 4,000	
5/8 Balance	18,700	4,700	1,300	17,000		14,000	27,700

REVIEW (continued)

An improvement: separate columns for increases and decreases

Finally, we decided that we could improve this method by using a separate increase and decrease column for each item. Separate increase and decrease columns make it much easier to see all the increases and decreases for each element in the accounting equation. No "+" or "−" signs are required. Also, this is what is actually done in practice.

Because assets are on the left side of the equation, we agree to make left-side columns positive for assets. Because liabilities and owner's equity are on the right side of the equation, we agree to make right-side columns positive for liabilities and owner's equity. This is the usual accounting custom.

If we omit the explanation column to save space, the Nevada Company record of transactions will now look like this (beginning and ending balances are on May 2 and May 8):

	Assets								=	Liabilities + Owner's Equity			
	Cash		Accounts Receivable		Supplies		Equipment			Note Payable		C. Goldman, Capital	
	Increase	Decrease	Increase	Decrease	Increase	Decrease	Increase	Decrease	Decrease	Increase	Decrease	Increase
5/2	bal. 17,300		bal. 4,500		bal. 900		bal. 12,000			bal. 10,000		bal. 24,700
5/4	800			800								
5/5			1,000									1,000
5/7		400			400							
5/7	2,000											2,000
5/8		1,000					5,000			4,000		
5/8	bal. 18,700		bal. 4,700		bal. 1,300		bal. 17,000			bal. 14,000		bal. 27,700

▼ *The Five Data Arrangements*

OVERVIEW

Transaction data are important	Transaction data are important. The data are the source of all financial information. Transaction data explain and verify changes in the business.
	The way data are organized and presented can make a tremendous difference in the efficiency of a business. Therefore, data must be organized so that it shows in the clearest possible way the kind of information that a business will need.
	Even if we use computers to electronically process information, the human brain still needs the final results to be presented in a clear, easy-to-use, and well-organized way.
Five data arrangements are necessary	Accountants, after many years of practice, discovered that transaction data must be arranged in a way that meets five basic information requirements. Look again at the table on page 368 showing the transactions of the Nevada Company. The information is arranged in a way that meets the five requirements presented below.

1) FIND A TRANSACTION BY DATE

Chronological listing	To easily locate a transaction by date, there must be a *chronological listing of the transactions* as they happened. The earliest transactions are shown first, and the more recent ones follow. From May 2 on, you can follow the sequence of events and easily locate a transaction by date.
Example	Suppose that you want to find all transactions that happened on May 7. Look at the date column. It is easy to follow it down until you come to May 7 (5/7). It turns out that there were two transactions on May 7. You can now examine the details of each transaction.

2) SEE ALL PARTS OF A TRANSACTION

All parts are easy to see	Once you locate a transaction, it is easy to see *all the individual items in each transaction*. This is because all parts of the transaction appear on the same line.
Example	In the May 8 transaction, the company purchased $5,000 of equipment using some cash and borrowing the balance. If you look on the line for May 8, you can easily see all three items that are affected: Cash decreased by $1,000, Equipment increased by $5,000, and Notes Payable increased by $4,000.

3) SEE IF THE EQUATION STAYS IN BALANCE

Increases and decreases in each transaction	You can easily prove that each transaction keeps the equation in balance. If you look on any line with a transaction, you can quickly see that the increases and decreases in the equation items keep the equation in balance.
Example	In the May 8 transaction, Cash decreased by $1,000 and Equipment increased by $5,000. This is a net $4,000 increase in total assets. On the right side of the equation for May 8, you can see that the liabilities increased by $4,000. The equation remains in balance.

4) SEE THE HISTORICAL DETAIL OF EACH ITEM

A record of all increases and decreases	There is a permanent record of both *the increases and decreases in every item*.

4) SEE THE HISTORICAL DETAIL OF EACH ITEM (continued)

Example

You can select any item in the equation. Suppose you want to know the changes in the cash account for the week beginning May 2. You can see that there was an increase of $800, a decrease of $400, an increase of $2,000, and a decrease of $1,000. Increases and decreases are not netted. Each one is shown separately.

> *Note:* If you want to explain why the cash changed with a particular transaction, then you can examine the parts of any transaction in which you are interested. You could also add an explanation column.

5) DETERMINE THE BALANCE OF EACH ITEM

Calculate the balance whenever you want

You can easily find the *balance of each item* in the equation. A balance can be calculated at any time.

Examples

- Suppose you want to know the balance of Supplies on May 8. Look on the May 8 date line. Under Supplies, the balance shows as $1,300.
- Suppose you want to know how much cash you had on May 6. Just take the beginning balance ($17,300), add any increases through May 6 ($800), and subtract the decreases through May 6 (none). The cash balance on May 6 is $18,100.

"… and I'm telling you, we want FIVE kinds of data arrangements."

CHECK YOUR UNDERSTANDING

?

Fill in each blank space with the correct word. The answers are on page 373.

Transaction data must be arranged in a way that meet five basic information requirements. First of all, transactions are recorded in _____ order. Second, it must be easy to see all the _____ of each transaction. Third, it must be easy to verify that the transaction keeps the accounting _____ in _____. Fourth, there must be a permanent historical record of all the _____ and _____ of each item. Fifth, it must be easy to find the _____ of each item.

What data arrangement is needed? *For each separate situation in the table below, mark the correct box to indicate which information arrangement(s) is (are) required in each situation.*

Situation	Five Basic Information Arrangements				
	(1) Find a transaction by date	**(2)** See all parts of a transaction	**(3)** See if the equation stays in balance	**(4)** See the historical detail of each item	**(5)** Determine the balance of each item
1) The owner wants to know how much cash the business has today.					
2) A tax auditor wants to know for what purpose a large check was written.					
3) The manager wants to know if the property tax payments were made before December 10, to avoid a late payment penalty.					
4) A customer is disputing the balance we are showing in our account receivable from him.					
5) Our business has purchased another business. It is a complex transaction with many changes to the accounting equation.					
6) Before deciding on a loan, the bank wants to know the amount of debt that our business has.					
7) The owner wants to know if the May 3 cash deposit was from a revenue or from a customer advance payment.					

ANSWERS

✓

Transaction data must be arranged in a way that meet five basic information requirements. First of all, transactions are recorded in chronological order. Second, it must be easy to see all the parts of each transaction. Third, it must be easy to verify that the transaction keeps the accounting equation in balance. Fourth, there must be a permanent historical record of all the increases and decreases of each item. Fifth, it must be easy to find the balance of each item.

Situation	Five Basic Information Arrangements				
	(1) Find a transaction by date	(2) See all parts of a transaction	(3) See if the equation stays in balance	(4) See the historical detail of each item	(5) Determine the balance of each item
1) The owner wants to know how much cash the business has today.					X
2) A tax auditor wants to know for what purpose a large check was written.	X	X			
3) The manager wants to know if the property tax payments were made before December 10, to avoid a late payment penalty.	X	X			
4) A customer is disputing the balance we are showing in our account receivable from him.				X	X
5) Our business has purchased another business. It is a complex transaction with many changes to the accounting equation.		X	X		
6) Before deciding on a loan, the bank wants to know the amount of debt that our business has.					X
7) The owner wants to know if the May 3 cash deposit was from a revenue or from a customer advance payment.	X	X			

LEARNING GOAL 20
Learn to Use Accounts

OVERVIEW

Introduction

At the most basic level, an accounting system is simply a way of recording increases and decreases. Why? Because the financial condition of every business is described by the accounting equation $A = L + OE$, and there are only two possible ways that the items in the equation can change: either increase or decrease.

The means of keeping a record of all increases and decreases of each item in the accounting equation is the "account." This learning goal explains the account.

In Learning Goal 20, you will find:

▼ *The Account and How It Is Used*

EXAMPLE

Example of recording increases and decreases

Look again at the last table that we used to record the transactions for the Nevada Company (see page 367). This table uses separate increase and decrease columns for all the items in the accounting equation. For each item, notice that the increase and decrease columns form a "T."

For example, the cash item in the accounting equation of Nevada Company for the week beginning May 2 shows the following entries:

Cash

	Increase	Decrease
5/2 beginning balance	17,300	
	800	400
	2,000	
		1,000
	———	
5/8 ending balance	18,700	

An item can change in only two possible ways—either increase or decrease. By putting an increase column on one side and a decrease column on the other side, a "T" is formed. All the increases are shown on one side and the decreases are shown on the other side. The ending balance of 18,700 is calculated by subtracting the total of the decrease side (1,400 on the right side) from the total of the positive (increase) side (20,100 on the left side).

THE ACCOUNT

Definition

Each one of these increase/decrease "T" arrangements is called an account. An **account** is a detailed, historical record that shows all the increases and all the decreases of a specific item in the accounting equation.

THE ACCOUNT (continued)

The T account	The simplest form of an account is called a ***T account*** (see example on page 375). It shows only the most basic information: name, increases, and decreases. (Later on, we will add useful information to the account.)

Entry	Each recording on the left side or right side of an account is called an ***entry***.

Footing	Because an account keeps a record of all increases and all decreases, an account can also show a balance. The balance of an account is called a ***footing***, and to total an account is ***to foot*** it.

Note: The word "footing" also refers to a total of a column of numbers. |

Examples	Refer back to the last table for the Nevada Company on page 367.

• Cash, Accounts Receivable, Supplies, and Equipment are asset accounts.
• Note Payable is a liability account.
• C. Goldman, Capital is an owner's equity account.

The Cash account shows four entries: two increases and two decreases. The footing (the balance) of the Cash account on May 8 is \$18,700. |

Two information requirements are fulfilled	An account meets two of the five information requirements. The two requirements are:

• An account keeps a record of all increases and decreases of a specific item in the accounting equation (the "historical detail").
• An account shows the balance of a specific item in the accounting equation. |

RULES FOR INCREASING AND DECREASING THE ACCOUNTS

Concept

This is the idea behind all the rules for recording increases and decreases in the accounts:

> • We agree that one side of an account will be the positive side. This is called the *"normal"* or *"natural" side* of the account, and is used for increases.
> • Therefore, the other side of the account will be the negative side, for recording decreases.

It is actually this simple.

Positive sides

Over many years, accountants have agreed on the positive sides:

• For left-side accounts in the accounting equation (assets), the left side of an account shall be the positive side.
• For right-side accounts in the accounting equation (liabilities and owner's capital), the right side of an account shall be the positive side.

RULES FOR INCREASING AND DECREASING THE ACCOUNTS (continued)

Examples

The following table and illustration show you how this rule affects each type of account, when recording changes:

Change	Assets	Liabilities	Owner's Capital
Positive (increase)	Left side	Right side	Right side
Negative (decrease)	Right side	Left side	Left side

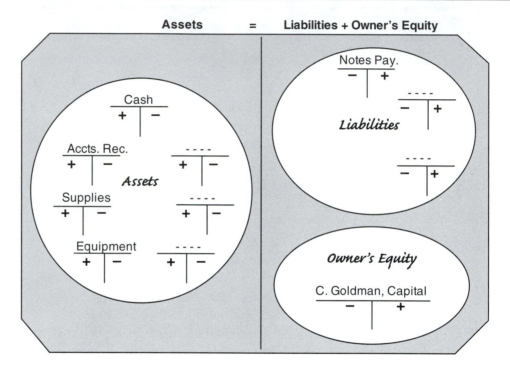

Nothing magic here!

There is nothing magic or mysterious about this method. We could just as easily agree that the natural positive location should be the top part of an account and decreases should be on the bottom part of an account. To keep a record of increases and decreases that the human brain can see, all we need are two separate locations in each account. Most people find left and right to be easiest, probably because the accounting equation is divided into left and right parts.

RULES FOR INCREASING AND DECREASING THE ACCOUNTS (continued)

Assets and liabilities cannot have negative balances. For example, can you imagine negative equipment or negative supplies? Of course not—balances are positive. However, as a shortcut, sometimes accountants will *temporarily* show cash with a negative balance if the cash account is overdrawn, or *temporarily* show accounts receivable with a negative balance because of an overpayment by a customer. Both of these situations are really liabilities, not negative assets.

☞*QUICK REVIEW*☜

- An account meets two of the five information requirements: it keeps a historical record of all the increases and decreases of an item in the accounting equation, and it shows the balance of the item.

- To record increases in accounts, accountants have agreed on the following rules:
  — An item that belongs on the left side of the equation will be increased by a left-side entry.
  — An item that belongs on the right side of the equation will be increased by a right-side entry.

- Once we agree on increases, then decreases are on the opposite side from the increases.

☞*VOCABULARY*☜

Account: a detailed, historical record of all the increases and decreases of a specific item in the accounting equation (page 375)

Entry: the recording of a change in an account; usually refers to recording in ledgers or journals (page 376)

Footing: the balance of an account; the total of a column of numbers (page 376)

"Normal" or *"natural" side:* the side of an account which records increases (page 377)

T account: the simplest form of an account, in the form of a T, showing name and increases on one side, and decreases on the opposite side (page 376)

To foot: to total an account or a column of numbers (page 376)

PRACTICE FOR LEARNING GOAL 20

SOLUTIONS FOR LEARNING GOAL 20 BEGIN ON PAGE 387.

Learning Goal 20 is about learning to use accounts. Use these problems to practice how to record the increases and decreases in accounts.

REINFORCEMENT PROBLEMS

1)   **Identify natural positive sides of accounts.** The T accounts below are randomly shown—there is no particular order. Identify the natural positive side of each account by writing a plus sign (+) on the side that is the natural positive side (the "normal" side).

Cash	Dean Jones, Capital	Supplies	Notes Payable	Wages Payable

Equipment	Accounts Receivable	Accounts Payable	Notes Receivable	Land

---

2)   **Explain the meaning and use of the natural positive side.** What is the importance of the natural positive side (the "normal" side) of an account? What is the natural positive side used for?

---

3)   **Identify the changes in the accounts.** Shown below are accounts that have been increased and/or decreased by certain transactions. (If you have difficulty, *remember the natural positive sides* of the accounts you are looking at.)

- Write one sentence to identify which accounts have increased and which have decreased.
- Write one sentence that accurately describes the transaction.

Example:

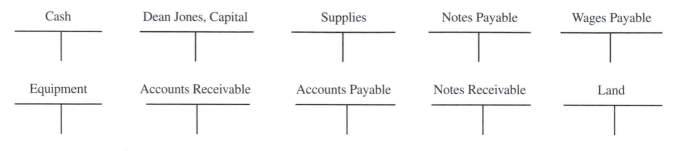

Cash	Anna Chan, Capital
5,000	5,000

- **Increase/decrease:** Cash increases and Anna Chan, Capital increases.
- **Description:** The owner invested $5,000 in her business.

A)

Cash	Accts. Receivable
750	750

- **Increase/decrease:**
- **Description:**

SOLUTIONS FOR LEARNING GOAL 20 BEGIN ON PAGE 387.

3) *continued*

B)

Supplies		Accts. Payable	
1,000			1,000

- **Increase/decrease:**
- **Description:**

C)

Cash		Supplies	
	500	500	

- **Increase/decrease:**
- **Description:**

D)

Equipment		Cash		Notes Payable	
15,000			5,000		10,000

- **Increase/decrease:**
- **Description:**

E)

Cash		Accts. Payable	
	300	300	

- **Increase/decrease:**
- **Description:**

4) **Practice recording changes in the accounts.** Each question below describes a separate transaction. Blank T accounts are arranged under the accounting equation with each question. For each individual question, do the following:

- **Analysis:** identify which accounts increase and/or which accounts decrease.
- **Rules:** specify what entries on the left or right side of the accounts are required.
- **Entry:** write the names of the accounts affected above the T accounts, and record the dollar amounts into the accounts. (*Remember:* the entries must keep the equation in balance!)

P
R
A
C
T
I
C
E
■
P
R
A
C
T
I
C
E
■
P
R
A
C
T
I
C
E
■
P
R
A
C
T
I
C
E
■
P
R
A
C
T
I
C
E
■
P
R
A
C
T
I
C
E

PRACTICE FOR LEARNING GOAL 20

SOLUTIONS FOR LEARNING GOAL 20 BEGIN ON PAGE 387.

4) *continued*

Example: San Antonio Company purchases $500 of office supplies for cash.

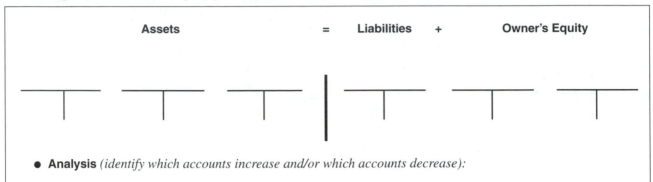

- **Analysis** *(identify which accounts increase and/or which accounts decrease):*

- **Rules** *(specify what entries on the left or right side of the accounts are required):*

Solution:

	Assets		=	Liabilities	+	Owner's Equity	
Cash	Supplies						
500	500						

- **Analysis** *(identify which accounts increase and/or which accounts decrease):* The **asset** Cash **decreases** by $500 and the **asset** Supplies **increases** by $500.

- **Rules** *(specify what entries on the left or right side of the accounts are required):* Assets are increased by a left-side entry, so record $500 on the left side of Supplies. Assets are decreased by a right-side entry, so record $500 on the right side of Cash.

A) St. Phillips Company purchases $800 of supplies "on account."

	Assets		=	Liabilities	+	Owner's Equity	

- **Analysis** *(identify which accounts increase and/or which accounts decrease):*

- **Rules** *(specify what entries on the left or right side of the accounts are required):*

PRACTICE FOR LEARNING GOAL 20

SOLUTIONS FOR LEARNING GOAL 20 BEGIN ON PAGE 387.

4) *continued*

B)　Bryan Company collects $1,000 from customers "on account."

Assets	=	Liabilities	+	Owner's Equity

- **Analysis** *(identify which accounts increase and/or which accounts decrease)*:

- **Rules** *(specify what entries on the left or right side of the accounts are required)*:

C)　Dave Mason, owner of Mountain View Company, invests $10,000 in his business.

Assets	=	Liabilities	+	Owner's Equity

- **Analysis** *(identify which accounts increase and/or which accounts decrease)*:

- **Rules** *(specify what entries on the left or right side of the accounts are required)*:

D)　Richland Company receives a $400 advance payment from a customer.

Assets	=	Liabilities	+	Owner's Equity

- **Analysis** *(identify which accounts increase and/or which accounts decrease)*:

- **Rules** *(specify what entries on the left or right side of the accounts are required)*:

PRACTICE FOR LEARNING GOAL 20

SOLUTIONS FOR LEARNING GOAL 20 BEGIN ON PAGE 387.

4) *continued*

E) North Harris Company purchased a $5,000 computer by paying $3,000 cash and signing a note payable for the balance.

		Assets	=	Liabilities	+	Owner's Equity

- **Analysis** *(identify which accounts increase and/or which accounts decrease):*

- **Rules** *(specify what entries on the left or right side of the accounts are required):*

F) San Jacinto Company pays $250 owing to a supplier "on account."

		Assets	=	Liabilities	+	Owner's Equity

- **Analysis** *(identify which accounts increase and/or which accounts decrease):*

- **Rules** *(specify what entries on the left or right side of the accounts are required):*

G) Diane Lee, owner of El Paso Company, recorded $750 of revenue "on account."

		Assets	=	Liabilities	+	Owner's Equity

- **Analysis** *(identify which accounts increase and/or which accounts decrease):*

- **Rules** *(specify what entries on the left or right side of the accounts are required):*

SOLUTIONS FOR LEARNING GOAL 20 BEGIN ON PAGE 387.

4) *continued*

H)   Tarrant Company uses up $100 of supplies during its operations (an expense).

Assets			=	Liabilities	+	Owner's Equity

- **Analysis** *(identify which accounts increase and/or which accounts decrease)*:

- **Rules** *(specify what entries on the left or right side of the accounts are required)*:

I)   Kingwood Company receives a $500 invoice for repair services. The invoice is not paid immediately (an expense).

Assets			=	Liabilities	+	Owner's Equity

- **Analysis** *(identify which accounts increase and/or which accounts decrease)*:

- **Rules** *(specify what entries on the left or right side of the accounts are required)*:

J)   Grayson Company receives $750 cash upon completion of a job for a customer (a revenue).

Assets			=	Liabilities	+	Owner's Equity

- **Analysis** *(identify which accounts increase and/or which accounts decrease)*:

- **Rules** *(specify what entries on the left or right side of the accounts are required)*:

PRACTICE FOR LEARNING GOAL 20

SOLUTIONS FOR LEARNING GOAL 20 BEGIN ON PAGE 387.

5) **Calculate account balances.** Each of the items below gives information about an account. Calculate the ending balance of the account. State if the ending balance is on the right side or left side. All beginning balances are normal balances.

Beginning Balance	Account Changes
A) Cash: $5,000	Received payment from customer: $1,200; paid accounts payable: $750; paid employees: $2,500; owner investment: $5,000
B) Accounts Payable: $550	Purchases supplies on account: $500; received bill from repair service: $3,000; made payment to supplies vendor: $850
C) Owner's Capital: $3,500	Owner invested $5,000; earned $950 revenue; incurred $350 advertising expense; owner withdrew: $2,000
D) Owner's Capital: $5,000	Earned $1,000 revenue; paid $5,000 wages expense; owed $2,000 utility expense "on account"
E) Supplies: $150	Purchased supplies on account: $500; used $300 of supplies
F) Wages Payable: $500	Employees earned $4,000 which has not yet been paid

6) **Analyzing accounts.** Once you understand how accounts are used, then you can begin to answer questions about why and how accounts have changed. For each of the four separate situations below, answer the questions about the accounts.

A) The Supplies account of Spokane Enterprises had a normal balance on October 1 of $4,500. The October 31 balance was a normal balance of $3,100, and the income statement shows October Supplies Expense of $5,500. What was the amount of supplies purchased?

B) The Accounts Receivable account of Everett Company shows a normal ending balance of $15,900 on January 31, and a normal January 1 balance of $7,800. If credit sales during the month were $12,500, what is the amount of collections from customers during January?

C) Seattle Service Company had $8,850 of Accounts Payable owing on August 1. During August, the company made $12,000 of payments to creditors and owed $3,300 on August 31. How much did the company purchase on credit during August?

D) Bellevue Corporation shows a February 28 normal cash balance of $75,700. If, during February, the company received $55,200 of cash and paid $81,000 of cash, what was the cash balance on February 1?

PRACTICE QUESTIONS FOR LEARNING GOAL 20 BEGIN ON PAGE 380.

REINFORCEMENT PROBLEMS

1)

Cash	Dean Jones, Capital	Supplies	Notes Payable	Wages Payable
+	+	+	+	+

Equipment	Accounts Receivable	Accounts Payable	Notes Receivable	Land
+	+	+	+	+

2) The natural positive side of an account is an essential common point of reference. Once the natural positive side is agreed upon, then both the increases and decreases can be recorded in a consistent and accurate way. The natural positive side is used to: 1) record account increases; and 2) show account balances. The opposite side then becomes the side used for decreases.

3) A)

Cash		Accounts Receivable	
750			750

- **Increase/decrease:** Cash increases and Accounts Receivable decreases.
- **Description:** The business collected $750 cash from customers who owed the business on account.

B)

Supplies		Accounts Payable	
1,000			1,000

- **Increase/decrease:** Supplies increases and Accounts Payable increases.
- **Description:** The business purchased $1,000 of supplies on account (on credit).

C)

Cash		Supplies	
	500	500	

- **Increase/decrease:** Cash decreases and Supplies increases.
- **Description:** The business purchased $500 of supplies for cash.

D)

Equipment		Cash		Notes Payable	
15,000			5,000		10,000

- **Increase/decrease:** Equipment increases, Cash decreases, and Notes Payable increases.
- **Description:** The business purchased $15,000 of equipment, paying $5,000 cash and signing a note payable for $10,000.

PRACTICE QUESTIONS FOR LEARNING GOAL 20 BEGIN ON PAGE 380.

3) *continued*

E)

Cash		Accts. Payable	
	300	300	

- **Increase/decrease:** Cash decreases and Accounts Payable decreases.
- **Description:** The business used $300 cash to pay $300 owing of accounts payable.

4)

A) St. Phillips Company

	Assets ↑		=	Liabilities ↑	+	Owner's Equity	
Supplies				Accounts Payable			
800					800		

- **Analysis** *(identify which accounts increase and/or which accounts decrease)*: The **asset** Supplies **increases** by $800 and the **liability** Accounts Payable **increases** by $800.
- **Rules** *(specify what entries on the left or right side of the accounts are required)*: Assets are increased by a left-side entry, so record $800 on the left side of Supplies. Liabilities are increased by a right-side entry, so record $800 on the right side of Accounts Payable.

B) Bryan Company

	Assets ↑ ↓		=	Liabilities	+	Owner's Equity	
Cash	Accts. Rec.						
1,000		1,000					

- **Analysis** *(identify which accounts increase and/or which accounts decrease)*: The **asset** Cash **increases** by $1,000 and the **asset** Accounts Receivable **decreases** by $1,000.
- **Rules** *(specify what entries on the left or right side of the accounts are required)*: Assets are increased by a left-side entry, so record $1,000 on the left side of Cash. Assets are decreased by a right-side entry, so record $1,000 on the right side of Accounts Receivable.

PRACTICE QUESTIONS FOR LEARNING GOAL 20 BEGIN ON PAGE 380.

4) *continued*

C) Mountain View Company

Assets ↑		=	Liabilities	+	Owner's Equity ↑
Cash					D. Mason, Capital
10,000					10,000

- **Analysis** *(identify which accounts increase and/or which accounts decrease)*: The **asset** Cash **increases** by $10,000 and the **owner's equity** D. Mason, Capital **increases** by $10,000.
- **Rules** *(specify what entries on the left or right side of the accounts are required)*: Assets are increased by a left-side entry, so record $10,000 on the left side of Cash. Owner's equity is increased by a right-side entry, so record $10,000 on the right side of D. Mason, Capital.

D) Richland Company

Assets ↑		=	Liabilities ↑	+	Owner's Equity
Cash			Unearned Revenue		
400			400		

- **Analysis** *(identify which accounts increase and/or which accounts decrease)*: The **asset** Cash **increases** by $400 and the **liability** Unearned Revenue **increases** by $400.
- **Rules** *(specify what entries on the left or right side of the accounts are required)*: Assets are increased by a left-side entry, so record $400 on the left side of Cash. Liabilities are increased by a right-side entry, so record $400 on the right side of Unearned Revenue.

E) North Harris Company

Assets ↓ ↑		=	Liabilities ↑	+	Owner's Equity
Cash	Equipment		Notes Payable		
3,000	5,000		2,000		

- **Analysis** *(identify which accounts increase and/or which accounts decrease)*: The **asset** Cash **decreases** by $3,000, the **asset** Equipment **increases** by $5,000, and the **liability** Notes Payable **increases** by $2,000.
- **Rules** *(specify what entries on the left or right side of the accounts are required)*: Assets are decreased by a right-side entry, so record $3,000 on the right side of Cash. Assets are increased by a left-side entry, so record $5,000 on the left side of Equipment. Liabilities are increased by a right-side entry, so record $2,000 on the right side of Notes Payable.

SOLUTIONS FOR LEARNING GOAL 20

PRACTICE QUESTIONS FOR LEARNING GOAL 20 BEGIN ON PAGE 380.

4) *continued*

F) San Jacinto Company

Assets ↓	=	Liabilities ↓	+	Owner's Equity
Cash		Accounts Payable		
250		250		

- **Analysis** *(identify which accounts increase and/or which accounts decrease)*: The **asset** Cash **decreases** by $250 and the **liability** Accounts Payable **decreases** by $250.
- **Rules** *(specify what entries on the left or right side of the accounts are required)*: Assets are decreased by a right-side entry, so record $250 on the right side of Cash. Liabilities are decreased by a left-side entry, so record $250 on the left side of Accounts Payable.

G) El Paso Company

Assets ↑	=	Liabilities	+	Owner's Equity ↑
Accts. Rec.				Diane Lee, Capital
750				750

- **Analysis** *(identify which accounts increase and/or which accounts decrease)*: The **asset** Accounts Receivable **increases** by $750 and the **owner's equity** Diane Lee, Capital **increases** by $750.
- **Rules** *(specify what entries on the left or right side of the accounts are required)*: Assets are increased by a left-side entry, so record $750 on the left side of Accounts Receivable. Owner's equity is increased by a right-side entry, so record $750 on the right side of Diane Lee, Capital.

H) Tarrant Company

Assets ↓	=	Liabilities	+	Owner's Equity ↓
Supplies				xxx, Capital
100				100

- **Analysis** *(identify which accounts increase and/or which accounts decrease)*: The **asset** Supplies **decreases** by $100 and the **owner's equity** xxx, Capital **decreases** by $100.
- **Rules** *(specify what entries on the left or right side of the accounts are required)*: Assets are decreased by a right-side entry, so record $100 on the right side of Supplies. Owner's equity is decreased by a left-side entry, so record $100 on the left side of xxx, Capital.

SOLUTIONS FOR LEARNING GOAL 20

PRACTICE QUESTIONS FOR LEARNING GOAL 20 BEGIN ON PAGE 380.

4) *continued*

I) Kingwood Company

Assets	=	Liabilities ↑	+	Owner's Equity ↓
		Accts. Pay.		xxx, Capital
		500		500

- **Analysis** *(identify which accounts increase and/or which accounts decrease)*: The **liability** Accounts Payable **increases** by $500 and the **owner's equity** xxx, Capital **decreases** by $500.
- **Rules** *(specify what entries on the left or right side of the accounts are required)*: Liabilities are increased by a right-side entry, so record $500 on the right side of Accounts Payable. Owner's equity is decreased by a left-side entry, so record $500 on the left side of xxx, Capital.

J) Grayson Company

Assets	↑	=	Liabilities	+	Owner's Equity ↑
Cash					xxx, Capital
750					750

- **Analysis** *(identify which accounts increase and/or which accounts decrease)*: The **asset** Cash **increases** by $750 and the **owner's equity** xxx, Capital **increases** by $750.
- **Rules** *(specify what entries on the left or right side of the accounts are required)*: Assets are increased by a left-side entry, so record $750 on the left side of Cash. Owner's equity is increased by a right-side entry, so record $750 on the right side of xxx, Capital.

5)   A) $7,950 left side
      B) $3,200 right side
      C) $7,100 right side
      D) $1,000 left side
      E) $350 left side
      F) $4,500 right side

SOLUTIONS FOR LEARNING GOAL 20

PRACTICE QUESTIONS FOR LEARNING GOAL 20 BEGIN ON PAGE 380.

6) Whenever you are asked to analyze an account, you have two good choices:
    - Use a formula that calculates the balance of an account: **beginning balance + increases – decreases = ending balance**.
    - You can also draw a T account. Fill in what you know, and then calculate what is missing. Each of the solutions below show both approaches.

A) $4,500 + X – 5,500 = 3,100$. So, X = **4,100** of purchases.   Or:

(supplies expense is the amount of supplies used up)

Supplies	
4,500	
	5,500
___?___	
3,100	

B) $7,800 + 12,500 – X = 15,900$. So, X = **4,400** of collections.   Or:

(increases to A/R are from making credit sales)

Accounts Receivable	
7,800	
12,500	?
___	
15,900	

C) $8,850 + X – 12,000 = 3,300$. So, X = **6,450** of purchases.   Or:

Accounts Payable	
	8,850
12,000	
	___?___
	3,300

D) $X + 55,200 – 81,000 = 75,700$. So, X = **101,500**.   Or:

Cash	
?	
55,200	
	81,000
___	
75,700	

Your Questions?

It is *very* important to be aware of what you need to understand better. What do you need to understand better about this learning goal? Use this space to write the questions that you want to discuss with your classmates, instructor, or supervisor. Try to be very specific about what is bothering you, such as explanations that you do not fully understand.

LEARNING GOAL 21
Use the Owner's Capital Accounts

In Learning Goal 21, you will find:

▼ *The Parts of Owner's Equity*

OVERVIEW OF OWNER'S EQUITY

The individual owner's equity accounts

As you know, the owner's equity account is subdivided, to show the specific kinds of changes that affect owner's equity.

Revenues, expenses, owner drawing, and owner investment are the recurring changes that affect the owner's capital. The first three of these changes—revenues, expenses, and owner drawing—happen frequently and need to be carefully monitored. Therefore, in practice, the owner's capital is subdivided by creating individual accounts for revenues, expenses, and owner drawing.

Rule

Because owner's equity is on the right side of the accounting equation, all increases to owner's equity and the specific accounts that increase owner's equity are always recorded on the right side of an account. Decreases are left-side entries.

OVERVIEW OF OWNER'S EQUITY (continued)

Capital account expanded

In the diagram below, the owner's capital is expanded to show you the individual owner equity accounts. These separate accounts are a subdivision of the owner's capital. Because investments do not happen frequently and are therefore easy to follow, they are recorded directly into the owner's capital account.

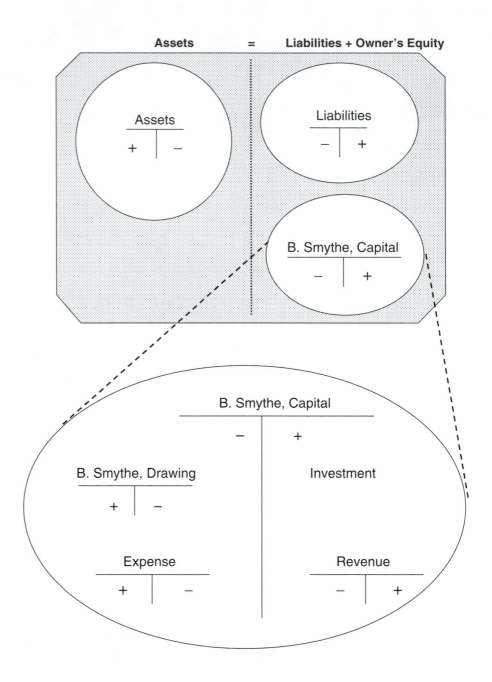

▼ *Rules and Examples of Increases and Decreases*

DECREASING THE OWNER'S CAPITAL ACCOUNT

Expenses and withdrawals	Drawings and expenses reduce the owner's capital. That is why they are shown as part of the *left side* of the owner's capital account. That is also why increases to drawings and expenses are recorded on the left side of these accounts.

- The more the owner withdraws, the greater the reduction in the owner's capital.
- The more expenses that are recorded, the greater the reduction in the owner's capital.

Rule for expenses and withdrawals	The "natural positive side" of the drawing account and expense accounts is the *left side*.

A common confusion	One of the most common confusions of students who are first learning about increasing and decreasing accounts is understanding why expense accounts and the drawing account are increased with left-side entries. In effect, they are asking: "Why is the normal balance of an expense or drawing account on the left side?"

The reason that people temporarily become confused about this is that they forget something important: expense transactions and withdrawal transactions are really just particular types of decreases in the owner's capital, and decreases in the owner's capital are *always* recorded by left-side entries. So, expenses and withdrawals have to be recorded by left-side entries.

DECREASING THE OWNER'S CAPITAL ACCOUNT (continued)

Example

Assume that the owner's capital balance of Watson Company is $25,000. Then, the business pays $1,000 of rent expense. When we record the expense directly in the capital account, this is what we will see:

	John Watson, Capital	
	$25,000	Beginning Balance
Rent Expense $1,000		

Why the owner's equity decreased

The owner's capital has decreased by $1,000 because business resources were used up to pay the rent. Or, you could also say: "Rent expense increased by $1,000." Whichever way you prefer to describe it, a left-side entry was needed to show the reduction in John Watson, Capital.

Example, continued

Suppose that some time passes, and there are more expense and withdrawal transactions. For now, we will continue to record these transactions as direct decreases in the owner's capital.

	John Watson, Capital	
	$25,000	Beginning Balance
Rent Expense $1,000 $1,000		
Repairs Expense $750		
Withdrawals $2,500		
Advertising Expense $3,000		

DECREASING THE OWNER'S CAPITAL ACCOUNT (continued)

Example, continued	The owner's capital has now been decreased by transactions that we describe as another $1,000 of rent expense, $750 of repairs expense, $2,500 of withdrawals, and $3,000 of advertising expense. There are now three types of expenses and a withdrawal.
	John Watson, Capital is reduced to $16,750. The more left entries we record, the more the owner's capital decreases. At the same time, the total of the expenses and drawing is increasing.
More transactions ...	Suppose that more time goes by, and the business has more expenses and withdrawals.

John Watson, Capital

	$25,000 Beginning Balance
Rent Expense $1,000 $1,000	
Repairs Expense $750 $1,220 $175	
Withdrawals $2,500 $1,000	
Advertising Expense $3,000 $525	

Now, the expenses and withdrawals have increased to $11,170 and the owner's capital balance is down to $13,830 ($25,000 – $11,170). The more expenses and withdrawals, the more the capital balance decreases. We are recording *increases in negative things*—things that decrease the owner's capital. Each left entry increases the total amount of expense or drawing but, at the same time, it decreases the owner's capital.

Learning Goal 21: Use the Owner's Capital Accounts

DECREASING THE OWNER'S CAPITAL ACCOUNT (continued)

Clean up the capital account

The left (decrease) side of the capital account is starting to become very messy and crowded, isn't it? This overcrowding is starting to happen with only three types of expenses and a drawing account. In a real business, think what would happen if there were many more expense accounts, each with dozens or hundreds of transactions!

Individual accounts

You can see that trying to record expenses and withdrawals directly into the owner's capital account will become messy and difficult, because of limited space. The solution to this problem is simply to give each type of decrease in the capital account its own separate account.

Even though the expenses and withdrawals will now be recorded in their own individual accounts, we still understand that they are really just particular types of decreases in the owner's capital. We can continue to record their increases with left-side entries, just as if they were still being recorded directly into the capital account.

John Watson, Withdrawals	
2,500	
1,000	

Rent Expense		Repairs Expense		Advertising Expense	
1,000		750		3,000	
1,000		1,220		525	
		175			

Reducing a drawing or expense account

You may be wondering when a drawing or expense account would ever be decreased—that is, an amount recorded on the right side. In practice, this is usually the result of some kind of adjustment, correction, or year-end closing. It does not happen very often. You will study this later (Volume 2 of this series).

CHECK YOUR UNDERSTANDING

Fill in each blank space with the correct word. The answers are below.

An expense or withdrawal transaction is always recorded by a _____-side entry. The reason people sometimes become confused about this is they forget that an expense or a withdrawal transaction is really just a particular type of _____ in the owner's capital. A decrease in owner's capital is always recorded by a _____-side entry.

However, because of the large number of expense and withdrawal transactions, it (is/is not) _____ feasible to record expenses and withdrawals directly in the owner's capital account. Instead, individual expense accounts and a drawing account are used, all of which have _____-side normal balances.

ANSWERS

An expense or withdrawal transaction is always recorded by a left-side entry. The reason people sometimes become confused about this is they forget that an expense or a withdrawal transaction is really just a particular type of decrease in the owner's capital. A decrease in owner's capital is always recorded by a left-side entry.

However, because of the large number of expense and withdrawal transactions, it is not feasible to record expenses and withdrawals directly in the owner's capital account. Instead, individual expense accounts and a drawing account are used, all of which have left-side normal balances.

INCREASING THE OWNER'S CAPITAL ACCOUNT

Introduction

Investments and revenues increase the owner's capital. That is why they are shown on the right side of the owner's capital account.

- The more the owner invests, the greater the increase in the owner's capital.
- The more revenues that are recorded, the greater the increase in the owner's capital.

INCREASING THE OWNER'S CAPITAL ACCOUNT (continued)

Separate accounts	Because of space limitations, it is not practical to enter all the revenues directly into the right side of the owner's capital account. Therefore, a separate account is used to record each type of revenue transaction. For example, service revenue and interest revenue transactions would be recorded in two separate revenue accounts.
Rule for revenues	Revenue accounts always have normal right-side balances. Increases are always recorded on the right of revenue accounts.
Decreases in revenues	You may be wondering when a revenue account would ever be decreased— that is, an amount recorded on the left side. In practice, this is usually the result of some kind of adjustment, correction, or year-end closing. It does not happen very often. You will study this later (Volume 2 in this series).

EXAMPLES OF OWNER'S EQUITY TRANSACTIONS

Introduction	Here are some typical examples of owner's equity transactions using just a few accounts. To remind you that they are really subdivisions of owner's capital, we will show the revenue, expense, and drawing accounts under the owner's capital account.

Suppose that on June 5, Jill Hirata decides to start her own business by investing cash. Therefore, the asset Cash increases $10,000 and Jill Hirata, Capital increases $10,000.

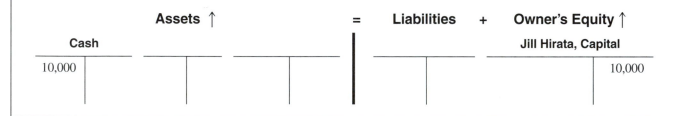

EXAMPLES OF OWNER'S EQUITY TRANSACTIONS (continued)

On June 7, the business buys $500 of supplies on account. Therefore, the asset Supplies increases $500 and the liability Accounts Payable increases $500. Owner's capital is not affected.

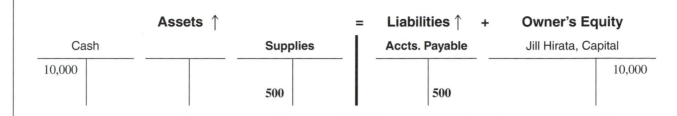

On June 8, the business uses up $100 of supplies. The asset Supplies decreases. The account Supplies Expense increases, thereby decreasing total owner's capital to $9,900.

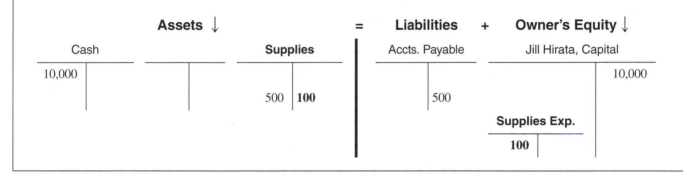

On June 10, the business earns $800 of revenue on account. So, the asset Accounts Receivable increases $800. The revenue account Fees Earned increases by $800, thereby increasing total owner's capital to $10,700.

Learning Goal 21: Use the Owner's Capital Accounts

EXAMPLES OF OWNER'S EQUITY TRANSACTIONS (continued)

On June 15, the business receives a $300 bill for equipment rental. The bill will be paid early next month, so the liability Accounts Payable increases $300. The expense account Rent Expense increases $300, thereby decreasing total owner's capital to $10,400.

Assets			=	Liabilities ↑	+	Owner's Equity ↓
Cash	Accts. Rec.	Supplies		Accts. Payable		Jill Hirata, Capital
10,000						10,000
	800	500 | 100		500		
				300		
				Supplies Exp.		Fees Earned
				100		| 800
				Rent Exp.		
				300		

On June 19, Jill withdraws $250 cash from the business, so the asset Cash decreases $250. The drawing account increases $250, thereby decreasing total owner's capital to $10,150.

Assets ↓			=	Liabilities	+	Owner's Equity ↓	
Cash	Accts. Rec.	Supplies		Accts. Payable		Jill Hirata, Capital	
10,000						**J. Hirata, Draw.**	10,000
	800	500 | 100		500		**250** |	
250				300			
						Supplies Exp.	Fees Earned
						100 |	| 800
						Rent Exp.	
						300 |	

⌒QUICK REVIEW⌒

● The owner's capital account is subdivided into three additional types of accounts: revenues, expenses, and owner drawing. There are usually many different types of expenses and several different types of revenues.

● Expenses and drawing are always decreases to the owner's capital. Therefore, the natural positive side of expense and drawing accounts is the left side.

● Revenues are always an increase to owner's capital. Therefore, the natural positive side of revenue accounts is the right side.

● Investments are recorded directly into the right side of the owner's capital account.

"Left-side entry to record expenses and drawing, right-side entry to record revenues!"

● ●

PRACTICE FOR LEARNING GOAL 21

SOLUTIONS FOR LEARNING GOAL 21 BEGIN ON PAGE 406.

Learning Goal 21 is about learning the rules for increasing and decreasing the various owner's equity accounts. Use these questions and problems to practice what you have just read.

REINFORCEMENT PROBLEMS

1) **Explain concepts about owner's capital accounts.**

   A) Why is the natural positive side of the owner's capital the right side of the account?

   B) Why is the owner's capital subdivided into separate accounts for revenue, expense, and drawing, in addition to the owner's capital account?

   C) Why is the natural positive side of an expense account or drawing account the left side?

   D) The more an expense or drawing account increases, the more the total owner's capital decreases. Why?

   E) Why is the natural positive side of a revenue account the right side?

2) **Negative balance in owner's capital?** We know that assets and liabilities cannot really have negative balances, although sometimes assets such as Cash or Accounts Receivable might be temporarily shown with negative balances as a shortcut. However, can the owner's capital account ever have a negative balance? Why?

SOLUTIONS FOR LEARNING GOAL 21 BEGIN ON PAGE 406.

3) **Practice using owner's equity accounts.** Each question below describes a separate transaction. Below, blank T accounts are arranged under the accounting equation. For each individual question, do the following: Write the names of the accounts that are affected above the T accounts, and then make entries for the dollar amounts into the accounts. (*Remember:* the entries must keep the equation in balance!)

A) On October 1, David Jefferson invests $15,000 to start a new business called Reliable Real Estate Appraisal Company.

B) On October 5, the business spends $5,000 cash to purchase $4,000 of computer equipment and $1,000 of office supplies from a vendor.

C) On October 7, the business uses up $500 of supplies in performing an appraisal for a client.

D) On October 20, the business receives a $200 bill from the electric company. The bill will be paid early next month.

E) On October 28, the business completes an appraisal job and the client pays $1,500 cash.

F) On October 31, David Jefferson withdraws $750 cash from his business.

| Assets | = | Liabilities | + | Owner's Equity |

SOLUTIONS FOR LEARNING GOAL 21

PRACTICE QUESTIONS FOR LEARNING GOAL 21 BEGIN ON PAGE 404.

REINFORCEMENT PROBLEMS

1) A) Accountants use the accounting equation as a reference to decide which side of an account will be the natural positive side. Because the owner's capital is on the right side of the equation, the natural positive side of the owner's capital account is its right side.

   B) Revenues, expenses, and owner withdrawals are all types of changes in the owner's capital. Because these changes are numerous and frequent, and because they have a powerful effect on the success or failure of a business, they must be monitored very closely. In order to follow these changes carefully, they are assigned individual accounts. This permits more accurate observation than simply recording them all together in the owner's capital account.

   C) Decreases in the owner's capital account are recorded on the left side of the account. So, if the decreases in the owner's capital are subdivided into expense and drawing accounts, these "decrease accounts" should have left natural positive sides, because the amounts recorded are decreases in the owner's capital.

   D) Expenses and owner drawings decrease the owner's capital.

   E) Revenues are sales transactions that cause the owner's capital to increase. Increases to owner's capital are recorded on the right side of the account. Therefore, since revenues increase owner's capital, revenue increases should be recorded on the right side of an individual revenue account.

2) Yes. The owner's capital account can have a negative balance. This happens when liabilities exceed assets. This situation happens when a business consumes resources in a way that does not add value, so little or no assets are received from customers in return. A negative balance is the amount of money an owner must invest so the business will have enough assets to pay off all the debts.

SOLUTIONS FOR LEARNING GOAL 21

PRACTICE QUESTIONS FOR LEARNING GOAL 21 BEGIN ON PAGE 404.

3) *Note:* To help you remember the previous changes, the prior transactions are recorded in light gray.

A)

On October 1, David Jefferson invests $15,000 to start a new business called Reliable Real Estate Appraisal Company.

Assets ↑   =   Liabilities   +   Owner's Equity ↑

Cash   David Jefferson, Capital

15,000   15,000

B)

On October 5, the business spends $5,000 cash to purchase $4,000 of computer equipment and $1,000 of office supplies from a vendor.

Assets ↓ ↑   =   Liabilities   +   Owner's Equity

Cash   Supplies   Equipment   David Jefferson, Capital

15,000 | 5,000   1,000 | 4,000 | 15,000

C)

On October 7, the business uses up $500 of supplies in performing an appraisal for a client.

Assets ↓   =   Liabilities   +   Owner's Equity ↓

Cash   Supplies   Equipment   Davie Jefferson, Capital

15,000 | 5,000   1,000 | 500   4,000 | 15,000

Supplies Exp.

500 |

Learning Goal 21: Use the Owner's Capital Accounts

SOLUTIONS FOR LEARNING GOAL 21

PRACTICE QUESTIONS FOR LEARNING GOAL 21 BEGIN ON PAGE 404.

3) *continued*

D)

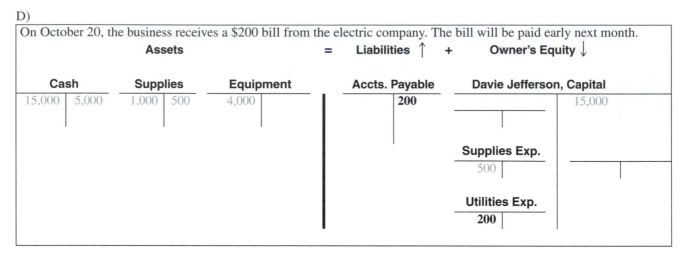

On October 20, the business receives a $200 bill from the electric company. The bill will be paid early next month.

	Assets		=	Liabilities ↑	+	Owner's Equity ↓

Cash	Supplies	Equipment		Accts. Payable	Davie Jefferson, Capital
15,000 | 5,000	1,000 | 500	4,000		**200**	15,000

Supplies Exp.
500

Utilities Exp.
200

E)

On October 28, the business completes an appraisal job and the client pays $1,500 cash.

	Assets ↑		=	Liabilities	+	Owner's Equity ↑

Cash	Supplies	Equipment		Accts. Payable	Davie Jefferson, Capital
15,000 | 5,000	1,000 | 500	4,000		200	15,000
1,500					

Supplies Exp. — 500 · Service Revenue — **1,500**

Utilities Exp.
200

F)

On October 31, David Jefferson withdraws $750 cash from his business.

	Assets ↓		=	Liabilities	+	Owner's Equity ↓

Cash	Supplies	Equipment		Accts. Payable	Davie Jefferson, Capital
15,000 | 5,000	1,000 | 500	4,000		200	15,000
1,500 | **750**					D. Jefferson Draw. — **750**
bal. 10,750	bal. 500				

Supplies Exp. — 500 · Service Rev. — 1,500

Utilities Exp.
200

Learning Goal 21: Use the Owner's Capital Accounts

LEARNING GOAL 22

"Debits on the left, credits on the right!"

In Learning Goal 22, you will find:

▼ *The Words "Debit" and "Credit"*

WHAT DEBIT AND CREDIT REALLY MEAN

Introduction

Every occupation has its own special terminology. Two of the accounting terms that most people have heard at one time or another are the terms *debit* and *credit*. Even though these words only refer to the left and right sides of an account, there seems to be much confusion and even anxiety about the meaning of these two words.

The truth is really quite simple. Accounting was first developed in Italy during the 1400s. At that time, educated business people spoke Latin. The root word of the Latin term for "left" was "debere." The root word for "right" was "credere." Today, those words have changed into "debit" and "credit" in English, but the meaning is still the same—left and right. The word "debit" is often abbreviated as *Dr.,* and the word "credit" is often abbreviated as "*Cr.*"

Rule

- Instead of saying "left side," say "debit."
- Instead of saying "right side," say "credit."

WHAT DEBIT AND CREDIT REALLY MEAN (continued)

**Do not make
these mistakes!**

People who should know better (financial writers, TV broadcasters, and even some nonaccounting teachers) often use debit and credit terminology in completely mistaken ways. They think that the words debit and credit mean things like good or bad, or always increase, always decrease, etc. Ignore these people. The words debit and credit *only refer to* **location**—left or right.

The words debit and credit *do not mean* "good" or "bad" or "favorable" or "unfavorable" or "always increase" or "always decrease" or "gain" or "loss" or anything else!

Debit means "left" and credit means "right." And that is all.

▼ *Debit and Credit Rules Applied to All Account Types*

APPLY DEBITS AND CREDITS TO THE ACCOUNTS

Introduction

If you have already practiced recording transactions in other learning goals, you will be happy to know that applying "debit" and "credit" to accounts does not really involve doing anything much different. *All you need to do is remember to say "debit" instead of "left," and "credit" instead of "right." The rules for increasing and decreasing accounts are* **still the same**.

> *Note:* To **charge** an account means to debit it. There is no alternative word for credit.

**Review of basic
recording rules**

If you have not yet studied the basic recording rules, they are repeated here:

● **Increases:** Any account that is a *left-side* account in the accounting equation (assets) is increased with a *left-side entry* (debit). Any account that is a *right-side* account in the accounting equation (liabilities and owner's capital) is increased with a *right-side entry* (credit).

● **Decreases:** Learn increases first. Decreases are then recorded on the opposite side from increases. (So, assets are decreased with credits, and liabilities and owner's capital are decreased with debits.)

APPLY DEBITS AND CREDITS TO THE ACCOUNTS (continued)

Rules illustrated

The expanded illustration below shows the rules for recording all transaction types, using the "debit" and "credit" terminology.

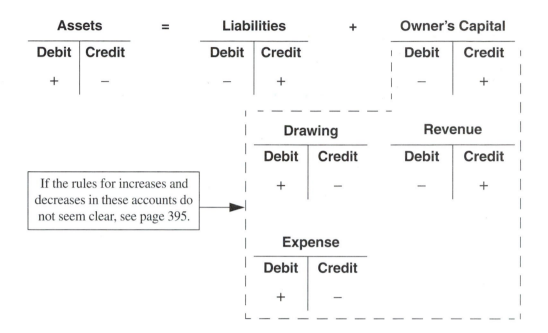

If the rules for increases and decreases in these accounts do not seem clear, see page 395.

DEBIT AND CREDIT RULES FOR THE SIX BASIC ACCOUNT TYPES

Summary

The table below shows a summary of the rules for debits and credits for each of the six basic account types in the accounting equation. This is exactly the same information that you see in the illustration above.

	Assets	Liabilities	Owner's Capital	Revenue	Expense	Drawing
Debit (left)	Increase (and natural positive balance)	Decrease	Decrease	Decrease	Increase (and natural positive balance)	Increase (and natural positive balance)
Credit (right)	Decrease	Increase (and natural positive balance)	Increase (and natural positive balance)	Increase (and natural positive balance)	Decrease	Decrease

Learning Goal 22: "Debits on the left, credits on the right!"

DEBIT AND CREDIT RULES FOR THE SIX BASIC ACCOUNT TYPES (continued)

Examples

Philadelphia Company performs $3,000 of consulting services and mails a bill to the client. The bookkeeper debits Accounts Receivable for $3,000 and credits Fees Earned for $3,000.

Assets ↑	=	Liabilities	+	Owner's Equity ↑
Accts. Receivable				

				John Jefferson, Capital

Dr.   Cr.

3.000

Fees Earned

Dr.   Cr.

3.000

Allegheny Company spends $5,000 cash to purchase $4,000 of computer equipment and $1,000 of office supplies. The bookkeeper records the transaction with a debit to Supplies for $1,000, a debit to Equipment for $4,000, and a credit to Cash for $5,000.

Assets ↓ ↑   =   **Liabilities**   +   **Owner's Equity**

Cash	Supplies	Equipment				David Jefferson, Capital
Dr. Cr.	Dr. Cr.	Dr. Cr.				
5,000	1,000	4,000				

Learning Goal 22: "Debits on the left, credits on the right!"

⁓Quick Review⁓

● The words "debit" and "credit" only refer to location. Debit means left and credit means right. They do not have any other meaning.

● The rules for increasing and decreasing accounts are:

— left-side accounts are increased with left-side entries, and right-side accounts are increased with right-side entries

— learn increases first; then decreases are on the opposite sides

⁓Vocabulary⁓

Charge: to debit an account (page 410)

Credit: a right-side entry or the right side of an account (page 409)

Cr.: the abbreviation for the word "credit" (page 409)

Debit: a left-side entry or the left side of an account (page 409)

Dr.: the abbreviation for the word "debit" (page 409)

"They will love it! 'Debit' for left and 'credit' for right!"

● ●

Learning Goal 22: "Debits on the left, credits on the right!"

PRACTICE FOR LEARNING GOAL 22

SOLUTIONS FOR LEARNING GOAL 22 BEGIN ON PAGE 419.

Learning Goal 22 is about using debit and credit terminology when recording transactions. Answer the questions and problems below to practice what you have just read.

MULTIPLE CHOICE
On the line provided, enter the letter of the best answer for each question.

1) Which of the following is not true? _____
   A) Items on the left side of the accounting equation are increased with debits, and items on the right side are increased with credits.
   B) Items on the left side of the accounting equation are decreased with credits, and items on the right side are decreased with debits.
   C) Both sides of the accounting equation are decreased with debits and increased with credits.
   D) Both A and B.

2) Albuquerque Company receives a bill for advertising services, which will be paid next week. The company will have to _____
   A) debit Owner's Capital and credit Cash.
   B) debit Advertising Expense and credit Accounts Payable.
   C) debit Advertising Expense and credit Cash.
   D) wait until payment is made.

3) How are decreases to accounts distinguished from increases? _____
   A) Decreases are always on the side opposite from the side for increases.
   B) Decreases are always right-side (credit) entries.
   C) Decreases are always left-side (debit) entries.
   D) Decreases are always shown with a minus sign.

4) If the Santa Fe Art Shoppe collected $500 of cash from Accounts Receivable, then it would have to _____
   A) debit Accounts Receivable $500 and credit Cash $500.
   B) debit Cash $500 and credit Accounts Receivable $500.
   C) debit Cash $500 and credit Owner's Equity $500.
   D) none of the above.

5) An account that is increased with a credit is _____
   A) Cash.
   B) Equipment.
   C) Accounts Payable.
   D) both A and B.

6) The Luna Voc Tour Company purchased $100 of supplies on account. It should _____
   A) debit Supplies $100 and credit Cash $100.
   B) debit Supplies $100 and credit Owner's Equity $100.
   C) debit Supplies $100 and debit Cash $100.
   D) debit Supplies $100 and credit Accounts Payable $100.

7) Which of the following is not true? _____
   A) Debits increase assets.
   B) Credits decrease assets.
   C) Credits increase liabilities.
   D) Credits decrease liabilities.

8) A credit to Accounts Payable is _____
   A) an increase to Accounts Payable.
   B) a decrease to Accounts Payable.
   C) an unfavorable entry.
   D) both A and C.

Learning Goal 22: "Debits on the left, credits on the right!"

SOLUTIONS FOR LEARNING GOAL 22 BEGIN ON PAGE 419.

9) A credit to Unearned Revenue is ____
A) an increase to a revenue.
B) an increase to a liability.
C) an increase to an asset.
D) none of the above.

10) Las Cruces Enterprises shows a Service Revenue account with a credit balance of $44,200. Accounts Payable has a normal balance of $11,000, owner's drawing has a normal balance of $5,000, and expenses total $37,100 normal balance. Las Cruces has ____
A) a net loss of $8,900.
B) a net loss of $3,900.
C) a net income of $2,100.
D) a net income of $7,100.

11) Debits record ____
A) decreases in liabilities and assets.
B) decreases in assets and increases in liabilities.
C) decreases in liabilities and increases in assets.
D) increases in liabilities and assets.

12) Accounts payable was debited and cash was credited. Which of the following best describes what happened? ____
A) The company borrowed cash.
B) The company used cash to pay accounts payable that was owing.
C) The company reduced accounts payable by earning income.
D) The company is owed money for services rendered.

13) Cash is credited and supplies is debited. Which of the following best describes what happened? ____
A) The company bought some supplies.
B) The company used up some supplies.
C) The company sold some supplies to another business which owes the cash.
D) The company sold some supplies and received the cash.

14) Cash is debited and unearned revenue is credited. Which of the following best describes what happened? ____
A) The company is owed cash for services rendered to a customer.
B) The company receives cash for services rendered.
C) The company receives cash for services not yet performed.
D) None of the above.

15) Cash is debited and accounts receivable is credited. Which of the following best describes what happened? ____
A) The company collects cash owing from a customer(s).
B) The company collects cash prior to rendering services.
C) The company borrows cash and owes the money to the creditor.
D) None of the above.

16) Equipment is debited and notes payable is credited. Which of the following best describes what happened? ____
A) The company sold equipment and is owed the money by the buyer.
B) The company purchased equipment for cash.
C) The owner personally purchased equipment and then contributed it to the company.
D) None of the above.

PRACTICE FOR LEARNING GOAL 22

SOLUTIONS FOR LEARNING GOAL 22 BEGIN ON PAGE 419.

REINFORCEMENT PROBLEMS

1) **Identify the natural positive side.** For each of the accounts listed below, place a mark in either the "Dr." space or the "Cr." space to indicate if the natural positive side is the debit side or the credit side of the account.

Account	Natural Positive Side	
	Dr.	Cr.
A) Supplies		
B) Accounts Payable		
C) Service Revenue		
D) Cash		
E) R. Penland, Drawing		
F) R. Penland, Capital		
G) Accounts Receivable		
H) Rent Expense		
I) Prepaid Rent		
J) Equipment		
K) Unearned Revenue		
L) Notes Payable		

2) **The six elements of the accounting equation: identify the debit and credit rules.** Complete the following table by writing the word "increase" or "decrease" in the spaces in each column of the six elements in the accounting equation. At the bottom of each column, also write "Dr." or "Cr." to identify which side of an account for each element shows the natural positive balance (the "normal balance").

	Assets	Liabilities	Owner's Capital	Revenue	Expense	Drawing
Debit						
Credit						
Natural Positive Balance?						

3) **Record debit and credit entries into accounts.** In each of the separate transactions listed below, use T accounts to record transactions. Before recording each transaction, complete the "analysis" and "apply the rule" sections. The first transaction is presented as an example.

Note: Remember that you can visualize each transaction by either drawing a picture of the condition of the business or by using the accounting equation. Then place T accounts in the picture or under the equation.

Learning Goal 22: "Debits on the left, credits on the right!"

SOLUTIONS FOR LEARNING GOAL 22 BEGIN ON PAGE 419.

3) *continued*

Example: Annapolis Enterprises pays $550 to purchase office supplies.

Analysis (account type, account name, and increase or decrease):
The *asset Supplies increases* by $550. The *asset Cash decreases* by $550.

Apply the rule (debits and credits):
Assets are decreased with credits: credit Cash $550.
Assets are increased with debits: debit Supplies $550.

Record in T account:

Cash		Supplies	
	550	550	

A) Essex Company receives $1,000 from a customer before the services are provided.

Analysis (account type, account name, and increase or decrease):

Apply the rule (debits and credits)

Record in T account:

B) Montgomery Enterprises receives a $200 electric bill. The bill is not paid immediately.

Analysis (account type, account name, and increase or decrease):

Apply the rule (debits and credits)

Record in T account:

C) Prince Georges Company finishes consulting services for a client and sends the client a bill for $5,000.

Analysis (account type, account name, and increase or decrease):

Apply the rule (debits and credits)

Record in T account:

Learning Goal 22: "Debits on the left, credits on the right!"

SOLUTIONS FOR LEARNING GOAL 22 BEGIN ON PAGE 419.

3) *continued*

D) Cecil Company prepays six months of fire insurance for $2,500.

Analysis (account type, account name, and increase or decrease):
Apply the rule (debits and credits)
Record in T account:

E) James Lafayette, owner of Anchorage Company, invests $9,000 in his business.

Analysis (account type, account name, and increase or decrease):
Apply the rule (debits and credits)
Record in T account:

F) Soldotna Company pays a $1,000 account payable.

Analysis (account type, account name, and increase or decrease):
Apply the rule (debits and credits)
Record in T account:

G) Nome Commercial Company purchases $10,000 of equipment, paying $3,000 cash and signing a note payable for the balance.

Analysis (account type, account name, and increase or decrease):
Apply the rule (debits and credits)
Record in T account:

PRACTICE QUESTIONS FOR LEARNING GOAL 22 BEGIN ON PAGE 414.

MULTIPLE CHOICE

1) C.
2) B.
3) A.
4) B. This is giving up one asset (Accounts Receivable) for another asset (Cash).
5) C.
6) D.
7) D. Debits (left-side entry) decrease liabilities.
8) A.
9) B.
10) D. Net income (or loss) is simply revenues – expenses ($44,200 – $37,100 = $7,100).
11) C.
12) B, because Accounts Payable decreased and Cash decreased.
13) A, because Cash decreased and Supplies increased.
14) C, because Cash increased and Unearned Revenue increased.
15) A, because Cash increased and Accounts Receivable decreased.
16) D. Equipment increased and Notes Payable increased, so the company purchased equipment and signed a note payable.

REINFORCEMENT PROBLEMS

1)

Account	Natural Positive Side	
	Dr.	**Cr.**
A) Supplies	✗	
B) Accounts Payable		✗
C) Service Revenue		✗
D) Cash	✗	
E) R. Penland, Drawing	✗	
F) R. Penland, Capital		✗
G) Accounts Receivable	✗	
H) Rent Expense	✗	
I) Prepaid Rent	✗	
J) Equipment	✗	
K) Unearned Revenue		✗
L) Notes Payable		✗

Learning Goal 22: "Debits on the left, credits on the right!"

SOLUTIONS FOR LEARNING GOAL 22

PRACTICE QUESTIONS FOR LEARNING GOAL 22 BEGIN ON PAGE 414.

2)

	Assets	Liabilities	Owner's Capital	Revenue	Expense	Drawing
Debit	Increase	Decrease	Decrease	Decrease	Increase	Increase
Credit	Decrease	Increase	Increase	Increase	Decrease	Decrease
Natural Positive Balance?	Dr.	Cr.	Cr.	Cr.	Dr.	Dr.

3)   A) Essex Company receives $1,000 from a customer before the services are provided.

Analysis:
The *asset Cash increases* by $1,000. The *liability Unearned Revenue increases* by $1,000.

Apply the rule:
Assets are increased with debits: debit Cash $1,000.
Liabilities are increased with credits: credit Unearned Revenue $1,000.

Record in T account:

	Cash		Unearned Revenue
	1,000		1,000

B) Montgomery Enterprises receives a $200 electric bill. The bill is not paid immediately.

Analysis:
The *expense Utility Expense increases* by $200. The *liability Accounts Payable increases* by $200.

Apply the rule:
Expenses are increased with debits: debit Utility Expense $200.
Liabilities are increased with credits: credit Accounts Payable $200.

Record in T account:

	Utility Expense		Accounts Payable
	200		200

Learning Goal 22: "Debits on the left, credits on the right!"

PRACTICE QUESTIONS FOR LEARNING GOAL 22 BEGIN ON PAGE 414.

3) *continued*

C) Prince Georges Company finishes consulting services for a client and sends the client a bill for $5,000.

Analysis:
The *asset Accounts Receivable increases* by $5,000. The *revenue Fees Earned* (or similar name, such as Service Revenue, etc.) *increases* by $5,000.

Apply the rule:
Assets are increased with debits: debit Accounts Receivable $5,000.
Revenues are increased with credits: credit Fees Earned $5,000.

Record in T account:

Accounts Receivable		Fees Earned	
5,000			5,000

D) Cecil Company prepays six months of fire insurance for $2,500.

Analysis:
The *asset Prepaid Insurance increases* by $2,500. The *asset Cash decreases* by $2,500.

Apply the rule:
Assets are increased with debits: debit Prepaid Insurance $2,500.
Assets are decreased with credits: credit Cash $2,500.

Record in T account:

Prepaid Insurance		Cash	
2,500			2,500

E) James Lafayette, owner of Anchorage Company, invests $9,000 in his business.

Analysis:
The *asset Cash increases* by $9,000. The *owner's equity James Lafayette, Capital increases* by $9,000.

Apply the rule:
Assets are increased with debits: debit Cash $9,000.
Owner's equity is increased with credits: credit James Lafayette, Capital $9,000.

Record in T account:

Cash		James Lafayette, Capital	
9,000			9,000

Learning Goal 22: "Debits on the left, credits on the right!"

SOLUTIONS FOR LEARNING GOAL 22

PRACTICE QUESTIONS FOR LEARNING GOAL 22 BEGIN ON PAGE 414.

3) continued

F)   Soldotna Company pays a $1,000 account payable.

Analysis:
The *asset Cash decreases* by $1,000. The *liability Accounts Payable decreases* by $1,000.

Apply the rule:
Assets are decreased with credits: credit Cash $1,000.
Liabilities are decreased with debits: debit Accounts Payable $1,000.

Record in T account:

	Cash		Accounts Payable	
		1,000	1,000	

G)   Nome Commercial Company purchases $10,000 of equipment, paying $3,000 cash and signing a note payable for the balance.

Analysis:
The *asset Equipment increases* by $10,000. The *asset Cash decreases* by $3,000. The *liability Notes Payable increases* by $7,000.

Apply the rule:
Assets are increased with debits: debit Equipment $10,000.
Assets are decreased with credits: credit Cash $3,000.
Liabilities are increased with credits: credit Notes Payable $7,000.

Record in T account:

Equipment		Cash		Notes Payable	
10,000			3,000		7,000

Your Questions?

It is *very* important to be aware of what you need to understand better. What do you need to understand better about this learning goal? Use this space to write the questions that you want to discuss with your classmates, instructor, or supervisor. Try to be very specific about what is bothering you, such as explanations that you do not fully understand.

Learning Goal 22: "Debits on the left, credits on the right!"

LEARNING GOAL 23
Explain the Ledger

OVERVIEW

Introduction

In the prior three learning goals, you learned about accounts, and that individual accounts fulfill Items #4 and #5 of the five information requirements (page 365). In this learning goal, you will learn how the accounts are arranged. This is done to save space and make it easy to add new accounts.

Our present arrangement

So far, we have used to a table to record transactions, and to meet the five information requirements.

	Assets								=	Liabilities + Owner's Equity			
	Cash		Accounts Receivable		Supplies		Equipment			Note Payable		C. Goldman, Capital	
	Increase	Decrease	Increase	Decrease	Increase	Decrease	Increase	Decrease	Decrease	Increase	Decrease	Increase
5/2	bal. **17,300**		bal. **4,500**		bal. **900**		bal. **12,000**			bal. **10,000**		bal. **24,700**
5/4	800			800								
5/5			1,000									1,000
5/7		400			400							
5/7	2,000											2,000
5/8		1,000					5,000			4,000		
5/8	bal. **18,700**		bal. **4,700**		bal. **1,300**		bal. **17,000**			bal. **14,000**		bal. **27,700**

The table is not practical

Unfortunately, there is one serious problem in the way we are recording transactions in tables. SPACE! Even though we nicely satisfy all five requirements, we are going to quickly run out of space for accounts. Because we are placing the accounts across a page, we are limited by the width of a page. Already we need to show the different owner's capital subaccounts, and this could include several different revenues and many individual expenses. We will also have additional assets and liabilities. Even if we went across two pages we would never have enough space! However, remain calm … you only have to read the next page to find the solution to the problem.

SEPARATE BOOKS FOR DIFFERENT PURPOSES

Two books: the journal and the ledger	To solve the space problem and to still satisfy all five of the information requirements, accountants have found that they need to enter the transaction information into *two* separate kinds of records. These records are usually kept in two separate books, called a journal and a ledger. In a computerized system, they are shown as two separate files.
Journal defined	A *journal* is like a daily diary that keeps a list of all the transactions as they happen. We will discuss the journal in depth in the next learning goal, starting on page 430.

THE GENERAL LEDGER

Ledger defined	The ***ledger*** is a book that contains individual accounts. The general-purpose kind of ledger that we study here is also called the ***general ledger*** because it contains all the accounts. The accounts in the ledger are sometimes called ***ledger accounts***. A ledger fulfills two information requirements because with a ledger you can: • see a record of all the increases and decreases in each account • see the balance of each account
The structure of the ledger	A ledger solves the space problem by placing each account on its own page. The accounts as individual pages are then placed into the book (the ledger). We can have as many accounts as we want. The book is designed so that the back can be separated and new pages can be added. So, any time we need a new account, we can just add another page for the new account! The diagram on the next page illustrates this idea.

THE GENERAL LEDGER (continued)

Every account has its own page. All the pages are placed together in a book called the ledger.

This makes it possible to keep as many accounts as necessary in one convenient place.

In a computerized system, a computer file is used instead of a book.

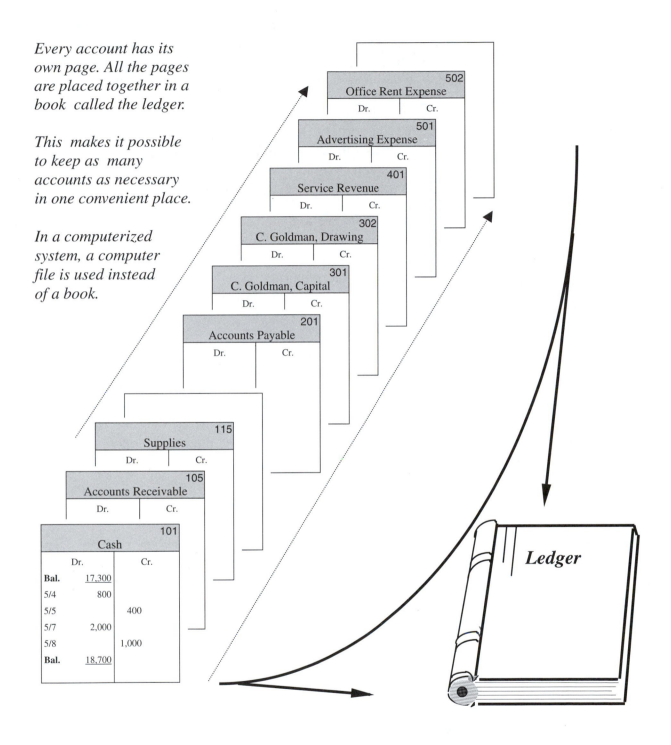

THE GENERAL LEDGER (continued)

How many accounts?	How many accounts a business needs depends upon the size and the nature of a particular business, what kinds of transactions it usually has, and how much detail the owners and managers want to know about the operations.
Account identification numbers	In the upper-right corner of each account in the illustration on page 425, you will notice a number. Each account has its own permanent identification number. These are called ***account numbers***.
Rule for assigning account numbers	The account numbers are assigned to accounts in the approximate ordering sequence that the accounts normally appear on the financial statements. • The balance sheet accounts are assigned the first numbers, in the same order that they would appear on the balance sheet. For example, assets are shown first, beginning with cash, then liabilities, and then finally the owner's capital account. • The drawing account is numbered next. • The income statement accounts are next. • Expense accounts are numbered last.
Rule for placing accounts in the ledger	Account pages are placed in the ledger in the same sequence as their account numbers. *Note:* In a computerized system, accounts also appear in the same sequence.
The chart of accounts	The names of all the accounts and the numbers assigned to them can be found in a listing called the ***chart of accounts***. The chart of accounts is usually located on the first page of a ledger.

THE GENERAL LEDGER (continued)

Example: chart of accounts

Although there is no one format for every chart of accounts, here is an example of how the chart of accounts might look for the Nevada Company:

**Nevada Company
Chart of Accounts**

Asset Accounts: numbers 101–199
#101	Cash
#105	Accounts Receivable
#115	Supplies
#140	Office Equipment
#160	Building
#170	Land

Liability Accounts: numbers 201–299
#201	Accounts Payable
#205	Wages Payable
#210	Unearned Revenue

Owner's Capital Accounts: numbers 301–399
| #301 | C. Goldman, Capital |
| #302 | C. Goldman, Drawing |

Revenue Accounts: numbers 401–499
| #401 | Service Revenue |
| #405 | Interest Earned |

Expense Accounts: numbers 501–599
#501	Advertising Expense
#502	Office Rent Expense
#507	Equipment Rent Expense
#510	Wages Expense
#515	Utilities Expense
#520	Supplies Expense
#525	Insurance Expense
#550	Miscellaneous Expense

Gaps in the numbering sequence

You can see that there are large gaps of unused numbers in the sequence of numbers assigned to the accounts. This is done intentionally. The gaps are for numbers that might be needed later when new accounts are added. For example, the number 111 might be used later if Nevada Company wanted to create an account called "Cleaning Supplies."

Learning Goal 23: Explain the Ledger

QUICK REVIEW

A ledger ...	
meets these two information requirements ...	**arranges data by ...**
● keeps a historical record of *all the increases* and *all the decreases* in each account. ● shows the *balance* of each account at any time.	● accounts, which are all placed in a single book or file. ● keeping numbered accounts in numerical sequence.

VOCABULARY

Account numbers: unique identification numbers assigned to accounts (page 426)

Chart of accounts: a listing of account names and identification numbers (page 426)

General ledger: a book or computer file that contains all the ledger accounts (page 424)

Journal: a chronological record of transactions (page 424)

Ledger: a book or computer file that contains accounts (page 424)

Ledger accounts: accounts which are found in a ledger (page 424)

PRACTICE FOR LEARNING GOAL 23

Learning Goal 23 is about the purpose and function of a ledger. Use these questions to practice what you have just read.

MULTIPLE CHOICE

1) A ledger is ____
   A) an individual record of increases and decreases of a particular item in the accounting equation.
   B) a book or a file that contains all the accounts of a business.
   C) a chronological record of transaction data.
   D) both B and C.
2) The purpose of a ledger is to ____
   A) maintain normal balances in accounts.
   B) prove that debits equal credits.
   C) maintain a detailed record of all the increases and decreases in each account.
   D) serve as a source of business transaction documentation.
3) An account number will always be found ____
   A) in a record of transactions.
   B) on a ledger account.
   C) in the part of the ledger called the "chart of accounts."
   D) both B and C.
4) Which kind of account would you normally expect to see last in a ledger? ____
   A) Revenues
   B) Liabilities
   C) Assets
   D) Expenses
5) Accounts are usually placed into a ledger in the following order: ____
   A) in the sequence of their account numbers
   B) by size
   C) alphabetically
   D) by type of account
6) If you only had the number of an account, and wanted to find out the account name, the best plan would be to ____
   A) look through the ledger until you found the account with the correct number.
   B) look in the chart of accounts.
   C) look in the journal.
   D) speak with the accountant who recorded the transactions.
7) Information in the ledger is arranged by ____
   A) account.
   B) transaction.
   C) size (largest to smallest).
   D) chronological record.
8) A ledger fulfills which of the following information needs? ____
   A) You can easily see all parts of each transaction and the balance of each account.
   B) You can see that the accounting equation stays in balance with each transaction.
   C) You can see a historical record of the increases and decreases in each account and the account balance.
   D) You can easily see all parts of each transaction and a historical record of each account.

SOLUTIONS FOR LEARNING GOAL 23

MULTIPLE CHOICE

1) B. Not to be confused with A, which is an account.
2) C.   3) D.   4) D.   5) A.   6) B.   7) A.   8) C.

LEARNING GOAL 24
Use a Journal

In Learning Goal 24, you will find:

▼ The Purpose and Structure of a General Journal

OVERVIEW

Introduction

A *journal* is like a daily transaction diary. A journal is where transaction information is first recorded in an accounting system.

Accountants have discovered that it is actually more efficient to first record the transaction information into the journal. For that reason, the journal is often called the **book of original entry**. After transaction information is entered into the journal, the same information is then recorded into the ledger accounts.

Both the journal and the ledger contain exactly the same information. However, each book *arranges* the information differently, in order to meet different information needs.

OVERVIEW (continued)

A journal meets three information needs	A journal arranges data in order to meet information needs #1, #2 and #3 (see page 365). With a journal, you can: • find a transaction by date • see all the accounts affected by each transaction • see if the accounting equation stays in balance with each transaction
General journal	Most businesses have more than one kind of journal. However, we will study the most common kind of journal that all businesses use. This is an all-purpose journal that is called the ***general journal***. Recording information into a journal is called ***journalizing***.

THE STRUCTURE OF A GENERAL JOURNAL

Why the journal is different	Like a ledger, a journal is a book with individual pages. However, the journal is different because it arranges the transaction information differently. In a journal, the journal pages record *all of the complete transactions* in the order in which they happen. This is different than a ledger, which uses each page to record information about only one account.
Example	In the example below, you see the top part of a journal page. On the page are two transactions of the Jill Hirata Company, for the week of June 5.

Date	Account	Dr.	Cr.
2000 June 5	Cash Jill Hirata, Capital Owner made investment to start business	10,000	 10,000
June 7	Supplies Accounts Payable Purchase supplies on account	500	 500

THE STRUCTURE OF A GENERAL JOURNAL (continued)

Notice that these three information requirements are met:

- Transactions can be located by date, because they are recorded chronologically.
- All the accounts in each separate transaction are easily identified.
- It is easy to see if the debits and credits are keeping the equation in balance.

▼ *Recording Transactions in a General Journal*

HOW TRANSACTIONS ARE RECORDED IN A GENERAL JOURNAL

Using the example above ...

We can use the transaction on page 431 for June 5 to see how an entry should be recorded into a journal.

Rule for date

Date: The date that is entered is always the date of transaction, not the date that it is being recorded, which may be later.

Date	Account	Dr.	Cr.
2000 June 5			

Rules for recording the debits

- Debits are always recorded first.
- Use the *exact name* of the account that needs to be debited. Do not put something like "cash investment" because there is no account by that name.
- Write the name of the account next to the left margin.
- If there is more than one account to debit, write the name of the next account to be debited on the next line. There is no particular order for entering account names.

Dollar amount: Write the dollar amount being debited into the debit (Dr.) column on the same line as the name of the account. Dollar signs are not used.

Date	Account	Dr.	Cr.
2000 June 5	**Cash**	**10,000**	

HOW TRANSACTIONS ARE RECORDED IN A GENERAL JOURNAL (continued)

Rules for recording the credits

- Credit entries are recorded after all debits are recorded.
- Use the *exact name* of the account that needs to be credited. Do not put something like "increase in capital" because there is no account by that name.
- It is customary to *indent the name of a credited account,* so it is easy to identify.
- If there is more than one account to credit, write the name of next account to be credited on the next line. There is no particular order for entering account names.

Dollar amount: Write the dollar amount being credited into the credit (Cr.) column on the same line as the name of the account.

Date	Account	Dr.	Cr.
2000 June 5	Cash **Jill Hirata, Capital**	10,000	**10,000**

Check equality

Check to see that the dollar value of debits equals the dollar value of the credits. In this example, it is pretty obvious, but in bigger journal entries with multiple debits and credits, it is not always so easy to see. If debits do not equal credits, the transaction being recorded will cause the accounting equation to be out of balance.

Equality OK!

Date	Account	Dr.	Cr.
2000 June 5	Cash Jill Hirata, Capital	10,000	10,000

Explanation is a good idea

Check with your teacher or supervisor to find out if an explanation is required. However, it is usually a good idea to write an explanation. This is especially true in complicated or unusual transactions where you should also *identify the source of the information.* Weeks, months, or years later, when someone asks you for an explanation (like the IRS), you will thank yourself for being so careful.

Learning Goal 24: Use a Journal

HOW TRANSACTIONS ARE RECORDED IN A GENERAL JOURNAL (continued)

Date	Account	Dr.	Cr.
2000 June 5	Cash	10,000	
	Jill Hirata, Capital		10,000
	Owner made investment to start business		

Explanation

Skip a line

Skip a line before you journalize the next transaction. This makes all the individual transactions much easier to identify. Your tired teacher or supervisor will be very grateful.

CHECK YOUR UNDERSTANDING

?

Fill in each blank space with the correct word. The answers are below.

The journal is a chronological record of _____. The journal meets these information requirements: 1) you can locate any transaction by _____, 2) you can see all the _____ in each transaction, and 3) you can see if the accounting equation stays in _____. The procedure of recording information into the journal is called _____.

The journal and ledger are different because the journal organizes data by _____, while the ledger organizes data by _____. Information is always recorded into the journal (before/after) _____ the ledger.

ANSWERS

The journal is a chronological record of transactions. The journal meets these information requirements: 1) you can locate any transaction by date, 2) you can see all the accounts in each transaction, and 3) you can see if the accounting equation stays in balance. The procedure of recording information into the journal is called journalizing.

The journal and ledger are different because the journal organizes data by transaction, while the ledger organizes data by account. Information is always recorded into the journal before the ledger.

▼ *Recording in Both the Journal and Ledger*

THREE STEPS FOR RECORDING TRANSACTIONS

Overview

You now understand what a journal is, what a ledger is, and how to record transaction data into each of them. Because both the journal and ledger are needed, but have different functions, the complete recording procedure must record the same data in both of them. You are now ready to do this, so you can see all steps in recording a transaction. There are three basic steps.

Before you begin ...

Be sure that you have analyzed the event, to determine that it is a transaction.

Procedure

To record a transaction …	
Step	**Action**
1	**Visualize the transaction:** This is a very important step that verifies that the event is a transaction and determines exactly how it will be recorded. Use the accounting equation, like the examples in the grey shaded boxes (below) to visualize the complete change: • account type • account name • increase/decrease
2	**Journalize:** Use the debit and credit rules to enter the transaction into the journal.
3	**Record in ledger accounts:** Use the debit and credit rules to record the same information into the affected ledger accounts.

Example

Let us imagine that we are doing the bookkeeping for David Lilliput, who is going to start a small business called "David's tiny little Bodyguard Service."

THREE STEPS FOR RECORDING TRANSACTIONS (continued)

● **June 1:** David invests $20 to start his business. (This is going to be a very small business!)

Step 1	Visualize the transaction	
Account Type	**Account Name**	**Increase/Decrease**
Asset	Cash	Increase $20
Owner's Equity	David Lilliput, Capital	Increase $20

$$A \uparrow \quad = \quad L \quad + \quad OE \uparrow$$
Cash   David Lilliput, Capital
+20   +20

Step 2	Journalize		

Assets are increased with debits: debit Cash $20.
Owner's equity is increased with credits: credit David Lilliput, Capital $20.

Date	Account	Dr.	Cr.
2000 June 1	Cash	20	
	David Lilliput, Capital		20
	Owner made investment to start business.		

Step 3	Record in ledger accounts

Assets are increased with debits: debit Cash $20.
Owner's equity is increased with credits: credit David Lilliput, Capital $20.

Cash	David Lilliput, Capital
20	20

THREE STEPS FOR RECORDING TRANSACTIONS (continued)

- **June 2:** The business purchases $5 of office supplies and $20 of office equipment, all on account, from London Company.

Step 1	Visualize the transaction	
Account Type	**Account Name**	**Increase/Decrease**
Asset	Office Supplies	Increase $5
Asset	Office Equipment	Increase $20
Liability	Accounts Payable	Increase $25

$$A \uparrow \qquad = \qquad L \uparrow \qquad + \quad OE$$

Office Supplies +5   Accounts Payable +25
Office Equipment +20

Step 2	Journalize

Assets are increased with debits: debit Office Supplies $5.
Assets are increased with debits: debit Office Equipment $20.
Liabilities are increased with credits: credit Accounts Payable $25.

Date	Account	Dr.	Cr.
2000 June 2	Office Supplies Office Equipment Accounts Payable Purchase supplies and equipment from London Company	5 20	 25

Step 3	Record in ledger accounts

Assets are increased with debits: debit Office Supplies $5.
Assets are increased with debits: debit Office Equipment $20.
Liabilities are increased with credits: credit Accounts Payable $25.

Office Supplies		Office Equipment		Accts. Payable			
5		20			25		

THREE STEPS FOR RECORDING TRANSACTIONS (continued)

Journal and ledger entries with three or more accounts are called *compound entries*. Compound entries are quite common.

● **June 3:** The business receives a $7 advance payment from Houyhnhnm Company.

Step 1	Visualize the transaction	
Account Type	**Account Name**	**Increase/Decrease**
Asset	Cash	Increase $7
Liability	Unearned Revenue	Increase $7

$$A \uparrow \quad = \quad L \uparrow \quad\quad\quad + \quad OE$$
$$\text{Cash} +7 \quad\quad \text{Unearned Revenue} +7$$

Step 2	Journalize		
Assets are increased with debits: debit Cash $7. Liabilities are increased with credits: credit Unearned Revenue $7.			
Date	**Account**	**Dr.**	**Cr.**
2000 June 3	Cash Unearned Revenue Advance payment from Houyhnhnm Company	7	7

Step 3	Record in ledger accounts
Assets are increased with debits: debit Cash $7. Liabilities are increased with credits: credit Unearned Revenue $7.	

Cash   Unearned Revenue

7   7

THREE STEPS FOR RECORDING TRANSACTIONS (continued)

- **June 4:** The business uses up $3 of office supplies.

Step 1	Visualize the transaction	
Account Type	**Account Name**	**Increase/Decrease**
Asset	Office Supplies	Decrease $3
Owner's equity	Supplies Expense	Increase $3

$$A \downarrow \quad = \quad L \quad + \quad OE \downarrow$$
Office Supplies (3)   Supplies Expense +3

Step 2	Journalize		

Expenses are increased with debits: debit Supplies Expense $3.
Assets are decreased with credits: credit Office Supplies $3.

Date	Account	Dr.	Cr.
2000 June 4	Supplies Expense Office Supplies Office supplies used up for the Swift report	3	3

Step 3	Record in ledger accounts

Expenses are increased with debits: debit Supplies Expense $3.
Assets are decreased with credits: credit Office Supplies $3.

Office Supplies		Supplies Expense
3		3

Note: Remember that an expense is a decrease in owner's equity— caused by operations. The more expenses, the more owner's equity decreases.

THREE STEPS FOR RECORDING TRANSACTIONS (continued)

- **June 5:** The company provided security services to Shadow Company for $5 "on account."

Step 1	Visualize the transaction	
Account Type	**Account Name**	**Increase/Decrease**
Asset	Accounts Receivable	Increase $5
Owner's equity	Security Service Revenue	Increase $5

$$A \uparrow \quad = \quad L \quad + \quad OE \uparrow$$
Accounts Receivable +5   Security Service Revenue +5

Step 2	Journalize

Assets are increased with debits: debit Accounts Receivable $5.
Revenues are increased with credits: credit Security Service Revenue $5.

Date	Account	Dr.	Cr.
2000 June 5	Accounts Receivable Security Service Revenue Security services for Shadow Company	5	5

Step 3	Record in ledger accounts

Assets are increased with debits: debit Accounts Receivable $5.
Revenues are increased with credits: credit Security Service Revenue $5.

Accounts Receivable		Security Service Revenue
5		5

THREE STEPS FOR RECORDING TRANSACTIONS (continued)

● **June 6:** The company signed a contract to provide Security Services to Green Hornet Company.

Step 1	Visualize the transaction	
Account Type	**Account Name**	**Increase/Decrease**
A = L +OE **Not a transaction**		

Note: Nothing of value has yet been provided or received, so this is a business event that is not an accounting transaction. There may be legal implications, but there are no recordable economic effects.

● **June 6:** The company paid $3 owing on the account payable.

Step 1	Visualize the transaction	
Account Type	**Account Name**	**Increase/Decrease**
Asset	Cash	Decrease $3
Liability	Accounts Payable	Decrease $3
A ↓ = L ↓ + OE Cash (3) Accounts Payable (3)		

Step 2	Journalize
Assets are decreased with credits: credit Cash $3. Liabilities are decreased with debits: debit Accounts Payable $3.	

Date	Account	Dr.	Cr.
2000 June 6	Accounts Payable Cash Payment on Accounts Payable—London Company	3	3

THREE STEPS FOR RECORDING TRANSACTIONS (continued)

Step 3	Record in ledger accounts

Assets are decreased with credits: credit Cash $3.
Liabilities are decreased with debits: debit Accounts Payable $3.

Cash	Accounts Payable	
3	3	

● **June 7:** The company paid $10 for liability insurance coverage until the end of September.

Step 1	Visualize the transaction

Account Type	Account Name	Increase/Decrease
Asset	Cash	Decrease $10
Asset	Prepaid Insurance	Increase $10

$$A \downarrow \uparrow \qquad = \quad L \ + \ OE$$
Cash (10)
Prepaid Insurance +10

Step 2	Journalize

Assets are decreased with credits: credit Cash $10.
Assets are increased with debits: debit Prepaid Insurance $10.

Date	Account	Dr.	Cr.
2000 June 7	Prepaid Insurance Cash Prepaid Old Bailey Insurance Company— liability insurance coverage until September 30	10	10

THREE STEPS FOR RECORDING TRANSACTIONS (continued)

Step 3	Record in ledger accounts

Assets are decreased with credits: credit Cash $10.
Assets are increased with debits: debit Prepaid Insurance $10.

Cash	Prepaid Insurance			
10	10			

● **June 7:** The company received $15 from T & P Company for security services.

Step 1	Visualize the transaction

Account Type	Account Name	Increase/Decrease
Asset	Accounts Receivable	Increase $15
Owner's equity	Security Service Revenue	Increase $15

$$A \uparrow \qquad = \quad L \quad + \quad OE \uparrow$$
Cash +15   Security Service Revenue +15

Step 2	Journalize

Assets are increased with debits: debit Cash $15.
Revenues are increased with credits: credit Security Service Revenue $15.

Date	Account	Dr.	Cr.
2000 June 7	Cash	15	
	Security Service Revenue		15
	Services provided to T & P Company		

THREE STEPS FOR RECORDING TRANSACTIONS (continued)

Step 3	Record in ledger accounts
Assets are increased with debits: debit Cash $15. Revenues are increased with credits: credit Security Service Revenue $15.	

☞*QUICK REVIEW*☜

A journal …	
meets these three information requirements …	**arranges data by …**
● find a transaction by date. ● see all parts of a transaction. ● see if the equation stays in balance.	● transactions, which are recorded chronologically.

● The three steps for recording transactions are:
— visualize
— journalize
— record in the ledger

☞*VOCABULARY*☜

Book of original entry: a journal (page 430)

Compound entries: entries containing three or more accounts (page 438)

General journal: an all-purpose journal that can record all types of transactions (page 431)

Journal: a chronological record of transactions (page 430)

Journalizing: recording information into a journal (page 431)

"Stranger, did you mean 'journal' or did you mean 'ledger'?"

•   •

PRACTICE FOR LEARNING GOAL 24

SOLUTIONS FOR LEARNING GOAL 24 BEGIN ON PAGE 458.

Learning Goal 24 is about learning to use the general journal. Use these questions and problems to practice what you have just read.

MULTIPLE CHOICE

1) When using the general journal _____
   A) the name of the account used must be exactly the same as the name used in the chart of accounts.
   B) account numbers must always be entered immediately.
   C) credits are recorded before debits.
   D) both A and B.

2) When using the general journal, it is good form to _____
   A) skip a line between transactions.
   B) always place the name of the debit account on the left margin and indent the credit account name.
   C) always place the name of the credit account on the left margin and indent the debit account name.
   D) both A and B.

3) If the San Mateo Sales Company purchased $100 of supplies for cash, and the bookkeeper debited prepaid insurance and credited cash in the journal, then _____
   A) total assets would not be affected.
   B) total assets would be understated.
   C) total assets would be overstated.
   D) prepaid insurance would be understated.

4) Which of the following functions does a journal *not* do? _____
   A) The journal shows in one place all the parts of each transaction.
   B) The journal provides a chronological record of all the transactions as they occurred.
   C) The journal is a way of calculating the balance in any account.
   D) The journal provides a single, convenient location to first enter transaction data into the accounting system.

5) Which of the following accounts should be entered first in a correct journal entry? _____
   A) Cash, when it is decreased.
   B) Accounts Payable, when it is increased.
   C) Expense, when it is increased.
   D) Revenue, when it is increased.

6) If you saw a journal entry that was a debit to Cash and a credit to Unearned Revenue, then you would conclude that _____
   A) cash was received when revenue was earned.
   B) cash was borrowed.
   C) cash was advanced by a customer before services were completed.
   D) none of the above.

7) A journal entry that contains three or more accounts is called a _____
   A) compound entry.
   B) complex entry.
   C) multiple-account entry.
   D) combined entry.

8) Which of the following statements about journal entries is true? _____
   A) Assets should always be recorded before liabilities.
   B) A line must be skipped between each debit and credit.
   C) The date must always show when the entry was recorded.
   D) Credits should be indented.

SOLUTIONS FOR LEARNING GOAL 24 BEGIN ON PAGE 458.

9) The proper procedure for recording a journal entry is ____
   A) debit accounts should always be entered last and written next to the left margin.
   B) debit accounts should always be entered first and indented.
   C) the exact name of accounts must always be used, with no exceptions.
   D) always check the balance of each account that is debited or credited.

10) Which of the following statements about a journal is true? ____
   A) Accounts that are increased should be entered first.
   B) Explanations in the journal are seldom done.
   C) Transactions should never cause the accounting equation to be out of balance.
   D) Explanations must always be written under each individual debit and credit.

11) The proper sequence for recording transaction information is ____
   A) visualize, record in accounts, journalize.
   B) journalize, visualize, record in accounts.
   C) visualize, journalize, record in accounts.
   D) visualize and journalize.

12) The journal entry to record a cash receipt from a customer on account would include a ____
   A) debit to Accounts Receivable.
   B) credit to Cash.
   C) credit to Revenue.
   D) credit to Accounts Receivable.

13) The journal entry to record purchase of supplies on account would include a ____
   A) debit to Accounts Payable
   B) debit to Cash.
   C) debit to an expense.
   D) credit to Accounts Payable.

14) The Pelissippi Company wants to record a cash payment for repairs expense and rent expense. Which of the following entries is correct? ____

   A) Cash   500
       Rent Expense   275
             Repairs Expense   325

   B) Rent Expense   275
       Repairs Expense   325
             Cash   500

   C) Rent Expense   275
             Repairs Expense   325
       Cash   500

   D) None of the above.

PRACTICE FOR LEARNING GOAL 24

SOLUTIONS FOR LEARNING GOAL 24 BEGIN ON PAGE 458.

15) The journal entry to record the purchase of equipment by signing a note payable and making a cash down payment would include a _____
   A) debit to Cash and credit to Equipment.
   B) credit to Notes Payable and a credit to Cash.
   C) credit to Equipment and a debit to Cash.
   D) debit to Equipment and a debit to Notes Payable.

REINFORCEMENT PROBLEMS

1) **Practice visualizing a transaction using the accounting equation and pictures.** Before recording a transaction, it is necessary to visualize the transaction.

   After each transaction, see if you can visualize the effect on the accounting equation two ways:
   - Write the accounting equation using both arrows and numbers to show what parts of the equation are increasing or decreasing.
   - Draw a picture of a business, and enter the changes in the picture. Use the first transaction as an example.

Example: Bryce Jones, owner of Sacramento Company, invests $10,000 in his business.

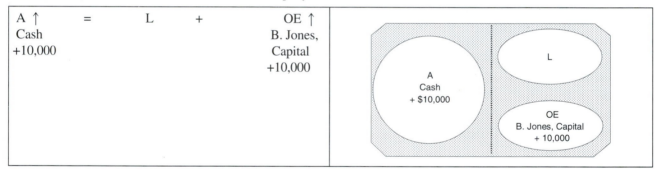

A) Palomar Company uses up $200 of supplies.

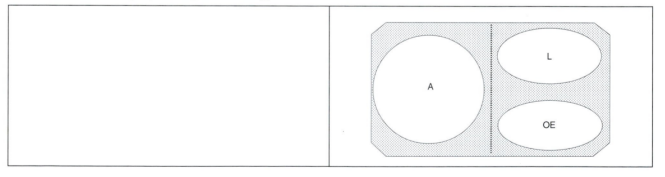

PRACTICE FOR LEARNING GOAL 24

SOLUTIONS FOR LEARNING GOAL 24 BEGIN ON PAGE 458.

1) *continued*

B) Mira Costa Enterprises collects $850 owing from customers.

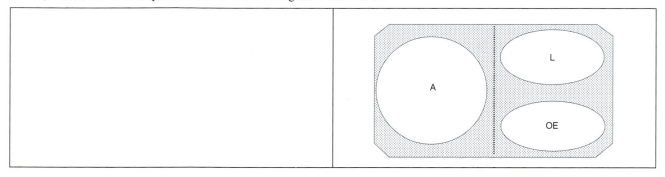

C) Santa Monica Corporation purchases $10,000 of equipment by paying $1,000 cash and signing a $9,000 note payable.

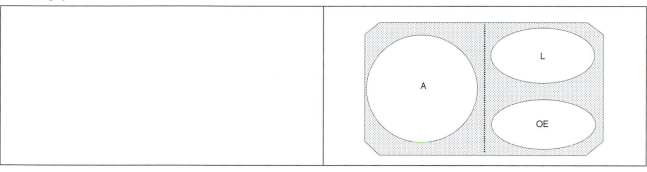

D) Fairfield Partnership prepays three months' office rent for $9,000.

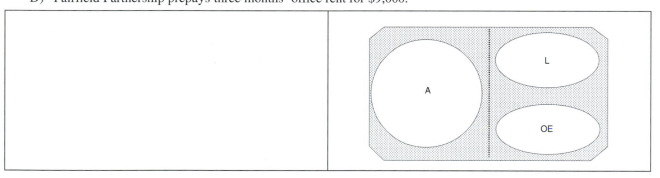

PRACTICE FOR LEARNING GOAL 24

SOLUTIONS FOR LEARNING GOAL 24 BEGIN ON PAGE 458.

1) *continued*

E)   Sonoma Company receives a $300 advance payment from a customer.

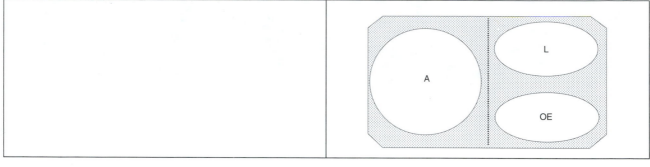

F)   Salinas Enterprises pays a $400 account payable.

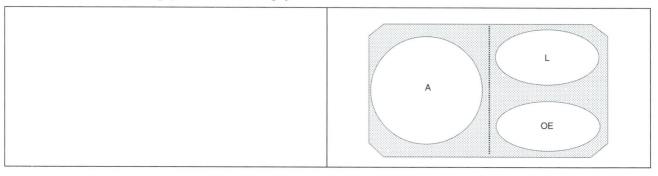

G)   Fairfield Company (in D, above) uses up one month's worth of prepaid office rent.

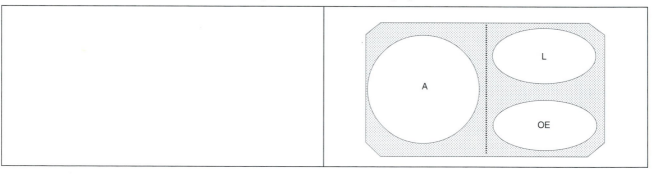

H)   Riverside Company earns $500 on account.

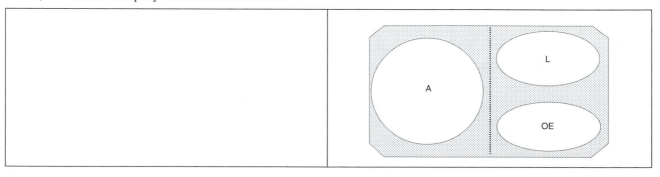

Learning Goal 24: Use a Journal

SOLUTIONS FOR LEARNING GOAL 24 BEGIN ON PAGE 458.

2) **Prepare general journal entries.** For each of the transactions described below for the Macon Cove Information Technology Company in November 2001, prepare general journal entries in the blank journal on page 452. You may omit explanations in this exercise. Remember to take time to analyze/visualize before you make the entry.

November 1: Laurie Shelby invests $8,500 to start her new business, Macon Cove Information Technology Services.

November 1: Macon Cove Information Technology Services rented office space and paid three months' rent in advance for $1,050.

November 4: The business purchases $2,300 of office equipment and $700 of office supplies by making a $1,000 cash down payment and signing a $2,000 note payable.

November 5: Paid Acme Cleaning Services $100.

November 6: Purchased advertising in the month's computer magazine, $500 on credit.

November 7: Completed analysis services for Nashville Company, $980 on account.

November 11: Pays $700 to an employee for wages.

November 12: The business performs $1,500 of services on account for Chattanooga Computer Research Company.

November 14: Laurie Shelby invests an additional $5,000 cash into the business, plus $4,000 of office equipment and $2,000 of office supplies.

November 15: The business paid an account payable, $500.

November 17: Received a $980 check from Nashville Company, on account.

November 19: The business pays $250 for gardening services for the owner's home, a personal expense of the owner, Laurie Shelby.

November 24: Received $2,000 cash for consulting services to Morristown Company.

November 27: Laurie Shelby withdraws $500 cash from her business.

November 30: A count of the supplies shows that the business used up $1,200 of supplies during the month of November.

SOLUTIONS FOR LEARNING GOAL 24 BEGIN ON PAGE 458.

2) *continued*

Date	Account	Dr.	Cr.
2001			

SOLUTIONS FOR LEARNING GOAL 24 BEGIN ON PAGE 458.

3) **Prepare general journal entries.** The general journal that you see below contains explanations but no journal entries. Using the explanations, prepare the correct journal entries.

Date	Account	Dr.	Cr.
2001			
Feb. 8			
	Ken Peters invests $25,000 cash to begin new business, Du Page Delivery Enterprises		
9			
	Prepaid 1 year of insurance for $1,500		
10			
	Purchased office supplies from Jolliet Company, $250 on account		
12			
	Paid $1,000 and signed a $2,000 note payable for an office computer		
14			
	Ken Peters invests an additional $5,000 cash in the business, plus a van worth $15,000.		
	With the van is a note payable of $7,000		
15			
	Billed Morraine Valley Company for services, $575 on account		
17			
	Paid $200 owing to Jolliet Company from February 10		

PRACTICE FOR LEARNING GOAL 24

SOLUTIONS FOR LEARNING GOAL 24 BEGIN ON PAGE 458.

3) *continued*

Date	Account	Dr.	Cr.
20			
	Used up $200 of supplies.		
24			
	Wrote $520 check to Sunshine Day Care for owner's child-care expense.		
27			
	Collected $300 from Morraine Valley Company on account.		

4) **Write explanations to journal entries.** After you have practiced enough journal entries, you should be able to look at a journal entry and know what has happened. This exercise helps you practice this skill. In the general journal below, there are journal entries without explanations. Write a brief, complete, and accurate explanation under each entry.

Date	Account	Dr.	Cr.
2000			
July 11	Accounts Payable, Grants Pass Company	1,000	
	Cash		1,000
12	Andrea Sheaffer, Drawing	750	
	Cash		750
14	Supplies Expense	190	
	Supplies		190
15	Cash	3,500	
	Accounts Receivable, Portland Enterprises		3,500

SOLUTIONS FOR LEARNING GOAL 24 BEGIN ON PAGE 458.

4) *continued*

Date	Account	Dr.	Cr.
17	Accounts Receivable, Gresham Corporation	4,100	
	Fees Earned		4,100
20	Computer Equipment	10,300	
	Cash		2,500
	Notes Payable		7,800
22	Cash	850	
	Unearned Revenue		850
24	Rent Expense	1,500	
	Prepaid Rent		1,500
25	Land	145,000	
	Building	90,000	
	Cash		50,000
	Notes Payable		185,000
27	Repairs Expense	175	
	Accounts Payable		175

PRACTICE FOR LEARNING GOAL 24

SOLUTIONS FOR LEARNING GOAL 24 BEGIN ON PAGE 458.

5) **Reconstruct journal entries from ledger accounts.** You know that in the normal recording procedure, journal entries are always prepared first, before transferring data into the ledger accounts. However, in this exercise we will test your understanding by working backwards from ledger accounts. Using the information in the T accounts shown below, prepare the general journal entries for the month of May, and include explanations.

Cash				Accounts Receivable				Supplies				Prepaid Rent		
May				May				May				May		
5		900		6		330		7	250			18		700
6	330			15	500			17	250					
10	750													
12		450												
17		1,050												

Equipment			Accounts Payable			Notes Payable		
May			May			May		
17	2,800		7		250	17		2,000
			10		1,500			
			12	450				

Service Revenue			Wages Expense			Advertising Expense			Rent Expense		
May			May			May			May		
10		750	5	900		10	1,500		18	700	
15		500									

5)

Date	Account	Dr.	Cr.
2000			

PRACTICE FOR LEARNING GOAL 24

SOLUTIONS FOR LEARNING GOAL 24 BEGIN ON PAGE 458.

5) *continued*

Date	Account	Dr.	Cr.
2000			

6) **Review: Distinguish between the journal and the ledger.** Complete the following table to contrast the essential features of a journal and a ledger.

	A journal …	A ledger …
meets these five information needs …		
and does not meet these information needs …		
and the data is primarily arranged by …		

SOLUTIONS FOR LEARNING GOAL 24

PRACTICE QUESTIONS FOR LEARNING GOAL 24 BEGIN ON PAGE 446.

MULTIPLE CHOICE

1) A.
2) D.
3) A. Total assets are the same, but Supplies is understated by $100 and Prepaid Insurance is overstated by $100.
4) C. Account balances are only found in the ledger.
5) C, because increasing an expense is a debit entry, and debits are placed first. All the other examples are credits.
6) C.
7) A.
8) D. A is incorrect because the rule for which to record first is to record debits before credits. B is incorrect because a line should be skipped between transactions, not between each debit and credit. C is incorrect because the date to use is the date the transaction occurred, not the date it was recorded.
9) C.
10) C.
11) C.
12) D.
13) D.
14) D. All the entries are either debited or credited incorrectly, or do not balance.
15) B.

REINFORCEMENT PROBLEMS

1)   A) Palomar Company uses up $200 of supplies.

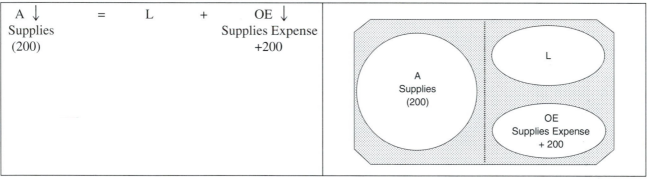

A ↓	=	L	+	OE ↓
Supplies				Supplies Expense
(200)				+200

   B)   Mira Costa Enterprises collects $850 owing from customers.

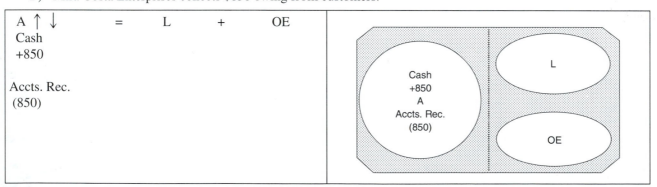

A ↑ ↓	=	L	+	OE
Cash				
+850				
Accts. Rec.				
(850)				

SOLUTIONS FOR LEARNING GOAL 24

PRACTICE QUESTIONS FOR LEARNING GOAL 24 BEGIN ON PAGE 446.

1) *continued*

C) Santa Monica Corporation purchases $10,000 of equipment by paying $1,000 cash and signing a $9,000 note payable.

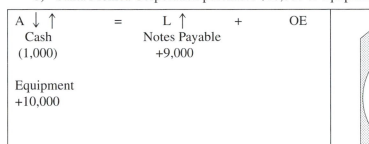
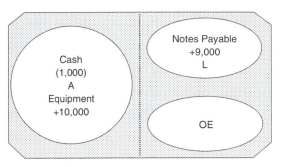

```
A ↓ ↑         =      L ↑        +      OE
  Cash              Notes Payable
  (1,000)              +9,000

Equipment
+10,000
```

D) Fairfield Partnership prepays three months' office rent for $9,000.

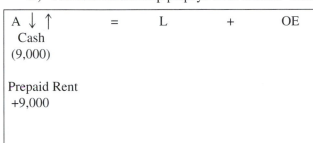
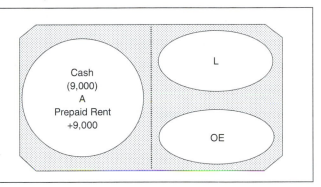

```
A ↓ ↑         =      L          +      OE
  Cash

  (9,000)

Prepaid Rent
+9,000
```

E) Sonoma Company receives a $300 advance payment from a customer.

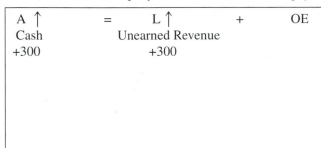
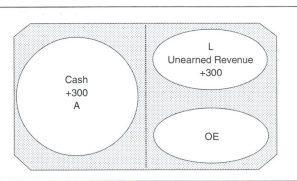

```
A ↑           =      L ↑        +      OE
  Cash              Unearned Revenue
  +300                 +300
```

SOLUTIONS FOR LEARNING GOAL 24

PRACTICE QUESTIONS FOR LEARNING GOAL 24 BEGIN ON PAGE 446.

1) *continued*

F)   Salinas Enterprises pays a $400 account payable.

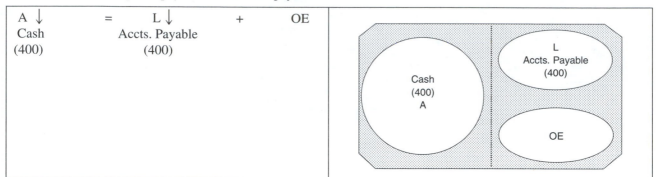

G)   Fairfield Company (in D, above) uses up one month's worth of prepaid office rent.

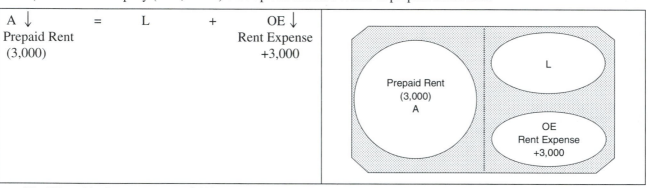

H)   Riverside Company earns $500 on account.

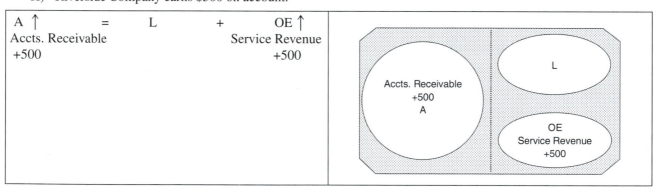

PRACTICE QUESTIONS FOR LEARNING GOAL 24 BEGIN ON PAGE 446.

2)

Date	Account	Dr.	Cr.
2001			
Nov. 1	Cash	8,500	
	Laurie Shelby, Capital		8,500
1	Prepaid Rent	1,050	
	Cash		1,050
4	Office Equipment	2,300	
	Office Supplies	700	
	Cash		1,000
	Notes Payable		2,000
5	Cleaning Expense	100	
	Cash		100
6	Advertising Expense	500	
	Accounts Payable		500
7	Accounts Receivable	980	
	Service Revenue		980
11	Wages Expense	700	
	Cash		700
12	Accounts Receivable	1,500	
	Service Revenue		1,500
14	Cash	5,000	
	Office Equipment	4,000	
	Office Supplies	2,000	
	Laurie Shelby, Capital		11,000
15	Accounts Payable	500	
	Cash		500
17	Cash	980	
	Accounts Receivable		980

SOLUTIONS FOR LEARNING GOAL 24

PRACTICE QUESTIONS FOR LEARNING GOAL 24 BEGIN ON PAGE 446.

2) continued

Date	Account	Dr.	Cr.
2001			
19	Laurie Shelby, Drawing	250	
	Cash		250
24	Cash	2,000	
	Service Revenue		2,000
27	Laurie Shelby, Drawing	500	
	Cash		500
30	Supplies Expense	1,200	
	Supplies		1,200

3)

Date	Account	Dr.	Cr.
2001			
Feb. 8	Cash	25,000	
	Ken Peters, Capital		25,000
	Ken Peters invests $25,000 cash to begin new business, Du Page Delivery Enterprises		
9	Prepaid Insurance	1,500	
	Cash		1,500
	Prepaid 1 year of insurance for $1,500		
10	Office Supplies	250	
	Accounts Payable		250
	Purchased office supplies from Jolliet Company, $250 on account		
12	Office Equipment	3,000	
	Cash		1,000
	Notes Payable		2,000
	Paid $1,000 and signed a $2,000 note payable for an office computer		

SOLUTIONS FOR LEARNING GOAL 24

PRACTICE QUESTIONS FOR LEARNING GOAL 24 BEGIN ON PAGE 446.

3) *continued*

Date	Account	Dr.	Cr.
14	Cash	5,000	
	Van	15,000	
	Notes Payable		7,000
	Ken Peters, Capital		13,000
	Ken Peters invests an additional $5,000 cash in the business,		
	plus a van worth $15,000 with the van is a note payable of $7,000		
15	Accounts Receivable	575	
	Service Revenue		575
	Billed Morraine Valley Company for services, $575 on account		
17	Accounts Payable	200	
	Cash		200
	Paid $200 owing to Jolliet Company from February 10		
20	Supplies Expense	200	
	Supplies		200
	Used up $200 of supplies		
24	Ken Peters, Drawing	520	
	Cash		520
	Wrote $520 check to Sunshine Day Care for owner's child-care expense		
27	Cash	300	
	Accounts Receivable		300
	Collected $300 from Morraine Valley Company on account		

4)

July 11: Paid on account owing to Grants Pass Company.

July 12: The owner (or possibly, partner) Andrea Sheaffer, withdrew cash.

July 14: The business used up of supplies.

July 15: Collected cash on account owing from Portland Enterprises.

July 17: Earned service revenue on account from Gresham Corporation.

July 20: Purchased computer equipment by paying $2,500 cash down and signing a $7,800 note payable for the balance.

July 22: Received an advance payment from a customer.

July 24: Used up prepaid rent, for the period of _____.

July 25: Purchased $145,000 of land and $90,000 building by paying $50,000 cash and signing a note payable for the balance.

July 27: Used repair services. Balance owing on account was $175.

SOLUTIONS FOR LEARNING GOAL 24

PRACTICE QUESTIONS FOR LEARNING GOAL 24 BEGIN ON PAGE 446.

5)

Date	Account	Dr.	Cr.
2000			
May 5	Wages Expense	900	
	Cash		900
	Paid wages		
6	Cash	330	
	Accounts Receivable		330
	Collected amount owing on account from xxxx		
7	Supplies	250	
	Accounts Payable		250
	Purchased supplies on account from xxxx		
10	Advertising Expense	1,500	
	Accounts Payable		1,500
	Used advertising services. Balance owing to xxxx		
10	Cash	750	
	Service Revenue		750
	Completed services for xxxx		
12	Accounts Payable	450	
	Cash		450
	Paid on account owing to xxxx		
15	Accounts Receivable	500	
	Service Revenue		500
	Completed services on account to xxxx		
17	Supplies	250	
	Equipment	2,800	
	Cash		1,050
	Notes Payable		2,000
	Purchased supplies and equipment for $1,050 cash down payment and $2,000 note payable		
	for the balance		
18	Rent Expense	700	
	Prepaid Rent		700
	Used up Prepaid Rent		

Learning Goal 24: Use a Journal

SOLUTIONS FOR LEARNING GOAL 24

PRACTICE QUESTIONS FOR LEARNING GOAL 24 BEGIN ON PAGE 446.

6)

	In a journal ...	In a ledger ...
meets these information needs ...	• you can find a transaction by date • you can easily see all parts of each transaction • you can see if the equation stays in balance	• you can see the historical detail of each account item • you can determine the balance of each account item
and does not meet these information needs ...	• you cannot see the historical detail of each account item • you cannot determine the balance of each account item	• you cannot find a transaction by date • you cannot easily see all parts of each transaction • you cannot see if the equation stays in balance
and the data is primarily arranged by ...	transaction	account

Your Questions?

It is *very* important to be aware of what you need to understand better. What do you need to understand better about this learning goal? Use this space to write the questions that you want to discuss with your classmates, instructor, or supervisor. Try to be very specific about what is bothering you, such as explanations that you do not fully understand.

In Learning Goal 25, you will find:

▼ *Practical Form of the Account and General Journal*

A MORE REALISTIC JOURNAL

Two improvements

Only two improvements are needed in order to make our journal realistic and fully usable. Shown below is the general journal for David's tiny little Bodyguard Service for the first week of operations after all the transactions are recorded. Notice the following two improvements in the journal:

Journal Page Number: Every journal has page numbers. The "J1" that you see as a shaded box in the upper right corner of the journal means page 1 of the general journal. (Sometimes the letters "G" or "GJ" are used instead.)

"Posting Reference" Column: The new column that is titled "Post. Ref." is only used during the posting procedure which will be explained. When data is transferred from the journal to a ledger account, that account's identification number is entered in the "Post. Ref." column. (Sometimes the "Posting Reference" column is titled "LP" for ledger page, or "folio.")

A MORE REALISTIC JOURNAL (continued)

	GENERAL JOURNAL			J1
Date	**Account Titles and Explanation**	**Post. Ref.**	**Debit**	**Credit**
2000				
June 1	Cash		20	
	David Lilliput, Capital			20
	Owner made investment to start business			
2	Office Supplies		5	
	Office Equipment		20	
	Accounts Payable			25
	Purchase supplies and equipment from London Company			
3	Cash		7	
	Unearned Revenue			7
	Advance payment from Houyhnhnm Company			
4	Supplies Expense		3	
	Office Supplies			3
	Office supplies used up for the Swift report			
5	Accounts Receivable		5	
	Security Service Revenue			5
	Security services for Shadow Company			
6	Accounts Payable		3	
	Cash			3
	Payment on Accounts Payable—London Company			

A MORE REALISTIC JOURNAL (continued)

	GENERAL JOURNAL (continued)				J1
Date	Account Titles and Explanation	Post. Ref.	Debit	Credit	
2000					
7	Prepaid Insurance		10		
	Cash			10	
	Prepaid Old Bailey Insurance Company—				
	liability insurance coverage until September 30				
7	Cash		15		
	Security Service Revenue			15	
	Security services for T & P Company				

A MORE REALISTIC LEDGER ACCOUNT

We expand the basic "T"

The simple T accounts that we have been using are very useful for analyzing the effects of transactions and for illustrations. However in practice, a real ledger account needs more features to it than a simple T account that is used for analysis. Although the format of real ledger accounts will vary somewhat, you can see a typical example in the illustration on page 469.

To assist you in making the connection to a T account, in the illustration there is a darker line that forms the basic "T" that is the essential part of every ledger account.

A MORE REALISTIC LEDGER ACCOUNT (continued)

New features

You can see that a ledger account is really just an expanded T account, with the following features added:

- **A "Date" column:** This is the date the transaction occurred. This may not be the same date that the transaction is recorded into the ledger account.
- **An "Explanation" column**, for additional information. In practice, this is seldom used.
- **The "Post. Ref." column** is an important source reference. A number is placed in this column to show what *page of the journal* the dollar amount came from. In this way, the change in the account can be traced back to the transaction from which it originated.
- **A "Balance" column** to update the balance every time there is an entry. This makes it easy to instantly see the balance, instead of retotaling debits and credits with each new entry. The "Balance" column shows the "natural" ("normal") balance of the account. For example, we would know that the normal balance in this cash account should always be a debit because cash is an asset. (On the occasion that an accountant might show a temporary negative balance, the amount in the "Balance" column can be put in brackets ( ), circled, or written in red, to show that it is negative.)

Note: This ledger account is known as a *three-column account form* ledger account, because it has three money-amount columns: a debit, a credit, and a balance column. There are also other forms and variations.

	CASH				ACCOUNT NO. 101
Date	Explanation	Post. Ref.	Debit	Credit	Balance

▼ *Posting—Information Transfer from Journal to Ledger*

THE POSTING PROCESS

Introduction

In the prior discussion of the three steps in the recording procedure, you learned that the third step was recording the transaction information in the ledger accounts. In actual practice, the information that is recorded in the ledger accounts is taken directly from what is recorded in the journal. This process of transferring account information from the journal to the ledger is known as "posting." There are five steps to the posting process. The table below is a summary.

When done

In manual accounting systems, posting is done at regular, frequent intervals (such as weekly). In a computerized system, posting is usually done daily.

Step	Action
1	In the journal, locate the first account for which there is no entry in the "Post. Ref." column.
2	Open the ledger and locate the same account.
	In the ledger (using the journal information): • In the "Date" column, record the transaction date from the journal. • If the journal entry is a debit, record the dollar amount in the "Debit" column. If the journal entry is a credit, record the dollar amount in the "Credit" column. • In the "Balance" column, record the new account balance. • In the "Post Ref." column, record the page number of the general journal where the information came from.
4	Return to the journal and enter the ledger account number in the "Post. Ref." column on the same line as the account just posted.
5	• Move to the next unposted account in the journal (Step 1). • Repeat actions in Steps 2-5.

THE POSTING PROCESS (continued)

Chart of accounts for David's ...

In order to demonstrate the posting process for you, we need a chart of accounts from David's tiny little Bodyguard Service.

David's tiny little Bodyguard Service
Chart of Accounts

Asset Accounts: numbers 101–199
#101	Cash
#105	Accounts Receivable
#107	Notes Receivable
#110	Office Supplies
#115	Prepaid Insurance
#140	Office Equipment

Liability Accounts: numbers 201–299
#201	Accounts Payable
#205	Wages Payable
#210	Unearned Revenue
#220	Notes Payable

Owner's Capital Accounts: numbers 301–399
| #301 | David Lilliput, Capital |
| #302 | David Lilliput, Drawing |

Revenue Accounts: numbers 401–499
| #401 | Security Service Revenue |
| #405 | Interest Earned |

Expense Accounts: numbers 501–599
#501	Advertising Expense
#505	Rent Expense
#507	Legal Expense
#510	Accounting Expense
#515	Wages Expense
#520	Insurance Expense
#525	Utilities Expense
#530	Supplies Expense

THE POSTING PROCESS (continued)

Example

The following example shows you the five steps and detailed posting procedures for David's tiny little Bodyguard Service.

GENERAL JOURNAL				J1
Date	**Account Titles and Explanation**	**Post. Ref.**	**Debit**	**Credit**
2000				
June 1	Cash		20	
	David Lilliput, Capital			20
	Owner made investments to start business			
2	Office Supplies		5	
	Office Equipment		20	
	Accounts Payable			25
	Purchase supplies and equipment from London Company			

Step 1 **Identify account that needs to be posted.** In the journal, locate the first account for which there is no entry in the "Post. Ref." column. The first account for which there is no entry in the "Post. Ref." column is the Cash account in the June 1 transaction (see dotted circle above).

Step 2 **Locate the same account in the ledger.** Open the ledger and locate the same account. (To save space, we will only look at the part of the ledger account we need to use.)

THE POSTING PROCESS (continued)

Step 3 **Transfer data from journal to ledger.**
- In the "Date" column, record the transaction date from the journal ("June 1").
- If the journal entry is a debit, record the dollar amount in the "Debit" column ("20"). (If a credit, record in the "Credit" column.)
- In the "Balance" column, record the new account balance. In this example, there was no prior balance, so the new balance is $20.
- In the "Post Ref." column, record the page number of the general journal where the information came from. This entry came from J1. This is a source reference, should we ever need to find where the $20 came from.

	CASH				ACCOUNT NO. 101
Date	**Explanation**	**Post. Ref.**	**Debit**	**Credit**	**Balance**
2000					
June					
1		**J1**	**20**		**20**

Step 4 **Cross-reference to the journal.** Return to the journal and enter the ledger account number in the "Post. Ref." column on the same line as the account just posted ("101"). This entry serves as a reference if later you need to prove that the amount was correctly posted into the proper account.

	GENERAL JOURNAL			J1
Date	**Account Titles and Explanation**	**Post. Ref.**	**Debit**	**Credit**
2000				
June 1	Cash	**101**	20	
	David Lilliput, Capital			20
	Owner made investments to start business			
2	Office Supplies		5	
	Office Equipment		20	
	Accounts Payable			25
	Purchase supplies and equipment from London Company			

Learning Goal 25: Use Realistic Accounting Records

THE POSTING PROCESS (continued)

Step 5 **Process repeats.** Move to the next unposted account in the journal (Step 1), and repeat actions in Steps 2-5.

GENERAL JOURNAL				J1
Date	Account Titles and Explanation	Post. Ref.	Debit	Credit
2000				
June 1	Cash	101	20	
	David Lilliput, Capital			20
	Owner made investment to start business			
2	Office Supplies		5	
	Office Equipment		20	
	Accounts Payable			25
	Purchase supplies and equipment from London Company			

THE COMPLETED JOURNAL AND LEDGER

Completed transactions

On the following pages are the posted journal and ledger accounts for David's tiny little Bodyguard Service transactions from June 1 to June 4. The June 5, 6, 7, and 8 transactions have not yet been posted.

GENERAL JOURNAL				J1
Date	Account Titles and Explanation	Post. Ref.	Debit	Credit
2000				
June 1	Cash	101	20	
	David Lilliput, Capital	301		20
	Owner made investment to start business			
2	Office Supplies	110	5	
	Office Equipment	140	20	
	Accounts Payable	201		25
	Purchase supplies and equipment from London Company			

Learning Goal 25: Use Realistic Accounting Records

THE COMPLETED JOURNAL AND LEDGER (continued)

Date	Account Titles and Explanation	Post. Ref.	Debit	Credit
3	Cash	101	7	
	Unearned Revenue	210		7
	Advance payment from Houyhnhnm Company			
4	Supplies Expense	530	3	
	Office Supplies	110		3
	Office supplies used up for the Swift report			
5	Accounts Receivable		5	
	Security Service Revenue			5
	Security services for Shadow Company			
6	Accounts Payable		3	
	Cash			3
	Payment on Accounts Payable—London Company			
7	Prepaid Insurance		10	
	Cash			10
	Prepaid Old Bailey Insurance Company—			
	liability insurance coverage until September 30			
7	Cash		15	
	Security Service Revenue			15
	Security services for T & P Company			
8	Unearned Revenue		3	
	Security Service Revenue			3
	Performed part of the services for the customer			
	who paid in advance on June 3			

THE COMPLETED JOURNAL AND LEDGER (continued)

LEDGER ACCOUNTS

CASH					ACCOUNT NO. 101
Date	Explanation	Post. Ref.	Debit	Credit	Balance
2000					
June 1		J1	20		20
3		J1	7		27

ACCOUNTS RECEIVABLE					ACCOUNT NO. 105
Date	Explanation	Post. Ref.	Debit	Credit	Balance
2000					

OFFICE SUPPLIES					ACCOUNT NO. 110
Date	Explanation	Post. Ref.	Debit	Credit	Balance
2000					
June 2		J1	5		5
4		J1		3	2

PREPAID INSURANCE					ACCOUNT NO. 115
Date	Explanation	Post. Ref.	Debit	Credit	Balance
2000					

OFFICE EQUIPMENT					ACCOUNT NO. 140
Date	Explanation	Post. Ref.	Debit	Credit	Balance
2000					
June 2		J1	20		20

THE COMPLETED JOURNAL AND LEDGER (continued)

LEDGER ACCOUNTS (continued)

ACCOUNTS PAYABLE					ACCOUNT NO. 201	
Date	Explanation	Post. Ref.	Debit	Credit	Balance	
2000						
June 2		J1		25	25	

UNEARNED REVENUE					ACCOUNT NO. 210	
Date	Explanation	Post. Ref.	Debit	Credit	Balance	
2000						
June 3		J1		7	7	

DAVID LILLIPUT, CAPITAL					ACCOUNT NO. 301	
Date	Explanation	Post. Ref.	Debit	Credit	Balance	
2000						
June 1		J1		20	20	

SECURITY SERVICE REVENUE					ACCOUNT NO. 401	
Date	Explanation	Post. Ref.	Debit	Credit	Balance	
2000						

SUPPLIES EXPENSE					ACCOUNT NO. 530	
Date	Explanation	Post. Ref.	Debit	Credit	Balance	
2000						
June 4		J1	3		3	

☙ QUICK REVIEW ☙

- Two added features to the journal are:
    - journal page numbers
    - a "Posting Reference" column
- Four added features to the ledger account are:
    - a "Date" column
    - an "Explanation" column
    - a "Posting Reference" column
    - an account "Balance" column
- The posting process is the transfer of information from entries on the journal into the ledger accounts. Posting occurs at regular intervals such as weekly or monthly. In computerized systems, it often occurs daily (or even more frequently).

"I like a man who knows all the procedures."

• • •

SOLUTIONS FOR LEARNING GOAL 25 BEGIN ON PAGE 480.

Learning Goal 25 is about using realistic journal and ledger accounts. Use these questions and problems to practice what you have just read.

MULTIPLE CHOICE
On the line provided, enter the letter of the best answer for each question.

1) When a journal entry is posted, which of the following is *not* true? ____
   A) The same information that is in the journal is recorded again in the ledger.
   B) The reference column of the ledger account will show a journal page number.
   C) The reference column of the journal will show either a "Dr." or a "Cr."
   D) Account numbers must be used as part of the posting procedure.
2) Posting is performed ____
   A) after the transaction, but before the information is recorded in the journal.
   B) after transaction information is recorded in the journal.
   C) only when ledger accounts need updating.
   D) in the order of the numbers on the chart of accounts.
3) The "Posting Reference" column in the journal ____
   A) should be filled in at the same time that transaction information is journalized.
   B) is filled in immediately after a transaction is posted into the ledger.
   C) is seldom used in practice.
   D) none of the above.
4) The "Explanation" column of a ledger account ____
   A) should be filled in at the time transaction information is journalized.
   B) is an important part of the posting procedure.
   C) is seldom used in practice.
   D) none of the above.
5) The procedure of transferring information from the journal to ledger accounts is called ____
   A) posting.
   B) journalizing.
   C) balancing the books.
   D) recording.
6) After a journal entry is posted, the ____
   A) reference column in the journal will contain a page number of the ledger.
   B) reference column in the ledger will contain an account number of the journal.
   C) both A and B.
   D) none of the above.
7) The general journal does not have a column with the title ____
   A) "Account," or sometimes "Description."
   B) "Date."
   C) "Balance."
   D) "Post. Ref."

REINFORCEMENT PROBLEM

1) **Complete the posting.** Return to the journal (J1) beginning on page 474 in the "Completed transactions" discussion. Using the journal, and the ledger accounts following the journal, complete the posting for the June 5, 6, 7, and 8 transactions by writing directly on the journal and on the ledger accounts that are affected.

SOLUTIONS FOR LEARNING GOAL 25

PRACTICE QUESTIONS FOR LEARNING GOAL 25 BEGIN ON PAGE 479.

MULTIPLE CHOICE

1) C. It should show the ledger account number to which the debit or credit was posted.
2) B.
3) B.
4) C.
5) A.
6) D. The reference column in the *ledger* will contain the page number of the journal to show where the information came from, and the reference column in the *journal* will contain the ledger account number to show where the information was posted.
7) C. Balances are only found in ledger accounts.

REINFORCEMENT PROBLEM

1)

Date	Account Titles and Explanation	Post. Ref.	Debit	Credit
5	Accounts Receivable	105	5	
	Security Service Revenue	401		5
	Security services for Shadow Company			
6	Accounts Payable	201	3	
	Cash	101		3
	Payment on Accounts Payable—London Company			
7	Prepaid Insurance	115	10	
	Cash	101		10
	Prepaid Old Bailey Insurance Company—liability insurance coverage until September 30			
7	Cash	101	15	
	Security Service Revenue	401		15
	Security services for T & P Company			
8	Unearned Revenue	210	3	
	Security Service Revenue	401		3
	Performed part of the services for the customer who paid in advance on June 3			

SOLUTIONS FOR LEARNING GOAL 25

PRACTICE QUESTIONS FOR LEARNING GOAL 25 BEGIN ON PAGE 479.

1) *continued*

	CASH				ACCOUNT NO. 101
Date	**Explanation**	**Post. Ref.**	**Debit**	**Credit**	**Balance**
2000					
June 1		J1	20		20
3		J1	7		27
6		J1		3	24
7		J1		10	14
7		J1	15		29

	ACCOUNTS RECEIVABLE				ACCOUNT NO. 105
Date	**Explanation**	**Post. Ref.**	**Debit**	**Credit**	**Balance**
2000					
June 5		J1	5		5

	PREPAID INSURANCE				ACCOUNT NO. 115
Date	**Explanation**	**Post. Ref.**	**Debit**	**Credit**	**Balance**
2000					
June 7		J1	10		10

	ACCOUNTS PAYABLE				ACCOUNT NO. 201
Date	**Explanation**	**Post. Ref.**	**Debit**	**Credit**	**Balance**
2000					
June 2		J1		25	25
6		J1	3		22

	UNEARNED REVENUE				ACCOUNT NO. 210
Date	**Explanation**	**Post. Ref.**	**Debit**	**Credit**	**Balance**
2000					
June 3		J1		7	7
8		J1	3		4

SOLUTIONS FOR LEARNING GOAL 25

PRACTICE QUESTIONS FOR LEARNING GOAL 25 BEGIN ON PAGE 479.

1) *continued*

Date	SECURITY SERVICE REVENUE		Post. Ref.	Debit	Credit	ACCOUNT NO. 401
	Explanation					Balance
2000						
June 5			J1		5	5
7			J1		15	20
8			J1		3	23

Did you remember to:

- write the date of the transaction in the ledger account?
- update the balance in the ledger account after each posting?
- record the journal page number in the ledger account?
- record the ledger account number in the "Post. Ref." column *in the journal* after you posted each account?

Your Questions?

It is *very* important to be aware of what you need to understand better. What do you need to understand better about this learning goal? Use this space to write the questions that you want to discuss with your classmates, instructor, or supervisor. Try to be very specific about what is bothering you, such as explanations that you do not fully understand.

LEARNING GOAL 26

The Trial Balance—Prepare It and Use It Two Ways

In Learning Goal 26, you will find:

▼ *What Is a Trial Balance?*

▼ *What Is a Trial Balance?*

THE TRIAL BALANCE

Trial balance defined

A trial balance is a listing of all the ledger account names with their balances. The account names are listed in a column. Next to the name of each account is *the balance of that account* as either a debit or credit. Accounts with zero balances are not usually included. Turn to page 484 for an example.

"What is a trial balance?"

• •

THE TRIAL BALANCE (continued)

The East Lake Street Company
Trial Balance
June 30, 2000

Account Name	Dr.	Cr.
Cash..	$ 7,580	
Accounts Receivable...................................	4,207	
Office Supplies...	533	
Accounts Payable......................................		$ 2,500
Wages Payable		750
Cindy Walczak, Capital		8,220
Cindy Walczak, Drawing.............................	500	
Fees Earned..		5,550
Rent Expense	1,200	
Supplies Expense.......................................	300	
Wages Expense	2,700	
Total..	**$17,020**	**$17,020**

When is it prepared?

A trial balance can be prepared at any time, but normally it is prepared at the end of an accounting period, just before the financial statements are prepared.

Where does the information come from?

The amounts listed in the trial balances are the ending balances of all the individual ledger accounts. Therefore, the source of the information is the general ledger.

The two purposes of the trial balance

The trial balance:

- *tests* whether or not the total of all the debit balance accounts equals the total of all the credit balance accounts. This proves that both sides of the accounting equation are equal, which is necessary in double-entry accounting.
- is the *source of the financial statements*. If all the account balances in the trial balance are correct, then we can prepare a balance sheet, income statement, and statement of owner's equity from the trial balance. All the accounts with balances are in the trial balance.

EXAMPLE OF PREPARING A TRIAL BALANCE

| *Example* | On page 486, you will find all the completed ledger accounts for David's tiny little Bodyguard Service for the entire month of June, as of June 30. Using these accounts, you can prepare a trial balance like this: |

Step	Action	Example
1	Prepare the trial balance headings. Be sure the date is correct. *Note:* The trial balance is a point in time, not a period of time.	**David's tiny little Bodyguard Service** **Trial Balance** **June 7, 2000** **Account Title**　　　　**Dr.**　　**Cr.**
2	Beginning with the first account in the ledger, list the names of the accounts and their balances in the same order that they appear in the ledger. Do not list any zero-balance accounts.	**David's tiny little Bodyguard Service** **Trial Balance** **June 7, 2000** see table below

David's tiny little Bodyguard Service
Trial Balance
June 7, 2000

Account Title	Dr.	Cr.
Cash	15	
Accounts Receivable	7	
Prepaid Insurance	10	
Office Equipment	20	
Accounts Payable		25
Unearned Revenue		4
David Lilliput, Capital		20
David Lilliput, Drawing	3	
Security Service Revenue		30
Advertising Expense	3	
Rent Expense	9	
Accounting Expense	2	
Insurance Expense	4	
Utilities Expense	1	
Supplies Expense	5	

Learning Goal 26: The Trial Balance—Prepare It and Use It Two Ways

EXAMPLE OF PREPARING A TRIAL BALANCE (continued)

LEDGER

CASH — ACCT. NO. 101

Date	Explan.	Post. Ref.	Debit	Credit	Balance
2000					
June 1		J1	20		20
3		J1	7		27
6		J1		3	24
7		J1		10	14
7		J1	15		29
15		J2		9	20
23		J3		2	18
25		J3		4	14
27		J3		1	13
28		J3	5		18
30		J3		3	15

ACCOUNTS RECEIVABLE — ACCT. NO. 105

Date	Explan.	Post. Ref.	Debit	Credit	Balance
2000					
June 5		J1	5		5
28		J3		5	–0–
30		J3	7		7

OFFICE SUPPLIES — ACCT. NO. 110

Date	Explan.	Post. Ref.	Debit	Credit	Balance
2000					
June 2		J1	5		5
4		J1		3	2
11		J2		2	–0–

PREPAID INSURANCE — ACCT. NO. 115

Date	Explan.	Post. Ref.	Debit	Credit	Balance
2000					
June 7		J1	10		10

OFFICE EQUIPMENT — ACCT. NO. 140

Date	Explan.	Post. Ref.	Debit	Credit	Balance
2000					
June 2		J1	20		20

ACCOUNTS PAYABLE — ACCT. NO. 201

Date	Explan.	Post. Ref.	Debit	Credit	Balance
2000					
June 2		J1		25	25
6		J1	3		22
12		J2		3	25

UNEARNED REVENUE — ACCT. NO. 210

Date	Explan.	Post. Ref.	Debit	Credit	Balance
2000					
June 3		J1		7	7
8		J1	3		4

DAVID LILLIPUT, CAPITAL — ACCT. NO. 301

Date	Explan.	Post. Ref.	Debit	Credit	Balance
2000					
June 1		J1		20	20

DAVID LILLIPUT, DRAWING — ACCT. NO. 302

Date	Explan.	Post. Ref.	Debit	Credit	Balance
2000					
June 30		J3	3		3

SECURITY SERVICE REVENUE — ACCT. NO. 401

Date	Explan.	Post. Ref.	Debit	Credit	Balance
2000					
June 5		J1		5	5
7		J1		15	20
8		J1		3	23
30		J3		7	30

ADVERTISING EXPENSE — ACCT. NO. 501

Date	Explan.	Post. Ref.	Debit	Credit	Balance
2000					
June 12		J2	3		3

RENT EXPENSE — ACCT. NO. 505

Date	Explan.	Post. Ref.	Debit	Credit	Balance
2000					
June 15		J2	9		9

ACCOUNTING EXPENSE — ACCT. NO. 510

Date	Explan.	Post. Ref.	Debit	Credit	Balance
2000					
June 23		J3	2		2

INSURANCE EXPENSE — ACCT. NO. 520

Date	Explan.	Post. Ref.	Debit	Credit	Balance
2000					
June 25		J3	4		4

UTILITIES EXPENSE — ACCT. NO. 525

Date	Explan.	Post. Ref.	Debit	Credit	Balance
2000					
June 27		J3	1		1

SUPPLIES EXPENSE — ACCT. NO. 530

Date	Explan.	Post. Ref.	Debit	Credit	Balance
2000					
June 4		J1	3		3
11		J2	2		5

Learning Goal 26: The Trial Balance—Prepare It and Use It Two Ways

EXAMPLE OF PREPARING A TRIAL BALANCE (continued)

Step	Action	Example
3	Add the trial balance columns and compare the totals.	**David's tiny little Bodyguard Service** **Trial Balance** **June 30, 2000**

Account Title	Dr.	Cr.
Cash	$15	
Accounts Receivable	7	
Prepaid Insurance	10	
Office Equipment	20	
Accounts Payable		$25
Unearned Revenue		4
David Lilliput, Capital		20
David Lilliput, Drawing	3	
Security Service Revenue		30
Advertising Expense	3	
Rent Expense	9	
Accounting Expense	2	
Insurance Expense	4	
Utilities Expense	1	
Supplies Expense	5	
Total	**$79**	**$79**

Step	Action
4	If the totals are equal and you know that the individual account balances are correct, then you can use the trial balance to prepare the financial statements. • *Income statement:* Use the revenue and expense accounts. • *Statement of owner's equity:* Use the owner's capital account, the drawing account, and the net income (or loss) from the income statement. • *Balance sheet:* Use the asset and liability accounts, and the final balance of owner's capital from the statement of owner's equity.

PREPARE FINANCIAL STATEMENTS FROM THE TRIAL BALANCE

Example

The financial statements below were prepared from the June 30 trial balance of David's tiny little **Bodyguard Service** on page 487.

David's tiny little Bodyguard Service
Income Statement
For the Month Ended June 30, 2000

Revenues		
Security service revenue		$30
Expenses		
Rent expense	$9	
Supplies expense	5	
Insurance expense	4	
Advertising expense	3	
Accounting expense	2	
Utilities expense	1	
Total expenses		24
Net income		$ 6

David's tiny little Bodyguard Service
Statement of Owner's Equity
For the Month Ended June 30, 2000

David Lilliput, Capital, June 1	$ 0
Add: Owner investment	20
Net income	6
	26
Less: Drawings	(3)
David Lilliput, Capital, June 30	$23

David's tiny little Bodyguard Service
Balance Sheet
June 30, 2000

Assets		Liabilities	
Cash	$15	Accounts payable	$25
Accounts receivable	7	Unearned revenue	4
Prepaid insurance	10	Total liabilities	29
Office equipment	20		
		Owner's Equity	
		David Lilliput, Capital	23
Total assets	$52	Total liabilities and owner's equity	$52

Learning Goal 26: The Trial Balance—Prepare It and Use It Two Ways

PREPARE FINANCIAL STATEMENTS FROM THE TRIAL BALANCE (continued)

To find out if the owner made an investment, you will need to look into the ledger account for the owner's capital. For example, by just looking at the $20 of David Lilliput, Capital on the trial balance, you cannot be sure if it includes any current investment or not. This makes a difference, because any owner's investments must be disclosed separately on the statement of owner's equity.

LOCATING ERRORS IN THE TRIAL BALANCE

How to locate errors

What if the totals are not equal? In a manual accounting system, locating errors in the trial balance can be a slow process. In a faulty computerized accounting system that requires a programming fix, the process of finding the source of an error in the trial balance can be even more difficult. Here is how to proceed: *work backwards from the trial balance.*

Step	Action	Possible Errors
1	Examine the trial balance.	• Columns were added incorrectly. • An account balance was omitted. • A balance was placed into the wrong column. • Amounts were written down incorrectly.
	Note: Check the difference between the totals:	If the difference between the totals is evenly divisible by 9, a transposition (like 51 instead of 15) or a slide (like 10 instead of 100) may be the only problem. If the difference is evenly divisible by 2, an amount written in the wrong column may be the only problem. Look for exactly half the difference.
2	Check the individual ledger accounts.	• The balance of an account was calculated incorrectly. • The balance is shown incorrectly (debit instead of credit, or credit instead of debit).
3	Check the posting.	• Debit was posted as a credit, or credit posted as a debit. • The same amount was posted more than once. • Part of a transaction posting was omitted. • A wrong amount was posted.
4	Check the journalizing.	• Debits did not equal credits when a transaction was journalized.

LOCATING ERRORS IN THE TRIAL BALANCE (continued)

**What the trial balance
DOES NOT detect!**

A correct trial balance proves that the total debits equal the total credits. However, the trial balance does not detect these kinds of errors:

- any transaction that was not journalized
- any transaction that was not posted
- journal entries that balance, but using wrong amounts or wrong accounts
- multiple journalizing or posting of the same transaction
- in a computerized system, failing to choose the correct default settings

All of these errors can occur and the trial balance will still balance! These errors must be corrected before the financial statements are prepared and given to investors, lenders, and other stakeholders. You will learn how to deal with some of these problems in the second book in this series (Volume 2), when we discuss adjusting and correcting entries.

**NO debits or credits
on financial
statements**

Even though the trial balance uses debits and credits, *financial statements never have debits and credits*. This is because most people who use financial statements do not understand debits and credits.

☙ QUICK REVIEW ☙

- The trial balance is a listing of all accounts and their ending balances. (Accounts with zero balances are not usually included.)

- A trial balance can be prepared at any time, but normally it is prepared at the end of an accounting period, just before the financial statements are prepared.

- A trial balance serves two important functions:

    — It proves that the accounting equation is in balance for all the ledger accounts. The total of all debit balances must equal the total of all credit balances.

    — It is the source of the account balances used on the income statement, statement of owner's equity, and balance sheet.

- The trial balance does not identify errors in which the accounting equation still balances.

- Never use debits or credits on financial statements.

Learning Goal 26: The Trial Balance—Prepare It and Use It Two Ways

PRACTICE FOR LEARNING GOAL 26

SOLUTIONS FOR LEARNING GOAL 26 BEGIN ON PAGE 496.

Learning Goal 26 is about learning to prepare a trial balance, and the two ways of using the trial balance. Use these questions and problems to practice what you have learned.

MULTIPLE CHOICE
On the line provided, enter the letter of the best answer for each question.

1) A trial balance is prepared _____
   A) usually just before financial statements are prepared.
   B) at any time the accountant desires to verify that the books are in balance.
   C) using the ending balances in all nonzero accounts.
   D) all the above.

2) A trial balance is used _____
   A) to test if all the debit account balances equal the total credit account balances.
   B) as the source of information that is used to prepare financial statements.
   C) as a financial statement.
   D) both A and B.

3) A trial balance would help in detecting which error? _____
   A) A journal entry that was not posted.
   B) A journal entry that was posted twice.
   C) A journal entry that was posted to the wrong accounts.
   D) None of the above.

4) If a trial balance does not balance, it could mean that _____
   A) a ledger account was added incorrectly.
   B) a journal entry was posted twice.
   C) a journal entry was posted to the wrong accounts.
   D) none of the above.

5) If a $700 credit to Accounts Receivable was posted as a $700 credit to Cash, then on the trial balance _____
   A) total debits would exceed total credits by $700.
   B) total credits would exceed total debits by $700.
   C) the trial balance would be completely unaffected.
   D) none of the above.

6) If a $500 debit to Cash was posted as a $50 debit to Cash, then on the trial balance _____
   A) the cash is understated by $500.
   B) total debits will exceed total credits by $450.
   C) total credits will exceed total debits by $450.
   D) the cash is overstated by $500.

7) If $250 of supplies are consumed, but this is journalized and posted as a $250 debit to Supplies Expense and a $25 credit to Supplies, then on the trial balance _____
   A) total debits will be overstated.
   B) total debits will exceed total credits.
   C) total credits will exceed total debits.
   D) total credits will be overstated.

8) Debits and credits are _____
   A) used only on the balance sheet.
   B) used only on the income statement.
   C) never used on any financial statements.
   D) are optional on financial statements.

PRACTICE FOR LEARNING GOAL 26

SOLUTIONS FOR LEARNING GOAL 26 BEGIN ON PAGE 496.

REINFORCEMENT PROBLEMS

1) **Prepare a trial balance.** Listed below in random order are various ledger accounts with balances for the Overland Park Company, as of December 31, 2000. On a separate piece of paper, prepare a trial balance in good form. Account numbers are in brackets ( ).

(#150) Land: $35,780

(#115) Supplies: 425

(#130) Prepaid Insurance: 800

(#101) Cash: 4,281

(#515) Wages Expense: 3,500

(#415) Interest Earned: 125

(#201) Wages Payable: $1,500

(#401) Service Revenue: 8,400

(#510) Utility Expense: 202

(#505) Rent Expense: 800

(#301) R. Wills, Draw: 1,000

(#215) Unearned Revenue: $1,250

(#520) Repairs Expense: 1,315

(#110) Accounts Receivable: 7,227

(#300) R. Wills, Capital: 54,555

(#140) Equipment: 10,500

2) **You be the teacher—grade the financial statement (report form balance sheet).** You have just given a weekly quiz which requires your students to prepare financial statements from a trial balance. Below is a report form balance sheet prepared by one of your students. Preparation of a correct balance sheet is worth 10 points. Identify the mistakes and grade this balance sheet. How many points would you give? (Mistakes are from actual exams.)

Wayne Grey-Eagle Company Balance Sheet		
	Dr.	**Cr.**
Assets:		
Cash	$21,500	
Accounts receivable	7,150	
Office supplies	325	
Prepaid rent	2,800	
Equipment	15,900	
Total assets	47,675	
Liabilities and Owner's Equity		
Liabilities:		
Wages payable		3,300
Accounts payable		4,470
Notes payable		22,500
Total liabilities		30,270
Owner's Equity:		
Wayne Grey-Eagle, Capital, January 1		17,925
Wayne Grey-Eagle, Drawing		(5,000)
Net income		4,480
Wayne Grey-Eagle, Capital, January 31		17,405
Total	$47,675	$47,675

SOLUTIONS FOR LEARNING GOAL 26 BEGIN ON PAGE 496.

3) **Prepare financial statements from a trial balance; analyze the business.** Your friend Frank Wade is an expert mechanical engineer. Early this year, he started a new engineering design and consulting business called Wade Engineering, in which he invested all the cash that the business needed to begin the consulting operations.

The first year of operations has just ended, and Frank meets you for lunch. During lunch, he tells you that he is looking for a partner to invest an additional $25,000 cash in the business. He would make you an equal partner for only the investment. You would not have to do any work in the business. He says that he has been quite busy with many clients, and has not done any financial work himself. He did, however, hire a reliable bookkeeper who prepared the trial balance which he lets you keep to review. Frank says he is hoping for an answer from you within the next 7 to 10 days.

Wade Engineering Trial Balance December 31, 2000		
Account Name	**Dr.**	**Cr.**
Cash...	$ 3,100	
Accounts Receivable...	17,100	
Office Supplies..	1,100	
Design Supplies	1,200	
Prepaid Rent...	650	
Office Equipment..	3,500	
Design Equipment	14,700	
Wages Payable		$ 4,900
Accounts Payable..		2,900
Frank Wade, Capital		25,000
Frank Wade, Drawing..	4,400	
Design Fees...		27,800
Interest Earned		100
Rent Expense	1,400	
Wages Expense	12,500	
Utilities Expense...	380	
Supplies Expense (Office).....................................	140	
Supplies Expense (Design)....................................	530	
Total	**$60,700**	**$60,700**

Instructions:

● **Prepare financial statements.** On a separate piece of paper, prepare the balance sheet, the income statement, and the statement of owner's equity for the year ended December 31, 2000. Prove the amount of Frank's original investment when you prepare the financial statements.

● **Analyze the statements and make a decision.** After you prepared the three financial statements, you realized that you would also like to have a statement of cash flows to analyze, but you have not yet learned to prepare one. Fortunately, you have a friend in a more advanced accounting class who can prepare this statement, which you see on page 494.

PRACTICE FOR LEARNING GOAL 26

SOLUTIONS FOR LEARNING GOAL 26 BEGIN ON PAGE 496.

3) *continued*

Wade Engineering		
Statement of Cash Flows		
For the Year Ending December 31, 2000		
Cash flows from **operating** activities:		
Receipts:		
Cash collections from customers		$10,700
Interest earned		100
Payments:		
Rent expense	$2,050	
Utilities expense	380	
Wages expense	7,600	
Supplies expense	70	
Total cash payments		10,100
Net cash provided by operating activities		700
Cash used in **investing** activities:		
Purchase of equipment		(18,200)
Cash flows from **financing** activities:		
Owner investment	25,000	
Less: withdrawals	(4,400)	
Net cash provided by financing activities		20,600
Net increase in cash		3,100
Cash balance January 3, 2000		-0-
Cash balance December 31, 2000		$ 3,100

Now that you have all four financial statements available, answer the following questions to help you decide if you should invest.

A) The income statement shows the change in the company's wealth that resulted from operating the business. Was there an increase or decrease in total wealth as a result of operations? How much?

B) The statement of cash flows shows the sources and uses of cash for the business. Frank Wade claims he actually invested $25,000 cash to start the business. If the beginning cash balance was zero, and Frank invested $25,000, then why is the December 31 cash balance only $3,100?

C) How much cash did the business obtain from its operations?

Learning Goal 26: The Trial Balance—Prepare It and Use It Two Ways

SOLUTIONS FOR LEARNING GOAL 26 BEGIN ON PAGE 496.

3) *continued*

D) Look at the fees earned on the income statement, and look at the statement of cash flows. What do you think of the ability of the business to collect cash from its customers?

E) What was the biggest use of cash during the year? Is it likely to happen again next year?

F) Take a close look at the balance sheet. What do you think about the company's ability to pay current liabilities when they come due? What are the immediate sources of cash? Why do you think Frank wants an answer from you in the next 7 to 10 days?

G) What might cause a company to show on the income statement that it increased its wealth from operations, and yet on the statement of cash flows show that it did not receive the same amount of cash from operations?

H) Every business always has **two** *abiding and overriding issues* that dictate its ability to survive. From the questions so far, can you guess what these two survival issues are?

I) So what do you think? Are you going to invest $25,000 to be an equal partner and not have to work in the business? What are your reasons?

SOLUTIONS FOR LEARNING GOAL 26

PRACTICE QUESTIONS FOR LEARNING GOAL 26 BEGIN ON PAGE 491.

MULTIPLE CHOICE

1) D.
2) D.
3) D. Choices A, B, and C all keep total debits equal to credits, so a trial balance would stay in balance.
4) A. This is the only choice in this question that would cause the trial balance to not balance.
5) D. Tricky question. The trial balance would remain in balance, but it would not be "completely unaffected" because one account would be overstated and another would be understated.
6) C. Total debits are understated by $450, because Cash was debited for $50 instead of $500.

Use T accounts to visualize this:

	Cash		Some other account	
50				500

7) B. Use T accounts to visualize:
(Total credits are understated by $225)

	Supplies Expense		Supplies	
250				25

8) C.

SOLUTIONS FOR LEARNING GOAL 26

PRACTICE QUESTIONS FOR LEARNING GOAL 26 BEGIN ON PAGE 491.

REINFORCEMENT PROBLEMS

1)

Overland Park Company
Trial Balance
December 31, 2000

Account Name	Dr.	Cr.
Cash..	$ 4,281	
Accounts Receivable.....................................	7,227	
Office Supplies..	425	
Prepaid Insurance...	800	
Equipment..	10,500	
Land	35,780	
Wages Payable		$ 1,500
Unearned Revenue..		1,250
R. Wills, Capital...		54,555
R. Wills, Drawing	1,000	
Service Revenue		8,400
Interest Earned..		125
Rent Expense	800	
Utilities Expense..	202	
Wages Expense	3,500	
Repairs Expense..	1,315	
Total	**$65,830**	**$65,830**

2) The major problem with this "balance sheet" is that the student has become confused between a trial balance and a balance sheet. The entire format is incorrect.

Errors:
- Financial statements **NEVER** have debits and credits! Most people do not know what they are.
- This statement is prepared in the columnar format of a trial balance, showing the debit and credit totals. Debits and credits have nothing whatsoever to do with where numbers are written on a financial statement.
- Owner's equity should just be one number, showing the final balance of Wayne Grey-Eagle, Capital. This statement has made the owner's equity section into a miniature version of the statement of owner's equity.
- The title of the statement does not show the date.

SOLUTIONS FOR LEARNING GOAL 26

PRACTICE QUESTIONS FOR LEARNING GOAL 26 BEGIN ON PAGE 491.

2) *continued*

All of these are serious mistakes. I would give this statement a score of about 4 out of 10. Although there are some minor variations in report format, here is one correct way the report form of the statement should look:

Wayne Grey-Eagle Company
Balance Sheet
January 31, 2000

Assets

Cash	$21,500	
Accounts receivable	7,150	
Office supplies	325	
Prepaid rent	2,800	
Equipment	15,900	
Total assets		47,675

Liabilities and Owner's Equity

Liabilities:

Wages payable	$ 3,300	
Accounts payable	4,470	
Notes payable	22,500	
Total liabilities		30,270

Owner's Equity:

Wayne Grey-Eagle, Capital		17,405
Total liabilities and owner's equity		$47,675

---

3)

Wade Engineering
Balance Sheet
December 31, 2000

Assets		Liabilities	
Cash	$ 3,100	Wages payable	$ 4,900
Accounts receivable	17,100	Accounts payable	2,900
Office supplies	1,100	Total liabilities	7,800
Design supplies	1,200		
Prepaid rent	650	**Owner's Equity**	
Office equipment	3,500	Frank Wade, Capital	33,550
Design equipment	14,700		
Total assets	$41,350	Total liabilities and owner's equity	$41,350

Learning Goal 26: The Trial Balance—Prepare It and Use It Two Ways

PRACTICE QUESTIONS FOR LEARNING GOAL 26 BEGIN ON PAGE 491.

3) *continued*

Wade Engineering
Income Statement
For the Year Ending December 31, 2000

Revenues		
Design fees	$27,800	
Interest earned	100	
Total revenues		$27,900
Expenses		
Wages expense	12,500	
Rent expense	1,400	
Supplies expense (Design)	530	
Supplies expense (Office)	140	
Utilities expense	380	
Total expenses		14,950
Net income		$12,950

Wade Engineering
Statement of Owner's Equity
For the Year Ending December 31, 2000

Frank Wade, Capital, January 3		$ –0–
Add: Owner investment	$25,000	
Net income	12,950	
		37,950
Less: Withdrawals		4,400
Frank Wade, Capital, December 31		$33,550

Question: How could you verify the amount of Frank Wade's investment? Use the formula for the statement of owner's equity: **Beginning capital + investment + net income – drawings = ending capital.** This was: $0 + X +12,950 – 4,400 = 33,550$. So $X = 25,000$.

A) Business operations caused the total wealth of the company to increase by $12,950.

B) We can examine the statement of cash flows to learn what happened to cash during the current period of operations. The statement of cash flows shows us that the *operations* only provided $700 of cash. *Investing activities* (equipment was purchased) used up $18,200 of cash. Finally, the *financing activities* shows us that the main source of cash was Frank's investment, *less what he drew back out of the business*. This was a net of $20,600.
To summarize: A zero beginning cash balance + 700 – 18,200 + 20,600 = 3,100 ending cash balance.

C) $700 was generated from operations (see Operating Activities on statement of cash flows on page 494).

D) The income statement shows design revenues of $27,800, yet the statement of cash flows reveals that only $10,700 was collected from the customers. Uncollected receivables must be building up. This is a serious problem. The business is making sales but is not able to collect cash from the customers. As the receivables build up, the business begins to experience cash flow difficulties. The cause? There could be several:
1) Poor selection of customers; they do not have the ability to pay on time.
2) Slow billing procedures and no reminders.
3) Disputes arising from poor work.
4) Fraud. Nonexistent sales are being reported.

Learning Goal 26: The Trial Balance—Prepare It and Use It Two Ways

SOLUTIONS FOR LEARNING GOAL 26

PRACTICE QUESTIONS FOR LEARNING GOAL 26 BEGIN ON PAGE 491.

3) *continued*

E) The biggest use of cash was the purchase of equipment—$18,200. This is understandable, because this is a new business, and it needs equipment to begin operations. This cash expenditure probably will not have to be repeated next year, so cash flow is likely to be more positive. However, small businesses are always in need of cash to expand operations.

F) The balance sheet shows only $3,100 of cash. There is $4,900 of wages payable. Employees want to be paid on time. If the business cannot do this, the employees will leave. This is probably why Frank is hoping to hear from you quickly. Another source of cash is the accounts receivable, but the statement of cash flows warns us that receivables are building up, so this is a questionable source of cash. Moreover, there are also other short-term payables of $2,900 due in the near future. The business is having a cash-flow crisis.

G) Assuming that there is no fraud, and only poor cash flow management, it appears that a lot of effort has been devoted to finding customers and doing jobs. Very little effort has been devoted to getting payment from customers. Although operations have created $12,950 of new wealth, much of this still remains in the form of accounts receivable.

H) The two survival issues are *profitability* and *liquidity*. Profitability means operating the business in such a way that wealth is accumulated. Liquidity means having enough cash available to: 1) pay debts as they come due, and 2) take advantage of opportunities and grow.

I) **Well, it's your money, but I wouldn't put in a nickel without finding out what is happening here. IF there is no fraud, the customers are good, and the quality of work is good, then I would be interested, but with the provision that I would manage financial operations, while Frank concentrated on doing the engineering work.**

Your Questions?

It is *very* important to be aware of what you need to understand better. What do you need to understand better about this learning goal? Use this space to write the questions that you want to discuss with your classmates, instructor, or supervisor. Try to be very specific about what is bothering you, such as explanations that you do not fully understand.

LEARNING GOAL 27
Explain the Accounting Cycle

THE ACCOUNTING CYCLE

Definition

Accounting activity occurs in a recurring, sequential kind of pattern. The recurring, sequential pattern of accounting activity is known as the "accounting cycle."

The main elements of the cycle are analyzing, processing, and communicating.

What you have learned so far

The parts of the cycle that you have learned to perform so far are:

Analyze: Business events are analyzed to see if they have affected the accounting equation. This analysis is also called "measurement." Any event that changes the accounting equation is called a "transaction," and must be recorded.

Process: Processing refers to recording and organizing data. This consists of journalizing, posting, summarizing, adjusting, and correcting procedures. So far, you have learned:

- recording ("journalizing") transactions
- posting
- preparing a trial balance

You will learn more about the remaining steps in processing in the next book in this series (Volume 2).

Communicate: Communication refers to the preparation of financial reports and disclosures and interpretations. So far, you have practiced preparing three reports: the income statement, the statement of owner's equity, and the balance sheet.

Some variations

Not every business and not every accountant is exactly the same. So, you can expect some small differences in the exact steps of the cycle. However, a useful overview of the cycle is on page 503 for you to study.

THE ACCOUNTING CYCLE (continued)

Manual accounting compared to computerized accounting

The accounting cycle is essentially the same for both a computerized and manual accounting system. A computerized system automates some specific mechanical procedures and saves time. This is especially true about the way transaction data is entered into a computerized system.

However, computers can never perform the analysis part of the cycle. Analysis is your most important skill. Computers are also very poor communicators.

You need to have a clear understanding of all the steps in the accounting cycle. Just because a computer is doing much of the work, *this does not mean that you do not need to understand what is happening.* You do!

For these reasons, it can be a good idea to practice with and understand how a *manual accounting system* functions. This is because …

● many people learn and remember better by practicing manually for the first time;
● most parts of a computerized system are essentially the same as a manual system; and
● you may actually be involved in using a manual accounting system.

THE ACCOUNTING CYCLE (continued)

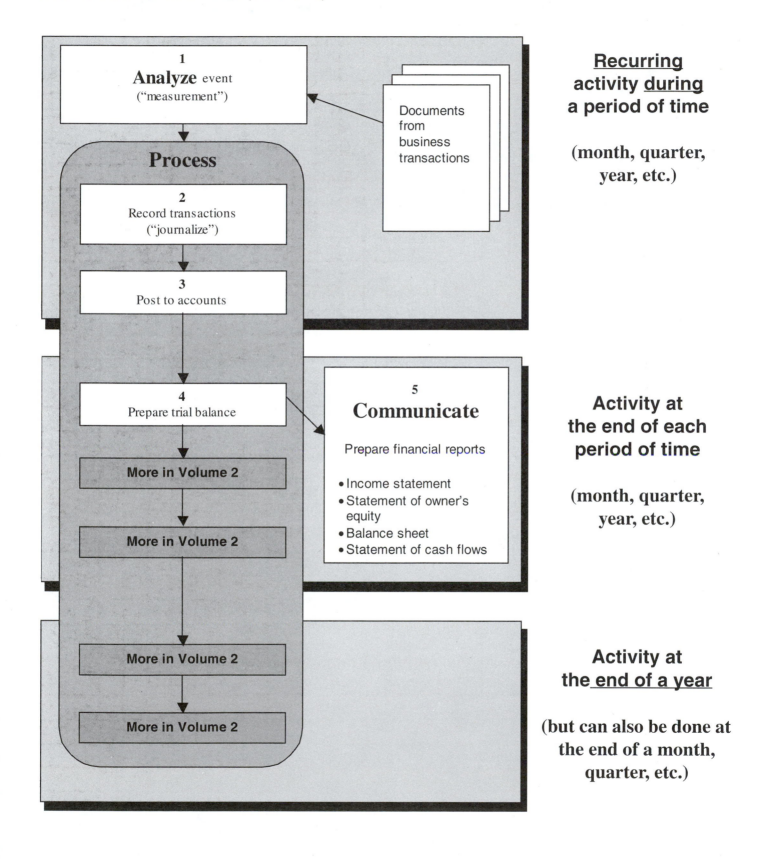

PRACTICE FOR LEARNING GOAL 27

SOLUTIONS FOR LEARNING GOAL 27 BEGIN ON PAGE 506.

Learning Goal 27 is about the accounting cycle. Use these questions and problems to practice what you have just read.

MULTIPLE CHOICE
On the line provided, enter the letter of the best answer for each question.

1) The accounting cycle consists of these steps in this order: _____
   A) analyze, journalize, and post
   B) analyze, process, and communicate
   C) communicate, analyze, journalize, and post
   D) none of the above

2) Recording, posting, and preparing a trial balance are all part of _____
   A) communicating.
   B) analyzing.
   C) transactions.
   D) processing.

3) Preparing financial statements is the most important part of _____
   A) communicating.
   B) analyzing.
   C) transactions.
   D) processing.

4) Analyzing, journalizing, and posting are activities that happen _____
   A) on a recurring basis throughout a period of time.
   B) only at the end of a designated period of time.
   C) usually at the end of a year.
   D) none of the above.

5) Preparing financial statements is an activity that usually happens _____
   A) on a recurring basis throughout a period of time.
   B) only at the end of a designated period of time.
   C) usually at the end of a year.
   D) none of the above.

PRACTICE FOR LEARNING GOAL 27

P R A C T I C E · P R A C T I C E · P R A C T I C E · P R A C T I C E · P R A C T I C E · P R A C T I C E · P R A C T I C E

SOLUTIONS FOR LEARNING GOAL 27 BEGIN ON PAGE 506.

REINFORCEMENT PROBLEM

1) The illustration you see below only contains diagrams of the five steps that you have learned up to this point. Fill in each of the five empty parts of the illustration by writing in a description for the five steps that you have learned.

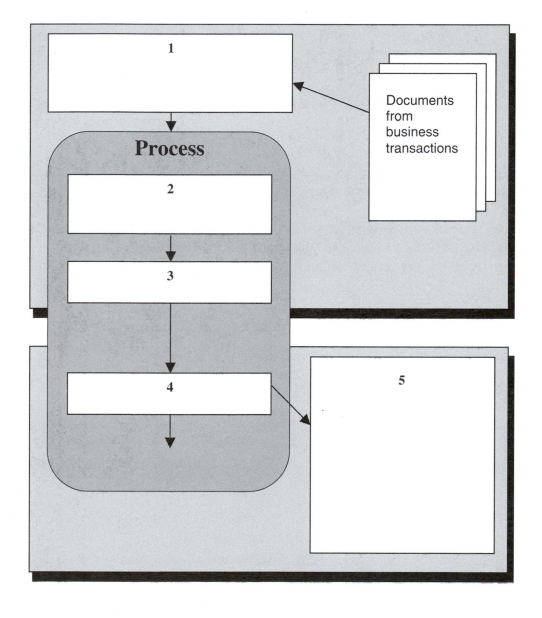

SOLUTIONS FOR LEARNING GOAL 27

PRACTICE QUESTIONS FOR LEARNING GOAL 27 BEGIN ON PAGE 504.

MULTIPLE CHOICE

1) B.
2) D.
3) A.
4) A.
5) B.

REINFORCEMENT PROBLEM

1) See the accounting cycle diagram on page 503 for the solution.

Your Questions?

It is *very* important to be aware of what you need to understand better. What do you need to understand better about this learning goal? Use this space to write the questions that you want to discuss with your classmates, instructor, or supervisor. Try to be very specific about what is bothering you, such as explanations that you do not fully understand.

CUMULATIVE VOCABULARY REVIEW

Match each description with the term that it describes. Enter the letter of the correct description in the space provided next to each term on the left. The answer for each term is in the right column.

	Term	Description	Answers
____	1) Footing	A) A listing of all nonzero ledger account names and balances.	1H
____	2) Debit	B) A right-side entry or balance.	2N
____	3) Journalize	C) A simple form of an account used for analysis.	3L
____	4) Accounting cycle	D) A journal.	4J
____	5) Posting	E) An entry consisting of three or more accounts.	5O
____	6) Account	F) An abbreviation for "debit."	6K
____	7) Journal	G) To debit.	7M
____	8) Cr.	H) The balance or total of a column of numbers.	8P
____	9) To charge	I) A book or computer file containing all the accounts of a business.	9G
____	10) Dr.	J) Analyze, process, and communicate.	10F
____	11) General ledger	K) An historical record of all changes in an item in the accounting equation.	11I
____	12) Book of original entry	L) To record a transaction in a journal.	12D
____	13) Compound entry	M) A chronological recording of transactions, like a diary.	13E
____	14) Trial balance	N) A left-side entry or balance.	14A
____	15) Ledger account	O) Transferring information from a journal into a ledger.	15Q
____	16) T account	P) An abbreviation for "credit."	16C
____	17) Credit	Q) An account showing debit, credit, balance, date, explanation, and posting reference.	17B

CUMULATIVE TEST SOLUTIONS BEGIN ON PAGE 514.

TIME LIMIT: 55 MINUTES

INSTRUCTIONS

*In the space provided, enter the best answer to each question. Do **not** look back in the book when taking the test. (If you need to do this, you are not ready.) After you finish the test, refer to the answers and circle the number of each question that you missed. Then go to the* **Help Table** *(on page 516) to identify your strong and weak knowledge areas by individual learning goal.*

MULTIPLE CHOICE

On the line provided, enter the letter of the best answer for each question.

1) Which one of the following is not one of the five basic data arrangements? ____
   A) seeing the balance of any item in the accounting equation
   B) seeing the audit trail posting reference of an entry in a ledger account
   C) seeing all the parts of a transaction together in one place
   D) keeping a historical record of all increases and decreases for each item in the accounting equation

2) The natural positive balance (normal balance) of an account is ____
   A) the minimum balance that must always be maintained in an account.
   B) always located on the side of the account used for increases.
   C) always located on the side of the account used for decreases.
   D) always calculated by excluding the beginning balance of the account.

3) Owner's equity accounts that would be increased by a debit would be ____
   A) revenues and expenses.
   B) capital and revenue.
   C) expenses and drawing.
   D) revenue and drawing.

4) To record a decrease in an account, use ____
   A) debits.
   B) credits.
   C) credits, if the normal balance is debit, and debits if the normal balance is credit.
   D) credits, if the normal balance is credit, and debits if the normal balance is debit.

5) All the accounts of a business are grouped together in a book or file called the ____
   A) ledger.
   B) journal.
   C) trial balance.
   D) accounting system.

6) The general journal does not do which of the following? ____
   A) provide a chronological record of all transactions
   B) show all the accounts involved in each transaction together
   C) show the balance of each account
   D) help locate recording errors by showing debits and credits together for each transaction

7) You are looking at the Accounts Payable account in the ledger, and you see an entry in the "Posting Reference" column (sometimes called the "LP" or "Folio" column). This entry ____
   A) refers to the account number of that account.
   B) refers to a page number in the journal.
   C) refers to the sequential number of the journal entry.
   D) is a reference to the date of the original transaction.

8) "Posting" means that transaction information is transferred from the ____
   A) journal to the trial balance.
   B) ledger to the trial balance.
   C) ledger to the journal.
   D) journal to the ledger.

CUMULATIVE TEST: LEARNING GOALS 19 THROUGH 27

CUMULATIVE TEST SOLUTIONS BEGIN ON PAGE 514.

9) A trial balance is _____
   A) a listing of accounts and their balances, usually prepared at any point in time.
   B) a listing of the names of accounts with their account numbers, prepared before a new account is added.
   C) a listing of accounts and their balances, usually prepared at the end of an accounting period.
   D) another name for the book of accounts.

10) Which of the following account types should show a normal credit balance? _____
    A) asset, liability, and expense
    B) asset, revenue, and liability
    C) liability, revenue, and owner's capital
    D) liability, expense, and drawing

11) The usual sequence in the recording of transaction data is _____
    A) analyze the event, post into the ledger, journalize, prepare the trial balance.
    B) journalize the transaction, analyze the event, prepare a trial balance, post into the ledger.
    C) analyze the event, journalize, post into the ledger, prepare a trial balance.
    D) analyze the event, journalize, post into the ledger.

12) Use the journal entry below to answer the next question.

Date	Account Titles and Explanation	Post. Ref.	Debit	Credit
2000				
August 3	Supplies		220	
	Accounts Payable			220

This journal entry is recording _____
A) the purchase of supplies.
B) the payment of a liability.
C) the using up of supplies.
D) an owner investment of personal supplies into the business.

13) A manager needs to know how much merchandise inventory the company has available. This is an example of needing to use which kind of data arrangement? _____
    A) a chronological record of transactions
    B) an historical record of all increases and decreases for each item in the accounting equation
    C) the balance of any item in the accounting equation
    D) all the accounts involved in each individual transaction

14) An account is _____
    A) an historical record of transactions, like a diary.
    B) a listing of all balances for each asset, liability, or owner's equity item in the equation.
    C) a description of recordable business events.
    D) an historical record of all changes and the balance of an asset, liability, or owner's equity item.

15) Increases in the owner's capital are usually the result of _____
    A) debits to revenue accounts and debits to expense accounts.
    B) credits to revenue accounts and debits to the capital account.
    C) debits to expense accounts and debits to revenue accounts.
    D) none of the above.

CUMULATIVE TEST SOLUTIONS BEGIN ON PAGE 514.

16) Use the illustration below to answer the next question.

Accounts Receivable

bal. 2,000	
15,000	10,000

The best explanation of what happened in this account is _____
A) credits increased the account by $15,000, resulting in a $7,000 credit balance.
B) credits decreased the account by $10,000 and debits increased the account by $15,000, resulting in a $7,000 credit balance.
C) credits decreased the account by $10,000 and debits increased the account by $15,000, resulting in a $2,000 debit balance.
D) credits decreased the account by $10,000 and debits increased the account by $15,000, resulting in a $7,000 debit balance.

17) If you wanted to know the amount of the accounts payable owing as of today, you would look in _____
A) the journal.
B) the ledger.
C) the book of original entry.
D) the trial balance.

18) Which of the following journal entries has been recorded correctly? _____

A)	Cash		500
	Wages Expense	500	

B)	Equipment	3,700	
	Cash		1,650
	Notes Payable		1,950

C)	Supplies Expense	500	
	Telephone Expense	900	
	Accounts Payable		1,400

D)   None of the above.

19) Tempe Service Company shows a normal accounts payable balance of $10,500 on December 31. During December, there were payments to creditors of $11,900 and new purchases on account of $10,700. The balance of accounts payable on December 1 was a _____
A) credit balance of $1,200.
B) debit balance of $11,700.
C) credit balance of $11,700.
D) credit balance of $9,300.

CUMULATIVE TEST SOLUTIONS BEGIN ON PAGE 514.

20) Which error would not cause the total credits in a trial balance to be greater than the total debits? ____
    A) Cash sales of $5,000 recorded in the journal is accidentally posted twice into the ledger by debiting Land $5,000 and crediting notes payable $5,000.
    B) A journal entry recording cash collections from customers of $200 is posted as a debit to the cash account in the ledger for $200 and as a credit to accounts receivable for $2,000.
    C) The account balance of accounts receivable is a normal balance of $950, and is entered in the trial balance "Credit" column for $950.
    D) None of the above.

21) A journal entry that consists of three or more accounts is called a ____
    A) complex entry.
    B) simple entry.
    C) compound entry.
    D) group entry.

22) A partner of the Burlington and Champlain partnership wants to know why the Notes Payable account shows increases of $20,000 during September. This is an example of needing which kind of accounting data arrangement? ____
    A) a chronological record of transactions
    B) an historical record of all increases and decreases for each item in the accounting equation
    C) the balance of any item in the accounting equation
    D) all the accounts involved in each individual transaction

23) Which of the following is not true about the words "debit" and "credit"? ____
    A) Debits are increases and credits are decreases.
    B) Debits and credits can describe the balance of an account.
    C) Debits and credits can describe increases and decreases in an account.
    D) The left side of an account is called the debit side, and the right side is called the credit side.

24) The usual sequence of accounts in the ledger is ____
    A) assets, expenses, owner's capital, revenues, drawing.
    B) revenues, expenses, drawing, assets, liabilities.
    C) liabilities, assets, revenues, drawing, expenses.
    D) assets, liabilities, owner's capital, revenues, expenses.

25) Which of the following is not true? ____
    A) Assets are increased by credits.
    B) Liabilities are decreased by debits.
    C) Revenues are increased by credits.
    D) Expenses are increased by debits.

26) The trial balance would not detect which error? ____
    A) Recording revenue on account by debiting Service Revenue and debiting Accounts Receivable.
    B) Incorrectly totaling the balance in a ledger account.
    C) Debiting Cash and forgetting to credit Accounts Receivable.
    D) Forgetting to post an entire transaction already recorded in the journal.

27) The correct general journal entry to record the purchase of supplies for cash would include ____
    A) a debit to Cash recorded just above the credit to Supplies.
    B) a debit to Cash recorded just below the credit to Supplies.
    C) a credit to Supplies recorded just below the debit to Cash.
    D) a debit to Supplies recorded just above the credit to Cash.

28) The ending balance of any account can be calculated as ____
    A) the total debits, minus the total credits.
    B) the beginning balance, minus the total credits, plus the total debits.
    C) the beginning balance, plus the total increases, minus the total decreases.
    D) the beginning balance, plus the total credits, minus the total debits.

512

CUMULATIVE TEST SOLUTIONS BEGIN ON PAGE 514.

29) The Concord Company shows revenues with credit balances totaling $38,000, total debits to Accounts Receivable of $10,000, expenses with debit balances totaling $42,000, and debits to the drawing account totaling $5,000. The company had a ____
A) net income of $6,000.
B) net income of $1,000.
C) net loss of $4,000.
D) net loss of $9,000.

30) In October, the Supplies account of Dover Company has a normal beginning balance of $7,300, total debits of $12,950, and a normal ending balance of $14,400. What was the October Supplies Expense? ____
A) $5,850
B) $1,450
C) $12,950
D) none of the above

31) If you wanted to find the ledger account number for Rent Expense, you would look in ____
A) the chart of accounts.
B) the journal.
C) the ledger.
D) none of the above.

32) The correct general journal entry to record fees earned on account would include ____
A) a debit to Cash recorded just above the credit to a revenue.
B) a credit to a revenue recorded just below the debit to Accounts Receivable.
C) a debit to a revenue recorded just below the credit to Accounts Receivable.
D) a credit to Accounts Receivable recorded just below the debit to a revenue.

33) The reason that entries are made in the "Posting Reference" column in the journal is to ____
A) show the account numbers when transactions are being journalized.
B) show that transaction information has been recorded into specific ledger accounts.
C) show that transaction information has been recorded on specific ledger pages.
D) both A and B.

34) Financial statements are prepared from the ____
A) general journal.
B) general ledger.
C) trial balance.
D) none of the above.

35) Which of these accounts is not a subdivision of the owner's capital? ____
A) revenues
B) liabilities
C) drawing
D) expenses

Use this table for the next two questions:

	Assets	Liabilities	Owner's Capital	Revenue	Expense	Drawing
Debit	1	2	3			
Credit			4	5	6	

36) The boxes labeled "1," "2," and "3" in the table above should contain the words ____
A) decrease, increase, increase.
B) increase, decrease, increase.
C) decrease, decrease, increase.
D) increase, decrease, decrease.

CUMULATIVE TEST SOLUTIONS BEGIN ON PAGE 514.

37) The boxes labeled "4," "5," and "6" in the table above should contain the words _____
   A) increase, increase, decrease.
   B) increase, decrease, increase.
   C) decrease, decrease, decrease.
   D) decrease, decrease, increase.

CUMULATIVE TEST QUESTIONS BEGIN ON PAGE 508.

MULTIPLE CHOICE

1) B.
2) B.
3) C, because expenses and drawing are reducing the owner's capital.
4) C. *Remember:* decreases are simply the side opposite from increases.
5) A.
6) C.
7) B. An entry in the ledger should always be traceable to the page of the journal where it originated.
8) D.
9) C.
10) C.
11) C.
12) A.
13) C.
14) D.
15) D. The correct answer is credits to revenue accounts and credits to the owner's capital account.
16) D. This is an asset account, so credits decrease it and debits increase it.
17) B, because the ledger contains all the accounts and their balances.
18) C. A is wrong because the credits have been recorded before the debits. B is wrong for two reasons: first, the names of the accounts being credited are not indented; second, the total credits add up to 3,600 but the debit is for 3,700.
19) C. When calculating a missing amount in an account, *you have two good choices:* 1) you can use the formula that applies to all accounts: **beginning balance + increases – decreases = ending balance** or 2) you can set up a T account, plug in the information that you know, and look for the missing amount. If you use the first approach, then: X + 10,700 – 11,900 = 10,500. Therefore, X = 11,700. The natural positive balance (normal balance) of accounts payable is a credit balance.

    If you use the T account method, then:

Accounts Payable	
	?
	11,900
10,700	
	10,500

20) A. Even though mistakes were made in the entry A, total debits equal total credits. In entry B, credits will exceed debits by $1,800. In C, a $950 debit is entered as a $950 credit, making the credits in the trial balance exceed debits by $1,900.
21) C.
22) B.
23) A.
24) D.
25) A.
26) D. Forgetting to post an entry does not cause total debits and credits to be unequal in the ledger accounts. All the other situations will cause the total debits and credits in the ledger to be unequal: in A, there are two debits and no credits; in B, the incorrect total will cause total debits and credits in the ledger to be unequal; in C, there is a debit but no credit.
27) D. *Always try to visualize the entry.* Write it down it you have to:

Supplies	xxx	
Cash		xxx

CUMULATIVE TEST QUESTIONS BEGIN ON PAGE 508.

28) C. Debits and credits do not mean increase or decrease, only left and right.

29) C. The formula for net income (or loss) is: **Revenues – Expenses = Net Income (or loss)**. Therefore, $38,000 – $42,000 = – $4,000. The debits to the accounts receivable are already included as part of the total revenue. Drawings are not expenses, and do not affect the net income.

30) A. Supplies expense means the amount of supplies used up. You need to calculate the decrease in the Supplies account. So, this is like #19.

A) You can use the formula for an account: **beginning balance + increases – decreases = ending balance**. Because Supplies is an asset account, debits are increases, so therefore: $7,300 + 12,950 – X = 14,400$. This gives: $– X = – 5,850$. So, $X = 5,850$.

B) Using the T account approach:

Supplies	
7,300	
12,950	?
14,400	

31) A.

32) B. *Always try to visualize the entry.* Write it down it you have to:

Accounts Receivable	xxx	
Fees Earned		xxx

33) B. Posting reference entries are not part of journalizing.

34) C.

35) B.

36) D.

37) A.

HELP TABLE

Identify Your Strengths and Weaknesses

The questions in this test cover the nine learning goals of Section V. After you have circled the number of each question that you missed, look at the table below.

Go to the first learning goal category in the table: "Explain the Five Kinds of Information." The second column in the table shows which questions on the test covered this learning goal. Look on the test to see if you circled numbers 1, 13, or 22. How many did you miss? Write this number in the "How Many Missed?" column. Repeat this process for each of the remaining learning goal categories in the table.

If you *miss **two** or more questions* for any learning goal, you are too weak in that learning goal and you need to *review*. The last column shows you where to read and practice so you can improve your score.

Some learning goal categories have more questions because you need to be especially well prepared in these areas. More questions means your performance must be better.

Learning Goal	Questions	How many missed?	Material begins on ...
SECTION V			
19) Explain the Five Kinds of Information	1, 13, 22		page 365
20) Learn to Use Accounts	2, 14, 16, 19, 28, 30		page 374
21) Use the Owner's Capital Accounts	3, 15, 29, 35		page 393
22) "Debits on the left, credits on the right!"	4, 10, 23, 25, 36, 37		page 409
23) Explain the Ledger	5, 17, 24, 31		page 423
24) Use a Journal	6, 12, 18, 21, 27, 32		page 430
25) Use Realistic Accounting Records	7, 8, 33		page 466
26) The Trial Balance—Prepare It and Use It Two Ways*	9, 20, 26, 34		page 483
27) Explain the Accounting Cycle	11		page 501

* For Learning Goal 26, you should also practice preparing a balance sheet, an income statement, and a statement of owner's equity on a blank piece of paper from the information on a trial balance. Use problems in any book for which you also have a solution.

Essential Math for Accounting

BRIEF OVERVIEW

Introduction

This section is designed to give you a review of all the math you will need for this book and for beginning your work in any introductory accounting text. Combined with the math review in the next book of this series (Volume 2), you will have a review of all the math you will need for your entire first year of accounting study … and more.

How to use this section

You do not need to read the entire math review. Simply study those topics that you feel you need to practice.

● Read the topic that you feel you need to practice.
● When you finish reading, work the "Practice" problems for that topic.
● Review the solutions and highlight the problems you missed, so you can try them again or ask your instructor or classmates for more help.

Math review in the next volume …

This book is the first book in a series of two books. The second book (Volume 2) continues the math review, which includes:

● explanation and use of fractions
● continuation of basic algebra topics

In this section, you will find:

▼ *Percent*

▼ *Positive and Negative Numbers*

▼ *Introduction to Algebra and Equations*

▼ *General Introduction: Numerals are Symbols for Amounts*

NUMERALS

Importance of numerals	We all see and use numerals every day, usually without giving them much thought. However, the individual numerals are really a foundation of all of our mathematics! Let's take a moment to be sure that we are comfortable about what numerals really mean and how they function.
Numerals are symbols	A numeral is a symbol for an amount of something. In the number system with which most of us are familiar, there are ten symbols. For example, suppose that some of us are hungry. I suggest that we order pizza. How many pizzas? We can use symbols to express the number of pizzas we want:

Numeral Symbol	Written as ...	Number of Pizzas
0	"zero"	
1	"one"	●
2	"two"	● ●
3	"three"	● ● ●
4	"four"	● ● ● ●
5	"five"	● ● ● ● ●
6	"six"	● ● ● ● ● ●
7	"seven"	● ● ● ● ● ● ●
8	"eight"	● ● ● ● ● ● ● ●
9	"nine"	● ● ● ● ● ● ● ● ●

You can see that there is a numeral symbol for each individual amount from zero units to nine units or, in this case, pizzas.

NUMERALS (continued)

Only ten symbols are used	Suppose that we wanted to order ten pizzas, or eleven, or twelve … or twenty. Could we invent more symbols for more units? Yes, that would be possible. For example, we could create a symbol like "*" for the number ten, or perhaps the symbol "Y" for the number eleven, and so on; however, this is not practical. We would need an unimaginably large number of symbols for all the possible numbers, and we could never remember them! For this reason, our number system uses only ten symbols, but in a very clever way.

▼ *The Place-Value Numeral System*

WHAT THE SYSTEM IS

Introduction	So far, we have only been able to express amounts up to nine units of something. Clearly, this is not enough. But if we are limited to only ten symbols, what can we do? A long, long time ago, the clever people who invented our number system gave this problem a great deal of thought. Their solution was something called the "place-value" numeral system.
Definition: the place-value numeral system	The place-value numeral system is a method that determines the value of a numeral by how it is positioned relative to other numerals.
Numeral groups	In the place-value numeral system, the basic ten symbols are placed into groups. The position—or place—of each group determines the size of the numerals within the group. Below is a chart of some number groups as they are positioned in a place-value system.

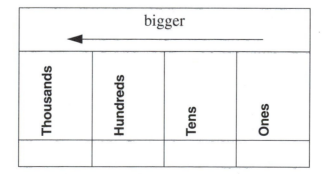

READING AND WRITING NUMERALS IN EACH PLACE

The "ones" place   The first, and smallest, place begins on the right. This is called the "ones" place because all the numerals are counted in units of one.

Examples   Below are examples with the numeral "three" and the numeral "seven," which are three units of one and seven units of one.

The numeral "three" is placed like this:			
Thousands	Hundreds	Tens	Ones
			3

The numeral "seven" is placed like this:			
Thousands	Hundreds	Tens	Ones
			7

The "tens" place   The next place is the "tens" place. All numerals written in this position are counted in *units of ten*, rather than units of one as in the "ones" place. For example, in the "tens" place, a "2" means two units of ten; in other words, twenty. A "3" in the "tens" place means three units of ten, which is thirty, and so on. Each greater numeral in the "tens" place adds another unit of ten.

Examples   These examples show you how to write and say some numerals in the "tens" place.

The number "ten"			
Thousands	Hundreds	Tens	Ones
		1	0

Saying the number:
- One unit of ten is "ten"
- No units of one is silent

The number is called "ten"

The number "twelve"			
Thousands	Hundreds	Tens	Ones
		1	2

Saying the number:
- One unit of ten is "ten"
- Two units of one is "two"

The number is called "twelve"

READING AND WRITING NUMERALS IN EACH PLACE (continued)

The number "twenty-two"			
Thousands	Hundreds	Tens	Ones
		2	2

Saying the number:
- Two units of ten is "twenty"
- Two units of one is "two"

The number is called "twenty-two"

The number "thirty-five"			
Thousands	Hundreds	Tens	Ones
		3	5

Saying the number:
- Three units of ten is "thirty"
- Five units of one is "five"

The number is called "thirty-five"

The number "forty-eight"			
Thousands	Hundreds	Tens	Ones
		4	8

Saying the number:
- Four units of ten is "forty"
- Eight units of one is "eight"

The number is called "forty-eight"

The number "ninety-nine"			
Thousands	Hundreds	Tens	Ones
		9	9

Saying the number:
- Nine units of ten is "ninety"
- Nine units of one is "nine"

The number is called "ninety-nine"

Note: All the numbers from twenty-one to ninety-nine are always hyphenated whenever they are spelled.

How about fourteen pizzas? So are we ready to order our pizzas now? Suppose that we have decided to order fourteen pizzas. The place-value number system neatly allows us to put a "1" in the "tens" place to signify ten, and then put a "4" in the "ones" place to signify four. Presto! We have easily expressed a total of **fourteen** pizzas!

"Digits"

When a number is represented by several numerals, each individual numeral is often called a "digit." For example, we represent the number eighty-three by using the numerals "8" and "3" like this: 83. The numeral "8" is one digit and the numeral "3" is another digit.

READING AND WRITING NUMERALS IN EACH PLACE (continued)

The "hundreds" place   The next place is the "hundreds" place. All numbers written in this position are counted in *units of one hundred*. For example, in the "hundreds" place, a "2" means two units of one hundred; in other words, two hundred. A "3" in the "hundreds" place means three units of one hundred, which is three hundred, and so on. In the "hundreds" place, each greater numeral adds another unit of one hundred.

Examples   Below are examples of some numbers in the "hundreds" place.

The number "one hundred thirty-two"			
Thousands	Hundreds	Tens	Ones
	1	3	2

Saying the number:
- One unit of one hundred is "one hundred"
- Three units of ten is "thirty"
- Two units of one is "two"

The number is called "one hundred thirty-two"

The number "two hundred fifty"			
Thousands	Hundreds	Tens	Ones
	2	5	0

Saying the number:
- Two units of one hundred is "two hundred"
- Five units of ten is "fifty"
- Zero units of one is silent

The number is called "two hundred fifty"

The number "three hundred four"			
Thousands	Hundreds	Tens	Ones
	3	0	4

Saying the number:
- Three units of one hundred is "three hundred"
- Zero units of ten is silent
- Four units of one is "four"

The number is called "three hundred four"

Note: The word "and" is not used.

The number "eight hundred ninety-nine"			
Thousands	Hundreds	Tens	Ones
	8	9	9

Saying the number:
- Eight units of one hundred is "eight hundred"
- Nine units of ten is "ninety"
- Nine units of one is "nine"

The number is called "eight hundred ninety-nine"

READING AND WRITING NUMERALS IN EACH PLACE (continued)

The "thousands" place

The next place is the "thousands" place. All numbers written in this position represent units of one thousand. For example, in the "thousands" place, a "2" means two units of one thousand; in other words, two thousand. A "3" in the "thousands" place means three units of one thousand, which is three thousand, and so on. Each greater numeral adds one thousand.

Examples

Below are examples of some numbers in the "thousands" place.

The number "one thousand seven hundred fifty-six"			
Thousands	Hundreds	Tens	Ones
1,	7	5	6

The number "two thousand thirty"			
Thousands	Hundreds	Tens	Ones
2,	0	3	0

Saying the number:
- One unit of one thousand is "one thousand"
- Seven units of one hundred is "seven hundred"
- Five units of ten is "fifty"
- Six units of one is "six"

The number is called "one thousand seven hundred fifty-six"

Saying the number:
- Two units of one thousand is "two thousand"
- Zero units of one hundred is silent
- Three units of ten is "thirty"
- Zero units of one is silent

The number is called "two thousand thirty"

Using commas

When numbers become larger, it is more difficult to quickly identify the number places. To make it easier to see the number places, a comma is entered after every third number place, beginning from the right.

Examples:
- The number "one thousand seven hundred fifty-six" is written "1,756."
- The number "two thousand thirty" is written "2,030."

READING AND WRITING NUMERALS IN EACH PLACE (continued)

Places are multiples of ten

Notice that each greater place in the place-value table is a multiple of ten times the preceding place value. This is sometimes called a "base ten" system.

- "10" is ten ones
- "100" is ten tens
- "1,000" is ten hundreds

… and so on, with each new place being ten times the preceding one.

A bigger place-value table

You can see that each time we have looked at a new place of numbers, the size of the numbers at the new place in the chart is ten times greater than the numbers in the previous place. Below is a place-value chart that shows place-value numerals up to one billion. Of course, you could continue to increase the chart to ten billion, one hundred billion, one trillion, and so on.

Billions	Hundred Millions	Ten Millions	Millions	Hundred Thousands	Ten Thousands	Thousands	Hundreds	Tens	Ones
7,	5	7	4,	3	0	8,	2	9	1

The amount you see above is written as "7,574,308,291." It is called "seven billion, five hundred seventy-four million, three hundred eight thousand, two hundred ninety-one."

PRACTICE

SOLUTIONS FOR THE PLACE-VALUE SYSTEM BEGIN ON PAGE 528.

REINFORCEMENT PROBLEMS: THE PLACE-VALUE SYSTEM

1) **Write the words in numbers.** For each amount on the left that is expressed in words, express that same amount using numbers. The first item is an example.

Amount written in words	Amount written in numbers
A) Three thousand four hundred eighty-eight	3,488
B) Eighty-nine	
C) Two hundred twelve	
D) Nine hundred seven	
E) Twenty-two thousand, six hundred seventy-two	
F) Eleven thousand three	
G) One hundred fifty-four thousand, seven hundred thirty-three	
H) Two million, sixty-five thousand, ninety-one	
I) Ten million, two hundred eighty-six thousand, four hundred thirty-three	
J) Thirty-nine thousand, one hundred thirty-nine	
K) Seventeen thousand, four hundred twenty-seven	
L) Five thousand, seven hundred thirty-five	

2) **Write the numbers in words.** For each amount, express the number using words.

Amount written in numbers	Amount written in words
A) 257	
B) 33	
C) 4,079	
D) 7,294	
E) 12,370	
F) 97	
G) 909	
H) 54	
I) 47,882	

3) **Identify the place-value.** For each number in bold type, identify what place value place it is part of. The first two items are examples.

Number	Place-Value		Number	Place-Value
2,422	hundreds		19**8**	ones
3**5**,077			28,00**9**	
846			1**1**,305	
239,**5**55			4,**5**80,423	
7,3**9**7,137			9,**2**22	
5,00**2**			8**1**2,331	
1,**8**72			1**7**,999	

SOLUTIONS

PRACTICE QUESTIONS FOR THE PLACE-VALUE SYSTEM BEGIN ON PAGE 527.

REINFORCEMENT PROBLEMS: THE PLACE-VALUE SYSTEM

1)

	Amount written in words	Amount written in numbers
A)	Three thousand four hundred eighty-eight	3,488
B)	Eighty-nine	89
C)	Two hundred twelve	212
D)	Nine hundred seven	907
E)	Twenty-two thousand, six hundred seventy-two	22,672
F)	Eleven thousand three	11,003
G)	One hundred fifty-four thousand, seven hundred thirty-three	154,733
H)	Two million, sixty-five thousand, ninety-one	2,065,091
I)	Ten million, two hundred eighty-six thousand, four hundred thirty-three	10,286,433
J)	Thirty-nine thousand, one hundred thirty-nine	39,139
K)	Seventeen thousand, four hundred twenty-seven	17,427
L)	Five thousand, seven hundred thirty-five	5,735

2)

	Amount written in numbers	Amount written in words
A)	257	two hundred fifty-seven
B)	33	thirty-three
C)	4,079	four thousand seventy-nine
D)	7,294	seven thousand two hundred ninety-four
E)	12,370	twelve thousand three hundred seventy
F)	97	ninety-seven
G)	909	nine hundred nine
H)	54	fifty-four
I)	47,882	forty-seven thousand eight hundred eighty-two

3)

Number	Place-Value		Number	Place-Value
2,**4**22	hundreds		19**8**	ones
35,077	thousands		28,0**0**9	tens
846	hundreds		**1**1,305	ten thousands
2**3**9,555	ten thousands		**4**,580,423	millions
3,397,137	hundred thousands		9,**2**22	hundreds
5,**0**02	hundreds		812,3**3**1	tens
1,**8**72	hundreds		17,99**9**	ones

▼ *Arithmetic Operations*

HOW TO ADD NUMBERS

Overview

Addition is the most common of all the arithmetic operations that you will do. The essential idea to remember is that when you are doing addition, you simply start at the top of a place-value column, and add the digits in that column. It really does not matter how big the numbers are that you are adding, because you are only adding one column at a time.

Symbol for addition

To signify that numbers are being added, the "+" symbol is used. If numbers are shown vertically, the symbol is placed to the left of the last number. If numbers are shown horizontally, the symbol is placed between the numbers.

$$\text{Vertical:} \quad \begin{array}{r} 15 \\ 12 \\ + \underline{20} \end{array} \qquad \text{Horizontal:} \quad 15 + 12 + 20$$

Procedure

The following table shows you the steps for addition. Suppose that you want to add these numbers: 31, 5, 17, and 178.

Step	Action	Example
1	**Align the numbers** so that the individual digits in each place-value form a column. Draw a line under the bottom number.	$\begin{array}{r} 3\ 1 \\ 5 \\ 1\ 7 \\ +\ 1\ 7\ 8 \\ \hline \end{array}$
2	Beginning with the lowest place-value column that is not totaled, **add the numbers in a column**. Add from the top down. *Note:* It will be easiest if you develop the habit of keeping a mental "running total" as you add each number in the column. These totals are shown by the small numbers. Do not write these down. You would say to yourself: "1 plus 5 is 6." Then, "6 plus 7 is 13" and so on until the end of the column.	$\begin{array}{r} 3\ 1 \\ 5\ _{6} \\ 1\ 7\ _{13} \\ +\ 1\ 7\ 8\ _{21} \\ \hline \end{array}$

HOW TO ADD NUMBERS (continued)

Step	Action	Example
3	**Write the total** of the column (called the **sum**) at the bottom of the column. *Rule:* If the sum exceeds 9, put the digits of the sum into the columns to which they correspond. For example, the total of the "ones" column is 21. Here, we want to show this as one unit of "ones" and two units of "tens." Write the two units of ten at the top of the "tens" column, where it will later be added with the other "tens." The 1 remains in the "ones" unit column.	$$\begin{array}{ccc} & {}^{2} & \\ & 3 & 1 \\ & & 5 \\ & 1 & 7 \\ + & 1 & 7 & 8 \\ \hline & & & 1 \end{array}$$
4	If there are more place-value columns to add, **return to Step 2, and begin the next column**. **Adding the "tens" column:**	$$\begin{array}{cccc} {}^{1} & {}^{2} & & \\ & 3 & {}_{5}1 & \\ & & & 5 \\ & 1 & {}_{6}7 & \\ + & 1 & 7{}_{13} & 8 \\ \hline & 3 & & 1 \end{array}$$
	Adding the "hundreds" column: There are no more columns to add, so you are finished.	$$\begin{array}{cccc} {}^{1} & {}^{2} & & \\ & 3 & 1 & \\ & & & 5 \\ & 1 & 7 & \\ + & 1{}_{2} & 7 & 8 \\ \hline & 2 & 3 & 1 \end{array}$$

Checking your work

It is quite easy to make a mistake when adding a column of numbers, even if you are using a calculator. To check your totals, repeat the process, but add from the bottom to the top. Working in reverse order minimizes your chances of making the same mistake twice.

HOW TO ADD NUMBERS (continued)

Example with more numbers

Add the following five numbers: 2,196 + 13,099 + 350 + 12,454 + 41.

Step 1: Align the numbers	$$\begin{array}{r} 2,196 \\ 13,099 \\ 350 \\ 12,454 \\ +\quad 41 \\ \hline \end{array}$$

Steps 2 and 3: Add the "ones" place-value column. 20 is zero units of one and two units of ten. Write two units of ten into the "tens" column.

$$\begin{array}{r} \overset{2}{}\\ 2,1\;9\;6 \\ 13,0\;9\;9\;_{15} \\ 3\;5\;0\;_{15} \\ 12,4\;5\;4\;_{19} \\ +\quad 4\;1\;_{20} \\ \hline 0 \end{array}$$

Step 4: Add the "tens" column. Thirty-four tens is really four units of ten and three units of one hundred. Write the three units of one hundred into the "hundreds" column.

$$\begin{array}{r} \overset{3}{}\overset{2}{} \\ 2,1\;9_{11}\;6 \\ 13,0\;9_{20}\;9 \\ 3\;5_{25}\;0 \\ 12,4\;5_{30}\;4 \\ +\quad 4_{34}\;1 \\ \hline 4\;0 \end{array}$$

Step 4: Add the "hundreds" column. Eleven hundreds is really one unit of one hundred and one unit of one thousand. Write the one unit of one thousand into the "thousands" column.

$$\begin{array}{r} \overset{1}{}\overset{3}{}\overset{2}{} \\ 2,1_4\;9\;6 \\ 13,0_4\;9\;9 \\ 3_7\;5\;0 \\ 12,4_{11}\;5\;4 \\ +\quad 4\;1 \\ \hline 1\;4\;0 \end{array}$$

Step 4: Add the "thousands" column. Eight units of one thousand does not exceed nine, so no units need to be carried to the "ten thousands" column.

$$\begin{array}{r} \overset{1}{}\overset{3}{}\overset{2}{} \\ 2,_3 1\;9\;6 \\ 13,_6 0\;9\;9 \\ 3\;5\;0 \\ 12,_8 4\;5\;4 \\ +\quad 4\;1 \\ \hline 8,1\;4\;0 \end{array}$$

Step 4: Add the "ten thousands" column. There are two units of ten thousand, so this is twenty thousand. There are no more columns to add. The sum is 28,140.

$$\begin{array}{r} \overset{1}{}\overset{3}{}\overset{2}{} \\ 2,1\;9\;6 \\ 13,0\;9\;9 \\ 3\;5\;0 \\ 1_2\;2,4\;5\;4 \\ +\quad 4\;1 \\ \hline 2\;8,1\;4\;0 \end{array}$$

Characteristics of addition

Numbers can be added in any order
- Adding 5 + 12 + 8 is a sum of 25
- Adding 12 + 5 + 8 is also a sum of 25

Numbers can be added in any groups
- Adding (5 + 12) + 8 or 5 + (12 + 8) both give the same answer of 25

PRACTICE

REINFORCEMENT PROBLEM: ADDITION

1) Add the numbers shown in the left column of the table and show your answers in the right column.

Add the following numbers …	Answer
A) 4; 7; 9; 3	
B) 25; 189; 101; 56; 7	
C) 111; 390; 459; 285	
D) 1,003; 2,597; 144	
E) 2,091; 3,511; 9,972	
F) 1,461; 5,238; 9,499	
G) 19,884; 52,040; 27,318	
H) 299,351; 327,500	
I) 1,345,739; 12,905,476	
J) 11,005; 434; 899; 21,927	
K) 450; 50; 300	
l) 200; 1,000; 300	

SOLUTIONS

REINFORCEMENT PROBLEM: ADDITION

1)

Add the following numbers …	Answer
A) 4; 7; 9; 3	23
B) 25; 189; 101; 56; 7	378
C) 111; 390; 459; 285	1,245
D) 1,003; 2,597; 144	3,744
E) 2,091; 3,511; 9,972	15,574
F) 1,461; 5,238; 9,499	16,198
G) 19,884; 52,040; 27,318	99,242
H) 299,351; 327,500	626,851
I) 1,345,739; 12,905,476	14,251,215
J) 11,005; 434; 899; 21,927	34,265
K) 450; 50; 300	800
l) 200; 1,000; 300	1,500

HOW TO SUBTRACT NUMBERS

Overview	Subtraction is the process of finding the difference between two numbers. The difference between two numbers simply means the amount by which one number is greater than another number.
Example	If we subtract 7 from 10, we find that the difference is 3. This means that 10 is greater than 7 by the amount of 3.
Symbol for subtraction	To signify that numbers are being subtracted, the "−" symbol is used. If numbers are shown vertically, the symbol is placed to left of the bottom number. If numbers are shown horizontally, the symbol is placed between the numbers.

Vertical: 50   Horizontal: 50 − 20
           − 20

Procedure	The following table shows you the steps for subtraction. Suppose that you are planning a picnic. You have 195 paper plates and you will need 382. How many more do you need? (You need to find the difference between the numbers.)

Step	Action	Example
1	**Align the numbers** so that the individual digits are in the correct place-value columns. When aligning the numbers, put the larger number on top.	$\begin{array}{r} 3\ 8\ 2 \\ -\ 1\ 9\ 5 \\ \hline \end{array}$
2	**Go to the lowest place-value column** that has not been subtracted.	$\begin{array}{r} {}^{7}\ {}^{12} \\ 3\ \cancel{8}\ \cancel{2} \\ -\ 1\ 9\ 5 \\ \hline \end{array}$

If ...	Then ...
the bottom number in the column is smaller than the top number ...	... go to Step 3.
the bottom number in the column is bigger than the top number (here, the 5 is bigger than the 2) ...	... increase the top number in that column by borrowing a unit from the column next to it. One unit borrowed from the "tens" column adds ten to the "ones" column. So, the "ones" column increases to 12 (10 plus the 2). The 8 in the "tens" column is reduced to 7. Cross out the old numbers and write in the changed numbers.

HOW TO SUBTRACT NUMBERS (continued)

Step	Action	Example
3	**Subtract the bottom number in the column from the top number**, and write the difference under the line.	$\begin{array}{r} 7{}^{12} \\ 3\ \ 8\ \ \cancel{2} \\ -\ 1\ \ 9\ \ 5 \\ \hline 7 \end{array}$
4	If there are more columns to subtract, return to Step 2 and repeat the procedure with the other columns:	
	Subtracting the "tens" column: Because the 9 is greater than the 7, we need to borrow one unit from the "hundreds" column. One unit from the "hundreds" column adds 10 to the "tens" column, so the 7 is increased to 17. The difference between 9 and 17 is 8.	$\begin{array}{r} {}^{17} \\ 2\ \ \cancel{7}\ \ {}^{12} \\ \cancel{3}\ \ \cancel{8}\ \ \cancel{2} \\ -\ 1\ \ 9\ \ 5 \\ \hline 8\ \ 7 \end{array}$
	Subtracting the "hundreds" column: 1 is less than 2, and the difference is one. You need 187 more paper plates.	$\begin{array}{r} {}^{17} \\ 2\ \ \cancel{7}\ \ {}^{12} \\ \cancel{3}\ \ \cancel{8}\ \ \cancel{2} \\ -\ 1\ \ 9\ \ 5 \\ \hline 1\ \ 8\ \ 7 \end{array}$

Example without steps

Here is an example of subtraction without listing the steps:

Subtract 4,301 from 9,037:

$$\begin{array}{r} {}^{8}\ \ {}^{10} \\ \cancel{9},\ \ \cancel{0}\ \ 3\ \ 7 \\ -\ 4,\ \ 3\ \ 0\ \ 1 \\ \hline 4,\ \ 7\ \ 3\ \ 6 \end{array}$$

The difference is 4,736.

Example: moving two places to borrow

Occasionally, you may have to perform a subtraction operation with a number that makes it necessary to move two or more places to the left to find a number from which to borrow.

Example: Subtract 897 from 5,001.

HOW TO SUBTRACT NUMBERS (continued)

Step	Action	Example
1	**Align the numbers**.	$$\begin{array}{r} 5,\ 0\ \ 0\ \ 1 \\ -\ \ \ \ 8\ \ 9\ \ 7 \\ \hline \end{array}$$
2	**Go to the lowest place-value column** that has not been subtracted. If the bottom number is larger than the top number, it is necessary to borrow from the next place value; otherwise, subtract the bottom number from the top number. So, we need to borrow from the "tens" place, but there are no units in the "tens" place. Moving left, there are also not any units in the "hundreds" place. **We continue moving left until we find a place with units from which to borrow.** We first borrow a unit from "thousands" place, and put it the "hundreds" place. Now we are able to borrow a unit from the "hundreds" place and put it in the "tens" place. Finally, we can borrow a unit from the "tens" place and put it in the "ones" place.	$$\begin{array}{r} {\scriptstyle 9\ \ 9} \\ {\scriptstyle 4\ \ \cancel{10}\ \ \cancel{10}\ \ 11} \\ \cancel{5},\ \cancel{0}\ \ \cancel{0}\ \ \cancel{1} \\ -\ \ \ \ 8\ \ 9\ \ 7 \\ \hline \end{array}$$
3	Now we can subtract the 7 in the "ones" place from 11 in the "ones" place.	$$\begin{array}{r} {\scriptstyle 9\ \ 9} \\ {\scriptstyle 4\ \ \cancel{10}\ \ \cancel{10}\ \ 11} \\ \cancel{5},\ \cancel{0}\ \ \cancel{0}\ \ \cancel{1} \\ -\ \ \ \ 8\ \ 9\ \ 7 \\ \hline 4 \end{array}$$
4	Return to Step 2 and complete the subtraction process.	$$\begin{array}{r} {\scriptstyle 9\ \ 9} \\ {\scriptstyle 4\ \ \cancel{10}\ \ \cancel{10}\ \ 11} \\ \cancel{5},\ \cancel{0}\ \ \cancel{0}\ \ \cancel{1} \\ -\ \ \ \ 8\ \ 9\ \ 7 \\ \hline 4,\ 1\ \ 0\ \ 4 \end{array}$$

HOW TO SUBTRACT NUMBERS (continued)

Subtracting a sequence of numbers

The subtraction procedure is the same. Simply subtract the next number from the previous result.

Example: Subtract these numbers: 256 – 50 – 78 – 14.

First:	256	Next:	206	Next:	128	
	– 50		– 78		– 14	**Answer**
	206		128		114	

CHECKING SUBTRACTION ANSWERS

Checking your work: use addition

No one performs every calculation perfectly every time, even with a calculator. For this reason, it is important to know how to check your work. To check subtraction:

- Add the answer to the smaller number in the subtraction.
- If this total is equal to the larger number, the subtraction is correct.

Example

	5,001	To check:	4,104	
	– 897		+ 897	**Subtraction is correct**
	4,104		5,001	

REINFORCEMENT PROBLEM: SUBTRACTION

1) ● Subtract the numbers shown in the left column of the table and show your answers in the right column.
   ● Check by addition.

Subtract the following numbers ...	Answer	Check
A) 129 – 59		
B) 2,073 – 1,891		
C) 747 – 599		
D) 244 – 185		
E) 35,402 – 29,515		
F) 147,459 – 127,456		
G) 8,757,930 – 4,899,348		
H) 19,824 – 9,009		
I) 54,741 – 44,230		
J) 12,300 – 7,999		
K) 4,002 – 599		
L) 5,005 – 4,788		

SOLUTIONS

REINFORCEMENT PROBLEM: SUBTRACTION

1)

Subtract the following numbers ...	Answer	Check
A) 129 – 59	70	70 + 59 = 129
B) 2,073 – 1,891	182	182 + 1,891 = 2,073
C) 747 – 599	148	148 + 599 = 747
D) 244 – 185	59	59 + 185 = 244
E) 35,402 – 29,515	5,887	5,887 + 29,515 = 35,402
F) 147,459 – 127,456	20,003	20,003 + 127,456 = 147,459
G) 8,757,930 – 4,899,348	3,858,582	3,858,582 + 4,899,348 = 8,757,930
H) 19,824 – 9,009	10,815	10,815 + 9,009 = 19,824
I) 54,741 – 44,230	10,511	10,511 + 44,230 = 54,741
J) 12,300 – 7,999	4,301	4,301 + 7,999 = 12,300
K) 4,002 – 599	3,403	3,403 + 599 = 4,002
L) 5,005 – 4,788	217	217 + 4,788 = 5,005

HOW TO MULTIPLY NUMBERS

Introduction

Multiplication is really a fast way of doing addition, in the situation where there are numbers that are repeated. For example, suppose that you have seven boxes and each box contains five units of merchandise. To find the total units of merchandise, you could repeatedly add the number five until you have added it seven times:

$$
\begin{array}{r}
^3 5 \\
5 \\
5 \\
5 \\
5 \\
5 \\
\underline{5} \\
3\,5
\end{array}
$$

It is much easier to multiply five times seven:

$$
\begin{array}{r}
5 \\
\times\ \underline{7} \\
35
\end{array}
$$

Terminology

The following terms are normally used when referring to multiplication:

- Each of the numbers being multiplied are called **factors**.
- The bottom factor is usually called the **multiplier**.
- The answer is called the **product**.

$$
\begin{array}{r}
\text{factors} \longrightarrow\quad 5 \\
\times\ 7 \quad \textbf{multiplier} \\
\overline{35} \quad \textbf{product}
\end{array}
$$

Showing multiplication

Multiplication can be shown in several ways. The most common way to indicate multiplication is using the "✕" or "times" sign:

$$
\begin{array}{r}
7 \\
\times\ \underline{5} \\
35
\end{array}
\qquad \text{or: } 7 \times 5 = 35
$$

Other ways to show multiplication are: $7 \bullet 5 = 35$ or: $(7)\,(5) = 35$

HOW TO MULTIPLY NUMBERS (continued)

Memorizing multiplication for two single-digit numbers

If you have any trouble remembering how to multiply two single-digit numbers (such as "7 times 5" or "9 times 6"), you must get the basic multiples memorized. These multiples are found in the "Multiplication table" on page 568. It is not very difficult—you can make games out of the practice—and it is absolutely necessary. If you still need to memorize the multiples, do it.

How to multiply when one number is a single digit

The following table shows you how to multiply 135 by 7.

Step	Action	Example
1	**Align the factors** so that the individual digits are in the correct place-value columns. • Draw a horizontal line under the multiplier. *Rule:* The factor with the fewest digits is always placed on the bottom and becomes the multiplier.	$$\begin{array}{r} 1\ \ 3\ \ 5 \\ \times \qquad 7 \\ \hline \end{array}$$
2	**Multiply the right digit** of the multiplier with right digit of the top factor (7 times 5 is 35).	$$\begin{array}{r} {}^{3} \\ 1\ \ 3\ \boxed{5} \\ \times \qquad \boxed{7} \\ \hline 5 \end{array}$$

If …	Then, under the line …
the product is 9 or less,	write the product in the same place-value alignment as the digit in the multiplier.
the product is greater than 9,	• write the *right* digit (**5**) of the product (**35**) in the same place-value column as the digit in the multiplier. • write the *left* digit (**3**) of the product above the next number in the top factor.

Step	Action	Example
3	• Moving to the left, **multiply the next digit in the top factor** by the same digit in the multiplier (3 times 7 is 21). • Then *add* any number written above the top digit coming from the previous calculation (21 plus 3 is 24).	$$\begin{array}{r} \longleftarrow \\ {}^{2}\ \ {}^{3} \\ 1\ \boxed{3}\ 5 \\ \times \qquad \boxed{7} \\ \hline 4\ \ 5 \end{array}$$

(table continued on next page)

HOW TO MULTIPLY NUMBERS (continued)

Step	Action		Example
3 (cont.)	*If ...*	*Then, under the line ...*	
	the product is 9 or less,	• write the result in the next available place-value column to the left of the previous number in the answer.	
	the product is greater than 9,	• write the *right* digit (**4**) of the product (**24**) in the next available place-value column to the left of the previous number. • write the *left* digit (**2**) of the product above the next number in the top factor.	
4	Moving to the left in the top factor, **continue** using the same procedures in Step 3 until all the digits in the top factor have been multiplied by the multiplier.		⟵ ² ³ 1 3 5 × 7 ——— **9** 4 5

When both factors have multiple digits

The following six steps show you how to multiply when each factor has two or more digits.

Example: Multiply 135 and 287.

Step	Action	Example
1	**Align the factors** so that the individual digits are in the correct place-value columns. The factor with the fewest digits is the multiplier. Put it on the bottom, above a line. (In this case, either number can be on the bottom, because they both have the same number of digits.)	1 3 5 × 2 8 7 ————
2	**Complete the multiplication of the right digit** in the multiplier. (Use the method shown in the previous table.)	² ³ 1 3 5 × 2 8 7 ———— 9 4 5 *(table continued on next page)*

HOW TO MULTIPLY NUMBERS (continued)

Step	Action	Example
3	Move left to the **next digit in the multiplier** (8). Multiply this by the right digit in the top factor (5) (5 times 8 is 40).	<div align="right"><i>2 4 3</i> 1 3 5 × 2 8 7 ――――――― 9 4 5 **0** Notice the alignment ↑</div>

If ...	Then, under the line ...
the product is 9 or less,	write the product in the *same place-value column as the digit you are using in the multiplier.*
the product is greater than 9,	• write the *right* digit (**0**) of the product (**40**) *in the same place-value alignment as the digit you are using in the multiplier.* • write the *left* digit (**4**) of the product above the next number in the top factor. (Cross out any other number previously written here.)

Step	Action	Example
4	Using the same multiplier, **multiply the next digit to the left in top factor** (3 times 8 is 24). Then *add* the new number written above the top digit from the previous calculation (24 plus 4 is 28).	<div align="right">← <i>2 2 4 3</i> 1 3 5 × 2 8 7 ――――――― 9 4 5 **8** 0</div>

If ...	Then, under the line ...
the product is 9 or less,	write the product in the next available place-value column to the left of the previous number.
the product is greater than 9,	• write the *right* digit (**8**) of the product (**28**) in the next available place-value column to the left of the previous number. • write the *left* digit (**2**) of the product above the next number in the top factor.

Using the rules, finish multiplying all the digits in the top factor by the same digit (8) in the multiplier.	<div align="right"><i>2 2 4 3</i> 1 3 5 × 2 8 7 ――――――― 9 4 5 1 0 8 0</div>

(table continued on next page)

HOW TO MULTIPLY NUMBERS (continued)

Step	Action	Example
5	Return to Steps 3 and 4 until all the digits in the top factor have been multiplied by all the digits in the multiplier.	*1* 2 2 ~~4 3~~ 1 3 5 × 2 8 7 ————— 9 4 5 1 0 8 0 2 7 0
6	Add the place-value columns under the line to obtain the answer (in this example: 38,745). *Note:* The answer is called the **product**.	*1* 2 2 ~~4 3~~ 1 3 5 × 2 8 7 ————— 9 4 5 1 0 8 0 2 7 0 ————— 3 8, 7 4 5

When the multiplier has zeroes

If the multiplier is a number that contains one or more zeroes, do not multiply by a zero. Instead, put a zero under the line in the same place-value column as the zero in the multiplier. Then move left in the multiplier to the next number that is not a zero, and follow normal procedures.

Example 1: Multiply 573 by 250.
 	
The product is: 143,250.
	1 3 *1*
	  5 7 3
	× 2 5 0
	—————
	          0
	  2 8 6 5
	1 1 4 6
	—————
	1 4 3, 2 5 0

HOW TO MULTIPLY NUMBERS (continued)

Example 2: Multiply 573 by 205.	$\begin{array}{r} {}^{13}\ {}^{1}\ \\ 5\ 7\ 3 \\ \times\quad 2\ 0\ 5 \\ \hline 2\ 8\ 6\ 5 \\ \mathbf{0} \\ 1\ 1\ 4\ 6 \\ \hline 1\ 1\ 7,\ 4\ 6\ 5 \end{array}$
The product is: 117,465.	

Shortcut: when there are zeroes at the end of factors

Whenever a factor ends in zero, you can drop the zero before you multiply, then do the multiplication with the remaining digits. Attach the same number of zeroes to your answer as the number of zeroes you dropped. This saves time and reduces error.

Example: Multiply 4,500 and 320.	$\begin{array}{r} 4\ 5 \\ \times\quad 3\ 2 \\ \hline 9\ 0 \\ 1\ 3\ 5 \\ \hline 1,\ 4\ 4\ 0,\ \mathbf{0}\ \mathbf{0}\ \mathbf{0} \end{array}$
You can drop a total of three zeroes before you multiply. You will then attach three zeroes back to the product.	**Attach zeroes** ↑
Answer: 1,440,000.	

HOW TO MULTIPLY NUMBERS (continued)

Characteristics of multiplication

Numbers can be multiplied in any order and the answer is the same:
- Multiplying $7 \times 25 = 175$
- Multiplying $25 \times 7 = 175$

Numbers can be multiplied in any groups and the answer is the same:
- Multiplying $(9 \times 48) \times 22$ is $432 \times 22 = 9,504$
- Multiplying $9 \times (48 \times 22)$ is $9 \times 1,056 = 9,504$

The product of any number and zero is always zero:
- Multiplying $245 \times 0 = 0$

The product of any number and 1 is always the number itself:
- Multiplying $245 \times 1 = 245$

Multiplying a sequence of numbers

The multiplication procedure is the same. Simply multiply the next number times the previous result, until there are no more numbers to multiply.

Example: Multiply the following numbers: $27 \times 50 \times 219$

- First, multiply 27 times 50: $27 \times 50 = 1,350$
- Then multiply by the next number: $1,350 \times 219 = 295,650$

PRACTICE

SOLUTIONS FOR MULTIPLICATION BEGIN ON PAGE 546.

REINFORCEMENT PROBLEMS: MULTIPLICATION

1) In the table below, complete each indicated operation and write your answer in the "Answer" column next to the operation.

Multiply the following numbers …	Answer
A) 255×8	
B) 255×38	
C) 255×938	
D) $255 \times 2,938$	
E) 207×412	
F) $2,400 \times 3,500$	
G) 909×303	
H) 684×729	
I) 250×190	
J) $1,877 \times 300$	
K) 72×211	
L) 952×743	
M) $822 \times 3,005$	
N) 215×49	

2) A) If professor Gillis grades 4 tests per hour, how many tests can he grade in 8 hours?

B) A business collects $1 of sales tax for every $15 of sales. If the sales tax collection was $9,000, what was the total amount of sales?

C) The labor cost for manufacturing a computer is $52 per computer. What is the total labor manufacturing cost if 850 computers are manufactured this week?

SOLUTIONS

PRACTICE QUESTIONS FOR MULTIPLICATION BEGIN ON PAGE 545.

REINFORCEMENT PROBLEMS: MULTIPLICATION

1)

Operation	Answer
A) 255×8	2,040
B) 255×38	9,690
C) 255×938	239,190
D) $255 \times 2,938$	749,190
E) 207×412	85,284
F) $2,400 \times 3,500$	8,400,000
G) 909×303	275,427
H) 684×729	498,636
I) 250×190	47,500
J) $1,877 \times 300$	563,100
K) 72×211	15,192
L) 952×743	707,336
M) $822 \times 3,005$	2,470,110
N) 215×49	10,535

2) A) 4 tests $\times$ 8 = 32 total tests
    B) $15 $\times$ $9,000 = $135,000 total sales
    C) $52 labor $\times$ 850 = $44,200 total labor cost

HOW TO DIVIDE NUMBERS

Introduction	Division is the process of finding out how many times one number is contained in another number. It is the opposite of multiplication.
Example	Suppose that you have a loaded container that can hold 3,750 pounds, and the container is full. Each unit of your merchandise weighs 15 pounds. How many units of merchandise are in the container? In other words, we are asking how many times is the number 15 (for each unit) contained in the number 3,750.
Terminology	The following terms are normally used when referring to division:

- The "container" number is called the **dividend** (3,750 in this example).
- The number being contained is called the **divisor** (15 in this example).
- The result—the answer—is called the **quotient** (250 units in this example).

Showing division

Division can be shown in several ways. The most common way to indicate division are the following signs: ÷, or /, or ——, or $\overline{\big)}$

$$3,750 \div 15 = 250$$

dividend divisor quotient

or, 3,750 / 15 = 250

or, $\dfrac{3,750}{15} = 250$

or, $15\overline{\smash{\big)}\,3,750} = 250$

How to say division calculations

There are two equally correct ways of verbalizing division calculations:

- You can say the dividend amount, then say "divided by" the divisor amount ("3,750 divided by 15 equals 250") or,
- You can say the divisor amount, then say "divided into" the dividend amount ("15 divided into 3,750 equals 250").

HOW TO DIVIDE NUMBERS (continued)

How to do division

The table below shows the seven steps to use when you want to divide.

Example: Divide 4,259 by 23.

Step	Action	Example
1	Write the **dividend** inside a bracket, and write the **divisor** in front of the dividend. Ignore any commas.	**2 3 ⟌ 4 2 5 9**
2	Moving from left to right in the dividend, identify a partial dividend that is equal to or greater than the divisor, using the least possible digits. *Example:* "4" would not be correct because it is not equal to or greater than the divisor (23). "425" would not be correct, because a number with fewer digits is available (42), that is still equal to or greater than the divisor.	2 3 ⟌ **4 2** 5 9
3	Determine the **largest multiplier** of the divisor that will not result in a product greater than the partial dividend (here, not exceeding 42). Write this multiplier above the line, in the same place-value column as the right digit of the partial dividend. *Note:* Finding the correct multiplier may require a little trial and error. For example, 2 × 23 = 46, so 2 is too big of a multiplier because 46 exceeds 42.	multiplier → **1** 2 3 ⟌ 4 2 5 9
4	Write the **product** of the multiplier times the divisor under the partial dividend (1 × 23 = 23). Be sure that the place values are aligned correctly.	1 2 3 ⟌ 4 2 5 9 **2 3**
5	Subtract the product you just wrote down from the partial dividend. *Check:* The **difference** must be *less than the divisor.*	1 2 3 ⟌ 4 2 5 9 <u>2 3</u> **1 9** ← difference

HOW TO DIVIDE NUMBERS (continued)

Step	Action	Example
6	Create a new partial dividend. Bring down from the dividend, to the right of the previous partial dividend, the fewest numbers needed to make a new partial dividend that is equal to or greater than the divisor.	$$\begin{array}{r} 1 \\ 23\overline{)42\,5\,9} \\ 2\,3\downarrow \\ \hline 1\ 9\ 5 \end{array}$$
7	Return to Step 3 and repeat the procedures until there are no more digits left to bring down from the dividend. If there is a **remainder**, write it in brackets next to the quotient and label it as "remainder." (This means that the quotient contained slightly more than 185 units of 23.) The quotient (answer) is 185, with a remainder of 4.	$$\begin{array}{r} 1\ 8\ 5 \;\text{(4) remainder} \\ 23\overline{)42\,5\,9} \\ 2\,3 \\ \hline 1\,9\,5 \\ 1\,8\,4 \\ \hline 1\,1\,9 \\ 1\,1\,5 \\ \hline 4 \end{array}$$

Rule: when there is zero in a quotient

You will need to place a zero in the quotient whenever a digit brought down from the dividend does not make the partial dividend equal to or larger than the divisor.

Example: Calculate 67,320 / 33.

Step	Action	Example
1	Write the dividend inside a bracket, and write the divisor in front of the dividend. Ignore any commas.	$33\overline{)67320}$
2	Identify the partial dividend.	$33\overline{)67\,320}$
3	Determine the largest multiplier of the divisor that will not result in a product greater than the partial dividend.	$$\begin{array}{r} 2 \\ 33\overline{)67\,320} \end{array}$$
4	Write the product of the multiplier times the divisor under the partial dividend.	$$\begin{array}{r} 2 \\ 33\overline{)67\,320} \\ 6\,6 \end{array}$$

HOW TO DIVIDE NUMBERS (continued)

Step	Action	Example
5	Subtract the product you just wrote down from the partial dividend.	$$\begin{array}{r} 2 \\ 33\overline{)6\,7\,\,3\,2\,0} \\ \underline{6\,6} \\ 1 \end{array}$$
6	Create a new partial dividend. In this example, *two digits* must be brought down from the dividend, because bringing down only the 3 makes 13, which is not equal to or greater than the divisor of 33. *Rule:* You must place a **zero** above any number brought down that does not make the partial dividend equal to or greater than the divisor.	zero needed ———┐ ↓ $$\begin{array}{r} 2\,\,0 \\ 33\overline{)6\,7\,\,3\,2\,0} \\ \underline{6\,6}\,\downarrow\,\downarrow \\ 1\,3\,2 \end{array}$$
7	Return to Step 3 and repeat the procedures until there are no more digits left to bring down from the dividend. The quotient (answer) is 2,040.	$$\begin{array}{r} 2\,0\,4\,0 \\ 33\overline{)6\,7\,\,3\,2\,0} \\ \underline{6\,6}\,\downarrow\,\downarrow \\ 1\,3\,2\,\downarrow \\ \underline{1\,3\,2}\,\downarrow \end{array}$$ no remainder 0

Shortcut: when divisor and dividend end in zero

Whenever both the dividend and divisor end in zero, drop an equal number of zeroes from the ends of both numbers. Then do the division with the remaining digits. This saves time and reduces error.

Example: Evaluate 5,500 ÷ 50	$$\begin{array}{r} 1\,1\,0 \\ 5\overline{)\,5\,5\,0} \\ \underline{5} \\ 5 \\ \underline{5} \\ 5 \\ \underline{5} \end{array}$$
Example: Evaluate 11,790 / 170	$$\begin{array}{r} 6\,9\,\textbf{(6) remainder} \\ 17\overline{)\,1\,1\,7\,9} \\ \underline{1\,0\,2} \\ 1\,5\,9 \\ \underline{1\,5\,3} \\ 6 \end{array}$$

HOW TO DIVIDE NUMBERS (continued)

Example: Evaluate $\dfrac{4,200}{1,000}$	$$\begin{array}{r} 4 \ \textbf{(2) remainder} \\ 1\,0\,\overline{)\,4\,2} \\ \underline{4\,0} \\ 2 \end{array}$$

CHECKING DIVISION ANSWERS

Checking your work: use multiplication

No one performs every calculation perfectly every time, even with a calculator. For this reason, it is important to know how to check your work. To check division:

- **Step 1:** Multiply the quotient times the divisor.
- **Step 2:** If there is a remainder, add the remainder to the product in Step 1.

The answer will equal the dividend if the division is correct.

Examples

$550 \div 5 = 110$	Check: $110 \times 5 = 550$	**Quotient is correct**

$$1,179 \, / \, 17 = 69 \text{ r}6 \qquad \text{Check: } 69 \times 17 = \begin{array}{r} 1,173 \\ + \quad 6 \\ \hline 1,179 \end{array}$$ **Quotient is correct**

$$322 \div 11 = 29 \text{ r}3 \qquad \text{Check: } 29 \times 11 = \begin{array}{r} 319 \\ + \quad 3 \\ \hline 322 \end{array}$$ **Quotient is correct**

Note: The letter "r" indicates a remainder.

"BY" AND "INTO" ARE TWO IMPORTANT WORDS

Introduction

Here is a very common mistake when reading and listening to an explanation about division operations: confusing the meaning of "divide by" and "divide into."

"BY" AND "INTO" ARE TWO IMPORTANT WORDS (continued)

"Divide by"	When you read or hear the expression "divide *by*" followed by a number, that number refers to *the divisor*. *Examples:* • "Divide 350 by 25" means 350 ÷ 25. • "1,300 is divided by 200" means 1,300 ÷ 200.
"Divide into"	When you read or hear the expression "divide *into*" followed by a number, that number refers to *the dividend*. *Examples:* • "Divide 40 into 850" means 850 ÷ 40. • "1,400 is divided into 12,000" means 12,000 ÷ 1,400.

USING DIVISION IN "RATE" PROBLEMS

Definition: rate	The word **rate** refers to the comparison of two amounts of different things. *Note:* Sometimes the comparison is expressed as a percent. This is discussed in greater detail later on, page 589.
Rate per unit	Very often, rate information is given in a way that compares an amount of something to *one unit* of a different kind of thing. This is the clearest way to show a rate, and is often called "rate per unit."
Examples	The table below shows some examples of how rate can be expressed per unit.

Example	This amount ...	is being compared to this unit ...
"Marty earns $15 per hour."	15 (dollars)	1 (hour)
"In one hour the train can travel 80 miles."	80 (miles)	1 (hour)
"The car will travel 22 miles per gallon."	22 (miles)	1 (gallon of gas)
"For every dollar of profit the business needed $17 of sales."	17 (dollars of sales)	1 (dollar of profit)

USING DIVISION IN "RATE" PROBLEMS (continued)

Express totals as a rate per unit	Frequently, you may have information that shows two total amounts, but which would be very helpful to you if they would be compared as a rate per unit.

Examples	• Marty earned $255 for 17 hours of work. Marty would like to know how much he is being paid for each hour that he works (in other words, the rate of pay per hour). • This year, you earned $75,200 and paid $18,800 in taxes. It would be very revealing to find out how much income you had to earn for every dollar in tax that you paid (in other words, the rate of income earned per tax dollar paid). • You traveled 418 miles and used 19 gallons of gasoline. To check the efficiency of your car, you would like to know the miles traveled for each gallon of gasoline used (in other words, the rate of miles per gallon).

Procedure: calculate rate per unit	To compare two total amounts as a rate per unit: • Identify the amount you want to convert to the unit of reference. • Divide this amount into the other number.

Examples	Converting Marty's pay to a rate per hour: • To obtain the pay *per hour*, hours become the unit of reference. • Divide: $255 ÷ 17 hours = $15 wages per hour Converting your income to an amount per dollar of tax paid: • To obtain the income *per tax dollar*, the tax is the unit of reference. • Divide: $75,200 ÷ $18,800 = $4 of income per dollar of tax. Converting your travel mileage to a rate per gallon: • To obtain the rate *per gallon*, gallons become the unit of reference. • Divide: 418 miles ÷ 19 gallons = 22 miles per gallon.

Using the "/ "	Sometimes rate is expressed by using the "/ " sign. *Example:* "Marty earns $15/hour.

MORE USES FOR RATE PER UNIT

Two more uses

Once you know the rate per unit information, it can also be used in two more very handy ways.

- Specify any number of reference units to find a total.
- Specify a total to find the number of reference units.

Procedure: calculate a total from a specified number of units

Procedure:
- Specify an amount for the number of units.
- Multiply this amount by the rate per unit.

Example #1: "Marty earns $15 per hour. How much will he earn after 12 hours of work?"
- Specified amount of units: 12 (hours)
- 12 hours × $15 = $180 (total $)

Example #2: "Your gas mileage is 22 miles per gallon. How far could you travel on 50 gallons?"
- Specified amount of units: 50 (gallons)
- 50 gallons × 22 = 1,100 miles (total miles)

Procedure: calculate number of units from a specified total

Sometimes you need to find out the number of units of the reference item that will result from a specified total. After you know the rate per unit, do this:

Procedure:
- Specify a new "what if?" total.
- Divide this by the rate per unit.

Example #1: "Marty earns $15 per hour (rate per unit). How many hours will he have to work to earn $450?"
- Specified new total amount: $450
- $450 ÷ $15 per hour = 30 hours (amount of reference units—hours)

Example #2: "Your gas mileage is 22 miles per gallon (rate per unit). If you traveled 8,800 miles, how many gallons did you use?"
- Specified new total amount: 8,800 miles
- 8,800 miles ÷ 22 miles/gallon = 400 gallons (amount of reference units—gallons)

PRACTICE

SOLUTIONS FOR DIVISION BEGIN ON PAGE 556.

REINFORCEMENT PROBLEMS: DIVISION

1) In the table below, complete each indicated operation and write your answer in the "Answer" column next to the operation. Check your answers.

Divide the following numbers …	Answer	Check
A) 350 ÷ 25		
B) 2,576 ÷ 23		
C) 1,560 ÷ 15		
D) 1,218 ÷ 52		
E) 8,450 ÷ 241		
F) 11,250 ÷ 45		
G) 15,000 ÷ 3,000		
H) 3,200 ÷ 150		
I) 35,734 ÷ 17		
J) 79,184 ÷ 112		
K) 592 ÷ 38		
L) 4,200 ÷ 30		
M) 12,015 ÷ 252		
N) 980 ÷ 50		

2) A) Myer Company paid $8,250 for 750 pounds of raw materials. What is the cost per pound?

B) You paid $135 for 9 gallons of paint. What is the cost per gallon?

C) A storage tank is leaking toxic chemicals at the rate of 2 gallons per week. How many gallons will it leak after 52 weeks?

D) Our company sells Internet software packages for $35 per package. How many packages must be sold in order to have $42,000 of revenue?

E) Our company makes a profit of $50 for every computer that we sell. We had a profit of $375,000 this month. How many computers were sold?

F) If Lo Landscaping Service can mow the lawns for 3 homes in 1 hour, how many hours will be required to mow the lawns for 90 homes?

SOLUTIONS

PRACTICE QUESTIONS FOR DIVISION BEGIN ON PAGE 555.

REINFORCEMENT PROBLEMS: DIVISION

1)

Operation	Answer	Check
A) $350 \div 25$	14	$14 \times 25 = \underline{350}$
B) $2,576 \div 23$	112	$112 \times 23 = \underline{2,576}$
C) $1,560 \div 15$	104	$104 \times 15 = \underline{1,560}$
D) $1,218 \div 52$	23 r22	$23 \times 52 = 1,196 + 22 = \underline{1,218}$
E) $8,450 \div 241$	35 r15	$35 \times 241 = 8,435 + 15 = \underline{8,450}$
F) $11,250 \div 45$	250	$250 \times 45 = \underline{11,250}$
G) $15,000 \div 3,000$	5	$5 \times 3 = \underline{15}$
H) $3,200 \div 150$	21 r5	$21 \times 15 = 315 + 5 = \underline{320}$
I) $35,734 \div 17$	2,102	$2,102 \times 17 = \underline{35,734}$
J) $79,184 \div 112$	707	$707 \times 112 = \underline{79,184}$
K) $592 \div 38$	15 r22	$15 \times 38 = 570 + 22 = \underline{592}$
L) $4,200 \div 30$	140	$140 \times 3 = \underline{420}$
M) $12,015 \div 252$	47 r171	$47 \times 252 = 11,844 + 171 = \underline{12,015}$
N) $980 \div 50$	19 r3	$19 \times 5 = 95 + 3 = \underline{98}$

Note: The letter "r" indicates a remainder. Don't forget to use the shortcut of dropping zeroes (items G, H, L, and N)!

2) A) $8,250 / 750 pounds = $11 per pound
    B) $135 / 9 gallons = $15 per gallon
    C) 52 weeks × 2 gallons/week = 104 gallons
    D) $42,000 / $35 = 1,200 packages
    E) $375,000 / $50 = 7,500 computers
    F) 90 homes / 3 homes/hour = 30 hours

ROUNDING NUMBERS

What is "rounding"?	Rounding is the technique of simplifying a number by replacing a designated number of digits with zero.
The purpose of rounding	When a number is rounded, it is easier to use and remember, even though some precision is lost.

It is easier to remember ...	than ...
Rounded	**Not rounded or rounded less**
3,290	3,287
5,300	5,290
8,000	8,300

When is rounding used?	Rounding is very useful. The most important uses of rounding are:

- checking the reasonableness of calculations to avoid large errors
- making quick estimates of values
- simplifying financial and economic reports used for decision-making

Rounding procedure	The following three steps are used to round a number:

Step	Action
1	In the number selected, determine which place-value digit is to be rounded. *Note:* This information is often specified in a problem, or by an instructor or supervisor.
2	

	If ...	Then ...
	the digit to right of the digit to be rounded is 5 or greater,	add 1 to the digit to be rounded.
	the digit to the right of the digit to be rounded is less that 5,	the digit to be rounded remains unchanged.

Step	Action
3	Replace each digit to the right of the digit to be rounded with a zero.

ROUNDING NUMBERS (continued)

Examples   The following table illustrates examples of rounded numbers.

Rounding Specification	Rounded Number
Round 4,758 to the "tens" place	4,760
Round 4,758 to the "hundreds" place	4,800
Round 4,758 to the greatest place-value digit	5,000
Round 212, 954 to the "hundreds" place	213,000
Round 212, 954 to the "thousands" place	213,000
Round 212, 954 to the "ten thousands" place	210,000
Round 212, 954 to the "hundred thousands" place	200,000

REINFORCEMENT PROBLEM: ROUNDING NUMBERS

1) In each column, write the rounded number to the place value indicated. Use the first number as an example.

Number	Round to this place-value ...				
	tens	hundreds	thousands	ten thousands	greatest place-value
1,636	1,640	1,600	2,000	–0–	2,000
6,250					
15,975					
9,025,479					
821					
14,307					
5,825					
11,197					
272,889					

REINFORCEMENT PROBLEM: ROUNDING NUMBERS

1)

Number	Round to this place-value ...				
	tens	hundreds	thousands	ten thousands	greatest place-value
1,636	1,640	1,600	2,000	–0–	2,000
6,250	6,250	6,300	6,000	10,000	6,000
15,975	15,980	16,000	16,000	20,000	20,000
9,025,479	9,025,480	9,025,500	9,025,000	9,030,000	9,000,000
821	820	800	–0–	–0–	800
14,307	14,310	14,300	14,000	10,000	10,000
5,825	5,830	5,800	6,000	10,000	6,000
11,197	11,200	11,200	11,000	10,000	10,000
272,889	272,890	272,900	273,000	270,000	300,000

CHECKING THE REASONABLENESS OF AN ANSWER

Introduction

The ability to quickly check the reasonableness of an answer is a very important skill. It is especially useful in financial, accounting, and business calculations where money is involved. This is true **even if you use a calculator**. Large and embarrassing errors can be made on a calculator more easily than in hand-prepared calculations.

"Checking reasonableness" means ...

To "check reasonableness" means to do a quick estimate calculation for the purpose of avoiding large errors. You are checking that the answer is approximately the size that it should be. *This may be done before or after you do the exact calculation.*

How to check for reasonableness

The following procedure applies to addition, subtraction, multiplication, or division:

Step	Action
1	Round all numbers to the greatest place-value digit.
2	Using the rounded numbers, perform whatever calculation is required. This is your estimate.
3	Compare the estimate from Step 2 to the exact answer.

	If ...	Then ...
	the estimate is "reasonably close" to the exact answer,	there are probably no large errors.
	the estimate is very different than the exact answer,	recalculate for a new exact answer.

CHECKING THE REASONABLENESS OF AN ANSWER (continued)

Examples   The following examples show you how to check for reasonableness:

Calculation	Numbers	Exact Calculation	Reasonableness Check
addition	add: 4,579 + 1,926 + 11,842 + 3,875 rounded: 5,000 + 2,000 + 10,000 + 4,000	4, 5 7 9 1, 9 2 6 1 1, 8 4 2 + 3, 8 7 5 ――――― 2 2, 2 2 2	5, 0 0 0 2, 0 0 0 1 0, 0 0 0 + 4, 0 0 0 ――――― 2 1, 0 0 0
subtraction	subtract: 313,807 − 109,482 rounded: 300,000 − 100,000	3 1 3, 8 0 7 − 1 0 9, 4 8 2 ――――― 2 0 4, 3 2 5	3 0 0, 0 0 0 − 1 0 0, 0 0 0 ――――― 2 0 0, 0 0 0
multiplication	multiply: 17,947 × 582 rounded: 20,000 × 600	1 7, 9 4 7 × 5 8 2 ――――― 3 5 8 9 4 1 4 3 5 7 6 8 9 7 3 5 ――――― 1 0, 4 4 5, 1 5 4	**Using multiplication shortcut:** 2 × 6 ――― 1 2, 0 0 0, 0 0 0 **(Zeroes are dropped and then added back to the answer)**
division	divide: 39,850 / 420 rounded: 40,000 / 400	9 4 4 2 0 ⟌ 3 9 8 5 0 3 7 8 0 ――― 2 0 5 0 1 6 8 0 ――― **Remainder 3 7 0**	**Using division shortcut:** 1 0 0 4 ⟌ 4 0 0 4 ―― 0 0 **(An equal number of zeroes are dropped from each number)**

PRACTICE

REINFORCEMENT PROBLEM: DOING A REASONABLENESS CHECK

1) Complete the following table:

Calculation	Reasonableness Check	Exact Answer
$4,812 \times 3,499$		
$92,100 \div 217$		
$453,191 \div 72,647$		
807×354		
$7,985 \times 8,722$		

SOLUTIONS

REINFORCEMENT PROBLEM: DOING A REASONABLENESS CHECK

1)

Calculation	Reasonableness Check	Exact Answer
$4,812 \times 3,499$	15,000,000	16,837,188
$92,100 \div 217$	450	424 r92
$453,191 \div 72,647$	7 with remainder	6 r17,309
807×354	320,000	285,678
$7,985 \times 8,722$	72,000,000	69,645,170

Note: The letter "r" indicates a remainder.

WHICH OPERATION DO I USE?

Introduction

After you have practiced doing the calculations for the four operations of addition, subtraction, multiplication, and division, you are ready to apply what you have learned. Sometimes in a problem, the calculation signs will be given to you, such as: 475 – 224, or 845 × 22. In these kinds of situations, the operation symbols make it clear what to do.

However, very frequently you will be given the facts of a situation and you will have to decide which of the four operations you will need to apply to the facts. In other words, you will have to analyze the facts, and then decide which operation is needed. The guidelines below summarize when to apply the four operations.

Addition

The following table shows how to identify situations that require addition. In all cases, the underlying idea is to find the total of different numbers.

Add to ...	Examples
A) Find a total of different amounts	• Janice purchased items costing the following amounts: $4, $50, $122 and $435. What did she pay for all the purchases? ($104 + $50 + $122 + $435 = $711) • On the first three quizzes, Andrew scored 88, 79, and 91. What are his total points? (88 + 79 + 91 = 258)
B) Increase an amount by another amount	• Anselmo Company began the week with $10,532 in its savings account. During the week, it deposited $5,000 more into the account. How much does the company have at the end of the week? ($10,532 + $5,000 increase = $15,532) • Thuan Enterprises hired 112 new employees last year. How many employees does the company have now if it had 455 employees at the beginning of the year? (455 + 112 = 567)

WHICH OPERATION DO I USE? (continued)

Subtraction

The following table shows you how to identify situations that require subtraction. In all cases, the underlying idea is to calculate a numerical difference between two numbers.

Subtract to ...	Examples
A) Find a difference between two amounts	• If the cost of a vacation to Hawaii is $2,795 and the cost of a vacation to Bermuda is $3,977, how much more does the vacation to Bermuda cost? ($3,977 – $2,795 = $1,182)
B) Calculate a change	• Anselmo Company began the week with $10,532 in the savings account. At the end of the week, the company had $15,532 in the account. How much did the account change? ($15,532 – $10,532 = $5,000) • If the total debts of Lowjewski Company at the beginning of the month were $41,005, and $12,300 at the end of the month, how much did the debts change? ($41,005 – $12,300 = $28,705 decrease)
C) Find an excess or left-over amount	• Ames Company began the month with $4,190 in the office supplies account. If $3,850 of supplies were used during the month, how much is still in the account? ($4,190 – $3,850 = $340) • If the total assets of Diamond Enterprises are $443,250 and the total debts are $215,480, what is the owner's equity? ($443,250 – $215,480 = $227,770)
D) Find one part of a larger amount	• Senatobia Ventures spent $212,000, including sales tax, to purchase computers. If the sales tax was $19,000, what was the cost of the computers? ($212,000 – $19,000 = $193,000) • Holmes Company spent $500,000 to purchase land with a building and equipment. If the building was appraised at $273,000 and the equipment was appraised at $87,500, what was the cost of the land? ($500,000 – $273,000 – $87,500 = $139,500)

WHICH OPERATION DO I USE? (continued)

Multiplication

The following table shows you how to identify situations that require multiplication. In all cases, the underlying idea is that a single number is repeated a multiple number of times.

Multiply to ...	Examples
A) Find the total of a repeated number	• On each day of the week, Monday through Friday, your business purchased 85 units of merchandise. What are the purchases for the week? (The amount of 85 units is repeated 5 times, so 85 × 5 = 425 units)
B) Find the amount that is a "number of times" another number	• Dave earns **3 times as much** as John. If John earns $575 per week, how much does Dave earn per week? ($575 × 3 = $1,725) • If my car is traveling at 15 miles per hour and your car is traveling **4 times as fast** as my car, how fast is your car traveling? (15 mph × 4 = 60 mph)
C) Find the total for a specified number of units when you know the rate per unit	• Rasmussen Company pays wages at the rate of $450 per day. What total wages would be paid for 14 days? ("Per day" indicates that days are the units, and the rate per unit is $450. $450 × 14 = $6,300) • Hennepin Partnership purchased 500 shares of stock and each share cost $38. What is the total cost of the stock? ("Each share" indicates that shares are the units, and the rate per share is $38. $38 × 500 = $19,000)

WHICH OPERATION DO I USE? (continued)

Division   The following table shows you how to identify situations that require division. In all cases, the underlying idea is that division finds a multiple that one number (the dividend) is of another number (the divisor).

Divide to …	Examples
A) Find the number for which some amount is a multiple (a "number of times") that number. *Note:* This is opposite of item "B" in multiplication (see page 565).	• Two aircraft are flying away from Dallas. The first aircraft is 1,200 miles away and this is 4 times as far away from Dallas as the second aircraft. How far away from Dallas is the second aircraft? (You want to find the number for which the first aircraft's distance of 1,200 miles is 4 times that number. 1,200 miles / 4 = 300 miles) • Dave earns $1,725 per week. If Dave earns 3 times as much as John, how much does John earn? (You want to find the number for which Dave's $1,725 is 3 times that number. $1,725 / 3 = $575)
B) Find the size of equal parts when you know the total and the number of parts. *Note:* The answer can also be interpreted as a rate.	• If a rope is 24 feet long and divided into 8 pieces, how long is each piece? (24 **feet** / 8 **pieces** = 3 feet for each piece. The rate per unit is 3 **feet** per **piece**.) • Denise typed 2,250 words in 45 minutes. How many words does she type each minute? (2,250 **words** / 45 **minutes** = 50 words each minute. The rate per unit is 45 **words** per **minute**.)
C) Find the number of units, when you know the total units and the rate per unit. *Note:* Because you are dividing by similar kinds of units, the answer is never a rate.	• Roswell Company manufactured and shipped boxes containing 12,000 pens. If each box contains 8 pens, how many boxes were shipped? (The rate per unit is 8 pens per box. 12,000 **pens** / 8 **pens** per box = 1,500 boxes) • Clovis Corporation budgeted a total of $300,000 to purchase new computers. If each computer costs $2,000, how many new computers can be purchased? (The rate per unit is $2,000 per computer. $300,000 / $2,000 per computer = 150 computers) • D'Agostine's Catering Company is expecting 420 people for a party. The company is providing pizza for the guests. If one pizza serves 4 people, how many pizzas will be needed? (The rate per unit is 4 people per pizza. 420 **people** / 4 **people** per pizza = 105 pizzas)
D) Calculate a rate to compare the amount of any kind of thing to any another. *Note:* Rate is frequently described by using the word "per."	• Castlewood Company used up $185,000 over a period of 20 days. What was its rate of loss of cash per day? (You are comparing dollars to days. $185,000 / 20 **days** = 9,250 **dollars** per **day**)

CALCULATING AN AVERAGE

What is an average?	An **average** is just a special case of finding an amount per unit. The only special thing about an average is that the number that you are dividing into (the dividend) is a total that results from various different events. The answer (the average) is interpreted as the single number that is most typical or representative of all the events.
Procedure	• Find the total that results from adding the amount of each different event. • Divide the total by the number of events.
Example	Suppose that Sam had these four scores on accounting tests: 81, 92, 74, 88. What is his average score? *Answer:* The events are the four tests. • Add the scores: $(81 + 92 + 75 + 88) = 336$ • Divide by 4: $336 / 4 = 84$ Therefore, 84 is Sam's average score. This is interpreted as being the amount that is most typical or representative of all the scores.

MULTIPLICATION TABLE

The table below shows the multiples for all numbers from 0 to 10. The numbers in the table are the products to memorize.

Example: To multiply 7 by 4, find 7 in left margin and move to the right on that line until you come to column that has 4 at the top. The number 28 is the product that is the answer.

X	0	1	2	3	4	5	6	7	8	9	10	
0	0	0	0	0	0	0	0	0	0	0	0	
1	0	1	2	3	4	5	6	7	8	9	10	(numbers increase in units of 1)
2	0	2	4	6	8	10	12	14	16	18	20	(numbers increase in units of 2)
3	0	3	6	9	12	15	18	21	24	27	30	(numbers increase in units of 3)
4	0	4	8	12	16	20	24	28	32	36	40	(numbers increase in units of 4)
5	0	5	10	15	20	25	30	35	40	45	50	(numbers increase in units of 5)
6	0	6	12	18	24	30	36	42	48	54	60	(numbers increase in units of 6)
7	0	7	14	21	28	35	42	49	56	63	70	(numbers increase in units of 7)
8	0	8	16	24	32	40	48	56	64	72	80	(numbers increase in units of 8)
9	0	9	18	27	36	45	54	63	72	81	90	(numbers increase in units of 9)
10	0	10	20	30	40	50	60	70	80	90	100	(numbers increase in units of 10)

PRACTICE

SOLUTIONS FOR CHOOSING THE CORRECT OPERATION BEGIN ON PAGE 571.

REINFORCEMENT PROBLEM: CHOOSING THE CORRECT OPERATION

1) A) For each of the separate situations in the table, place an "✘" in the correct box to indicate which type of calculation is required. (For some items, more than one calculation is needed.)

   B) Calculate the answer to each item after you complete part "A."

Item	Add.	Sub.	Mult.	Div.	Answer
1) Texarkana Company began the week with $15,404 in its checking account. There is $3,400 in the account at the end of the week. By how much did the account change?					
2) McLennan Business Supplies sold 125 computers, 1,127 notebooks, 16 printers, 5 fax machines, 10 modems, and 422 pens. How many items did the company sell?					
3) K.C.'s barbecue restaurant cooked 350 meals and used up 25 gallons of barbecue sauce. How many meals per gallon did the company cook?					
4) Austin Company is creating a computer software product that it wants to finish in one year. The company has estimated that approximately 34,000 labor hours will be required to complete the project. If one employee works an average of 2,000 hours per year, how many employees will be required for the project?					
5) Cisco Partnership has 12 employees that earn $23.00 per hour. If each employee works 8 hours per day, what is the daily total pay for all employees? What is the weekly pay for a 5-day week?					
6) Cerritos Enterprises made sales to customers totaling $478,300. If total expenses were $312,500, what was the profit?					
7) Fullerton Company had advertising expense of $147,000 and Merced Company had advertising expense of $12,250. The expense for Fullerton was how many times that of Merced?					
8) The net income of Savannah Company was 4 times the net income of Barnesville Company. If Savannah Company earned $81,000, how much did Barnesville earn?					
9) Martinez Enterprises produces 3 times as many items as Cerritos Enterprises. If Cerritos produced 4,200 units last year, how many did Martinez produce?					

SOLUTIONS FOR CHOOSING THE CORRECT OPERATION BEGIN ON PAGE 571.

1) *continued*

Item	Add.	Sub.	Mult.	Div.	Answer
10) Chi paid $24,500 for a new car. This included $1,300 sales tax and $250 shipping. What was the cost of the car itself?					
11) Shawnee Company has 12 employees. The weekly payroll for all the employees is a total of $10,800. What is the average weekly wage of the employees?					
12) Sinclair Company had the following monthly sales in units: October: 3,205 units; November: 2,250 units; December: 2,249 units. Each unit sells for $14. What is the dollar sales for the three months?					
13) On May 1, El Camino Company had 417 units of supplies. During May, the company ordered and received 2,050 more units and used up 1,819 units. How many units were left on May 31?					
14) Manahoy Partnership constructed two buildings. One building cost $105,000 and the other building cost twice as much. What was the cost of both buildings?					
15) Manahoy Partnership has two partners that share profits. Partner A received $57,000 which was 3 times as much as Partner B. How much more money did Partner A earn?					
16) Dawson Company purchased $4,500 of office supplies. At the end of the month, an inventory shows that $715 of supplies are still on hand. How much was used up?					
17) Passaic Company has a net outflow of cash at the rate of $2,500 per day. If the company has $75,000 in the bank, how long will it be until the company runs out of money?					
18) The marketing department of Toms River Ventures is catering a party for the purchasing agents of its best customers. 354 people are expected at the party, and 118 bottles of sparkling water have been ordered. How many people does each bottle serve?					

SOLUTIONS

PRACTICE QUESTIONS FOR CHOOSING THE CORRECT OPERATION BEGIN ON PAGE 569.

REINFORCEMENT PROBLEM: CHOOSING THE CORRECT OPERATION

1)

	Item	Add.	Sub.	Mult.	Div.	Answer
1)	Texarkana Company began the week with $15,404 in its checking account. There is $3,400 in the account at the end of the week. By how much did the account change?		X			$12,004
2)	McLennan Business Supplies sold 125 computers, 1,127 notebooks, 16 printers, 5 fax machines, 10 modems, and 422 pens. How many items did the company sell?	X				1,705
3)	K.C.'s barbecue restaurant cooked 350 meals and used up 25 gallons of barbecue sauce. How many meals per gallon did the company cook?				X	14 meals per gallon (350 **meals** / 25 **gallons** = 14 meals per gallon)
4)	Austin Company is creating a computer software product that it wants to finish in one year. The company has estimated that approximately 34,000 labor hours will be required to complete the project. If one employee works 2,000 hours per year, how many employees will be required for the project?				X	17 employees (34,000 **hours** / 2,000 **hours** per employee = 17 employees)
5)	Cisco Partnership has 12 employees that earn $23.00 per hour. If each employee works 8 hours per day, what is the daily total pay for all employees? What is the weekly pay for a 5-day week?			X		$2,208 daily total ($23 × 12 = $276. $276 × 8 = $2,208) $11,040 weekly total ($2,208 × 5)
6)	Cerritos Enterprises made sales to customers totaling $478,300. If total expenses were $312,500, what was the profit?		X			$165,800
7)	Fullerton Company had advertising expense of $147,000 and Merced Company had advertising expense of $12,250. The expense for Fullerton was how many times that of Merced?				X	12 times ($12,250 is contained in $147,000 12 times)
8)	The net income of Savannah Company was 4 times the net income of Barnesville Company. If Savannah Company earned $81,000, how much did Barnesville earn?				X	$20,250 ($81,000 / 4 = $20,250)
9)	Martinez Enterprises produces 3 times as many items as Cerritos Enterprises. If Cerritos produced 4,200 units last year, how many did Martinez produce?			X		12,600 (4,200 × 3)
10)	Chi paid $24,500 for a new car. This included $1,300 sales tax and $250 shipping. What was the cost of the car itself?		X			$22,950

SOLUTIONS

PRACTICE QUESTIONS FOR CHOOSING THE CORRECT OPERATION BEGIN ON PAGE 569.

1) *continued*

Item	Add.	Sub.	Mult.	Div.	Answer
11) Shawnee Company has 12 employees. The weekly payroll for all the employees is a total of $10,800. What is the average weekly wage of the employees?				✗	$900 ($10,800 / 12 = $900)
12) Sinclair Company had the following monthly sales in units: October: 3,205 units; November: 2,250 units; December: 2,249 units. Each unit sells for $14. What is the dollar sales for the three months?	✗ (to find the total units)		✗ (to find the total dollar amount)		$107,856 (3,205 + 2,250 + 2,249 = 7,704. 7,704 × $14 = $107,856)
13) On May 1, El Camino Company had 417 units of supplies. During May, the company ordered and received 2,050 more units and used up 1,819 units. How many units were left on May 31?	✗ (to find the total available)	✗ (to find the amount left over after some were used)			648 (417 + 2,050 = 2,467. 2,467 – 1,819 = 648)
14) Manahoy Partnership constructed two buildings. One building cost $105,000 and the other building cost twice as much. What was the cost of both buildings?	✗ (to find the total cost of the two buildings)		✗ (to find the cost of the second building)		$315,000 ($105,000 × 2 = $210,000. $210,000 + $105,000 = $315,000)
15) Manahoy Partnership has two partners that share profits. Partner A received $57,000 which was 3 times as much as Partner B. How much more money did Partner A earn?		✗ (to find the difference between the earnings of the two partners)		✗ (to find how much Partner B earned)	$38,000 ($57,000 / 3 = $19,000. $57,000 – $19,000 = $38,000)
16) Dawson Company purchased $4,500 of office supplies. At the end of the month, an inventory shows that $715 of supplies are still on hand. How much was used up?		✗			$4,500 – $715 = $3,785
17) Passaic Company has a net outflow of cash at the rate of $2,500 per day. If the company has $75,000 in the bank, how long will it be until the company runs out of money?				✗	$75,000 / $2,500 per day = 30 days
18) The marketing department of Toms River Ventures is catering a party for the purchasing agents of its best customers. 354 people are expected at the party, and 118 bottles of sparkling water have been ordered. How many people does each bottle serve?				✗	354 / 118 = 3 people per bottle

▼ *Decimals*

WHAT ARE DECIMALS?

Introduction	**Decimals** are used to show numbers that are *between zero and one*. These kinds of numbers are important, and occur frequently.
The place values of decimals	We continue using the place-value table to express amounts, but now we expand the table by placing a period mark directly to the right of the "ones" place. This mark is called a **decimal point**. Any number that is located to the right of the decimal point is less than one. As before, the size of the number is determined by its placement.
Place-value table with decimals	The place-value table shows the decimal places for numbers less than one.

Each number increases by 10 times the previous number.					Decimal Point	Each number decreases by 10 times the previous number.				
Ten Thousands	Thousands	Hundreds	Tens	Ones		Tenths	Hundredths	Thousandths	Ten Thousandths	
					.					

The numbers to the left of the decimal point are called **whole numbers** and the numbers to the right of the decimal point are called **decimals**.

WHAT ARE DECIMALS? (continued)

How to say numbers that include decimals

- Say the whole number as you normally would.
- Use the word "and" for the decimal point.
- Say the decimal number as if it were also a whole number.
- Then say the name of the place value of the last decimal digit.

    Example: "74.915" would be said as: "seventy-four and nine hundred fifteen thousandths."

It is also acceptable to use the word "point" followed by the name of the digits. This is easier when there are many digits to the right of the decimal point.

    Example: You could say: "seventy-four *point* nine one five."

The "tenths" place

In the "tenths" place, one is divided into 10 parts. It takes 10 units in the "tenths" place to equal one.

Examples:
- ".1" is read "one tenth" (a pizza is divided into 10 pieces and you receive one piece).
- ".2" is read "two tenths" (a pizza is divided into 10 pieces and you receive two pieces).
- The number "1.4" is read "one and four tenths" (you have one full pizza and four parts out of 10 of another pizza).

The "hundredths" place

In the "hundredths" place, one is divided into 100 parts. It takes 100 units in the "hundredths" place to equal one, and 10 units in the "hundredths" place to equal one tenth.

Examples:
- ".01" is said as "one hundredth" (ten times smaller than .1).
- ".02" is said as "two hundredths" (ten times smaller than .2).
- The number "1.04" is said as "one and four hundredths" (or "one point zero four").
- The number "23.75" is said as "twenty-three and seventy-five hundredths" (or "twenty-three point seven five").

WHAT ARE DECIMALS? (continued)

The "thousandths" place	In the "thousandths" place, the amounts are 10 times smaller than the "hundredths" place. One is divided into one thousand parts.

Examples:
- ".001" is said as "one one thousandth" (ten times smaller than .01).
- ".002" is said as "two thousandths" (ten times smaller than .02).
- The number "1.004" is said as "one and four thousandths."
- The number "23.758" is said as "twenty-three and seven hundred fifty-eight thousandths" (or "twenty-three point seven five eight").

Use of commas	For some reason that no one seems to remember, commas are not used between digits that are to the right of the decimal point. Therefore, a number like 12.31295 is written without a comma.

Zeroes after the last number	When zeroes are placed *after* the last decimal number, the number is unchanged. The zero merely functions as a placeholder, and its use is optional.

Examples:
- .10 is the same as .1
- .100 is the same as .1
- .370 is the same as .37
- .3700 is the same as .37

Decimals are very popular	Decimals are the most common way of expressing numbers. Of course, money amounts are expressed using decimals, by placing a dollar sign ($) to the left of a decimal number.

PRACTICE

SOLUTIONS FOR EXPRESSING NUMBERS AS DECIMALS BEGIN ON PAGE 577.

REINFORCEMENT PROBLEMS: EXPRESSING NUMBERS AS DECIMALS

1) Identify the place value of the number written in **bold** type.

Number	Place value
A) 21.**3**	
B) 21.0**3**	
C) 21.00**3**	
D) 21.000**3**	

2) Say the following numbers. Use both methods of expression if possible.

A) 12.121	
B) 2.002	
C) $.75	
D) .75	
E) 498.10	
F) .333	
G) 3,529	
H) .845	
I) 3,492.07	
J) $3,492.07	
K) .5	
L) .05	
M) .005	

SOLUTIONS

PRACTICE QUESTIONS FOR EXPRESSING NUMBERS AS DECIMALS BEGIN ON PAGE 576.

REINFORCEMENT PROBLEM: EXPRESSING NUMBERS AS DECIMALS

1)

	Number	Place value
A)	21.**3**	tenths
B)	21.0**3**	hundredths
C)	21.00**3**	thousandths
D)	21.000**3**	ten thousandths

2)

A)	12.121	"twelve and one hundred twenty-one thousandths" or "twelve point one two one"
B)	2.002	"two and two thousandths" or "two point zero zero two"
C)	$.75	"seventy-five cents"
D)	.75	"seventy-five hundredths" or "point seven five"
E)	498.10	"four hundred ninety-eight and one tenth" or "four hundred ninety-eight point one"
F)	.333	"three hundred thirty-three thousandths" or "point three three three"
G)	3,529	"three thousand five hundred twenty-nine" (not a decimal number)
H)	.845	"eight hundred forty-five thousandths" or "point eight four five"
I)	3,492.07	"three thousand four hundred ninety-two and seven hundredths" or "three thousand four hundred ninety-two point zero seven"
J)	$3,492.07	"three thousand four hundred ninety-two dollars and seven cents"
K)	.5	"five tenths" or "point five"
L)	.05	"five hundredths" or "point zero five"
M)	.005	"five thousandths" or "point zero zero five"

ROUNDING DECIMALS

Introduction	The procedure for rounding decimals is the same as for any other number.

Step	Action
1	In the number selected, determine which place-value digit is to be rounded. *Note:* This information is often specified in a problem, or by an instructor or supervisor.
	<table><tr><th>If …</th><th>Then …</th></tr><tr><td>the digit to the right of the digit to be rounded is 5 or greater,</td><td>add 1 to the digit to be rounded.</td></tr><tr><td>the digit to the right of the digit to be rounded is less than 5,</td><td>the digit to be rounded remains unchanged.</td></tr></table>
2	Delete each digit to the right of the rounded digit.

Examples	The table below shows examples of rounding decimals.

Number	Round to this place value	Rounded number
.338	hundredths	.34
54.009	hundredths	54.01
.87220	hundredths	.872
14.847	tenths	14.8
39.08	tenths	39.1
4.7285	thousandths	4.729
9.040708	ten thousandths	9.0407
32.783	ones	33

ADDITION WITH DECIMALS

Overview	The addition of decimals is essentially the same procedure that you learned for addition of whole numbers. It is based upon aligning each digit in its correct place-value location.

Procedure for adding decimals	The table below shows you the procedure for adding decimal numbers.

Step	Action
1	Arrange the numbers vertically so that decimal points are exactly aligned.
2	For numbers with fewer digits to the right of the decimal point, insert zeroes to the right of the last digit until all numbers have the same number of digits on the right side of the decimal point.
3	Add the digits beginning with the right place-value column, and work to the left.
4	Align the decimal point in the answer with the decimal points above it.

Example	Add the following numbers: 15, 309.07, 711.3, .09, 10.885, and 53.007

Step	Action	Example
1	Arrange the numbers vertically so that decimal points are exactly aligned. (Notice how the whole number 15 is aligned.)	1 5. 3 0 9. 0 7 7 1 1. 3 . 0 9 1 0. 8 8 5 + 5 3. 0 0 7
2	For numbers with fewer digits to the right of the decimal point, insert zeroes after the last digit until all numbers have the same number of digits on the right side of the decimal point.	1 5. **0 0 0** 3 0 9. 0 7 **0** 7 1 1. 3 **0 0** . 0 9 **0** 1 0. 8 8 5 + 5 3. 0 0 7

ADDITION WITH DECIMALS (continued)

Step	Action	Example
3	Add the digits, beginning with the right place-value column, and work to the left.	*1 1 2 1* 1 5 . 0 0 0 3 0 9 . 0 7 0 7 1 1 . 3 0 0 . 0 9 0 1 0 . 8 8 5 + 5 3 . 0 0 7 —————— 1 , 0 9 9 3 5 2
4	Align the decimal point in the answer with the decimal points above it.	*1 1 2 1* 1 5 . 0 0 0 3 0 9 . 0 7 0 7 1 1 . 3 0 0 . 0 9 0 1 0 . 8 8 5 + 5 3 . 0 0 7 —————— 1 , 0 9 9 . 3 5 2 ↑ **Decimal point is correctly aligned**

SUBTRACTION WITH DECIMALS

Overview

Exactly the same procedure is used for subtraction of decimals as for addition, except that in Step 3 you subtract instead of add.

Example

What is the difference between 495.45 and 281.747?

$$
\begin{array}{r}
\scriptstyle 4\ \ 14\ \ 4\ \ 10 \\
4\ 9\ 5\ .\ 4\ 5\ 0 \\
-\quad 2\ 8\ 1\ .\ 7\ 4\ 7 \\
\hline
2\ 1\ 3\ .\ 7\ 0\ 3
\end{array}
$$

MULTIPLICATION WITH DECIMALS

Overview	Multiplication of numbers with decimals is practically the same as multiplication of whole numbers. The essential feature about multiplying numbers with decimals is that you must carefully count the total number of digits to the right of the decimal point.

Example	Multiply 85.73 and 8.4.

Step	Action	Example
1	Multiply the numbers just as if they were whole numbers. Ignore the decimal point.	4 5 2 2 2 7 8 5 . 7 3 × 8 . 4 ──── 3 4 2 9 2 6 8 5 8 4 ──── 7 2 0 1 3 2
2	Count the total number of digits that are to the right of the decimal point in both factors. Here: 2 in the top factor and 1 in the bottom factor = 3.	4 5 2 2 2 7 8 5 . 7 3 × 8 . 4 ──── 3 4 2 9 2 6 8 5 8 4 ──── 7 2 0 1 3 2
3	Begin with the right digit of the product, and count to the left the same total places that you obtained in Step 2. Insert the decimal point so that the product has the same number of digits to the right of the decimal point as the total in Step 2.	4 5 2 2 2 7 8 5 . 7 3 × 8 . 4 ──── 3 4 2 9 2 6 8 5 8 4 ──── 7 2 0 . 1 3 2 ↑ **The decimal point is three places to the left, starting at the right numeral**

MULTIPLICATION WITH DECIMALS (continued)

***Adding zeroes
in the product***

Sometimes extra zeroes have to be added to the product directly adjacent to the right of the decimal point.

> *Example:* If you multiply 2.18 times .035, you will need to count 5 places in the product, because there are 5 numbers to the right of the decimal point in the factors.

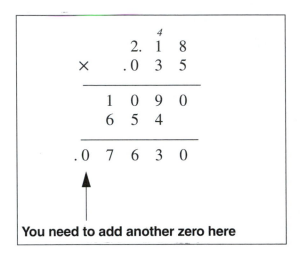

You need to add another zero here

DIVISION WITH DECIMALS

Overview

Dividing decimals is essentially the same as dividing whole numbers. However, decimal points in the divisor and dividend may have to be shifted to the right.

DIVISION WITH DECIMALS (continued)

Procedure	The following table shows you the procedure for dividing decimals.

Step	Action	Example
1	Determine if the divisor a whole number. ● If yes, only do Step 1: divide as you usually would with whole numbers, and be sure the decimal point in the quotient is aligned directly above the decimal point in the dividend. ● If no, go to Step 2.	**Divide 2.55 by 75** **Decimal points are aligned** $$\begin{array}{r} .034 \\ 75\overline{)2.550} \\ \underline{225} \\ 300 \\ \underline{300} \end{array}$$ **Adding one zero adds one place-value to the quotient**
2	If the divisor is a number with a decimal, make the divisor a whole number. Do this by moving the decimal point in the divisor to the right until the divisor becomes a whole number.	**Divide 32.5 by 1.75** 1 . 7 5 becomes 1 7 5
3	Move the decimal point in the dividend to the right by the same number of places as the decimal point was moved in the divisor. If there are not enough numbers, add zeroes to the dividend. *Note:* You can add extra zeroes beyond this, if you wish to show more places to the right of the decimal point in the quotient. Doing this gives a more precise answer.	3 2 . 5 becomes 3 2 5 0

DIVISION WITH DECIMALS (continued)

Step	Action	Example
4	Be sure the decimal point in the quotient is aligned directly above the decimal point in the dividend. Divide as usual.	**Decimal points are aligned** $$175\overline{)3250.00}$$ quotient 18.57 175 1500 1400 1000 875 1250 1225 **Remainder** 25 **2 extra zeroes are added**

Desired accuracy

In general, the custom is to carry out division one place value beyond the desired place value, and then round the desired place value.

Examples:
● In the example in Step 4 above, we will have accuracy to the tenths place value. The number will be rounded to 18.6.
● If we wanted accuracy to the hundredths place, we would add one more zero to the dividend (3250.000) and carry out the division to the thousandths place. This would result in 18.571, which would be rounded to 18.57.

Zeroes on the left side of the quotient

When the divisor is bigger than the dividend, the quotient that results will be such a small number that you need to place zeroes on the left side of the quotient, immediately after the decimal point. This follows exactly the same rule that you learned when dividing whole numbers.

Rule

You must place a zero above any number in the dividend that is brought down but does not make the partial dividend equal to or greater than the divisor.

DIVISION WITH DECIMALS (continued)

Example

The example below shows the application of the rule with a small decimal quotient.

Action	Example

Determine what is the largest multiplier of the divisor (9) that will not give a product that exceeds the partial dividend of 80. This amount is 8, because 8 times 9 gives a product of 72.	**Divide .801 by 9**
	
	       8
	9) .8 0 1
	     7 2

Because the multiplier of 8 had to be put in the hundredths place, it is necessary to clarify this location by placing a zero in the tenths place.	.0 8 9) .8 0 1 7 2

Continue the division in the normal way.	.0 8 9
	9) .8 0 1
	    7 2
	     8 1
	     8 1
	       0

Multiplying and dividing by numbers greater than 1 or less than 1

When multiplying and dividing, it is a good idea to know ahead of time whether the result is going to be a bigger number or a smaller number. This is very useful in avoiding mistakes.

Multiplication example

If the multiplier factor is …	then the answer is always …	Example
greater than 1	*bigger* than the other factor	Multiply 50 by 4 (multiplier). Answer: 200
less than 1	*smaller* than the other factor	Multiply 50 by .4 (multiplier). Answer: 20
exactly 1	the same number	Multiply 50 by 1. Answer: 50

DIVISION WITH DECIMALS (continued)

Division example

If the divisor is ...	then the answer is always ...	Example
greater than 1	*smaller* than the dividend	Divide 200 by 5 (divisor). Answer: 40
less than 1	*bigger* than the dividend	Divide 200 by .5 (divisor). Answer: 400
exactly 1	the same number	Divide 200 by 1 (divisor). Answer: 200

PRACTICE

SOLUTIONS FOR CALCULATING WITH DECIMALS BEGIN ON PAGE 588.

REINFORCEMENT PROBLEMS: CALCULATING WITH DECIMALS

1) **Various calculations.** Complete the following calculations without using a calculator:

Calculation	Answer
A) 718.852 + 224.36 + 141.039	
B) $731.44 × $289.03 (round to hundredths)	
C) .8975 ÷ 4 (round to thousandths)	
D) 214.072 − 99.39	
E) .0075 ÷ .05	
F) .08 × .07	
G) $1,100.98 + $384.66 + $903.21 + $288.17	
H) 108.49 − 17.136	
I) .27075 − .09057	
J) .725 × .083 (round to ten thousandths)	
K) $10,500 ÷ .4	
L) 75 ÷ 225 (round to thousandths)	
M) 550 ÷ .75 (round to thousandths)	
N) 550 × .75	
O) .55 ÷ 20 (to ten thousandths place)	
P) .09 ÷ 12	
Q) 7.85 × 12.42	
R) 29.5 × 21.009	

2) **Estimating results.** In the table below, indicate if the answer will be bigger or smaller:

Multiplication	A) 75 × 8	B) 75 × .8	C) 219 × .37	D) 219 × 3.7
Bigger or smaller than top factor?				

Division	E) $2,500 / 5	F) $2,500 / .5	G) 8,315 / .25	H) 8,315 / 2.5
Bigger or smaller than dividend?				

SOLUTIONS

PRACTICE QUESTIONS FOR CALCULATING WITH DECIMALS BEGIN ON PAGE 587.

REINFORCEMENT PROBLEMS: CALCULATING WITH DECIMALS

1)

Calculation	Answer
A) 718.852 + 224.36 + 141.039	1,084.251
B) $731.44 × $289.03 (round to hundredths)	$211,408.10
C) .8975 ÷ 4 (round to thousandths)	.224
D) 214.072 − 99.39	114.682
E) .0075 ÷ .05	.15
F) .08 × .07	.0056
G) $1,100.98 + $384.66 + $903.21 + $288.17	$2,677.02
H) 108.49 − 17.136	91.354
I) .27075 − .09057	.18018
J) .725 × .083 (round to ten thousandths)	.0602
K) $10,500 ÷ .4	$26,250
L) 75 ÷ 225 (round to thousandths)	.333
M) 550 ÷ .75 (round to thousandths)	733.333
N) 550 × .75	412.5
O) .55 ÷ 20 (to ten thousandths place)	.0275
P) .09 ÷ 12	.0075
Q) 7.85 × 12.42	97.497
R) 29.5 × 21.009	619.7655

2)

Multiplication	A) 75 × 8	B) 75 × .8	C) 219 × .37	D) 219 × 3.7
Bigger or smaller than top factor?	bigger (600)	smaller (60)	smaller (81.03)	bigger (810.3)

Division	E) $2,500 / 5	F) $2,500 / .5	G) 8,315 / .25	H) 8,315 / 2.5
Bigger or smaller than dividend?	smaller ($500)	bigger ($5,000)	bigger (33,260)	smaller (3,326)

▼ *Percent*

OVERVIEW OF PERCENT

Introduction	A percent is a very common way of expressing the relationship between two numbers. This is probably because when a number is expressed as a percent, the number often seems more natural or easier to understand than when it is expressed in a different way. Percents are used very frequently in business applications such as expressing profits, expenses, tax rates, markups and markdowns, probabilities, and changes in something.
Percent defined	**Percent** means "per 100" or "units per 100." When using the word "percent," you are saying that you are comparing a number to 100, which is considered a standard reference. The word "percent" derives from the Latin expression *per centum* that means "per 100." *Note:* The word "percentage" is often used instead of "percent."
Symbol	The symbol "%" means "percent."
"Rate" and percent	Since a percent is the result of comparing one number to another, percent is really just a particular way of expressing a rate, which you learned when studying division. In fact, the word "rate" is often used to refer to percent. This can be a little confusing. A careful reading of facts will usually clarify what is meant.
The whole amount of anything	Whenever we wish to refer to a whole amount of anything, we call it "100 percent." This serves as a standard reference. Any percent less than 100 percent is less than the reference amount. Any number more than 100 percent is greater than the reference amount.
Why use 100?	There is nothing magical or mysterious about using 100 as a point of reference. We could use any number. However, 100 is used because most people seem to find the round amount of 100 to be a simple and understandable point of reference, so it has become standardized.

OVERVIEW OF PERCENT (continued)

Examples	• To express the idea that 7 out of every 100 units are unsatisfactory, we would say, "We have a rejection rate of 7 percent." (We could also have said "seven hundredths.") • To say that $28 out of every $100 of income is paid as taxes, we would say that the "tax rate is 28%." (We could also have said "twenty-eight hundredths.") • To say that Jones Company has $125 of sales for every $100 of sales of Smith Company, we would say, "Jones Company sales are 125% of Smith Company sales." (We could also have said "one hundred twenty-five hundredths.")

CONVERTING NUMBERS TO AND FROM PERCENT

Any number can be 100%	It is not necessary to compare a number to exactly 100 in order to use percent. Any number can be expressed as a percent of any other number which represents a whole amount. Use the procedure below.
Procedure: convert a number into a percent	Imagine that we own a store that sells computer equipment. Suppose that we have 53 computers in our store, which are part of a total of 212 different items for sale in the store. The following table shows how to express 53 as a percent of 212.

Step	Action	Example
1	Identify a **base amount**. The base amount is the entire or whole amount of something, or a reference amount. It represents 100%. *Note:* The base amount often follows the word "of."	The base amount is 212 (units of merchandise).
2	Identify the **portion**. The portion is the number that you are comparing to the base amount.	The portion is 53 (units of merchandise).

CONVERTING NUMBERS TO AND FROM PERCENT (continued)

Step	Action	Example
3	Convert the portion to a decimal number by dividing the base amount into the portion.	53 / 212 = .25 (answer now in hundredths)
4	Convert the decimal to a percentage. Move the decimal point two places to the right by multiplying the decimal by 100.	.25 becomes 25
5	Add a percent symbol after the number.	25% (hundredths now expressed as percent)

Converting a percent to a decimal

If there is a number that is expressed as a percentage which you wish to convert to decimal, reverse the steps:

Step	Action	Examples	
1	Remove the percent symbol.	25% becomes 25	125% becomes 125
2	Move the decimal point two places to the left by dividing the number by 100.	25 / 100 = .25	125 / 100 = 1.25

Caution!

Numbers less than 1% are easy to misread!

When a number is less than 1%—that is, less than one part in a hundred—a decimal point is placed in front of the left digit of the percent. Be careful when reading these numbers. Examples:

	These …	both mean …	and NOT this …
Written as %	.8%	eight tenths of one percent	8% (eight percent)
Written as decimal	.008		

	These …	both mean …	and NOT this …
Written as %	.25%	twenty-five hundredths of one percent	25% (twenty-five percent)
Written as decimal	.0025		

REINFORCEMENT PROBLEM: CONVERTING TO AND FROM PERCENT

1) **Conversions.** Without using a calculator, convert the percent numbers to decimals and the decimal numbers to percent, and write your answers in the blank spaces:

Percent	Decimal	Percent	Decimal	Decimal	Percent	Decimal	Percent
82%		7.5%		.5		2.49	
8.2%		.75%		.05		12.49	
.82%		750%		.005		.78	
820%		.082%		.2788		.0333	
3.892%		44.175%		.0012		375	
.031%		1,749%		.084		3.75	

REINFORCEMENT PROBLEM: CONVERTING TO AND FROM PERCENT

1)

Percent	Decimal	Percent	Decimal	Decimal	Percent	Decimal	Percent
82%	.82	7.5%	.075	.5	50%	2.49	249%
8.2%	.082	.75%	.0075	.05	5%	12.49	1,249%
.82%	.0082	750%	7.5	.005	.5%	.78	78%
820%	8.2	.082%	.00082	.2788	27.88%	.0333	3.33%
3.892%	.03892	44.175%	.44175	.0012	.12%	375	37,500%
.031%	.00031	1,749%	17.49	.084	8.4%	3.75	375%

ROUNDING PERCENT

Procedure

The procedure for rounding percent is essentially the same as for any other number. The table below shows this procedure with examples.

Step	Action	Example
1	Determine which place-value digit you wish to round.	Round 45.3937% to the hundredths place.
2	• If the digit to the right of the rounded digit is 5 or greater, add 1 to the rounded digit. • If the digit to the right of the rounded digit is less than 5, the rounded remains unchanged.	45.39**37**%
3	Delete all the digits to the right of the rounded digit.	45.39%

ADDITION, SUBTRACTION, MULTIPLICATION, AND DIVISION

Convert to decimals

If you are given percentages to add, subtract, multiply, or divide, simply convert the percentages to decimals (see page 591). Then perform the operations in the same way that you learned about calculating with decimals.

Caution!

Confusing expressions!

Do these expressions have the same meaning?
- "What is 20% of ten?"
- "Ten is 20% of what?"

Answer: Different meanings!

Here are the correct calculations:
- "What is 20% of ten?" means $10 \times .2 = 2$
- "Ten is 20% of what?" means $10 \div .2 = 50$

Guideline

- A **"percent of" a number** means to multiply to obtain a portion of that number.
- A **number that is a "percent of"** *another number* means divide to find the other number.

ADDITION, SUBTRACTION, MULTIPLICATION, AND DIVISION (continued)

Quick practice

Calculate the answer to each question below:

Question	Answer
What is 25% of 125?	31.25
125 is 25% of what number?	500
.8 is 20% of what number?	4
What is 20% of .8?	.16
What is 120% of 120?	144
120 is 120% of what number?	100

USING PERCENT TO SOLVE PROBLEMS

Overview

Percent calculations are extremely useful, and have a lot of business applications. In general, percent is used to solve problems in the following four areas:

- the three basic types of percent calculation
- showing changes
- finding a base or a portion when they are combined
- comparing different bases

Each of these topics is discussed below.

THREE BASIC TYPES OF PERCENT CALCULATION

Introduction

When you are working in business situations, you will encounter three basic types of percent calculations which repeatedly occur. It is important that you become familiar and comfortable with these three calculations.

THREE BASIC TYPES OF PERCENT CALCULATION (continued)

Three basic types of percent calculations

These are three basic types of percent calculations:

- **Type 1: Finding the base amount**
You know the percent and you know the portion, but what was the base number?

   Example: Your business collected $45,000 in sales tax. You know that sales tax is 5% of total sales. What was the total sales?

- **Type 2: Finding the portion**
You know the rate (percent) and you know the base, but what was the portion?

   Example: Your business had $900,000 of sales. The sales tax is 5% of all sales. How much sales tax should you have collected?

   Note: Usually the portion is smaller than the base, but this is not always true. The portion can also be greater than the base, if the percent is greater than 100%.

- **Type 3: Finding the rate**
The percent amount is also called the **rate**. In this type of problem, you know the base and you know the portion, but you need to find the percent. This calculation is exactly the same as what you have already done to convert a number to a percent.

   Example: If $45,000 of sales tax was collected and total taxable sales was $900,000, what was the rate of tax (the percent)?

THREE BASIC TYPES OF PERCENT CALCULATION (continued)

Memory aid

Use the diagram below as a memory aid when doing calculations to solve the above three types of problems:

Portion	
Base	**Rate**

How to use the memory aid diagram

1) Identify which one of the three elements you need to find. Put your finger over the box that contains this element.

2) Use the other two remaining elements to solve the problem:

- If the two remaining elements are side by side, then multiply them.
- If one remaining element is above the other remaining element, then divide the lower element into the one above.

PRACTICE

REINFORCEMENT PROBLEM: IDENTIFY THE PORTION, BASE, AND RATE

1) This problem does not require any calculations. What is required is that you correctly *identify* the portion, base, and rate in each problem description. In the table below, write the amount of the portion, base, or rate for each separate situation. If one of these items is what must be calculated, write a check mark (✓) for the item that must be calculated. The first problem is an example.

Problem Description	Portion	Base	Rate
1) If 1,200 pink computers were sold, and this is 10% of all computer sales, how many computers were sold?	1,200	✓	10%
2) Andrea made a 20% down payment on a house. She paid $55,000. What did the house cost?			
3) Last year Kelly Company had sales of $485,000. The company forecasts a 7% increase in sales. How much will the increase be?			
4) Anandi Company had sales of $514,000 and a net income of $74,530. What percent is net income of sales?			
5) Jay earns $40 per hour and John earns $50 per hour. John's earnings are what percent of Jay's earnings?			
6) Diem Art Gallery paid an 8% commission when it sold a painting for $15,000. How much was the commission?			
7) Hobbs Enterprises purchased $75,000 of new equipment, which was 20% of the amount that had been budgeted for equipment. How much had been budgeted?			
8) .35 is 15% of what amount?			
9) What is 15% of .35?			

SOLUTIONS

REINFORCEMENT PROBLEM: IDENTIFY THE PORTION, BASE, AND RATE

1)

Problem Description	Portion	Base	Rate
1) If 1,200 pink computers were sold, and this is 10% of all computer sales, how many computers were sold?	1,200	✓	10%
2) Andrea made a 20% down payment on a house. She paid $55,000. What did the house cost?	$55,000	✓	20%
3) Last year Kelly Company had sales of $485,000. The company forecasts a 7% increase in sales. How much will the increase be?	✓	$485,000	7%
4) Anandi Company had sales of $514,000 and a net income of $74,530. What percent is net income of sales?	$74,530	$514,000	✓
5) Jay earns $40 per hour and John earns $50 per hour. John's earnings are what percent of Jay's earnings?	$50	$40	✓
6) Diem Art Gallery paid an 8% commission when it sold a painting for $15,000. How much was the commission?	✓	$15,000	8%
7) Hobbs Enterprises purchased $75,000 of new equipment, which was 20% of the amount it had been budgeted for equipment. How much had been budgeted?	$75,000	✓	20%
8) .35 is 15% of what amount?	.35	✓	15%
9) What is 15% of .35?	✓	.35	15%

EXAMPLES OF EACH TYPE OF CALCULATION

Finding the base

Your business collected $45,000 in sales tax. You know that sales tax is 5% of total sales. What was the amount of total sales?

Portion	
Base	**Rate**

We are asking: "$45,000 is 5% of what number?" The number we are trying to find is the base, so put your finger over the base (dark rectangle): $45,000 / .05 = $900,000 of sales.

Your travel expense for the year totaled $83,500. The accounting department tells you that your travel expense was 21.8% of the total travel expense for the entire business. How much was the total travel expense?

Portion	
Base	**Rate**

We are asking: "$83,500 is 21.8% of what number?" The number we are trying to find is the base, so put your finger over the base (dark rectangle). Following the procedure, divide the rate into the portion: $83,500 / .218 = $383,027.52 total travel expense.

Finding the portion

Your business had $900,000 of sales. The sales tax is 5% of all sales. How much sales tax should you have collected?

Portion	
Base	**Rate**

We are asking: "What number is 5% of $900,000?" The number that we are trying to find is the portion, so put your finger over the portion (dark rectangle). Following the procedure, multiply the base by the rate (percent): $900,000 × .05 = $45,000.

EXAMPLES OF EACH TYPE OF CALCULATION (continued)

Finding the portion (continued)

Acme Company has budgeted the product development expense as 12% of total expenses. If total expenses are budgeted at $715,000, how much will be budgeted for product development?

Portion	
Base	**Rate**

The reference (base) amount is $715,000. The rate is 12%. We are asking: "What number is 12% of $715,000?" The number that we are trying to find is the portion, so put your finger over the portion (dark rectangle). Following the procedure, multiply the base by the rate (percent): $715,000 × .12 = $85,800.

The portion can be bigger than the base: total utilities expense this month is $10,000. If we budget utilities expense for next month at 110% of this month, how much is budgeted for next month?

Portion	
Base	**Rate**

The reference (base) amount is $10,000. We are asking: "What number is 110% of $10,000?" The number that we are trying to find is the portion, so put your finger over the portion (dark rectangle). Following the procedure, multiply the base by the rate (percent): $10,000 × 1.10 = $11,000.

Finding the rate

Finding the rate is simply converting a number to a percent, which was presented to you on a previous page. Here is an additional example:

If $45,000 of sales tax was collected and total taxable sales was $900,000, what was the rate of tax (the percent)?

Portion	
Base	**Rate**

We are asking: "What percent is $45,000 of $900,000?" The number that we are trying to find is the rate, so put your finger over the rate (dark rectangle). Following the procedure, divide the portion by the base: $45,000 / $900,000 = .05 = 5%.

EXAMPLES OF EACH TYPE OF CALCULATION (continued)

Caution! *Converting to %*	Notice that in the above calculation, the .05 was converted to a percent format of 5%. The procedure to convert the decimal to a percent was: .05 × 100 = 5%. Multiplying by 100 moves the decimal point two places to the right, which results in the number 5. Only *after* you multiply by 100 do you add the % symbol. *Note:* The answer is *NOT* .05%; you cannot just add a % symbol!

PERCENT CALCULATIONS FOR SHOWING CHANGES

Overview of change situations	There are two common situations involving *change* that call for the use of percent: • express a change as a percent • calculate a new base amount
Situation #1: express change as a percent	People in business are always concerned about change. They frequently want to express change in percentage terms, rather than using only dollar amounts. This is because percent is easy to understand, and often comparison is more meaningful when percent is used instead of dollars.
Example	Company A had a $15,000 increase in sales during 2001. Company B had a $20,000 increase in sales in 2001. Which increase is better? Of course, $20,000 is greater than $15,000, but suppose I give you additional information: Company A sales in the prior year were $50,000 and Company B sales in the prior year were $500,000. Does this data change your opinion? To clarify the situation, you can express the change as a percent of the base amount in the prior year.

PERCENT CALCULATIONS FOR SHOWING CHANGES (continued)

Calculating the percent change	Calculating the percent change is really just a different use for the percent rate, which you already know how to do. In this situation, *the rate represents a % **change** from a base amount.*

Portion	
Base	Rate

Procedure	Using the information in the example, the following table shows you how to calculate the rate of change.

Step	Action	Examples	
		Company A	**Company B**
1	Identify the base amount (the year we are comparing to).	$50,000	$500,000
2	Identify or calculate the portion.	$15,000	$20,000
3	Divide the portion by the base.	$15,000 / $50,000 = .30 = 30%	$20,000 / $500,000 = .04 = 4%

	What a difference! Company A sales grew at the rate of 30% per year. Company B sales grew at the rate of only 4%.

Another example	In the year ending December 31, 2000, the total supplies expense was $22,100. In the next year, the total supplies expense was $27,500. What was the percent change in the supplies expense?

Step	Action	Example
1	Identify the base amount.	$22,100
2	Identify or calculate the portion.	$27,500 – $22,100 = $5,400 increase
3	Divide the portion by the base.	$5,400 / $22,100 = .244 = 24.4% increase

PERCENT CALCULATIONS FOR SHOWING CHANGES (continued)

Caution

This problem was a little tricky, because it only asked for the "change." It did not tell you if the change was an increase or decrease. *You had to decide.* For example, if the second year expense had been $16,700, the $5,400 would be a decrease. The calculation would be exactly the same, BUT you would have to label the answer as *decrease*, or it would be wrong. This is very common.

Situation #2: calculate a new base

In this situation, you are given the base amount. You are also given the percent of increase or decrease in the base amount. You have to calculate what the new total base amount will be by adding the amount of the increase or subtracting the amount of the decrease.

Increases in the base

There are two ways to calculate the increase in base kind of problem. The second way is faster.

Example: You are earning $3,800 per month. Because of your good work, you receive an 8% pay increase. What is the amount per month that you will be earning after the increase?

METHOD 1		
Step	**Action**	**Example**
1	Identify the base amount.	$3,800
2	Identify the percent change.	8% (increase)
3	Multiply the base by the percent to get **the amount of change.**	$3,800 × .08 = $304 (increase)
4	Add the increase to the old base to find the new base.	$3,800 + $304 = $4,104 *Warning:* It is NOT CORRECT to simply add 8 to $3,800 and get the result of $3,808.

METHOD 2 (Better)		
Step	**Action**	**Example**
1	Identify the base amount.	$3,800
2	Add the % increase to 100% and express as a decimal.	100% + 8% = 108% = 1.08
3	Multiply the old base by the decimal to get the new base.	$3,800 × 1.08 = $4,104

PERCENT CALCULATIONS FOR SHOWING CHANGES (continued)

Decreases in the base

There are two ways to solve the decrease in base kind of problem. The second way is faster.

Example: The supplies expense budget this year for your department is $8,500. You are told that next year this budget will be reduced by 15%. What will your supplies budget be for next year?

METHOD 1		
Step	**Action**	**Example**
1	Identify the base amount.	$8,500
2	Identify the percent change.	15% (decrease)
3	Multiply the base by the percent to get the amount of decrease.	$8,500 × .15 = $1,275 (decrease)
4	Subtract the decrease from the old base to find the new base.	$8,500 − $1,275 = $7,225

METHOD 2 (Better)		
Step	**Action**	**Example**
1	Identify the base amount.	$3,500
2	Subtract the % decrease from 100% and express as a decimal.	100% − 15% = 85% = .85
3	Multiply the old base by the decimal to get the new base.	$8,500 × .85 = $7,225

HOW TO FIND A BASE OR PORTION WHEN THEY ARE COMBINED

Introduction

Sometimes an unknown base and an unknown portion are combined together into one total. If you know what percent the portion is of the base, then you can calculate either the base or the portion, or both.

HOW TO FIND A BASE OR PORTION WHEN THEY ARE COMBINED (continued)

Example

You own a bookstore that calculates sales tax at the end of every month. At the end of June, total receipts including sales tax are $270,000. The sales tax rate is 8%. What is the amount of the sales tax? What is the amount of sales?

In this example, the base (the sales) is combined with the portion (the sales tax) which is 8% of the base. Together, the base and portion are $270,000.

Procedure

Follow the procedure in the table below to find a base or portion when both are combined into one total.

Step	Action	Example
1	Add the rate to 100% and convert to a decimal.	$100\% + 8\% = 108\% = 1.08$
2	Find the base first by dividing the total by the decimal from Step 1. *Note:* It is important to see that the base always represents 100%. Together, the portion and the base are 100% plus whatever additional percent of the base the portion is (in this case, another 8% of the base). In other words, $270,000 is 108% of the base.	$\$270,000 / 1.08 = \$250,000$ The amount of sales excluding tax is $250,000
3	To find the portion, subtract the base from the total.	$\$270,000 - \$250,000 = \$20,000$ (sales tax)

Caution

It may be tempting to simply multiply 8% times $270,000 to find the sales tax, but this will not work. Why? Because the $270,000 *already includes sales tax*. The tax should only be calculated on the actual sales (the true base). If you multiply $270,000 by 8%, you would be calculating sales tax on *both* the sales and sales tax! Your answer would overstate the sales tax.

HOW TO FIND A BASE OR PORTION WHEN THEY ARE COMBINED (continued)

Another example

This year, the attendance at the baseball world series was 885,320 people. This was a 9% increase from last year. How many people attended last year? How many more people attended this year than last year?

Solution:
885,320 / 1.09 = 812,220 (approximately) attended last year.
885,320 – 812,220 = a 73,100 increase.

Example with decrease

In the example above, suppose that the 885,320 attendance this year was a 9% decrease from last year. How many people attended last year? How many fewer people attended this year than last year?

Solution:
885,320 / .91 = 972,879 (approximately) attended last year.
972,879 – 885,320 = an 87,559 decrease.

COMPARISON WITH DIFFERENT BASES

Overview

In business, it is frequently necessary to compare portions that are related to different bases. Calculating a percent for the comparison provides a more useful comparison.

COMPARISON WITH DIFFERENT BASES (continued)

Example

Mega Company had $985,000 of sales last year. Its total operating expenses were $384,150. Mini Company had sales of $91,000 and its operating expenses were $37,310. Which company is operating more efficiently?

It is very difficult to compare the companies by just looking at the dollar amount of operating expenses. Clearly Mega Company had more expenses, but it is also a much bigger company.

Solution:
Compare the expenses (portions) as percentages of the base amounts (sales). Comparing percents, we see that Mega is operating more efficiently:

- Mega Company expenses: $384,150 / $985,000 = .39 = 39% of sales
- Mini Company expenses: $37,310 / $91,000 = .41 = 41% of sales

SOLUTIONS FOR PERCENT CALCULATIONS BEGIN ON PAGE 611.

REINFORCEMENT PROBLEMS: PERCENT CALCULATIONS

1) **Calculation with decimals, converting decimals and percents.** Convert the following percents to decimals and then do the indicated calculations. Show your answers as both decimals and percents.

Calculate …	Decimal Answer	Percent Answer
37% × 54%		
37% × 5.4%		
37% × .54%		
73.07% + 3.215%		
.95% + .85%		
143% + 100%		
35% ÷ 25%		
35% ÷ 2.5%		
35% ÷ .25%		
35% ÷ 250%		
99.9% − 82.3%		
152.7% − 42.875%		
.7% − .385%		

2) **Analyze common expressions.** Answer the following questions:

A) What number is 115% of 80?	
B) What number is 25% of 350?	
C) What number is 20% of 80%?	
D) $7,500 is 80% of what number?	
E) 350 is 25% of what number?	
F) 35% is 50% of what number?	
G) .20% × 80% is what number?	
H) .75% × 150 is what number?	
I) .9% × .8% is what number?	

PRACTICE

SOLUTIONS FOR PERCENT CALCULATIONS BEGIN ON PAGE 611.

3) **Identify the base, the portion, and the rate.** Before you can do a correct calculation involving a base, a portion, and a rate, you must first be able to identify them! In this problem, we do not care at all about doing calculations. Without doing any calculations, read each situation, then identify the base, the portion, and the rate by writing the amount of the item in the correct column. If the item is the amount we are trying to calculate, then place a check mark (✔) in the correct column. Use the first situation as an example.

Situation	Base	Portion	Rate
A) Anne purchased a new car for $20,000 and she made a 25% down payment. What was her down payment?	$20,000	✔	25%
B) In the year 2000, the revenue for Acme Company was $820,000. In 2001, the revenue increased by $98,400. What was the percent increase?			
C) At year end, the price of the stock of Jain Company was $22. This amount was 115% of last year's price. What was the price last year?			
D) O'Leary's Coffee Shoppe surveyed its customers. Of the 500 customers surveyed, 215 preferred decaffeinated brew instead of regular brew. What percent of customers want decaffeinated brew?			
E) Dennis just purchased a new truck, which the salesman claimed will have 5% better gas mileage than Dennis' old truck. The old truck got 14 miles per gallon. What *improvement* in mileage should Dennis expect?			
F) So far this year, Rapacious Corporation has spent $3,750 for supplies, which is 85% of its total supplies budget. What is the total supplies budget?			
G) Smilin' Norm Toy receives a 12% commission of the price of each used car that he sells. This month, Norm received $4,300 in commissions. What is the total price of all the cars that he sold this month?			
H) Passionate Poster Company sells three types of posters: small (15% of sales), medium (72%), and large (13%). The company sold 10,000 posters last month. How many were small posters?			

SOLUTIONS FOR PERCENT CALCULATIONS BEGIN ON PAGE 611.

4) **Answer typical business questions that involve percent.** Calculate the answer to each of the independent situations below. Show your calculation and answer in good form under each question.

A) At the California state fair, Bjork's hot dog stand began the day with 12 gallons of mustard. At the end of the day, 75% of the mustard is gone. How many gallons of mustard were used?

B) At the state fair, Chang's ice cream booth began the day with 200 gallons of rocky road ice cream, and at the end of the day, 45 gallons were still unsold. What percent is unsold?

C) At the state fair, Dorrance's Cotton Candy Concession has 15 pounds of sugar still unused when the day is over. This is 12% of the amount that was available in the morning. How much was available in the morning?

D) At the state fair, Porter's Fine Flower Shoppe recorded $13,330 of cash collections, which included both sales and sales tax. If the sales tax rate is 7.5% and all sales are taxable, what is the dollar amount of sales tax?

E) Rochelle purchased 100 shares of stock in a corporation for $35 per share. After a year, the total value of her investment was $3,920. What was the percent change in her investment for the year? (*Note:* the annual percent change in an investment is called annual **rate of return**.)

F) Miller's Hardware is having a sale. Paint is selling for 20% off the regular price. If the regular price of the paint you want is $24 per can, how much is the paint selling for now? Use the faster method to calculate your answer.

G) 1) If the price of merchandise changed from $200 to $150, what was the percent change?

2) If the price of merchandise changed from $150 to $100, what was the percent change?

3) If the price of merchandise changed from $100 to $50, what was the percent change?

The amount of each decrease was $50. But what is happening to the size of the percent change? Why?

H) The net income of Kona Company is 15% of the total revenue. If net income is $300,000, what is the total revenue?

I) Lansdale Company had net income of $200,000 and Lehigh Company had net income of $150,000. The Lansdale net income is what percent of Lehigh net income? The Lehigh net income is what percent of Lansdale net income?

PRACTICE

SOLUTIONS FOR PERCENT CALCULATIONS BEGIN ON PAGE 611.

4) *continued*

J) Lackawanna Enterprises had $700,000 of sales revenue this year. Last year, the sales revenue was $350,000. What is the percent change from last year to this year?

K) Your manager has just informed you that your supplies budget will increase 12% this year. Last year it was $27,300. What will the supplies budget be this year?

L) You have just been hired to work for the Summerdale Grocery Store. You are told that the coffee was marked up by 15% last month, and the manager wants it marked back down to its original price. The current price, which includes the markup, is $2.53 per pound. What price does the manager want?

M) Diana invested $5,200 and made a $1,700 profit on her investment. Kymberly invested $50,000 and made a $13,750 profit. Who had the greatest rate of return?

N) The Smith and Jones partnership allocates profits and losses 70% to Smith and 30% to Jones. If Baker enters the partnership and receives a 25% share of profits and losses,

   1)   what total percent share of the profits and losses do Smith and Jones receive together?

   2)   what percent share will Smith now receive? What percent share will Jones receive?

O) Merchandise is marked up from a cost of $1 to $1.45. What is the markup percentage based on cost? What is the markup percentage based on selling price?

P) **Challenging problem.** The Internal Revenue Service allows small businesses to deduct as an allowable business expense the payments made to certain retirement plans. The retirement deduction is limited to 15% of the net earnings of a business. However, the tax law, tricky as usual, states that the "net earnings" limit means what the net earnings would be after the deduction is subtracted. So, you don't know the amount of net earnings for purposes of the calculation unless you know the amount of the deduction. But you don't know the amount of the deduction unless you know the net earnings!

   1)   Suppose a business has $20,000 of "net earnings" before considering the deduction. What amount of net earnings can the 15% deduction be calculated on? What is the amount of the deduction? (*Hint:* View the net earnings before the deduction as some percent greater than what it would be after the deduction.)

   2)   What is the true deduction percent limit?

SOLUTIONS

PRACTICE QUESTIONS FOR PERCENT CALCULATIONS BEGIN ON PAGE 607.

REINFORCEMENT PROBLEMS: PERCENT CALCULATIONS

1)

Calculate ...	Decimal Answer	Percent Answer
37% × 54%	.1998	19.98%
37% × 5.4%	.01998	1.998%
37% × .54%	.001998	.1998%
73.07% + 3.215%	.76285	76.285%
.95% + .85%	.018	1.8%
143% + 100%	2.43	243%
35% ÷ 25%	1.4	140%
35% ÷ 2.5%	14.	1,400%
35% ÷ .25%	140	14,000%
35% ÷ 250%	.14	14%
99.9% − 82.3%	.176	17.6%
152.7% − 42.875%	1.09825	109.825%
.7% − .385%	.00315	.315%

2)

A)	What number is 115% of 80?	80 × 1.15 = 92
B)	What number is 25% of 350?	350 × .25 = 87.5
C)	What number is 20% of 80%?	.8 × .2 = .16 (or 16%)
D)	$7,500 is 80% of what number?	$7,500 / .8 = $9,375
E)	350 is 25% of what number?	350 / .25 = 1,400
F)	35% is 50% of what number?	.35 / .5 = .7 (or 70%)
G)	.20% × 80% is what number?	.0016 (or .16%)
H)	.75% × 150 is what number?	1.125
I)	.9% × .8% is what number?	.000072 (or .0072%)

3)

Situation	Base	Portion	Rate
A) Anne purchased a new car for $20,000 and she made a 25% down payment. What was her down payment?	$20,000	✓	25%
B) In the year 2000, the revenue for Acme Company was $820,000. In 2001, the revenue increased by $98,400. What was the percent increase?	$820,000	$98,400	✓
C) At year end, the price of the stock of Jain Company was $22. This amount was 115% of last year's price. What was the price last year?	✓	$22	115%
D) O'Leary's Coffee Shoppe surveyed its customers. Of the 500 customers surveyed, 215 preferred decaffeinated brew instead of regular brew. What percent of customers want decaffeinated brew?	500	215	✓

SOLUTIONS

PRACTICE QUESTIONS FOR PERCENT CALCULATIONS BEGIN ON PAGE 607.

3) *continued*

Situation	Base	Portion	Rate
E) Dennis just purchased a new truck, which the salesman claimed will have 5% better gas mileage than Dennis' old truck. The old truck got 14 miles per gallon. What *improvement* in mileage should Dennis expect?	14	✓	5%
F) So far this year, Rapacious Corporation has spent $3,750 for supplies, which is 85% of its total supplies budget. What is the total supplies budget?	✓	$3,750	85%
G) Smilin' Norm Toy receives a 12% commission of the price of each used car that he sells. This month, Norm received $4,300 in commissions. What is the total price of all the cars that he sold this month?	✓	$4,800	12%
H) Passionate Poster Company sells three types of posters: small (15% of sales), medium (72%), and large (13%). The company sold 10,000 posters last month. How many were small posters?	10,000	✓	15%

4) A) You are calculating the portion: 12 gallons × .75 = 9 gallons used
   B) You are calculating the rate: 45 gallons / 200 gallons = .225 = 22.5%
   C) You are calculating the base: 15 pounds / .12 = 125 pounds
   D) Combined base and portion; you want the portion: $13,330 / 1.075 = $12,400 $13,330 – 12,400 = $930 tax
   E) You are calculating the rate: $3,920 – $3,500 = $420 $420 / $3,500 = .12 = 12%
   F) You are calculating the new base: $24 × .8 = $19.20 per can
   G) 1) 50 / 200 = .25 (or a 25% change)
       2) 50 / 150 = .333 (or a 33.3% change)
       3) 50 / 100 = .5 = 50% change. The portion remains the same each time (50), but the base is decreasing. This makes the percent change greater.
   H) You are calculating the base: $300,000 / .15 = $2,000,000
   I) Lansdale is approximately 133% ($200,000 / $150,000) of Lehigh. Lehigh is 75% ($150,000 / $200,000) of Lansdale.
   J) You are calculating the rate: $350,000 (increase amount) / $350,000 (base) = 1 = 100% (100% increase)
   K) You are calculating the new portion: $27,300 × 1.12 = $30,576 or $27,300 × .12 = $3,276, so $27,300 + $3,276 = $30,576
   L) Combined base and portion, you need to know the base: $2.53 / 1.15 = $2.20
   M) Diana: $1,700 / $5,200 = approximately 32.7% Kymberly: $13,750 / $50,000 = 27.5%
   N) 1) If the new partner receives 25%, then Smith and Jones together receive 75% of partnership profits and losses.
       2) Smith will receive .75 × .7 = .525 which is 52.5%. Jones will receive .75 × .3 = .225 which is 22.5%.
   O) You are calculating the rate. If cost is the base, then the rate is $.45/$1.00 = .45 = 45% markup. If the selling price is the base, then $.45/$1.45 = approximately .31 = 31%.
   P) 1) You need to see that "net earnings" without the deduction is going to be 115% of what it would be after the deduction is subtracted, so this is a combined base and portion problem. $20,000/1.15 = $17,391 (base). The deduction is $17,391 × .15 = approximately $2,609 (portion).
       2) The true overall deduction percent is not really 15%. It is 1/1.15 = .86957, so .15 × .86957 = .13044, which is about 13.044%.

▼ *Positive and Negative Numbers*

OPPOSITES

Definition	Opposites are things that offset each other, cancel each other out, or go in opposite directions. Some things in the world are natural opposites.

Examples of opposites

- In a business, earning income and paying an expense are opposites, and have opposite effects on wealth of the business.
- In an election, a "yes" vote and a "no" vote have opposite effects on the outcome of a proposition.
- In an aircraft, climbing and descending have opposite effects on the altitude.
- Hours of daylight and hours of sunlight are opposites that have opposite effects on temperature.

Common feature of opposites

What all these things have in common is that the force of one opposing thing offsets or cancels out the effects caused by the other.

- Expenses offset the effects of income you earned; also, the more income you earn, the more the effects of expenses are offset.
- The more "no" votes there are, the effect of "yes" votes are offset; also, the more "yes" votes there are, the more the "no" votes are offset.

IDENTIFYING OPPOSITES

Overview

Because there are so many natural opposite things in business as well as in other activities, it is important to identify opposites and to measure them. When this is done, all the normal rules for mathematics will apply. That means that we can include opposites in any of our calculations.

"Positive" and "negative"

Opposites are usually described by the words "positive" and "negative."

- **"Positive"** means an amount greater than zero. This describes many conditions and situations such as wealth, progress towards a goal, things of substance, movement in a desired direction, and so on.
- **"Negative"** means an amount less than zero.

Note: The opposite of zero is zero.

IDENTIFYING OPPOSITES (continued)

Showing positive amounts	A positive amount is indicated either by a plus sign (+) or by a numeral. *Example:* To indicate a positive 5, you can write "+5" or "5." This would be interpreted by the words "positive five" or "five."
Showing negative amounts	A negative amount is indicated by writing a negative sign (–) in front of a numeral. *Example:* "–5" would be interpreted by the words "negative five" or "show the opposite of five."
Different meanings for a "–" sign!	A "–" sign (often called a "minus sign") can be used to indicate: • a negative number, or • show the opposite of a number, or • the operation of subtraction

IDENTIFYING OPPOSITES (continued)

Caution!

Interpreting minus signs

It is extremely easy to confuse the different meanings of a "–" sign. Here is how to distinguish what is intended:

- **When the symbol "–" is followed by a numerical amount, but there is no amount in front of the "–" symbol:** this indicates the negative of the number. It also means that you are to show the opposite of a number. The result is the same in either case.

    Example: "–5" indicates the amount of a negative 5. A –5 can also be interpreted as "show the opposite of 5," which is a negative 5.

    Example: "– (–5)" indicates the amount of the negative of negative 5, which is 5. This can also be interpreted as "show the opposite of –5," which is 5.

- **When the symbol "–" is between two amounts:** this indicates subtraction.

    Example: "8 – 5" means subtract 5 from 8.
    Example: "8 – (–5)" means subtract a negative 5 from 8.

Notice how the negative 5 was placed in brackets "( )" to prevent confusion with the subtraction sign. We will have more to say about subtraction later.

Synonym

A synonym for positive and negative numbers is "signed numbers."

PRACTICE

REINFORCEMENT PROBLEM: INTERPRETING THE MEANING OF + AND – SIGNS

1) For each of the expressions shown below, briefly interpret the meaning of the expression. Use the first item as an example.

Expression	Explanation
–5	The negative of 5 (or simply "negative five")
– (–3)	
10	
10 – 8	
–9	
7 – (–3)	
7 + (–3)	

SOLUTIONS

REINFORCEMENT PROBLEM: INTERPRETING THE MEANING OF + AND – SIGNS

1)

Expression	Explanation
–5	The negative of 5 (or simply "negative five")
– (–3)	The negative of negative 3 (the opposite of negative 3)
10	Positive 10 (or simply "ten")
10 – 8	Ten minus eight
–9	The negative of nine (or simply "negative nine")
7 – (–3)	Seven minus a negative three
7 + (–3)	Seven plus a negative three

MEASURING OPPOSITES

Overview

When something can be quantified in numbers, we can show the quantity of that thing using positive and negative amounts on a number line.

Number line

The example below shows a number line, in units of 1.

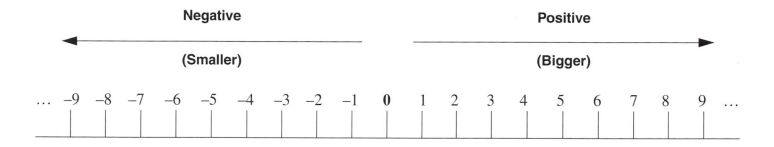

Comparing the numbers

Examples:
- 4 is more than 1, because 4 is to the right of 1.
- 1 is more than –2, because 1 is to the right of –2.
- –2 is more than –5 because –2 is to the right of –5.
- –5 is less than 5, because –5 is to the left of 5.

ABSOLUTE VALUE

Definition

Absolute value is the distance between any number on the number line and zero.

Examples

- The absolute value of –7 ("negative 7") is 7, because –7 is 7 units from 0.
- The absolute value of 3 is 3, because 3 is located 3 units from 0.

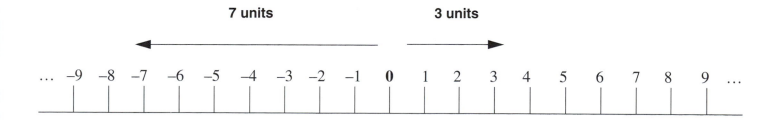

ABSOLUTE VALUE (continued)

Absolute value is positive

Of course, a distance cannot be negative. Therefore, the absolute value of any signed number is always positive. Absolute value is *never negative.*

> *Note: The absolute value of zero is zero.*

Symbol for absolute value

The symbol that indicates the absolute value of a number is a pair of vertical lines enclosing the number. The symbol looks like this: | |

Examples:
- "| 7 |" means the absolute value of 7 (which is 7).
- "| –7 |" means the absolute value of –7 (which is 7).

ADDITION OF SIGNED NUMBERS

Examples

The following four examples illustrate the addition of signed numbers by using income (which is positive) and expense (which is negative).

Example #1

- Suppose that you have a small business. You earn income from a sale of $5 (which is positive) and you earn income from another sale of $4 (which is also positive). What is the total effect on the wealth of the business?

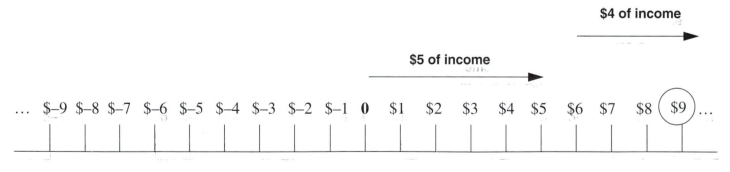

A positive $5 of income plus a positive $4 of income totals to a $9 increase in wealth (5 + 4 = 9).

ADDITION OF SIGNED NUMBERS (continued)

Example #2

● Suppose you earn $7 of income from a sale but you also have an expense of $3. What total effect do these two amounts have on the wealth of the business?

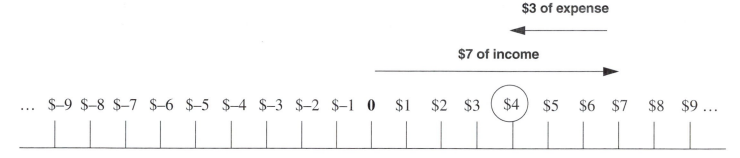

$3 of expense (a negative) added to a positive $7 of income partially offsets the income. The total of these two items results in $4 of wealth (7 + (–3) = 4). Adding numbers with opposite signs shows how naturally opposite things will offset each other.

Example #3

● Suppose that the business has an expense of $3 and another expense of $5, but has not yet earned any income. What is the total effect on the business wealth of both expenses?

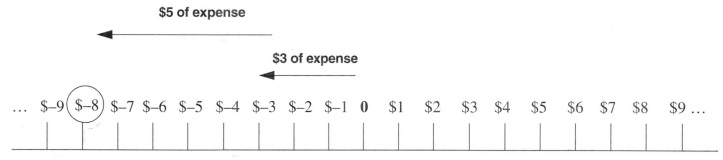

The expense of $3 plus another expense of $5 total to $–8. The wealth of the business was reduced by a total of $8 (–3 + (–5) = –8). Adding a negative to another negative results in a bigger negative total.

ADDITION OF SIGNED NUMBERS (continued)

Example #4

• Suppose that your business up to now has $2 of net profit. What is the total profit or loss if the business now incurs $3 of expenses followed by $8 of income?

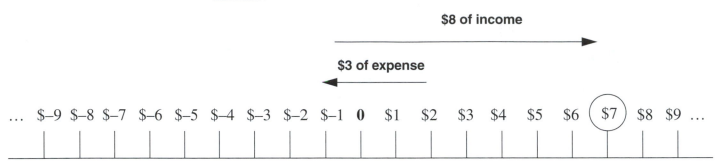

In this case, our starting point is a positive $2, instead of 0. Beginning with the positive $2, a negative $3 is added. The result is a negative $1 (a $1 loss). However, when a positive $8 of income is added, the final result is a positive $7 profit $(2 + (-3) + 8 = 7)$.

Rules for addition

The following table shows you the rules for adding signed numbers.

Rule	Examples
Same sign: To add two numbers with the same sign, add the absolute values, and then attach the common sign to the result.	• $7 + 4 = |7| + |4| = 11$ attaching the common sign, the answer is 11. • $-7 + (-4) = |-7| + |-4| = 11$ attaching the common sign, the answer is -11.
Different signs: To add two numbers with different signs, subtract the smaller absolute value from the larger absolute value, and attach the sign of the number with the larger absolute value.	• $7 + (-4) = |7| - |-4| = 3$ attaching the sign of larger number, the answer is 3. • $-7 + (4) = |-7| - |4| = 3$ attaching the sign of larger number, the answer is -3. *Note:* Notice how subtraction achieves the effect of combined opposites offsetting each other.
Any number + zero: The sum of any number and zero is the same number.	• $7 + 0 = 7$ • $-5 + 0 = -5$
Any number + its opposite: The sum of any number and its opposite is zero.	• $7 + (-7) = 0$ • $-7 + 7 = 0$

PRACTICE

SOLUTIONS FOR ADDING SIGNED NUMBERS BEGIN ON PAGE 622.

REINFORCEMENT PROBLEM: ADDING SIGNED NUMBERS

1) Calculate the totals of the expressions shown in the table:

Expression	Answer
A) 8 + 3	
B) 9 + (–3)	
C) –12 + (–10)	
D) –7 + 7	
E) –22 + (–30)	
F) –5 + (–9)	
G) 7 + 14	
H) 11 + 0	
I) 0 + 0	
J) –3 + 15	
K) 0 + (–5)	
L) 10 + (–20)	
M) –10 + (–20)	
N) 3 + (–3)	
O) –30 + 5	
P) –8 + (–3)	
Q) –38 + (–9) + 84	
R) 21 + (–15) + (–38)	
S) –39 + (–12) + (–45)	

SOLUTIONS

PRACTICE QUESTIONS FOR ADDING SIGNED NUMBERS BEGIN ON PAGE 621.

REINFORCEMENT PROBLEM: ADDING SIGNED NUMBERS

1)

Expression	Answer
A) 8 + 3	11
B) 9 + (−3)	6
C) −12 + (−10)	−22
D) −7 + 7	0
E) −22 + (−30)	−52
F) −5 + (−9)	−14
G) 7 + 14	21
H) 11 + 0	11
I) 0 + 0	0
J) −3 + 15	12
K) 0 + (−5)	−5
L) 10 + (−20)	−10
M) −10 + (−20)	−30
N) 3 + (−3)	0
O) −30 + 5	−25
P) −8 + (−3)	−11
Q) −38 + (−9) + 84	37
R) 21 + (−15) + (−38)	−32
S) −39 + (−12) + (−45)	96

SUBTRACTION OF SIGNED NUMBERS

Examples

The following four examples illustrate the subtraction of signed numbers by using income (which is positive) and expense (which is negative).

Example #1

Suppose that you have a small business and that you earned $7 of income. Then an unhappy customer cancels a $3 sale, so now you have less income. How much income do you have now?

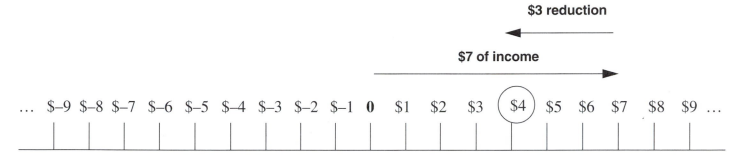

$7 of (positive) income minus the $3 decrease in the (positive) income leaves $4 of income, or $7 - 3 = 4$.

Example #2

Suppose that your business has recorded $9 of expense (a negative item). However, now you discover that $2 of expense was recorded in error, so now you have less expense. How much expense do you have now?

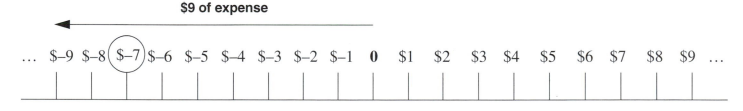

$9 of a negative item (the expense) is reduced by $2, resulting in $7 of expense or, in other words, $-9 - (-2) = -7$.

SUBTRACTION OF SIGNED NUMBERS (continued)

Example #3

Mechanically, subtraction is used to calculate the effects of *adding more of a negative (opposite) thing*. (See "Rules for addition" on page 620.)

For example, suppose that your business has earned $7 of income. Next, the business pays a $3 expense. The business now has *more of a negative thing* (an expense) which must be combined with the income to calculate the net profit or loss. So, 7 income + 3 expense = 4 profit.

Notice that the final result of adding more of a negative (the expense) is exactly the same as subtracting a positive (the income) of the same amount.

Adding more of a negative ($3 of expense) has exactly the same result on profit as subtracting a positive ($3 of revenue):

Add more of a negative	Subtract a positive
$7 + (-3) = 4$	$7 - 3 = 4$

Rule for subtraction

Distinguishing between adding opposite things and subtracting similar things can be confusing. Instead, it is much easier to use the following *simple rule* whenever you see a minus sign between two numbers.

The following table shows you the rule for subtracting signed numbers with examples:

Rule	Example	Apply the rule ...
Subtraction: To subtract two signed numbers, *add the opposite* of the number that is being subtracted. *Note:* Do *not* make any change to the number from which you are subtracting.	• $24 - 10$ • $15 - (-20)$ • $-15 - (-20)$ • $-15 - 20$ • $10 - 12$	• $24 + (-10) = 14$ • $15 + 20 = 35$ • $-15 + 20 = 5$ • $-15 + (-20) = -35$ • $10 + (-12) = -2$

SUBTRACTION OF SIGNED NUMBERS (continued)

Terminology: "subtract" and "from"

Example: "Subtract 15 from 12."
When you read or hear this kind of expression, it means that the number after the word "subtract" is being subtracted from the number after the word "from." In this case, it means: 12 – 15.

Other examples:
- "Subtract 22 from 100" means 100 – 22.
- "Subtract negative 9 from 15" means 15 – (–9).
- "From 33 subtract 12" means 33 – 12.

PRACTICE

SOLUTIONS FOR SUBTRACTING SIGNED NUMBERS BEGIN ON PAGE 627.

REINFORCEMENT PROBLEMS: SUBTRACTING SIGNED NUMBERS

1) Calculate the answer to each expression shown in the table below:

Expression	Answer	Expression	Answer
A) 12 – 3		I) 3 – (–1)	
B) 15 – 20		J) 30 – 20	
C) –9 – 9		K) 0 + (–5)	
D) –2 – (–15)		L) 10 – (–12)	
E) 0 – 3		M) –5 – (–3)	
F) 15 – 15		N) 5 – 5	
G) 15 – (–15)		O) 25 – 5	
H) –5 – 5		P) –8 – (–3)	

2) Calculate the answer to each of the following sentences:
   A) Subtract ten from thirty.
   B) Subtract twenty-five from three.
   C) Subtract a negative nine from five.
   D) Subtract a negative three from a negative eight.

3) **Addition and subtraction.** Calculate the answer to each expression in the table below:

Expression	Answer
A) 10 + 15 – 5	
B) –5 + (–7) – 3	
C) 5 – (–7) – (–5)	
D) –10 + (–3) – 8 + (–10)	
E) –4 + 3 – 2	
F) 30 – 15 + 8	
G) 15 + (–15)	
H) –50 – 10 + 12	
I) –5 + (–8) + 7 – 20	
J) 12 + (–5) – (–2)	
K) –8 – 2 + 4	
L) –5 – 7 – 10	
M) –25 + 5 + 10	
N) 25 – (–5)	

SOLUTIONS

PRACTICE QUESTIONS FOR SUBTRACTING SIGNED NUMBERS BEGIN ON PAGE 626.

REINFORCEMENT PROBLEMS: SUBTRACTING SIGNED NUMBERS

1)

Expression	Answer
A) 12 − 3	9
B) 15 − 20	−5
C) −9 − 9	0
D) −2 − (−15)	13
E) 0 − 3	−3
F) 15 − 15	0
G) 15 − (−15)	30
H) −5 − 5	0
I) 3 − (−1)	4
J) 30 − 20	10
K) 0 − (−5)	5
L) 10 − (−12)	22
M) −5 − (−3)	−2
N) 5 − 5	0
O) 25 − 5	20
P) −8 − (−3)	−5

2) A) Subtract ten from thirty = 20
   B) Subtract twenty-five from three = −22
   C) Subtract a negative nine from five = 14
   D) Subtract a negative three from a negative eight = −5

3)

Expression	Answer
A) 10 + 15 − 5	20
B) −5 + (−7) − 3	−15
C) 5 − (−7) − (−5)	17
D) −10 + (−3) − 8 + (−10)	−31
E) −4 + 3 − 2	−3
F) 30 − 15 + 8	23
G) 15 + (−15)	0
H) −50 − 10 + 12	−48
I) −5 + (−8) + 7 − 20	−26
J) 12 + (−5) − (−2)	9
K) −8 − 2 + 4	−6
L) −5 − 7 − 10	−22
M) −25 + 5 + 10	−10
N) 25 − (−5)	30

MULTIPLICATION OF SIGNED NUMBERS

Rules for multiplication

The table below shows you how to determine the sign of a product of two numbers:

Rule	Examples
Same signs: If the two numbers have the same sign, the product is positive.	• (3) (7) = 21 (two positives) • (–3) (–7) = 21 (two negatives)
Different signs: If the two numbers have different signs, the product is negative.	• (–3) (7) = –21 (negative and positive) • (3) (–7) = –21 (positive and negative)

Visual memory aid

$$(+) (+) = +$$
$$(-) (-) = +$$
$$(+) (-) = -$$
$$(-) (+) = -$$

Multiplying by 1 and by 0

The table below shows you some other important multiplication rules that involve multiplying by 1, by minus 1, and by 0.

Rule	Examples
Multiply by 1: The product of 1 and any number is that number.	• (1) (27) = 27 • (1) (22.459) = 22.459 • (1) (–7) = –7
Multiply by –1: The product of –1 and any number is that number, but with the opposite sign.	• (–1) (27) = –27 • (–1) (22.459) = –22.459 • (–1) (–7) = 7
Multiply by 0: The product of 0 and any number is 0.	• (0) (27) = 0 • (0) (22.459) = 0 • (0) (–7) = 0

DIVISION OF SIGNED NUMBERS

Rules for division

The table below shows you how to determine the sign of the quotient of two signed numbers.

Rule	Examples
Same signs: If the two numbers have the same sign, their quotient is positive.	• $20 / 5 = 4$ • $-20 / -5 = 4$
Different signs: If the two numbers have different signs, their quotient is negative.	• $20 / -5 = -4$ • $-20 / 5 = -4$

Visual memory aid

$$(+) \div (+) = +$$
$$(-) \div (-) = +$$
$$(+) \div (-) = -$$
$$(-) \div (+) = -$$

Division with 1 and 0 and the same number

The table below shows you some other important division rules that involve dividing by 1 and by 0.

Rule	Examples
Divide by 1: The quotient of any number divided by 1 is that number.	• $(27) \div (1) = 27$ • $(22.459) \div (1) = 22.459$ • $(-7) \div (1) = -7$
Divide by 0: The quotient of any number divided by zero cannot be determined, and is said to be "undefined."	• $(27) \div (0) =$ undefined • $(22.459) \div (0) =$ undefined • $(-7) \div (0) =$ undefined
Divide into 0: The quotient of zero divided by any number other than zero is zero.	• $0 \div 27 = 0$ • $(0) \div (-7) = 0$
Divide by the same number: Any number (except zero) divided by itself is 1.	• $5 \div 5 = 1$ • $.000719 \div .000719 = 1$

PRACTICE

REINFORCEMENT PROBLEMS: MULTIPLYING AND DIVIDING SIGNED NUMBERS

1) Calculate the product of each expression:

Expression	Answer
A) (7) (3)	
B) (–5) 4	
C) (–5) (–4)	
D) (–5) (–4) (–2)	
E) (8) (0)	
F) 8 (–8)	
G) (2) (–8) (–3)	
H) (8) (–1)	
I) –7 (–7)	
J) –7 (7)	
K) 5 (–3) (4)	
L) (8) • (4)	
M) (–8) • (–4)	
N) (–8) • (4)	
O) (–5) (–2) (–4)	
P) (–5) (–2) (–4) (–2)	

2) Calculate the quotient of each expression.

Expression	Answer
A) 8 ÷ 4	
B) –8 ÷ (–4)	
C) –8 ÷ (4)	
D) $14/_{-2}$	
E) $-25/_5$	
F) $-15/_{-15}$	
G) $12/_{-3}$	
H) $-12/_{-3}$	
I) $7/_0$	
J) $-8/_5$	
K) 30 ÷ 5 ÷ 2	
L) (–30) ÷ (–5) ÷ (–2)	
M) 0 ÷ 5	
N) –18 ÷ (–9)	
O) –20 ÷ (–4)	
P) 20 ÷ (–4)	

SOLUTIONS

REINFORCEMENT PROBLEMS: MULTIPLYING AND DIVIDING SIGNED NUMBERS

1)

Expression	Answer
A) (7) (3)	21
B) (–5) 4	–20
C) (–5) (–4)	20
D) (–5) (–4) (–2)	–40
E) (8) (0)	0
F) 8 (–8)	–64
G) (2) (–8) (–3)	48
H) (8) (–1)	–8
I) –7 (–7)	49
J) –7 (7)	–49
K) 5 (–3) (4)	–60
L) (8) • (4)	32
M) (–8) • (–4)	32
N) (–8) • (4)	–32
O) (–5) (–2) (–4)	–40
P) (–5) (–2) (–4) (–2)	80

2)

Expression	Answer
A) 8 ÷ 4	2
B) –8 ÷ (–4)	2
C) –8 ÷ (4)	–2
D) $14/_{-2}$	–7
E) $-25/_5$	–5
F) $-15/_{-15}$	1
G) $12/_{-3}$	–4
H) $-12/_{-3}$	4
I) $7/_0$	undefined
J) $-8/_5$	–1.6
K) 30 ÷ 5 ÷ 2	3
L) (–30) ÷ (–5) ÷ (–2)	–3
M) 0 ÷ 5	0
N) –18 ÷ (–9)	2
O) –20 ÷ (–4)	5
P) 20 ÷ (–4)	–5

MATHEMATICAL EXPRESSIONS

Definition	A **mathematical expression** is an arrangement of any numerals, letters, grouping symbols, and operational symbols which describes a value.

Symbols you are familiar with	Many of the symbols in a mathematical expression you already know:

- the numerals: 0, 1, 2, 3, 4, …
- common operational symbols such as add (+), subtract (−), multiply (•), and divide (÷)
- symbols indicating positive (+) and negative (−)

The equals symbol ("=")	The "=" symbol is very familiar, but technically it is not really part of a mathematical expression. Rather, the "=" shows the **equality** of two mathematical expressions.

Examples:
1) $4 + 8 = 4 • 3$ shows that the expression of 4 plus 8 is equal to the expression of 4 times 3. Each expression has the value 12.

2) $\frac{21}{3} = 12 − 5$ shows the expression of 21 divided by 3 is equal to the expression of 12 minus 5. Each expression has the value 7.

Variable symbols	Letters used in mathematical expressions are called **variables**. Whenever some amount is not known, a letter (a variable) is written into the expression in place of the unknown amount. Variables are used frequently in algebra.

Examples of variables	$4 + x = 7$ says that: "4 plus some amount is equal to 7." $4 + x$ is one mathematical expression and 7 is the other.

$\frac{y}{10} = 3 + x$ are expressions that show two unknown amounts. These two expressions say: "Some amount y divided by 10 is equal to 3 plus some other amount x."

MATHEMATICAL EXPRESSIONS (continued)

One of a variable

When a letter, such as x, is written by itself, it is understood that this represents 1 of x. This is the same as saying "1 times x." For example, writing "x" means exactly the same thing as writing "$1x$." For convenience, the numeral 1 is usually dropped.

Caution: Notice that "$1x$" is *NOT* the same as "$1 + x$," which means 1 plus x.

Grouping symbols

How numbers are grouped makes a big difference in a calculation. The most common grouping symbol is the parenthesis "( )." Other grouping symbols are the "{ }" and "[ ]" brackets, and fraction bars "——" or " / ".

Examples of grouping symbol

$(4 + 3) \cdot 2$
The 4 and 3 are grouped together and add to 7. So, the expression results in 7 times 2, which is 14.

$4 + (3 \cdot 2)$
Notice what a difference it makes if the 3 and 2 were grouped together. In this case, the 3 is multiplied by 2 and results in 6. When 6 is added to 4 the answer is 10.

Note: Operations within the parentheses are always done first.

More examples of mathematical expressions

- 25 is a numerical value, and therefore is a mathematical expression.
- $(x + 3)$ expresses the total of some amount plus 3.
- $25x - (x + 3)$ is a combination of symbols in an mathematical expression. This expression says "25 times an unknown amount x minus the sum of the unknown amount plus 3."

Basic operation symbols

When studying arithmetic, you learned the four basic operations of addition, subtraction, multiplication, and division. Here are examples of expressions using each operational symbol with the numeral 3 and the variable x.

MATHEMATICAL EXPRESSIONS (continued)

Operation	Mathematical Expression	English Descriptions
Addition	$3 + x$, or $(3 + x)$	• 3 plus x • x more than 3 • the total of 3 plus x
Subtraction	$x - 3$, or $(x - 3)$	• x minus 3 • 3 less than x • 3 subtracted from x
Multiplication	$3x$, or $3 \bullet x$, or $(3)(x)$, or $3(x)$, or $(3)x$, or	• 3 times x • 3 multiplied by x • x multiplied by 3 • 3 of x
Division	$\dfrac{x}{3}$ or $x/3$ or $x \div 3$	• x divided by 3 • 3 divided into x

Caution!

Notice that these two are different!

EXPONENTS

Exponents

An **exponent** is a small numeral placed slightly behind and above another numeral, to indicate that the preceding numeral must be multiplied by itself. For example, in the expression 3^2 the two indicates that 3 must be multiplied by itself twice. This is read as "three to the second power," or "three squared." The calculation is: $(3)(3) = 9$.

More examples

• 3^3 is read "three to the third power," which is $(3)(3)(3) = 27$.
• 3^4 is read "three to the fourth power," which is $(3)(3)(3)(3) = 81$.
• x^4 is read "x to the fourth power," which is $(x)(x)(x)(x)$.
• $3x^4$ is read "x to the fourth power, multiplied by three."

Caution

An exponent only applies to the value that **immediately precedes it**.

Examples

• $3 + 2^3 = 11$
• $(3 + 2)^3 = 125$
• $-3^2 = -9$ (the negative of 3 times 3)
• $(-3)^2 = 9$ (-3 times -3)
• $3x^2 = (3)(x)(x)$

PRACTICE

REINFORCEMENT PROBLEM: CALCULATING WITH EXPONENTS

1) Calculate the value of the following expressions:

Expression	Answer
A) 5^2	
B) 5^3	
C) -5^2	
D) -5^3	
E) $-(-5)^3$	
F) $(4-7)^2$	
G) $(-2)^3 + 5^2$	
H) $(-6+8)^3 + (7+1)^2$	
I) -2^4	
J) $4^2 - 2^2$	
K) $-(-10)^2$	
L) $(x+y)^2$ when $x=2$ and $y=3$	
M) $x+y^2$ when $x=2$ and $y=3$	
N) $-y^2$ when $y=2$	
O) $2^4/2^2$	
P) $-(-4)^2 - (-5)^2$	

SOLUTIONS

REINFORCEMENT PROBLEM: CALCULATING WITH EXPONENTS

1)

Expression	Answer
A) 5^2	25
B) 5^3	125
C) -5^2	–25
D) -5^3	–125
E) $-(-5)^3$	125
F) $(4-7)^2$	9
G) $(-2)^3 + 5^2$	17
H) $(-6+8)^3 + (7+1)^2$	72
I) -2^4	–16
J) $4^2 - 2^2$	12
K) $-(-10)^2$	–100
L) $(x+y)^2$ when $x=2$ and $y=3$	25
M) $x+y^2$ when $x=2$ and $y=3$	11
N) $-y^2$ when $y=2$	– 4
O) $2^4/2^2$	4
P) $-(-4)^2 - (-5)^2$	– 41

EVALUATING EXPRESSIONS

Introduction	Now that you have reviewed mathematical expressions and the key symbols in those expressions, you are ready to begin calculating the values of the expressions. This is an extremely important skill. You should practice it until you feel confident every time you do it.
Definition: "evaluate"	In mathematics, to **evaluate** an expression means to determine its value.
Order of operations	There are two elements involved in successfully evaluating an expression:

- a clear understanding of the mathematical operations
- knowing the *correct order* for performing these operations

The table below shows you the order of the steps that are performed to evaluate a mathematical expression. The operation to be evaluated is highlighted with a shaded box.

Step	Action	Examples
1	**Parenthesis ( ):** Evaluate the operations *within* parentheses or other grouping symbols. If there are two or more operations within a grouping symbol, do them in the order of Steps 2, 3, and 4 below.	*Evaluate:* $(9 \bullet 2 + 20) \bullet 3 - 5 \div 2^3$ $(9 \bullet 2 \div 20) \bullet 3 - 5 \div 2^3$ *Result:* $(38) \bullet 3 - 5 \div 2^3$
2	**Exponents:** Evaluate all the exponents.	*Evaluate:* $(38) \bullet 3 - 5 \div 2^3$ $38 \bullet 3 - 5 \div 2^3$ *Result:* $38 \bullet 3 - 5 \div 8$
3	**Multiply and Divide:** Evaluate all the multiplication and division operations as they occur from *left to right*.	*Evaluate:* $38 \bullet 3 - 5 \div 8$ $38 \bullet 3 - 5 \div 8$ *Result:* $114 - .625$
4	**Add and Subtract:** Evaluate all the addition and subtraction operations as they occur from *left to right*.	*Evaluate:* $114 - .625$ $114 - .625$ *Result:* 113.375

EVALUATING EXPRESSIONS (continued)

Follow the steps exactly	Knowing which operation to perform is an important skill that will always help you. The trick is to **follow the procedure exactly**. No matter how complicated the operations seem to be, if you slowly and carefully follow the procedure you will get the right answer.
Division bar is also a grouping symbol	If you see a division bar symbol, such as $\frac{20}{5 \cdot 2}$ or 20 / 5 • 2, treat the bar as a grouping symbol. This means that any expressions above or below the division bar are evaluated first as part of Step 1, just as if they were within parentheses, before any division is done. In this example, the 5 and 2 are evaluated first, to obtain 10. So, the final operation is 20 divided by 10.
Memory aid	A good memory aid for remembering the steps is to notice that the first letters of the operation steps spell the word "PEMDAS" (**P**arenthesis, **E**xponent, **M**ultiply, **D**ivide, **A**dd, and **S**ubtract). There are lots of cute expressions to help you remember the "PEMDAS" letters. One of them is "Popcorn Every Minute Doesn't Always Satisfy." Another real original is "Please Exhume Mr. Dracula At Sunrise."
Evaluating operations with variables	The use of letters (that is, variables) has no effect on the order of operations. The operations are performed in exactly the same steps. The only difference is that you must be given some value for each of the variables in order to determine the numerical value of the entire expression.
Example with variables	*Evaluate:* $4 \cdot y^2 - 10 + (8 - x) / 2$, when $y = .5$ and $x = 4$. Therefore, substitute the value .5 for y and the value 4 for x. The result is $4 \cdot .5^2 - 10 + (8 - 4) / 2$

Step	Action	Examples
1	**Parenthesis:** The only operation within the ( ) is to subtract 4 from 8.	$4 \cdot .5^2 - 10 + (\boxed{8 - 4}) / 2$ becomes $4 \cdot .5^2 - 10 + 4 / 2$
2	**Exponents:** Multiply .5 times .5, which results in .25.	$4 \cdot \boxed{.5^2} - 10 + 4 / 2$ becomes $4 \cdot .25 - 10 + 4 / 2$
3	**Multiply and Divide:** Moving from left to right, multiply 4 times .25, and then divide 4 by 2.	$\boxed{4 \cdot .25} - 10 + \boxed{4 / 2}$ becomes $1 - 10 + 2$
4	**Add and Subtract:** Moving from left to right, subtract 10 from 1, which is –9, and then add 2 to –9.	$\boxed{1 - 10 + 2}$ becomes -7

PRACTICE

SOLUTIONS FOR EVALUATING EXPRESSIONS BEGIN ON PAGE 638.

REINFORCEMENT PROBLEMS: EVALUATING EXPRESSIONS

1) Evaluate each of the expressions and write your answer next to the expression.

Expression	Answer	Expression	Answer
A) $10 - 7 + 2$		L) $\left[\dfrac{10}{2} \cdot \dfrac{4}{2}\right]^2$	
B) $10 - 7 \cdot 2$		M) $\left[\dfrac{1}{2} \cdot \dfrac{4}{10}\right] + 1.5^2$	
C) $(10 - 7) \cdot 2$		N) $\left(-.8^2 + \dfrac{3}{10}\right) \cdot \left[\left(\dfrac{10}{5}\right)^2\right]^2$	
D) $(10 - 7)^2 \cdot 2$		O) $81 - (5 - 8)^2 / 3 + 3^2 \div 3$	
E) $(5 - 3) + (7 + 3) / 2$		P) $8 \div 4 \cdot 8 \cdot 3^2$	
F) $(5 - 3^2)^2 + (7 + 3) / 2$		Q) $[8 - (-3 - 2)]^2$	
G) $9 \cdot 4^2 + 5 \cdot 8$		R) $4^2 + 1 / -3^2 + (-3)^2$	
H) $2 \cdot 3^3 - 10 \cdot 3$		S) $\dfrac{2 + 3 \cdot 2^3}{-8} - (3 \cdot 3)$	
I) $36 + (4^2 - 2) / 3 + 2^2$		T) $3 - (10 + 2)^2 / 3^2 - 12$	
J) $(2^3 \cdot 5 - 1) (2^2 + 1)$		U) $120 \div (-4) / 2$	
K) $5 + (3^3 - 17)^3 - 5$		V) $5 - 35 \cdot 2 / 2 + 3 \cdot 8$	

2) Evaluate each of the expressions and write your answer next to the expression.

Expression	Answer	Expression	Answer
A) $4x + 3$ when $x = 2$		I) $4r^2 (r - 1)$ when $r = -3$	
B) $4 (x + 3)$ when $x = 2$		J) $3 (x + y)$ when $x = 4, y = -8$	
C) $4 (x + 3)^2$ when $x = 2$		K) $3 (x - y) / (y - 1)$ when $x = 9, y = 3$	
D) $-4x^2 (x + 3)^2$ when $x = 2$		L) x^3 / x^2 when $x = 2$	
E) $-x^2 - 5x + 5$ when $x = 3$		M) $(x - y)^2$ when $x = 5, y = 2$	
F) $8y - 3$ when $y = 4$		N) x^y when $x = 2, y = 3$	
G) $y^2 - 5$ when $y = 2$		O) $p = r \cdot b$ when $r = .2, b = 100$	
H) $2a^2 - 5a + 4$ when $a = -2$		P) $a = l + e$ when $l = 2,000, e = 750$	

SOLUTIONS

PRACTICE QUESTIONS FOR EVALUATING EXPRESSIONS BEGIN ON PAGE 637.

REINFORCEMENT PROBLEMS: EVALUATING EXPRESSIONS

1)

Expression	Answer	Expression	Answer
A) $10 - 7 + 2$	5	L) $\left[\dfrac{10}{2} \bullet \dfrac{4}{2}\right]^2$	100
B) $10 - 7 \bullet 2$	-4	M) $\left[\dfrac{1}{2} \bullet \dfrac{4}{10}\right] + 1.5^2$	2.45
C) $(10 - 7) \bullet 2$	6	N) $\left(-.8^2 + \dfrac{3}{10}\right) \bullet \left[\left(\dfrac{10}{5}\right)^2\right]^2$	-5.44
D) $(10 - 7)^2 \bullet 2$	18	O) $81 - (5 - 8)^2 \Big/ 3 + 3^2 \div 3$	12
E) $(5 - 3) + (7 + 3) / 2$	7	P) $8 \div 4 \bullet 8 \bullet 3^2$	144
F) $(5 - 3^2)^2 + (7 + 3) / 2$	21	Q) $[8 - (-3 - 2)]^2$	169
G) $9 \bullet 4^2 + 5 \bullet 8$	184	R) $4^2 + 1 \Big/ -3^2 + (-3)^2$	undefined
H) $2 \bullet 3^3 - 10 \bullet 3$	24	S) $\dfrac{2 + 3 \bullet 2^3}{-8} - (3 \bullet 3)$	-12.25
I) $36 + (4^2 - 2) / 3 + 2^2$	38	T) $3 - (10 + 2)^2 \Big/ 3^2 - 12$	47
J) $(2^3 \bullet 5 - 1)(2^2 + 1)$	195	U) $120 \div (-4) / 2$	-15
K) $5 + (3^3 - 17)^3 - 5$	1,000	V) $5 - 35 \bullet 2 / 2 + 3 \bullet 8$	-2.5

2)

Expression	Answer	Expression	Answer
A) $4x + 3$ when $x = 2$	11	I) $4r^2 (r - 1)$ when $r = -3$	-144
B) $4(x + 3)$ when $x = 2$	20	J) $3(x + y)$ when $x = 4, y = -8$	-12
C) $4(x + 3)^2$ when $x = 2$	100	K) $3(x - y) \Big/ (y - 1)$ when $x = 9, y = 3$	9
D) $-4x^2 (x + 3)^2$ when $x = 2$	-400	L) $x^3 \Big/ x^2$ when $x = 2$	2
E) $-x^2 - 5x + 5$ when $x = 3$	-19	M) $(x - y)^2$ when $x = 5, y = 2$	9
F) $8y - 3$ when $y = 4$	29	N) x^y when $x = 2, y = 3$	8
G) $y^2 - 5$ when $y = 2$	-1	O) $p = r \bullet b$ when $r = .2, b = 100$	$p = 20$
H) $2a^2 - 5a + 4$ when $a = -2$	22	P) $a = l + e$ when $l = 2,000, e = 750$	$a = 2,750$

▼ *Introduction to Algebra and Equations*

OVERVIEW

Introduction

After you have mastered arithmetic, algebra is the most important kind of mathematics that you will learn. This is because algebra has so many practical uses. There are many activities and conditions in the world that can be described and then quantified by using algebra.

Algebra is the technique of writing a statement that uses mathematical expressions to numerically describe a relationship, an activity, or a condition. By doing this, algebra can provide exact answers to questions about many activities or conditions.

Examples of applications

Here are just a few examples of the almost unlimited activities and conditions that algebra can describe and calculate answers for:

- the balance of an account
- time needed to travel a specific distance
- what your loan payments will be
- the cost of insurance
- the amount of sod needed for a new lawn
- dosage formulas for medicine
- the amount of sales needed to earn a specified profit
- formula for the theory of relativity ($e = mc^2$)
- a balance sheet for a business

and the list could go on and on ...

OVERVIEW (continued)

Algebra compared to arithmetic

When someone studies algebra for the first time, that person often wants to know, "What is the difference between algebra and arithmetic?"

- In the operations for arithmetic, all the values that are used in the calculations are known and given to you. Each time you perform an operation or calculation in arithmetic, you know all the numerical values that you will use.
- Algebra uses the exact same kinds of calculations for the same exact situations that you learned in arithmetic. This is good news! What makes algebra different than arithmetic is that algebra generalizes the patterns or types of calculations without having to use specific numbers.

Algebra can be easily identified because in algebra, letters are often substituted for specific numbers, and an "=" sign is used. However, all of this is nothing more than a generalization of what you already learned in arithmetic.

As you will see, generalizing can be very, very powerful and very, very useful.

Variables

In algebra, missing or unknown values are represented by letters. These letters are called **variables**. Commonly used letters for variables are x, y, and z.

Examples

The table below shows some simple comparisons between arithmetic and algebra.

Arithmetic	Algebra	Difference
"5 + 3 is some amount"	$a + b = x$	Algebra generalizes the addition calculation. Any numbers can be substituted for a and b to get a correct answer, x.
"4 × 7 is some amount"	$a \bullet b = x$	Algebra generalizes the multiplication calculation. Any numbers can be substituted for a and b to get a correct answer, x.
"3 + 7 and 7 + 3 both equal 10"	$a + b = b + a$	Algebra generalizes the addition relationship for any numbers.

EQUATIONS

Definition

An **equation** is a statement which shows two mathematical expressions that are equal to each other. The symbol "=" is used to show the equality.

Examples

$10 + 2 = \dfrac{288}{24}$ is an equation.

$x + 5 = 3$ is an equation.

$p = b + r - 20$ is an equation.

The equation must always stay in balance

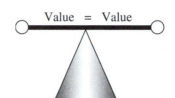

The most important thing about an equation is this: an equation must *always* remain in balance, no matter what. Think of an equation as a balance beam like you see below, with a value on each side of the beam. If some value is added to or removed from one side, the same thing must be done to the other side, or the beam will not balance.

TERMS OF AN EQUATION

Terms

When a mathematical expression in an equation has various parts, the parts of the equation that are *added or subtracted* are called **terms**.

Examples

The following table shows examples of various terms:

Mathematical Expression	Terms
$8 + 3 - x$	$8, 3, x$
$-4z + 8y$	$-4z, 8y$
$40 - (x + y) - 12x$	$40, (x + y), 12x$
$.7x + .9x - 3.5x$	$.7x, .9x, 3.5x$
$3(x + 8) - 5 + x^2$	$3(x + 8), 5, x^2$

TERMS OF AN EQUATION (continued)

Numerical coefficients

When a term is made up of both a variable and a numeral, the numeral part of the term is called a **numerical coefficient**. If a variable appears by itself, its numerical coefficient is 1, although by custom the 1 is not usually written.

Examples

The following table shows examples of terms and numerical coefficients:

Term	Numerical Coefficient	Which Means ...
$5x$	5	Five times x
x	1	1 times x
x^2	1	1 times x^2
$-3x$	-3	-3 times x
$-x^2$	-1	-1 times x^2
$3(x+8)$	3	3 times the quantity $(x+8)$

Like terms

Like terms are those terms that have the same variables and same exponents. The coefficients may be different.

Examples

The following table shows examples of like terms and unlike terms:

Mathematical Expression	Like Terms	Unlike Terms
$3x + 4y + 7x$	$3x, 7x$	$4y$
$8y + (-7y) + 5$	$8y, -7y$	5
$5x^2 + 3y^2$	none	$5x^2, 3y^2$
$5x^2 + 3x^2$	$5x^2, 3x^2$	none
$3y - 7 + 8x + 10$	7, 10	$3y, 8x$
$3x + 2 - 5x + 8$	$3x$ and $5x$, 2 and 8	none

Note: Numerals by themselves are like terms and may always be combined.

SOLVING EQUATIONS—OVERVIEW

Definition	"To solve an equation" means to find the value of a variable which makes the equation a true statement.

How to know if you have a correct solution	The way you can always know if you have a correct solution to an equation is to do the following:

- Replace the variable with the solution value.
- Evaluate the equation to determine the numerical value on each side.
- If the two sides are equal—if the equation stays in balance—the solution is correct.

Examples	The following table shows examples of how to check equations. (We will use the "=?" notation while we are checking to see if the solution is correct.)

Equation	Proposed Solution	Check By Replacing Variable
$12 - x = 9$	3	$12 - \mathbf{3} =? 9$ $9 = 9$ (true) Yes, 3 is a correct solution.
$100 + x - 250 = 720$	870	$100 + \mathbf{870} - 250 =? 720$ $720 = 720$ (true) Yes, 870 is a correct solution.
$4x + 42 = -8x$	-3.5	$4(-\mathbf{3.5}) + 42 =? -8(-\mathbf{3.5})$ $-14 + 42 =? 28$ $28 = 28$ (true) Yes, -3.5 is a correct solution.
$150 - 3x + 25 = 275$	40	$150 - 3(\mathbf{40}) + 25 =? 275$ $150 - 120 + 25 =? 275$ $55 = 275$ (false) No, 40 is not a correct solution.

PRACTICE

REINFORCEMENT PROBLEM: CHECKING THE SOLUTION

1) Check the proposed solutions to each of the equations below. Write "yes" if the proposed solution makes the equation a true statement, or write "no" if it does not make the equation a true statement.

Equation	Proposed Solution	Solution Makes Equation a True Statement?
A) $2x + 3 = 11$	$x = 4$	
B) $6x^2 - 9 = 45$	$x = -3$	
C) $\dfrac{30}{(x-1)} + 2 = -3$	$x = -5$	
D) $(x-1)(x+2) = 13.75$	$x = 3.5$	
E) $\dfrac{x^5}{x^2} = 8$	$x = 2$	
F) $-x - 3x \bullet 10 = 10$	$x = -.5$	
G) $\dfrac{x^2 + 5}{x - 5} + 3 = 39.2$	$x = 30$	
H) $x^2 + y - 12 = 15$	$x = 5, y = 3$	
I) $8(y - 5) + \dfrac{x^2}{x - 2} = -20$	$x = 4, y = -2$	

SOLUTIONS

REINFORCEMENT PROBLEMS: CHECKING THE SOLUTION

1)

Equation	Proposed Solution	Solution Makes Equation a True Statement?	
A) $2x + 3 = 11$	$x = 4$	yes	$8 + 3 = 11$ (true)
B) $6x^2 - 9 = 45$	$x = -3$	yes	$54 - 9 = 45$ (true)
C) $\dfrac{30}{(x-1)} + 2 = -3$	$x = -5$	no	$30 / -4 = -3$ (false)
D) $(x-1)(x+2) = 13.75$	$x = 3.5$	yes	$(2.5)(5.5) = 13.75$ (true)
E) $\dfrac{x^5}{x^2} = 8$	$x = 2$	yes	$32 / 4 = 8$ (true)
F) $-x - 3x \bullet 10 = 10$	$x = -.5$	no	$.5 + 15 = 10$ (false)
G) $\dfrac{x^2 + 5}{x - 5} + 3 = 39.2$	$x = 30$	no	$905 / 28 = 39.2$ (false)
H) $x^2 + y - 12 = 15$	$x = 5, y = 3$	no	$16 = 15$ (false)
I) $8(y - 5) + \dfrac{x^2}{x - 2} = -20$	$x = 4, y = -2$	yes	$-40 / 2 = -20$ (true)

SOLUTION PROCEDURES

Introduction to solution procedure	Now that you know how to verify whether or not a solution to an equation is correct, it is time to begin learning *how to* solve an equation, to get the solution. Solving equations is an extensive subject that will be continued in the next book of this accounting tutorial series. However, the following topics will show you how to deal with those equations that can be solved by simplifying and by adding and subtracting terms.
Overview of procedure steps	**The goal is to have the variable isolated on one side of the equation.** To accomplish this, we do the following, while always making sure that the equation stays in balance: **Step 1:** Simplify the terms of the equation. **Step 2:** Add or subtract the terms.

SIMPLIFYING TERMS

Overview	The terms of an equation can be simplified by doing the following: ● combining like terms ● removing parenthesis grouping whenever possible
Combining like terms	**Combining like terms** means to add or subtract the coefficients of whatever like terms appear on each side of an equation. The variable attaches to the result.
Example #1	Simplify $5x + 7x = 300$. ● $5x$ and $7x$ are like terms that have the same variable x. ● Adding the coefficients, we obtain 12. *Final result:* $12x = 300$, which is a simpler equation.

SIMPLIFYING TERMS (continued)

Example #2	Simplify $x + x^2 - 20x = 5x - 12x$.

- Left side: x and $-20x$ are like terms that have the same variable x.
- Subtracting the coefficients, we obtain -19.
- Result on left side: $x^2 - 19x$.

- Right side: $5x$ and $-12x$ are like terms that have the same variable x.
- Subtracting the coefficients, we obtain -7.
- Result on right side: $-7x$.

Final result: $x^2 - 19x = -7x$, which is a simpler equation.

Remove parenthesis

If the amount within a parenthesis is a term that is being added to or subtracted from other terms, then it is often useful to know how to remove the parenthesis. This is because after the parenthesis has been removed, there will frequently be like terms that can then be combined, or numbers that can be evaluated.

Procedure

The following table shows you the procedure for removing a parenthesis, or similar grouping symbols such as [ ] or { }, when the parenthesis term is being added to or subtracted from other expressions.

If ...	Then ...	Examples
No sign or a plus sign directly precedes the parenthesis,	The parenthesis may simply be removed. (The expression inside the parenthesis remains unaffected.)	• $(4x - 2) - 3x = 14$ is changed to: $4x - 2 - 3x = 14$ • $12 + (-2y + 8) = (7 - 3y)$ is changed to: $12 - 2y + 8 = 7 - 3y$
The parenthesis is directly **preceded by a minus sign**,	Reverse all the signs of the terms within the parenthesis when the parenthesis is removed.	• $3 - (4x - 2) - 3x = 14$ is changed to: $3 - 4x + 2 - 3x = 14$ • $12 - (-2y + 8) = -(7 + 3y)$ is changed to: $12 + 2y - 8 = -7 - 3y$

SIMPLIFYING TERMS (continued)

Note: In the third example, notice how the positive $4x$ within the parenthesis changed to a negative $4x$, and the -2 within the parenthesis changed to a $+2$. In the fourth example, notice how all the signs of the terms within the parenthesis also have been reversed when the parenthesis was removed. Also notice how the new sign of the first term in the parenthesis replaces the sign directly in front of the parenthesis when the parenthesis is removed.

Caution

Do *not* try to remove the parenthesis if the parenthesis term is being multiplied or divided by another term. A different procedure is needed, which is presented in the second book in this series.

Examples:
- $3(x + 2) = 10$
- $(x + 4) / 5 = 12$

PRACTICE

REINFORCEMENT PROBLEMS: SIMPLIFYING EXPRESSIONS

1) Remove parentheses where possible.

Equation	Rewritten Equation
A) $(2x + 10) - 3x = 230$	
B) $(4x - 3) + 10x = 50$	
C) $4x - (3 + 10x) = 50$	
D) $4(x - 3) + 10x = 50$	
E) $(2x + 10x) = x^2 - (3x - 8)$	
F) $(7x + 3) / 5x = 120 + x$	
G) $-(2x - 8) - (5y + 5) = 80$	

2) On a separate piece of paper, simplify the following equations by removing parentheses and combining like terms where possible.

Equation
A) $5 - x + 2x + 3 = 14$
B) $(5y - 3) - (2y + 10) = 20$
C) $50 = 5a - 6 + (10a - 12)$
D) $5(x - 3) + (5x + 2) = -30$
E) $-(x + 12 + 5x) + (x - 3) = 100$
F) $(x - 10) - (-x + 5) = 8$
G) $(x + 3)^2 - (x - 3) = 5$
H) $(a + b) - (5 - b) = -25$
I) $(x + 3) / 5 + 5 - 2 = 100$
J) $-75 = y^2 - 5y + 8 - (-4y - 10)$
K) $6 - 3x - 12 + 2x = 15$

SOLUTIONS

REINFORCEMENT PROBLEMS: SIMPLIFYING EXPRESSIONS

1)

Equation	Rewritten Equation
A) $(2x + 10) - 3x = 230$	$2x + 10 - 3x = 230$
B) $(4x - 3) + 10x = 50$	$4x - 3 + 10x = 50$
C) $4x - (3 + 10x) = 50$	$4x - 3 - 10x = 50$
D) $4(x - 3) + 10x = 50$	cannot remove parenthesis unless another procedure is used
E) $(2x + 10x) = x^2 - (3x - 8)$	$-2x + 10x = x^2 - 3x + 8$
F) $(7x + 3) / 5x = 120 + x$	cannot remove parenthesis unless another procedure is used
G) $-(2x - 8) - (5y + 5) = 80$	$2x + 8 - 5y - 5 = 80$

2)

Equation	Simplified Equation
A) $5 - x + 2x + 3 = 14$	$x + 8 = 14$
B) $(5y - 3) - (2y + 10) = 20$	$3y - 13 = 20$
C) $50 = 5a - 6 + (10a - 12)$	$50 = 15a - 18$
D) $5(x - 3) + (5x + 2) = -30$	$5(x - 3) + 5x + 2 = -30$
E) $-(x + 12 + 5x) + (x - 3) = 100$	$-5x - 15 = 100$
F) $(x - 10) - (-x + 5) = 8$	$2x - 15 = 8$
G) $(x + 3)^2 - (x - 3) = 5$	$(x + 3)^2 - x + 3 = 5$
H) $(a + b) - (5 - b) = -25$	$a + 2b - 5 = -25$
I) $(x + 3) / 5 + 5 - 2 = 100$	$(x + 3) / 5 + 3 = 100$
J) $-75 = y^2 - 5y + 8 - (-4y - 10)$	$-75 = y^2 - y + 18$
K) $6 - 3x - 12 + 2x = 15$	$-x - 6 = 15$

ADDING AND SUBTRACTING TERMS

Overview

Remember that the goal in solving an equation is to **isolate the variable** on one side of the equation. Up to now we have worked toward this objective by practicing procedures for simplifying an equation.

Now we will practice the next step: adding and subtracting terms. A very important way to isolate the variable and still maintain the equality of the equation is by adding or subtracting the same value to each side of the equation.

Procedure

The following table shows the procedure for adding and subtracting terms. The operation to be evaluated is highlighted with a shaded box.

Note: This procedure applies to isolating a single variable that appears on one side of an equation.

Step	Procedure	Example
1	Locate the variable and identify which side of the equation it is on.	$x + 3 = 28$ The variable is x and it is on the left side.
2	Remove the numbers on the same side of the equation as the variable. <table><tr><th>If …</th><th>Then …</th></tr><tr><td>the number is positive or added,</td><td>subtract it from both sides</td></tr><tr><td>the number is negative or subtracted,</td><td>add it to both sides</td></tr></table>	$x + 3 = 28$ $x + 3 - 3 = 28 - 3$ $x + 0 = 25$ $x = 25$ $x - 10 = 30$ $x - 10 + 10 = 30 + 10$ $x + 0 = 40$ $x = 40$
3	Check the solution by replacing the variable with the solution value.	$x + 3 = 28$ $25 + 3 = 28$ (true) $x - 10 = 30$ $40 - 10 = 30$ (true)

ADDING AND SUBTRACTING TERMS (continued)

More examples

- **The equation that describes the calculation of net income is:**
$r - e = i$, where r means revenue, e means expenses, and i means net income.

If the net income of our company was $1,000 and the expenses were $500, what were the revenues?

Solution:

$r - 500 = 1,000$	(values entered in equation)
$r - 500 + 500 = 1,000 + 500$	(removing the -500 on the side of the variable)
$r = 1,500$	(revenue)

Check: $1,500 - $500 = $1,000$
$1,000 = $1,000$ (true)

- **The equation that shows the ending balance of an account is:**
$b + i - d = e$, where the b means beginning balance, i means account increases, d means account decreases and e means ending balance.

Suppose that the beginning balance of the cash account was $10,000 and the company made cash payments of $47,000 during the month. The month-end cash balance was $2,500. What were the cash receipts during the month?

Solution:

$10,000 + i - 47,000 = 2,500$	(values entered in equation)
$10,000 - 10,000 + i - 47,000 = 2,500 - 10,000$	(isolating the variable)
$i - 47,000 = -7,500$	
$i - 47,000 + 47,000 = -7,500 + 47,000$	(isolating the variable)
$i = 39,500$	(the cash receipts)

Check: $10,000 + $39,500 - $47,000 = $2,500$
$2,500 = $2,500$ (true)

ADDING AND SUBTRACTING TERMS (continued)

When the isolated variable is negative

Suppose that you have this equation: $10 - x = 25$

Solution:
$10 - 10 - x = 25 - 10$
$0 - x = 15$
$-x = 15$

It may appear that the solution to this equation is $-x = 15$; however, that is not the case, because we are solving for x (positive x), not $-x$. From our discussion of signed numbers, we know that $-x$ means the negative of x. Therefore, the solution (the positive of x) will be the opposite, and so it must have opposite signs. The solution is $x = -15$.

Rule

When the isolated variable is negative, reverse the signs on all the terms to obtain the positive solution.

Caution: minus sign in front of a variable

Be careful to remember that a minus sign placed in front of a variable does not necessarily mean that the expression is negative. This is because the variable itself could be positive or negative. It is best to interpret this situation as "show the opposite of …" or "the negative of … ."

Example: The value of "$-x$" would be negative if x is positive, and would positive if x is negative.

PRACTICE

SOLUTIONS FOR SOLVING EQUATIONS BEGIN ON PAGE 653.

REINFORCEMENT PROBLEMS: SOLVING EQUATIONS

1) On a separate piece of paper, isolate the variable to solve each equation, and then check each solution. You may have to simplify some equations.

Equation	Answer
A) $x - 10 = 25$	
B) $x + 3 = 12$	
C) $x - 3 = -12$	
D) $3 - x = 15$	
E) $(-x - 8) = 32$	
F) $(-8x - 3) - (-7x + 1) = -49$	
G) $(15x - 8x) - (5x + x + 5) = 50$	
H) $-(-4x + 2) - 3x = 17$	

2) **True or false?** The expression "$-x$" represents a negative number. Explain your answer.

SOLUTIONS

PRACTICE QUESTIONS FOR SOLVING EQUATIONS BEGIN ON PAGE 652.

REINFORCEMENT PROBLEMS: SOLVING EQUATIONS

1)

Equation	Answer	Checking
A) $x - 10 = 25$	$x = 35$	$35 - 10 = 25$ ($25 = 25$, which is true)
B) $x + 3 = 12$	$x = 9$	$9 + 3 = 12$ ($12 = 12$, which is true)
C) $x - 3 = -12$	$x = -9$	$-9 - 3 = -12$ ($-12 = -12$, which is true)
D) $3 - x = 15$	$x = -12$	$3 - (-12) = 15$, which is $3 + 12 = 15$ ($15 = 15$, which is true)
E) $(-x - 8) = 32$	$x = -40$	$-(-40) - 8 = 32$, which is $40 - 8 = 32$ ($32 = 32$, which is true)
F) $(-8x - 3) - (-7x + 1) = -49$	$x = 45$	$(-8)(45) - 3 - [(-7)(45) + 1] = -49$, which is $-363 + 314 = -49$ (which is true)
G) $(15x - 8x) - (5x + x + 5) = 50$	$x = 55$	$[(15)(55) - (8)(55)] - [(5)(55) + 55 + 5] = 50$, which is $385 - 335 = 50$, which is true
H) $-(-4x + 2) - 3x = 13$	$x = 15$	$-[(-4)(15) + 2] - [(3)(15)] = 13$, which is $-(-58) - 45 = 13$, which is true

2)   False. We do not know if x itself is negative or positive, so there is no way to know if the expression is negative or positive.

Glossary

Account: A detailed, historical record of all the increases and decreases of a specific item in the accounting equation (page 375)

Account form: A balance sheet format in which assets are placed on the left side of page, and liabilities and owner's equity are placed on the right side (page 289)

Account numbers: Unique identification numbers assigned to accounts (page 426)

Accounts payable: The legal obligation to pay money, usually arising from receiving goods and services from vendors (page 165)

Accounts receivable: An amount owed by a customer to a business (page 7)

Accounting: A system of activities that provides financial information which is useful for decision-making (page 220)

Accounting cycle: The recurring, sequential pattern of accounting activity (page 501)

Added value: The value created when a new resource is created (page 13)

Annual report: A document, usually prepared by a large corporation, that contains audited financial statements, footnotes, and management discussion and analysis (page 272)

Asset: Business property (page 40)

Balance sheet: A report that shows the assets and claims on assets as of a specific date (page 289)

Book of original entry: A journal (page 430)

Bookkeeping: Another name for the processing functions in the accounting process (page 223)

Capital statement: Another name for the statement of owner's equity (page 284)

Charge: To debit an account (page 410)

Chart of accounts: A listing of account names and identification numbers (page 426)

Charter: The legal document that creates a corporation (page 75)

Common stock: Ownership shares of a corporation (page 75)

Comparability: The quality of information that makes it comparable between companies and over time (page 274)

Compound entries: Entries containing three or more accounts (page 438)

Conceptual framework: The organized reasoning that explains the basic nature of accounting (page 339)

Consistency: The quality of information that is prepared using the same methods and procedures (page 274)

Corporation: A business that is a combined legal and economic entity, and is owned by one or more individuals as stockholders (page 75)

Cr.: The abbreviation for the word "credit" (page 409)

Credit: A right-side entry or the right side of an account (page 409)

Debit: A left-side entry or the left side of an account (page 409)

Deferred revenue: Another name for unearned revenue (page 131)

Double-entry: A system of recording financial changes that requires at least two changes in the accounting equation, so it will stay in balance (page 97)

Dr.: The abbreviation for the word "debit" (page 409)

Economic entity: Any activity or operation for which the financial condition or financial information is to be reported (page 68)

Economic entity assumption: Assumption that it is possible to identify an individual economic entity for which financial reporting is to be done (page 69)

Economic resource: A resource that can be valued or measured in dollars (page 4)

Entity: Another term for economic entity (page 68)

Entry: The recording of a change in an account; usually refers to recording in ledgers or journals (page 376)

Equipment: Long-lived (more than a year) assets used in operations to produce goods or services (page 164)

Equity: A claim on asset value (page 51)

Expense: A decrease in owner's equity caused by using up resources in operations (pages 12, 115)

Financial Accounting Standards Board (FASB): The highest standard-setting authority in accounting (page 344)

Financing activities: Inflows and outflows of cash that are caused by borrowing, and by owner's investments and withdrawals (page 297)

Footing: The balance of an account; the total of a column of numbers (page 376)

Franchise: The right to operate someone else's business, usually in a particular location (page 164)

General journal: An all-purpose journal that can record all types of transactions (page 431)

General ledger: A book or computer file that contains all the ledger accounts (page 424)

General partnership: A partnership where all partners have personal liability and full management authority (page 75)

Generally Accepted Accounting Principles (GAAP): The rules and methods that accountants must follow (page 342)

Historical cost principle: The requirement that transactions be recorded at actual cost (page 43)

Income statement: A report that explains the operational changes in owner's equity for a specific period of time (page 276)

Intangible assets: Assets that have no physical substance (page 164)

Interest payable: Interest owed by a borrower (page 165)

Interest receivable: Interest that has been earned and that has not been received (page 164)

Inventory: Goods that a merchant has in stock (page 164)

Investing activities: Inflows and outflows of cash that are caused by acquiring and disposing of assets (page 297)

Journal: A chronological record of transactions (pages 424, 430)

Journalizing: Recording information into a journal (page 431)

Leasing: Renting property (page 43)

Ledger: A book or computer file that contains accounts (page 424)

Ledger accounts: Accounts which are found in a ledger (page 424)

Legal entity: The entity that has legal ownership of assets and legal responsibility for debts (page 73)

Liability: A debt; a creditor's claim on assets (page 52)

Limited partnership: A partnership in which certain partners do not have personal liability (page 75)

Liquidity: How quickly an asset can be turned into cash (page 292)

Managerial accounting: A kind of accounting that focuses on the detailed information needs of a specific company, rather than the general public (page 272)

MD & A: "Management discussion and analysis" found in annual reports (page 273)

Measurement: Another name for the analysis step in the accounting process (page 222)

Net assets: A synonym for owner's equity (pages 52, 195)

Net cash flow: The net change in cash during any specified time period (page 297)

Net income: When revenues are greater than expenses (pages 19, 280)

Net loss: When expenses are greater than revenues (pages 19, 280)

Net worth: A synonym for owner's equity (pages 52, 195)

"Normal" or "natural" side: The side of an account which records increases (page 377)

Notes payable: A written promise, made by a borrower, to repay a loan (page 165)

Notes receivable: A written promise to repay a loan, held by the lender, and made by a borrower (page 163)

Objective evidence: Proof provided by a past transaction (page 43)

Operating activities: Inflows and outflows of cash that are caused by regular business operations (page 296)

Operating guidelines: The principles, constraints, and assumptions part of the conceptual framework that gives guidance to accountants (page 341)

Operating statement: Another name for the income statement (page 277)

Owner's equity: An owner's claim on assets (page 52)

P & L statement: Another name for the income statement (page 277)

Partnership: A business with two or more owners acting as partners (page 74)

Personal liability: Being personally responsible to pay all business debts if they are not paid by the business (page 73)

Posting: Transferring information from journal to ledger (page 470)

Prepaid expense: An advance payment paid before goods or services are received (page 164)

Profit and loss statement: Another name for the income statement (page 277)

Property: Any resource that can be owned (page 5)

Proprietorship: A noncorporate business that is owned by one person (page 72)

Relevance: The quality of information that makes it significant or important (page 274)

Reliability: The quality of information that makes it free from material error or bias (page 274)

Report form: A balance sheet format in which assets are placed at the top of a page, and liabilities and owner's equity are placed underneath the assets (page 289)

Revenue: An increase in owner's equity caused by making sales to customers (pages 17, 119)

Security: The particular asset or assets a creditor can claim for nonpayment of a debt (page 53)

Service potential: The future benefits that any asset provides (page 41)

Shareholder: Another word for stockholder (page 75)

Single-entry: An outdated method of recording transactions in which only a part of the change in the accounting equation is recorded (page 97)

Stakeholders: People and organizations that use accounting information (page 223)

Statement of cash flows: A report that explains the change in the cash balance during a specific period of time (page 296)

Statement of condition: Another name for the balance sheet (page 290)

Statement of earnings: Another name for the income statement (page 277)

Statement of operations: Another name for the income statement (page 277)

Statement of owner's equity: The financial statement that explains all the changes in owner's equity (page 283)

Statement of position: Another name for the balance sheet (page 290)

Statements of Financial Accounting Standards (SFAS): The official pronouncements of the Financial Accounting Standards Board (page 344)

Stockholder: An owner of stock of a corporation (page 75)

Supplies: Materials that are frequently required for daily operations and used up relatively quickly (page 163)

T account: The simplest form of an account, in the form of a T, showing name and increases on one side, and decreases on the opposite side (page 376)

Trade receivable: Any receivable created by a sale to a customer (page 163)

Transaction: Any event that causes a change in the accounting equation (page 99)

Unearned revenue: A liability created by receiving a payment from a customer before services are performed (page 131)

Value chain: The sequence of activities that consumes resources for the purpose of adding value (page 16)

Vendor: Any seller of goods or services (page 53)

Withdrawals: A decrease in the owner's capital caused by the owner's withdrawal of cash or other assets out of the business for personal use (page 197)

Subject Index